SPIRITUAL PEOPLE, RADICAL LIVES

Gary Commins

SPIRITUAL PEOPLE, RADICAL LIVES:

Spirituality and Justice in Four 20th Century American Lives

Gary Commins

International Scholars Publications
San Francisco - London - Bethesda
1996

BR
1700.2
.C65
1996

Library of Congress Cataloging-in-Publication Data

Commins, Gary, 1952-
　　　Spiritual people, radical lives / Gary Commins.
　　　　　p. cm.
　　　Includes bibliographical references and index.
　　　ISBN 1-883255-43-0: $59.95 - ISBN (invalid) 1-883255-42-0 (pbk.):
$39.95.
　　　　　1. Christian biography--United States.　2. Radicals--United States--
Biography.　I. Title.
BR1700.2.C65　1994
277.3'082'0922--dc20
[B]　　　　　　　　　　　　　　　　　　93-47063
　　　　　　　　　　　　　　　　　　　　　CIP

Editorial Inquiries:
International Scholars Publications
7831 Woodmont Avenue #345
Bethesda,MD.20814

To order: (800) 55-PUBLISH

"The real Christian is always a revolutionary, belongs to a new race, and has been given a new name and a new song."

--Evelyn Underhill

"As the grain of mustard seed grew so large that the birds found shelter in it, so those who bear an awakened Seed into the world's suffering will grow until they become a refuge for many."

--Thomas Kelly

In memory of Matthew D. Ellington (1932-1989)

CONTENTS

ACKNOWLEDGEMENTS

I am indebted in more ways than I can remember or articulate to Larry Adams, Tim Vivian, Jeffrey Russell, and Rick Kennedy for their extensive help in guiding me through rough drafts of this book. I would also like to thank Will Wauters, Sarah Cline, Josh Acton, Fred Borsch, and Nat Pierce for their encouragement. I am indebted to Jane Hahn who taught me how to use a computer and who translated the manuscript from one computer language to another; Tim Vivian then helped edit the manuscript and got it camera-ready. I wish also to thank Tom Whitney for his proof-reading, and Robert M. West and Carole Bosch at Catholic Scholars Press for their editorial assistance.

This book would not have been possible without the financial support of the Commission on Ministry of the Diocese of Los Angeles, and the encouragement of Terry Lynberg and the Bishop's Committee and people of St. Michael's Episcopal Church, Isla Vista. My neverending thanks goes to the people of St. Michael's (1983-90) for the love and ministry we shared.

I would like to thank the staff at the libraries at the Graduate Theological Union, the University of California, Boston College, Boston University, and Andover

Newton Theological School. I also thank the Church Divinity School of the Pacific and Andover Newton Theological School for their hospitality during my sabbatical.

Matthew (Virgil, Larry, Duke) Ellington, a "homeless" (he abhorred the epithet), "recovered alcoholic" (his description), and a member of St. Michael's, tried to teach me in life many lessons I was more willing to absorb in the library at the feet of other great people. He was a difficult, confusing, challenging, angry, funny, grace-filled and redemptive presence for us all. I thank him for the power of resurrection and reconciliation made most visible in the last year of his life, and for the lessons I hope never to forget.

I dedicate this book to his blessed memory.

A Note About Language

In the past generation, our language has changed in speaking of both race and sex. I am personally committed to these improvements and have employed current usage whenever possible, but I have retained the original words of Muste, Day, King, and Merton without editorial comment in the hope that readers will understand that, like all of us, they were people of their time, and that they intended nothing derogatory in the word "negro" nor exclusive in the word "man."

All biblical citations are from the New Revised Standard Version unless otherwise noted.

                                        Gary Commins

Redondo Beach, California
Feast of Martin Luther King, Jr. 1994

INTRODUCTION

"Perfection is not for those who isolate themselves in ivory towers of an imaginary faultlessness, but only for those who risk the tarnishing of their supposed interior purity by plunging fully into life as it must inevitably be lived in this imperfect world of ours."

> --Thomas Merton

"[Saints] do not stand aside wrapped in delightful prayers and feeling pure and agreeable to God. They go right down into the mess; and there, right down in the mess, they are able to radiate God because they possess Him."

> --Evelyn Underhill

"What we plant in the soil of contemplation we shall reap in the harvest of action and thus the purpose of contemplation is achieved."

> --Meister Eckhart[1]

It began to come together. In the Fall of 1988 when I returned from my sabbatical (when I wrote the first draft of this book), I was to preach on the story of Jesus exorcising a young boy possessed by a demon (Mk 9:14-29). To their chagrin, the disciples had failed to dislodge the demon. When they had left behind the derisive sneers of their opponents, and the forgiving, forgetful joy of parent and child, the disciples asked their master: "Why could we not cast it out?" In other words, "What did we do wrong?" To get rid of this kind of demon, Jesus told them, you must pray.

It began to come together. Yet I suffer from a chronic suspicion of things that fit neatly in place when they pertain to God or the life of the spirit or the world in which we live, let alone to demons. Still, I cannot deny that the story in Mark's Gospel addresses my questions.

In the 1960s--my formative years--why did attempts to combat racism, militarism, and economic injustice grind to an unsuccessful halt? Why are those demons never completely expelled? Was it because the demons had not been properly identified? Was it because behind the stone walls of segregation, the Pentagon, the White House, and Wall Street, the demons remained unseen or unnamed? Had we not seen the powers giving life to war and systemic violence-- greed, insecurity, and self-hatred? Had we spoken of demons only to animate our own rhetoric? Had we mistaken for demons the projections of our own sins? Had we insisted too heartily on our own righteousness? Or was the more fundamental answer provided in the Gospel of Mark: You have not prayed. You have not prayed about the bombings in Birmingham and Hanoi. You have not prayed during the riots in the cities and on the campuses. You have not meditated on the incarnations, the transfigurations, the crucifixions and resurrections in your own era. And when you *have* prayed you have bowed before the projection of your own superego, to some god-the-great-liberal. Your false prayers to false gods have rendered you blind to the world as it is, deaf to the demons laughing in your own hearts.

Liberal American Christianity's tired activism lacked the faith, hope, and perspective to feed its love for others. So in the early 1970s, it drifted from activism to self-absorbed quietism. In the name of "spirituality," it ignored the attempt to cast out the world's demons and accommodated its own. A new, indoor fad replaced an old, outdoor one. An avaricious "spirituality" twisted honest desires for intimacy with God. In the 1970s, mainstream Christians wanted to build booths for themselves--never mind Moses, Elijah, and Jesus--and stay on the mount of the Transfiguration in never-ending bliss. In both sixties' activism and seventies' quietism, truth and deception lay together as uneasy bedfellows.

As it was for the Church, so it was with me. My thirst for a synthesis of a living activism and a healthy spirituality in my life and in the life of the Church had not been quenched. But where could I look, what could I find, to assuage this thirst?

There is a simple joke: a student is caught cheating on his metaphysics final by looking into the soul of the boy sitting next to him.[2] Behind the joke's silliness lies an unintended truth about Church history and the communion of saints. Often what we gain in the study of history are glimpses into the hearts and minds of those who have gone before us, those who have shared the same temptations and thirsts, those who have met the same demons, those who have wrestled with God. It is not "cheating" to study the ways that other Christians have integrated prayer and action. It is our assignment.

The purpose of my sabbatical was to discover how four twentieth-century figures had integrated spirituality with ministry. If they embodied that unity of spirit and life, then their spiritual biographies might uncover the hidden links within our lives. I set out to find the common threads in their lives, and find both an end and a new beginning in my search.

A. J. Muste (1885-1967), Dorothy Day (1897-1980), Martin Luther King, Jr.(1929-1968), and Thomas Merton (1915-1968) each blended Christian traditions into a unique personal synthesis. Every composer makes use of the same musical possibilities, each artist the same materials. They are influenced by the music they hear, the paintings and sculptures they see, yet they create music from what they hear in their own interior ear, art from sights envisioned in their own mind's eye. Like composers and artists, these four expressed their traditions in particular ways. Other twentieth-century Christians have had very different perceptions of themselves, God, and the world. Most have lived differently. Few have found the inner freedom and the passionate conviction to see as incisively or to act as boldly.

No one speaks, writes, or acts in a vacuum. Many of King's writings were ghostwritten or group efforts; many of his speeches addressed white *or* black audiences. Where does one find King's own ideas? Day corresponded with Merton; she worked with Muste. All four were well-read. Which ideas belong to whom? How is one to discern a person's spirituality, let alone trace its influences?

If it is difficult to discern a person's spirituality, the effort to define "spirituality" represents our need to understand the mystery more than its desire to be understood. A "systematic spirituality" is out of the question, yet we can seek more than a reverent silence. Even those who urged others to abandon images of God have used images of a "dark night" and a "cloud of unknowing" to describe the indescribable.

This biographically-rooted study does not imply that spirituality can be extracted from life. It is neither a limb to be amputated nor a part of the soul to be studied in a spiritual autopsy. It is the point at which faith and thought merge with action. Its audible and visible signs are repeated metaphors, phrases, stories, and constellations of insights embodied in actions, words, and plans for social transformation. A person's spirituality is discovered not only in word and deed but in the assumptions and inflections behind speech and action.

Spirituality includes more than a pious, privatized relationship, although intimacy with God is one part of it. It excludes a "me-centered" relationship with

God: there is, in reality, no such thing. Christian spirituality includes one's orientation not only to the Trinity but also to the community called Church, the web of societies called the world, and one's personal ministry within them. Spirituality is not a list of beliefs to which one assents but a cluster of intuitions which, when kindled by the Holy Spirit, spark a person to holy action.

An individual's spirituality is not born mature nor bred in isolation--even a hermit is an unfinished product of one or more religious traditions. Each Christian tradition has its own unique language and set of symbols to signify realities about God, faith, and life which others convey with different terms. Each is like a garden containing many kinds of seed. Each contains a range of insights about the character of God, the nature of the world, and priorities in choosing one's vocation. Muste, Day, King, and Merton inherited resources from various traditions, ascertained insights from secular wisdom, and adapted them in their interactions with a world of affluence and poverty, war and cold war.

One's spirituality does not evolve evenly from childhood to maturity. Before Paul's conversion, he "persecuted," after it he "proclaims" (Gal 1:11-24); once he was a child but now he is an adult (1 Cor 13:11). Paul's conversion may have occurred on the road to Damascus but his faith developed in confrontation with the Christian communities that caused him the most grief as, without prefabricated answers, he tried to work out their salvation in fear and trembling-- and with more than a little annoyance.

Everyone's spirit is shaped by life; everyone's spirituality is enacted in life. There are always fruits of the spirit, sweet or rotten. In these impressionistic portraits of four spiritual lives, I have drawn on specific events which may seem incidental, anecdotal, or even trivial. Yet they may reveal something concealed in better remembered or more dramatic events. And they may, as the Quaker tradition says, contain the sacred in the ordinary or, as Day said, sacramentally reveal the holy in the daily.

I began this study trying to connect two elements--interior spiritual life and outward social action--but after engaging these lives I consider such a theological model inadequate. I now prefer a more serviceable fourfold model of (1) spiritual guidance, (2) spiritual sustenance, (3) world-discernment, and (4) ministry. In part this merely breaks in half the "spiritual" component of the binary equation, but that same model has ignored--incredibly--the need to theologically interpret the world, to discern Zion from Babylon, the Wilderness from the Promised Land, to know how one is to live in the world without being of it. For all its traditional wear and tear, the Mary-Martha dichotomy does not help Jesus or his disciples choose their words to the Pharisee, the Sadducee, the tax collector, the Samaritan woman, or Pilate. Christians still live in a world peopled by religious and political authorities, by outcasts and Caesars. World-discernment is the missing element in most spiritualities.

It is helpful to see the four categories as points on a clock, the Christian life going round and round the circle as we learn from spiritual guidance and sustenance how to interpret the world and live accordingly. Then we bring these experiences back to reinterpret God and re-energize ourselves in a constant cycle of grace and faithful living. Yet this circle--while attractive--is untrue to our experience. The Christian life is not so contained or predictable. One does not start at one point and progress in a circle.

It is more helpful to imagine starting simultaneously at four points spread out randomly in space. Each sets off a molecular reaction which then propels matter in all directions at once. An event in one's ministry may become a source of spiritual guidance. A new way of looking at the world may help one re-evaluate an experience of spiritual consolation. When the secular and sacred intersect, there is bound to be a discovery of self, world, and God. When they continually meet, they can no longer be separated one from the other.

This wild and unpredictable interaction of spiritual guidance, spiritual sustenance, world-discernment, and ministry is characteristic of the lives of Muste, Day, King, and Merton--and of our own lives. It is less beautiful than a circle, more complicated than the dual relationship of action and reflection, yet more true to life.

It must also be said that spiritual guidance, spiritual sustenance, world-discernment, and ministry are more like clusters than individual points in space. Each is like a solar system or a molecule, made up of smaller constituent parts. Certain common elements, like themes in a symphony or threads in fabric, recur in the lives of Muste, Merton, King, and Day, and in the lives of most Christians.

SPIRITUAL GUIDANCE has always followed the formation of the people of God. Slaves right out of Egypt happen upon Mt. Sinai; Jesus' new disciples gather together to hear the Sermon on the Mount. Christians throughout the ages have found guidance from Jesus, the Cross, tradition, detachment, and their own interior canon.

All Christians wrestle with *Jesus*. Christianity is not, as some Protestants would have it, based on a revealed book, nor is it essentially, as some Roman Catholics and Orthodox might claim, a revealed tradition. Rather, it centers on a revealed person, Jesus, to whom the book and the tradition witness. One might honestly ask "which Jesus" each Christian sees: God incarnate? an itinerant preacher? the Son of David uniting people in a Kingdom of justice? the Son of Man without a place to rest his head? the Risen Lord reigning over creation? the crucified Savior forgiving the sins of the world?

Just as the Cross has always stood naked at the center of Christian faith, so the *way of the Cross* has been the icon of Christian discipleship. Yet, what does it mean to pick up one's cross and bear it? In the first century, the cross was the preferred instrument of political punishment and religious damnation. Since then, it has been spiritualized. Is it now a road to vulnerability? What is the relationship between Christ's Cross and ours?

Muste, Day, King, and Merton were not spiritual inventors or innovators in their *use of tradition*. They did not unearth their radicalism in esoteric corners of the faith. They found a treasure-trove of subversive social instruction in basic Christian assertions and practices, the common stuff of all believers. What did they find that so many others miss?

As Social Gospel theologian Walter Rauschenbusch said, "Each Christian has his own inner Bible, a narrower set of books and passages that speak to his spirit with the unmistakable sweetness and power of the Master, and from which he draws comfort and strength and holiness."[3] Each Christian uses certain *words as spiritual directors* to construct a way of life, words which spring forth in a crisis. Which words inspired Muste and Merton? Whose words inspired Day and King?

The Christian struggle with *detachment* is as old as Jesus' commands to "sell all you have," "let the dead bury the dead," and "come, follow me." How did King and Muste loosen their grip on the world, and its grip on them? How did Merton and Day make detachment a daily discipline?

The Israelites' cry for bread in the Wilderness and Jesus' petition for daily bread in the Lord's Prayer are as much prayers for SPIRITUAL SUSTENANCE as for physical needs. Spiritual sustenance takes different forms--community, a rule of life, vision, a sustaining presence, and hope--to feed many spiritual hungers.

Day called *community* the only antidote for the "long loneliness." Christians throughout the ages have gathered together in cities and in the desert, in monastic communities and sects and congregations. How did their very distinctive communities nourish Muste and Merton, Day and King?

Each of the four found his or her *rule of life* a source of nurture. Generally more a part of Catholic than Protestant tradition, a rule of life establishes a way of life incorporating prayer, work, study, and recreation. Protestants Muste and King, as much as Day and Merton, guided others along the lines of a typical rule. How did their success or failure in spiritual discipline affect their lives?

Sustenance also comes through a confidence in God's presence. The stories of biblical characters and of saints are punctuated with divine encounters giving people an indelible sense of God's *sustaining presence*. What were the formative encounters in the lives of Muste, Merton, Day, and King? How did those experiences sustain them?

As all four faced the horrors of violence and injustice, they were upheld by a *vision* of the future refuting one-dimensional world-views that would ordain a status quo. A vision of the future inspired slaves exiting Egypt and slaves in the American South, exiles in Babylon and Christian exiles in their own lands. King was not the only one who looked into the future from a mountaintop. What were the visions that energized each of them?

Liberals tend to have a warped understanding of *hope*. Some late nineteenth-century Liberal Protestants tended to equate technological progress with human perfection. Some post-Vatican II Roman Catholics have practically eradicated the concept of sin without doing much about its reality. How did the optimistic Muste and King and the pessimistic Day and Merton maintain hope after it had collided with evil?

Just as each of us has a singular relationship with God, so each person has a unique DISCERNMENT OF THE WORLD. The Gospel of John's sophisticated view of the "world" as beyond redemption yet worthy of redemption has rarely been equalled. Yet each individual has to come to his or her own stance regarding sin, chaos, redemption, imagination, the Church, and his or her own responsibility for the world.

The matrix of *sin, evil, and suffering* has, in Christian tradition, run the gamut from Satan-dominated theologies to Platonism's denial of evil's reality. Some people are spiritually near-sighted, seeing personal sin with clarity without observing collective evil. Others are far-sighted, focusing on evil out there without seeing it within. How clear-sighted were Muste and Merton, King and Day in their experience of sin, evil and suffering?

Part of world-discernment rests in one's analysis of the severity of social ills. Are we to call for reform or revolution? Social Gospel preachers reveled in either/or scenarios, offering damnation and perfection in consecutive breaths. King began his ministry in the same style. Day's words were more restrained. Muste and Merton believed they were surrounded by an *apocalyptic chaos*. Like the prophet Jeremiah, they believed they lived in a dying civilization in need of death-bed conversion.[4] How did their diagnoses affect their ministries?

To most Christians, the Church--or *a* Church--bears the power of Christ to redeem the world. Yet, in the Christian tradition *redemption* comes from surprising people and unusual places: through slaves out of Egypt, through a reviled small-town prophet dying a big-city criminal's death, through society's uneducated, unworldly, and unsuccessful. How did Merton, Muste, Day, and King understand the reality of redemption in their time?

Literature and imagination played a formative role in the lives of the young, white volunteers who helped register Southern black voters during Freedom Summer in 1964.[5] The *creative imagination* is forged in the terrible collision of evil and hope, and germinates in the friction between present suffering and a vision of future relief. How did imagination affect the lives and define the ministries of King, Day, Muste, and Merton?

Like Walter Rauschenbusch, Muste, Day, King, and Merton all wanted to "rechristianize" a Church which, like creation in Genesis, seemed both "good" and "fallen."[6] This *true and false Church* bruised each one of them. In return, they criticized its profligate infidelity to Christ. Yet they could not separate themselves from its selfish appetites without leaving behind its nurturing breasts. Was it possible for them to love the Church without hating it?

Although actively working to promote social change, each was profoundly aware of being what Merton called a *guilty bystander*. In classic fashion, all denounced the Pharisee in others and in themselves who rejoiced that, if not sinless, he is at least better than the tax collector (Lk 18:10-14). When so many people find guilt paralyzing, how did they find the admission of guilt a first step to freedom?

Experiences of God, perceptions of the world, and a sense of one's gifts help each Christian to discern her MINISTRY, to locate his part in the redemptive task. Christian ministry requires foolishness, risk, a transformed inner landscape, and a focus on a particular, scandalous vocation.

All Christians ask how they are to follow Jesus, how they are to interpret his words, how much they are to risk, how they are to balance those risks with daily responsibilities. Day answered that Christians are called to live *marginal*, *precarious lives*. With Merton, Muste, and King, she asked a question that countered the world's need: How to make their lives *more* precarious?

Had Nicodemus the pharisee asked Merton or Muste, King or Day, how he was to serve the world, each might have answered: First you must undergo *an inner revolution*, for unless you are born again you cannot assist at the birth of a new earth. Gandhi's demand for interior consistency with external action deeply influenced all four of them. How did they seek to embody this consistency in their lives?

All four cited Paul's words (1 Cor 1) about being *fools for Christ*. They knew the world considered them strange or irrelevant. They struggled to be content with the scandalous particularity of their callings. What could they say to a world that denounced or dismissed them as absurd?

In a complex world, how is a Christian to choose a particular *vocation*? Day's consistency contrasts with Muste, King, and Merton whose vocational questions rarely brought crystalline answers. Their Christian witness included Merton's solitary protest, Day's small-scale personal ministry, Muste's grand experiments, and King's politically transforming imagination. Monk, journalist, organizer, and preacher, their vocations begin to suggest the countless ways in which others can become co-liberators with God and Christ. What do their vocational struggles have to do with ours?

These threads, both common and diverse, tie together the spirit, faith, and life of Muste, Day, King, and Merton. Some of these elements may already uphold and direct us in our ministries. We may find other bonds between their lives and ours. Longer glimpses into their hearts and minds can help us search our traditions and consciences more thoroughly for other threads. More lasting looks into their intuitions about themselves, the Church, the world, and God can help us to understand why they lived as they did; why we live as we do. Nourished with tastes of their faith, hope, and love, we might find our lives snatched out of defeated assumptions and sparked with life-giving insights. Their lives can assist us to read anew our political landscape and--more significantly--lead us to compassion, prophecy, service, and love.

Muste, Day, King, and Merton did not live peaceful lives, for God's peace creates human strife. They were often torn by events, often restless in their vocations. The path to sanctity passes through anguish as well as inner peace, through confusion as well as clarity, and leads to frustration as often as joy. But is there anywhere else we would rather go?

NOTES

INTRODUCTION

1. Thomas Merton, *The Silent Life* (New York, 1957), 7; Evelyn Underhill, *The House of the Soul and Concerning the Inner Life* (Minneapolis, 1947 [repr.]), 150-51; Ray C. Petry, *Late Medieval Mysticism* (Philadelphia, 1957), 179.

2. Gary Commins, "Woody Allen's Theological Imagination," *Theology Today* 44: 2 (July 1987): 238.

3. Paul M. Minus, *Walter Rauschenbusch: American Reformer* (New York, 1988), 112.

4. Walter Brueggemann, *Hopeful Imagination* (Philadelphia, 1986), 32.

5. Robert Coles, *Dorothy Day: A Radical Devotion* (Reading, Massachusetts, 1987), 20-21.

6. Minus, 160.

CHAPTER ONE
A. J. MUSTE

April 15, 1967. Thousands of rain-drenched marchers walked Manhattan's wet streets to protest against the war in Vietnam. When asked, police officials estimated the crowd at 125,000. Protest organizers gauged their numbers at 350,000. Even the police estimate made this the largest demonstration the growing anti-war movement had yet produced. If asked who led the march, protest organizers might have pointed to a car near the head of the procession, a movable memorial to a man who had chaired planning meetings for the Spring Mobilization until his death two months before. Protest leaders had mounted a ten-foot high photograph of eighty-two-year-old A. J. Muste on top of the car and placed flowers in front of the photo--their tribute to the man who held together diverse and sometimes clashing groups in common opposition to the war. The organizers wanted the spirit of A. J.--the bemused detachment and the intense commitment--to lead the procession. If they could hold on to that spirit, the health of the movement was assured.[1]

The huge demonstration was one sign that Muste's work had born fruit. He achieved a second posthumous victory that day when Martin Luther King, Jr. gave his third major anti-war speech before a crowd in the United Nations plaza. They had known each other since the Montgomery bus boycott in 1956. For the previous three years the peace movement's elder statesman had told King, "there is a lynching going on in Vietnam," and urged him toward a more public stance against the war. King had declined Muste's previous invitations to join him on trips to Saigon in 1966 and to Hanoi in 1967. Now King put aside his ambivalence and took up Muste's longtime conviction that one could not "segregate" the cause of racial equality from the pursuit of peace.[2]

Muste's friends and fellow workers recognized that he died at the height of his influence and that his retirement years had been the most fruitful period of his life.[3] His fifty-year record of radicalism and pacifism, his personal integrity, and his ability to encourage cooperation among contentious factions enabled him to guide the peculiar amalgam that was the peace movement. He operated among traditional religious pacifists and secular radicals in the manner of the clerk at a Quaker meeting. As the clerk of the meeting listens to various points of view and finally sums up the "sense" of the meeting, so Muste quietly gathered various arguments together and unified divided discussions by stating the "sense" of the group.

Memories of Muste filled the pages of radical periodicals. Friends and co-workers remembered his self-discipline, his sense of humor, his detachment from possessions--the story of how he used to line the soles of his worn shoes with newspaper. Others remembered his interest in history and poetry, his love of baseball and the Marx brothers. Some could not reconcile the contradictions in his life--treating women as equals at work while retaining a traditional husband- and father-dominated family; his time-tested faith with his sporadic church attendance; his flippancy toward his dual membership in the Quaker meeting and the

Presbyterian Church. Those close to him argued whether his idealism had been realistic or naive.[4]

Perhaps because of this unresolved tension of realism and idealism, the elderly Muste communicated well with the generation that claimed it did not trust anyone over thirty. Twice he was invited to speak to gatherings of Students for a Democratic Society (SDS). His youthful anti-war co-workers admired him because he never invoked his half-century of experience as credentials for infallibility. Muste listened carefully to people sixty years his junior to discern their insights. After he died, one young man commented, "We are all sons of A. J."[5]

Late in life Muste referred to the years when he left Christian pacifism to follow Lenin as a "detour," a theme others picked up to interpret this chapter in his life. Colleague Sidney Lens, however, saw an elusive continuity: "His life had a central thread that combined inflexibility in ends with flexibility in means." Another commentator called Muste's a "surprisingly consistent life." On Muste's eightieth birthday, he received a telegram from Martin and Coretta King: "You have climbed the mountain and have seen the great and abiding truth to which you have dedicated your life."[6]

Throughout Muste's long and varied life he committed himself to help build the Kingdom of God on earth. The visions of the Hebrew prophets burned with earthy hopes of economic security, physical safety, long life, and freedom from fear. A "new heaven" had its place in Muste's heart, but visions of a "new earth" were his daily bread. The Quaker tradition, the labor movement, and Marxism-- each of which, in turn, claimed Muste's allegiance--all held the common intuition that history moves unevenly but inexorably toward that new earth.

Born in 1885, Abraham Johannes Muste left the Netherlands with his family at the age of six to join the on-going wave of migration across the Atlantic.

Raised in Michigan in the Calvinist tradition of the Dutch Reformed Church, Muste later reflected on his conservative upbringing: "In my own youth, one no more thought that a church member could vote the Democratic ticket than that he could beat his wife, or steal, or have extramarital sexual relations."[7]

Although he turned against his family's rigid dogmatism, he retained a conservative spiritual bent that became the foundation beneath his radical politics. He exchanged personal piety for the principles of the Social Gospel. The Sermon on the Mount and the so-called social teachings of the Hebrew prophets became the new cornerstones of his faith.

On an Easter Sunday afternoon when he was thirteen, Muste was walking outdoors when "the world took on a new brightness." He heard a voice within himself say, "Christ is risen indeed." For the first time in his life, God's presence felt real and appeared to him as an image of light.[8]

One of the few things young Muste never questioned was the feeling that led him to the ordained ministry. He graduated from a small college and attended a conservative seminary in New Jersey. In his first major shift within the Church, Muste moved away from rigid Calvinism. Another vision of light accompanied this change, this time in the halls of a New Jersey hotel:

> I was walking late one morning down the corridor of [the] hotel.
> Suddenly came again that experience of a great light flooding in
> upon the world making things stand forth "in sunny outline brave
> and clear" and of God being truly present and all-sufficient.[9]

He learned of liberal theology at Union Theological Seminary where, in 1912, he received a Bachelor in Divinity degree. Working in New York City, he came face-to-face with urban social problems and became acquainted with the Social Gospel movement.

Muste's second major shift within the Church came in the following years when he broke away from the dominant Christian ethics of the period:

> In all the study of the Scriptures through which I had been led in that
> citadel of orthodoxy, New Brunswick, and in the hotbed of heresy
> which was Union. . . .I had never been given an inkling that there
> might be such a thing as a pacifist interpretation of the Gospel.[10]

His shift in doctrine moved him from the Dutch Reformed tradition to the broader Congregational Church. His reading of scripture and his exposure to Social Gospel leaders like Walter Rauschenbusch and the Quaker pacifist Rufus Jones prepared him for pacifism just as the United States readied itself to enter World War I.

Muste assisted in the creation of a Boston branch of the newly organized Fellowship of Reconciliation (FOR) in 1916. Formed by a handful of English pacifists in response to the war, the FOR soon found sympathetic spirits in American pacifists and Social Gospel advocates like Rauschenbusch. They all exuded enthusiasm for the Sermon on the Mount's demands for nonviolence, love of enemies, and inner transformation, and shared the same confidence in a universal law of love and humanity's "essential teachability." Largely a liberal Protestant organization in its beginnings, the FOR quickly became a significant pacifist force in the U.S., acting "as a fulcrum" between social transformation and objection to war.[11]

Muste's preaching in his Congregational Church in Newtonville, Massachusetts turned in fits and starts toward nonviolence even as popular sentiment swung toward national zealotry. Muste knew that he might suffer the fate of other pacifist clergy. His sermons early in 1917 reveal a soul divided by his immigrant's patriotism and his evolving pacifism. Then he openly declared his pacifism. When a family in the congregation refused his pastoral care upon the death of their soldier son, Muste resigned in an atmosphere filled more with mutual disappointment than with malice.[12] Muste's ethical shift proved more revolutionary than its theological predecessor. Now he hungered for sanctification--the disciple's development into the likeness of Christ--for himself and for all Christians.

In 1919 and again in 1940, Muste associated with a pacifist fellowship concerned with sanctification. By 1919 Muste embraced the conventional Quaker style of pacifism that emphasized individual witness and pastoral ministry, and avoided political confrontation. He became the part-time minister of the Friends Meeting in Providence, Rhode Island. He visited imprisoned conscientious objectors who often suffered cruel mistreatment. Joining other ministers without pulpit, he became a part of "The Comradeship," a small group that lived together in Boston, made plans for a rural cooperative, and studied scripture's relevance for peace and social change. When Muste returned to pacifism after a long hiatus in the secular Left, he was persuaded by the gentle nudging of old friend and FOR leader John Nevin Sayre--and by war in Europe--to become the FOR's Executive Secretary in 1940. Just before the consummation of his relationship with the FOR that year, when pacifism still lay near one main strand in American political thought, *Time* named Muste America's "number one pacifist."[13]

Muste's restless convictions kept him skipping impatiently from one ideology and strategy to another in his search for a way to the new earth he envisioned. One of his young colleagues in the 1960s remembered that the old activist believed in trial and error. Muste defined his career as a series of "experiments," a word that punctuates his writings. In his adopted Quaker background, colonial Pennsylvania had been a "holy experiment" to create a new kind of social order. Mahatma Gandhi--who also influenced Muste--wrote of his own search for social, political, and spiritual change as an "experiment with truth." Muste asserted that Gandhi had turned nonviolence into "a science in the making."[14]

Muste liked to quote the Jewish theologian Martin Buber: "It is difficult, terribly difficult, to drive the plowshare of the normative principle into the hard soil of political reality."[15] Muste worked diligently to apply his principles and his vision of the new earth to social reality. While impressed by Thomas Merton's intellect, wisdom, and political commitment, when they met in 1964, Muste could not fathom the monastic vocation that seemed to remove moral principles from political reality. Merton, of course, understood his vocation as his own experiment with truth.[16]

Many religious pacifists entered the labor movement after the First World War to work against the injustices that bred violence. Muste's membership in The Comradeship led him to the Lawrence Strike in 1919, the first in a chain of experiments over fifty years that allowed him to exercise his ideals. After the strike's successful completion, he became the head of a new union, the Amalgamated Textile Workers, and began a slow transfer of allegiance from a Church uninterested in social redemption to the labor movement.

In 1921, Muste was named the first director of Brookwood Labor College. Teaching students historical and theoretical perspective on industrial society and training them for practical organizing, Brookwood resembled a seminary for labor leaders. It also bore a likeness to the Catholic Worker's "agronomic university" as it integrated workers with scholars, and action with reflection. At a poetry reading shortly before Muste began his twelve years at Brookwood, he read from Henry Vaughn: "I saw Eternity the other night/Like a great ring of pure and endless light/All calm as it was bright."[17] He felt the presence of the great light even as his pursuit of the new earth led him away from the Church.

Brookwood never endeared itself to the conservative wing of the labor movement, yet its influence exceeded its small size. It intentionally sought out blacks and women as students and gave Marx and Lenin equal billing with mainstream labor leaders. Always controversial, Brookwood shaped part of a new generation of aggressive labor organizing and won for Muste an important place in the development of American labor.

Muste chaired the FOR from 1926-29, but he abandoned pacifism and Christianity shortly thereafter. Frustrated with the Church's alliance with the powers-that-be and pacifism's failure to transform society, he yearned to act more directly to alleviate the suffering of the poor. He counted on the labor movement to build the new earth. Years of brutal labor conflict hardened him to accept political doctrines of violent revolution. As his Christian pacifism collided with Marxist revolution, he followed Marx.

By the early 1930s, Muste was like an explorer trying to find his way through an impenetrable mountain range to a promised land. Just as he tired of religious pacifism, so Brookwood wearied him of education separated from labor action. To bring them together he helped to start the Conference for Progressive Labor Action (CPLA) to embody the trade unionism advocated at Brookwood. When he tried to bring Brookwood into the CPLA in 1933, however, the college's board of directors forced him to resign.

Like his earlier move from The Comradeship to the labor movement, he again turned from education to action and edged from reform to revolution. The CPLA became involved in various strikes and formed Unemployed Leagues, which competed for hundreds of thousands of members with a parallel Communist organization. Just after Muste visited striking workers in Toledo, Ohio, he was arrested in Illinois on an amusing combination of charges--vagrancy and treason. The lighter charge was soon withdrawn but the more serious accusation hung over his head for almost a year before it, too, was dropped.

Muste soon realized that the CPLA could not achieve his goals and, seeing a fragmented Left, he began a brief foray into party politics with the founding of the American Workers' Party (AWP). Shortly after the formation of the AWP, Leon Trotsky's Communist League of America invited him to forge a new party--the Workers' Party of the United States--with Muste as its head. In spite of promises made before the merger, the new party promptly merged again--over Muste's objections--with the Socialist Party. Feeling used as a political pawn, Muste grew disgusted with his comrades' lack of ethics and disillusioned with the movement.

In the wake of this political debacle, some friends feared for his emotional health and chipped in to send A. J. and wife Anna on a European vacation in 1936. Muste met Trotsky in Norway where they spent a few days in mutual admiration, and Muste re-considered his position in the Left. Then he went to Paris where his life was irrevocably changed. While sitting in a church he heard an inner voice calling him back to Christian pacifism. After the previous evolutionary changes in his life, this transformation came like a sudden, blinding light. His long "detour" was over. Muste had come home.

Immediately upon his return to the U.S., he re-established his relationship with the FOR and became its Industrial Secretary. Having never revoked his credentials as a minister, he received a call to the Presbyterian Labor Temple in New York City. Founded twenty-five years earlier to address the unchurched through education and social service, the Labor Temple was Muste's Ellis Island back into the Church. He came into contact with the Catholic Worker and accepted invitations to speak to their community. His association with Dorothy Day led to shared civil disobedience in the 1950s, to work together on the Committee for Nonviolent Action (CNVA), and to a joint position in the 1960s as godparents to the anti-war movement.

As head of the FOR in the 1940s, Muste did not let World War II and the Cold War absorb all of his energies. The establishment of the FOR's Department of Race Relations in 1942 led to the founding of the Congress on Racial Equality (CORE) which formulated the nonviolent strategy for social change that became the hallmark of the civil rights movement.

Anna's ill health forced A. J. to cut back on his activities several years before her death in 1954. Her death and his retirement from the FOR opened the door to the most creative period of his life as he experimented with bringing together elements from his earlier work in the Church, the labor movement, politics, and pacifism. As he had moved from The Comradeship into the Lawrence Strike and from Brookwood to the CPLA and politics, once again he emphasized action over education.

After his disillusioning experience in the 1930s, Muste concluded there was more honor among thieves than among Communists. He refused to work with them in "united fronts" and painted the Soviet Union and the U.S. in the same critical hues. Yet, throughout the McCarthy era, he fought for Communists' civil liberties, a stand that bolstered his already impressive credentials as the ideal reconciler for the coming anti-war movement. In the 1950s, however, his opposition to McCarthyism merely won him J. Edgar Hoover's appellation as a Communist "front."

At the age of seventy-four, after spending nine days in jail and being put on one year's probation for a demonstration near Omaha, Muste joked that he did not know if he could last a whole year without taking part in another protest. Three years later, desirous of rest after returning from Dar es Salaam, he accepted an invitation to go to New Delhi the next month. In 1963, he organized a protest against apartheid at the South African consulate in New York City. At an Easter rally that same year he became one of the first Americans to speak out against military involvement in Vietnam. After his trip to Saigon in 1966, he told friends that he was too tired to travel again. When invited to North Vietnam, he averred that his earlier resolution had not included Hanoi.[18]

Muste's spirit of experimentation permeated every phase of his life. Never satisfied with existing institutions for reform or revolution, he felt compelled to create new ones and coined the same term for different kinds of organizations. In the 1930s, he wanted the American Workers' Party to be a "third way" between communism and the Socialist Party. In the fifties and sixties he searched for a "third camp," a "third force," a "third way"--an alliance among leaders of Asian and African independence movements, Western pacifists, Gandhians, and neutralists-- as an alternative to the violence of the capitalist and communist blocs.[19]

Most of Muste's experiments were creative but ineffective, and the measure of his failure is the degree to which he is forgotten outside of radical and pacifist circles. Gandhi's gospel had some success in India and again among African-Americans in the American South, but Muste failed to attract the white churches and privileged people he most often addressed.

Although Muste considered nonviolence a science and himself an experimenter, it would be more accurate to call nonviolence a search over largely uncharted terrain (in spite of Gandhi) and himself an explorer; or to call nonviolence a fine art and himself an artist. Yet despite his failures and his appropriation of an inexact analogy, the idea of the "experiment" had its practical and spiritual value. He did not invest his whole heart in any particular experiment and so was not easily disheartened or defeated. The attitude of experimentation encourages detachment from the need for immediate or dramatic results. In being freed from the anxiety to succeed, Muste guaranteed the resilience of his ministry.

The series of career migrations almost over, the new earth not yet found, Muste's inner light burned undimmed. One of his last experiments--his trip to Saigon at the age of 81--was especially trying. At a press conference, he and his fellow protesters became targets of eggs, tomatoes, and heckling. His small group's decision not to cooperate with arrest prior to an abortive demonstration at Saigon's American Embassy meant that they would be dragged away. One of his friends, Barbara Deming, had been especially concerned for the tall, thin, frail old man whose hands shook almost constantly. It was hot and humid. They were packed into a paddy wagon, then stuffed in a detention room at the airport as they awaited deportation. She "looked across the room at A. J. to see how he was doing. . . .He looked back with a sparkling smile and, with that sudden lighting up of his eyes which so many of his friends will remember, he said, 'It's a good life!'"[20]

Abraham

"Faith is the assurance of things hoped for, the conviction of things not seen...By faith Abraham obeyed when he was called to go out to a place which he was to receive as an inheritance; and he went out, not knowing where he was to go...For he looked forward to the city which has foundations, whose builder and maker is God."
   --Hebrews 11:1, 8, 10 (RSV)

"Show thy erring children at last the way from the City of Destruction to the City of Love."
   --Walter Rauschenbusch.[21]

An emigrant and immigrant as a child, Muste pictured himself as an emigrant and immigrant for life. It was part of his personal vocation, the Christian vocation, the world's vocation. He learned English without a trace of an accent, pledged allegiance to his new country, and established himself in his American home, but his life remained in perpetual migration. While Day, King, and Merton each stayed in one lifelong vocation, Muste's life contained enough dramatic exits to enliven several careers.

As a child Muste felt attracted to his American namesake, Abraham Lincoln, as an adult to his biblical namesake, Abraham. While traditional Christianity exalted Abraham as a model of piety, Muste found in Abraham's faith a "revolutionary concept of history." Abraham stood at the birth of sacred and secular history as the forefather of Israel and all nations. When he abandoned the status quo to obey God's voice and pursue a vision of the future, he inaugurated history's greatest revolution. Abraham was a fool, a gambler, a living critique of every status quo, and the progenitor of all revolutions.[22]

Abraham altered Muste's quasi-Calvinist understanding of destiny. The eighteenth-century Quaker John Woolman felt "drawn" to travel the American colonies and persuade his fellow Quakers to free their slaves. Destiny did not confine one to a pre-determined life; it invited a person toward a new destination.[23] Muste emulated his biblical namesake as he gambled that God was the impetus drawing him from one vocation and place to the next in an endless sequence of new ventures. At the celebration of his seventy-fifth birthday, he ended his address with a quote from the Battle Hymn of the Republic: "Be swift, my soul, to answer Him. Be jubilant, my feet." His glad eagerness to answer any call made him identify with Abraham.[24]

Abraham's journey became one of Muste's favorite texts. Before the American entry into World War II he advised fellow pacifists to be like Abraham who did not know where he was going but retained his commitment to God's will even as he struggled to discern it. God called pacifists, as God had called Abraham, to become instruments in redeeming the world. Pacifists did not have to define their goals with precision any more than Abraham had to draw a detailed map of the Promised Land. God provided no blueprints. If the Church and peace organizations were "not to a degree groping and confused" they did not understand the grave complexity of their situation. If they could but dimly discern the outlines of a new society lying ahead, they could confidently set out in the right general direction.[25]

Muste retold the story of Abraham as a tale of two cities, the "city-which-is and the city-which-is-to-be." God did not call the faithful to reform existing civilizations nor to move from one existing society to another. History moved toward "the perfect and holy city. . .whose 'builder and maker is God,'" and God sought out people as co-constructors to build this city. On his sixty-fifth birthday, Muste yearned to "symbolize and be faithful to the mad, relentless, joyous search for that city which is to be." If he could continue that race, he would be "more than content."[26]

Abraham departed from the city of Ur, a nondescript, morally neutral place known primarily for being left behind. Yet Muste often referred to the city-which-is as a doomed place, more akin to violent, pride-filled, and self-contradictory Babel. The Roman Empire in the age of apostolic Christianity, Oliver Cromwell's seventeenth-century regime at the dawning of the Quaker movement, the "City of Destruction" in the prayer of Walter Rauschenbusch, and the city-which-is were houses collapsing on rotten foundations. Muste likened Western Civilization to the city described by Augustine, the city that "seems to be able to dominate and destroy everything, but is itself dominated and destroyed by its own lust for power."[27]

In some ways, Muste's disdain for existing institutions equalled the antagonistic disregard other Christians, expecting the imminent return of Christ, felt for things passing away. But while they prepared for God's action through personal introspection and waited for God to deliver heaven to earth--or earth's faithful to heaven--Muste prepared to assist God in creating a new social order.

In its biblical context, the call of Abraham represents God's first step to repair a fragmented world after the fall of the tower of Babel. God called Abraham to counter the Babelization of the world, and from Sarah's womb came the beginnings of a new, redemptive community. Their children and children's children heard God repeat the promise of this community which was to be a blessing to all nations.

When God prepared to destroy Sodom because of its sins, Abraham interceded that God should save the whole city if it contained but fifty righteous people. And if God would save it for fifty, then why not for forty-five, or forty, or thirty, or twenty, or ten (Gen 18:22-32)? When in 1959 four demonstrators joined Muste to protest missile production by trespassing at Mead Air Force Base, one supporter said, "Perhaps God will spare us for the sake of five!"[28] Perhaps God would spare the world for the sake of the righteous few who sought the new earth.

In the middle of the McCarthy era, Muste persuaded fifty-five people, including Eleanor Roosevelt, to sign a petition calling for the release of Communists imprisoned under the Smith Act. When atomic scientists became concerned about the new atomic bomb, he wrote that if only two percent of them became conscientious objectors "multitudes" would follow. He predicted that a thousand recruits would make the World Peace Brigade, founded to resolve international conflicts through nonviolence, a viable political entity.[29]   Each generation gave birth to new forms of the redemptive community.

Muste felt that the great fellowship that would be the new earth required small fellowships like The Comradeship, Brookwood, and the secular coalitions of his retirement years. Although he sometimes questioned the practical effectiveness of alternative communities like The Comradeship and the Catholic Worker because they tended to emphasize community life over social impact, he felt drawn back into the nurturing community of the FOR.[30]

Remnant communities provided a "new spiritual dynamic" at critical junctures in history. They had outlasted Pharaoh, Nebuchadnezzar, Caesar, Barabbas, Hitler, Mussolini, and Stalin. A community relying solely on the power of God's love could still redeem the world.[31] Although they used different brands of leaven, Merton the Trappist monk, Day the Catholic Worker, and King the President of the SCLC saw the need for a remnant fellowship to redeem their society.

Christian traditions have usually attributed this role to the Church as a whole or to a certain sect within it. Strongly ambivalent about the Church, Day, King, and Merton sometimes questioned its own redeemability, yet Muste was the only one to actually leave it. All of them hated the Church for being an obstacle to God's will and loved it for being an instrument of grace. Muste was perennially disappointed with the Church--its dogmatism, its nationalism, its aloofness from workers and the poor. Even its rare, spasmodic interest in pacifism seemed to lift his hopes in order to dash them. He despaired of the Church when it forgot its mission to seek the new earth.

He often used the phrase "true church" to distinguish the institutional Church from the fellowship building the city-to-be. The Church assumed that its ontological existence constituted its witness to Christ's presence in the world. Muste had a functional view of the Church as an instrument of justice and reconciliation. If it did not perform that task, it failed. Jesus formed the Church around a mission and if it did not perform that mission, it lost its raison d'etre. Similar to King's "ekklesia," Muste's "true church" was the remnant within the institutional Church that received God's Word, repented, put down the sword, and sought reconciliation.[32]

During World War I, Muste said, "The real task of the church is to create the spiritual conditions that should stop the war and render all wars unthinkable"; a generation later, that it ought to proclaim a new society where God's will is done on earth as it is in heaven. Yet the Church still held the Gospel in one hand and a bomb in the other.[33]

To depend on the Church was like counting on squeezing a camel through the eye of a needle. Its entanglements with wealth, prestige, and power kept it from going where God called it. The Church in the West was like the Christian community of Laodicea--a church "neither hot nor cold," a church that made God sick (Rev 3:15-16). Muste repeatedly invited the Church to choose sacrificial love over power, to renounce violence and embrace the Cross, to become the world's saving remnant. A lifetime of letdowns did not completely deflate his hopeful nature. At the age of seventy-five he challenged the Church yet again: "The Church must itself be the *great Fellowship of Reconciliation* or be untrue to its Lord." But because the Church had lost the flavor of salt (Mt 5:13), the pacifist movement had to keep the taste of redemption fresh.[34]

In a 1929 address to the FOR, Muste preached on the Parable of the Two Sons. One son says he will obey his father but does not; the other says he will not serve his father yet he does: "Which of the two did the will of his father (Mt 21:31)?" The parable became a governing principle to discern the spiritual health of Christians. Some people sound Christian and are not; others do not sound like Christians, yet they serve God. Regardless of their religious or political affiliations, in Muste's true church, the one who worked for a new earth was the true Christian.[35]

In the next decade, Muste equated Marxist revolution with the coming of God's Kingdom and the Communist Party became his "one, holy catholic Church." The Christian Church had not done the job it said it would do. It had turned against its Father, so Muste transferred membership to the "church" which unknowingly sought to do God's will.[36]

As Muste began his "detour" into Marxism and compared the church of Christ unfavorably to the church of Lenin, he shared Day's experience of seeing radicals "doing something," unlike the Christians who had thoroughly adapted themselves to the city-which-is. He saw communists committed to a cause and willing to make personal sacrifices. He saw secular leftists dedicated to a vision of a classless, warless world, "a new earth in which righteousness dwelleth" (2 Pt 3:13), while Christians allied themselves with the forces of exploitation and war. The Christians of the first four centuries had not feared, bet on, sworn allegiance to, nor sought satisfaction from their era's dying order, but twentieth-century Christians had abandoned their apostolic heritage.[37]

The Comradeship had asked: How do you undo the conditions that create war? Muste called Brookwood College the "spiritual child" of The Comradeship because he believed it answered their question. Muste persisted in the same question every step of his circular path from pacifism to revolutionary violence and back to pacifism. In his labor-Marxist period, he believed that only a classless society could release the world from sin and undo conditions conducive to war. A warless world had a pre-requisite: the abolition of "capitalism which begets war."[38]

He launched the American Workers' Party to organize the laborers he saw as the instrument of social salvation. After his pacifism was resurrected, he continued to believe in the redemptive role of the oppressed in social transformation. In 1943, he wanted African-American churches to transplant Gandhian nonviolence onto American soil. He anticipated the intuition of Brazilian educator Paulo Freire: Because the oppressed have less to lose, they see that capitalism is "necrophilic." Freed from vested interests in maintaining the status quo, the oppressed--exploited laborers and oppressed blacks--could see alternatives to the City of Destruction and become agents of social change. As Muste put it, "the gulf between the peoples who have experienced humiliation as a people and those who have not is the deepest and most significant that we have to face." On one side of the gulf stood most of the world; on the other side stood most white Americans. How do you undo the conditions that create war? Jesus had founded "a worldwide fellowship of the lowly, the oppressed, the toilers, who were to be bound together in solidarity and affection for each other, and to devote themselves to the bringing in of a new social order." Muste kept coming back to the same realization. Redemption came through the humiliated, from the bottom of society up.[39]

When he returned to pacifism, Muste at first reversed his Marxist opinion: The abolition of war had to precede the demise of capitalism. Further reflection led him to see that the deaths of capitalism and war had a more subtle, dialectical relationship. One did not wait for a new economy to abolish war nor did one wait for the last truce to create a new economy. There were no either/ors when it came to peace, racial equality, and economic change. They all went "hand in hand" in one great transformation of the world-as-it-is. The Church was to battle against those "modern Leviathans" the superpowers, to announce the Christian hope of a new heaven and a new earth, and to proclaim that God's purposes for society were revealed in Jesus Christ.[40]

Muste found in the Abraham stories something that most Christians missed --an alternative to the war-making idolatry of his own time. He described a world that had to choose between two gods. The city-which-is worshipped Moloch, a god fed with the war dead of every generation from Abraham to World War II and ready to consume an older generation's offering of its young with peacetime conscription. The seekers of the city-which-is-to-be worshipped the God of Abraham. When God stopped Abraham from sacrificing his son Isaac, God forbade Abraham's descendants from sacrificing their children in war.[41] Muste also found in Abraham a model for his own vocation. Writing of her longtime ally, Day remembered that his "name Abraham means Father of a multitude, and he was that" and he traveled "to the ends of the earth. . .in search of peace."[42]

Abraham offered a revolutionary interpretation of history, a God to oppose all nationalistic and militaristic gods, and spiritual offspring to redeem the world. Israel's prophets later wrote of a remnant within God's unfaithful people, and Jesus established the apostolic Church as a saving remnant. In the Middle Ages, the mantle was worn by the Spiritual Franciscans and in Cromwell's England, by the Quakers. In the middle of the twentieth century, Muste saw the mantle of hope descending on the followers of Gandhi.

Choose Gandhi

"I call heaven and earth to witness against you today that I have set before you life and death, blessings and curses. Choose life so that you and your descendants may live. . . ."
   --Deuteronomy 30:19

"He that would save his life, in such a case, shall lose it. This people must cease to hold slaves, and to make war on Mexico, though it cost them their existence as a people."
   --Henry David Thoreau.[43]

In 1936, Muste returned to pacifism and spent much of the remainder of his life trying to guide radicals, liberals, and moderates, and Church and State to experience the same inner revolution that transformed his life. The reconverted pacifist debunked the popular dichotomies of capitalism and communism, West and East, Christianity and atheism. He envisioned a different set of choices: Totalitarianism or pacifism, total war or total pacifism.[44]

Religious pacifism had the tensile strength American capitalism lacked to challenge communism. The world of the late 1940s had a choice between two futures: Stalin or Gandhi. History, Muste believed, had conspired to set these choices before the world.

> [It was] part of the divine dispensation that the historic moment which saw the development of the atomic bomb--material violence to the nth degree--witnessed also the first large-scale triumph of Gandhian nonviolence, that the age of Lenin is the age also of Gandhi.[45]

The first "world" war and the first world pacifist organization--the FOR--both began in 1914. The 1940s produced a new height in violent destruction and the triumph of nonviolence. Like Day's mentor, Peter Maurin, who described Marx's materialist interpretation of history as the spiritual child of capitalism, Muste bluntly pronounced capitalism, as much as communism, a form of "death." The radical materialist interpretation of history and prescription of violent revolution merely echoed capitalism. Muste told radicals that if they wanted revolution, they had to choose the total revolution of Gandhi, not the superficial, cosmetic changes of Lenin. In the insane asylum of modern civilization, Jesus and Gandhi offered sanity, goodness, and hope.[46]

His conversion came suddenly--at the age of fifty-one--in the middle of his European vacation. As his ship pulled away from the dock in New York at the start of his trip, he raised his slender right arm in the clenched fist salute of violent revolution. Returning across the Atlantic, he showered his friends with letters announcing his "return to pacifism."[47]

He entered St. Sulpice Church in Paris as a Trotskyite tourist: "When you go sightseeing in Europe, you go to see churches even if you believe it would be better if there were no churches for anyone to visit." As he entered St. Sulpice, he felt a "deep and...singing peace." He sat down and noticed that this Catholic Church, cluttered with statues and saints, did not suit his Quaker tastes. "Without the slightest premonition of what was going to happen, I was saying to myself:

'This is where you belong.'" The inner voice added, "in the church, not outside it." The intuition came "without warning and transplanted me in an instant from one spiritual world, so to speak, into another." When he stood up he had been converted to the Christian pacifism he had sloughed aside.[48]

He later saw in his experience at St. Sulpice the image from Francis Thompson's "The Hound of Heaven," a God in relentless pursuit. It was one of Day's favorite poems. Muste's day in the Paris church paralleled a turning point in King's life. In a time of personal crisis, each heard an inner voice, felt an inner peace, and renewed his vocation.

> In coming back to faith in the way of non-violence and love I had returned to the true center of my own being, to God. Thus there was again peace within, whatever might happen outside. In a sense, what I might be able to do no longer mattered very much. I no longer needed to be anxious and preoccupied with the results of this campaign or that, since I was sure of the ultimate nature of the universe and realized that "the everlasting God, the Lord, the creator of the ends of the earth fainteth not, neither is weary." Paradoxically, however, I was able to go to work again with new enthusiasm and assurance, knowing that if there were a way to prevent war it was in a total pacifism, the actual practice of Jesus' way of life.[49]

This detached yet passionate commitment to nonviolent social change stayed with him the rest of his life.

In the previous decade and a half, the former preacher had become an apologist for violent revolution as he slowly qualified Jesus' words and actions with a worker's and then a Marxist's eye. Once again he believed that every use of violence tried to use Satan to cast out Satan. He regained the conservative spirit of his childhood and gave absolute authority to the words of Jesus. Each teaching provided spiritual direction to move from life-as-it-is to life-as-it-ought-to-be.[50]

Part of the convert's renewed vocation was to place a "radical choice" before the rest of the world so that it could choose life. His experience of his own human nature convinced him that people were free to choose life or death, blessing or curse, Marxism or pacifism. "A Christian can never be a fatalist," he said. The ability to choose, itself, became a linchpin of hope.[51] The Christian had to join with Herod to kill the Christ child *or* accept that child as King of Kings and Lord of Lords, and follow him to the Cross. Christians could wear the uniform of Caesar *or* carry the Cross of Christ. Western Christians approached the Soviet bloc with the Gospel in one hand and a nuclear weapon in the other. They had to leave one behind.[52]

In apocalyptic style, Muste set Christ's commands in opposition to orders from Winston Churchill. Theologians taking part in the Barmen Declaration of 1934 declared their time an historical crisis demanding an exclusive commitment to Christ. Martin Niemöller proclaimed Jesus Christ his "führer." And the Western Church has chosen to honor Christians who opposed Hitler. Muste's position was immeasurably more radical. The Christians who fought Nazism opposed what is popularly considered an aberration in Western Civilization. Muste saw democratic leaders like Churchill competing for loyalties that ought to belong solely to God. Niemöller and the crisis theologians considered their situation extraordinary. Muste asserted that the crisis existed in the West's ordinary, daily life. Western democracy was at odds with Christ. One had to choose between Christ or *Churchill.*[53]

In his years at the Labor Temple prior to World War II, Muste placed comparable choices before the labor movement. In his book *Non-Violence in an Aggressive World*, he often described Moses as a union organizer and the Exodus as a walkout. He pitted revolutionary Christianity against revolutionary Marxism like his allies at the Catholic Worker who considered the incarnation of Catholic social teachings the only radical alternative to communism. Workers had to choose the Communist International or the International of Goodwill and Nonviolence, the Church. After World War II, Muste said the United States had to choose between remaining a "bitter empire" or becoming a "redeemer nation," the politics of Machiavelli or the politics of the Hebrew prophets, "World War III or repentance and acceptance of God."[54]

The choices were clear: Blessing or curse, life or death. Foreshadowing Merton's language, he referred to the atomic bomb as the Beast of the Apocalypse. The nations could get rid of war or allow the apocalyptic horror to get rid of them. Yet the twentieth-century world seemed bent on making bad choices. In 1965, President Lyndon Johnson toured the U.S. using the quotation from Deuteronomy about choosing life (30:15-20) to justify military escalation in Vietnam. Muste was left to pick apart the contradictions in Johnson's Orwellian logic that death and war delivered life and peace.[55]

Muste's first assault on total war began prior to World War II and Hiroshima. Atomic weapons were not the root of the world's problems. They merely exacerbated the crisis. Muste did not practice "nuclear pacifism" nor was his opposition to war an adjustment to the nuclear age. He anticipated the temptation to total war before technology made it a practical possibility.[56]

Muste knew that the Gospel's paradoxical character made choosing life over death difficult: "For those who want to save their life will lose it, and those who lose their life for my sake, and for the sake of the gospel, will save it. For what will it profit them to gain the whole world and forfeit their life? Indeed, what can they give in return for their life?" (Mk 8:35-37) How could the individual or the nation save its life? One hundred years earlier, Thoreau said that to choose life the U.S. had to end its war in Mexico and abolish slavery. Territorial expansion and material prosperity--which most perceived as signs of life--were spiritual cancers. Physical increase led to spiritual decline; wealth impoverished the nation's soul.

The passage in Mark's Gospel connects Jesus' crucifixion and the disciple's Cross to words about life. Muste was never glib in referring to the Cross: Disciples risked death for the sake of the Gospel. Attachment to the things of the world brought spiritual death, and physical death--if offered in love--brought life. Similar words in the Gospel of John are preceded by another of Muste's--and Day's--favorite citations: "Very truly, I tell you, unless a grain of wheat falls into the earth and dies, it remains just a single grain; but if it dies, it bears much fruit" (Jn 12:24). Following some translations, Muste often used the word "seed" instead of "grain," for Seed in the Quaker tradition signifies Christ within each person.[57]

Muste's return to pacifism and Europe's return to war led to his first book, *Non-Violence in an Aggressive World*, published in 1940. Hiroshima and the Cold War made him put aside attempts at an autobiography to write his other book, *Not By Might*. Throughout the second book, he invited the United States to lose its life in order to save it, for there was an ironclad "law" that a nation's attempt to save its life meant losing it, that a grain of wheat bears fruit only by dying. The U.S. seemed bent on economic expansion and military ascendancy, so Muste asked: What does a nation gain "if it wins the whole world and loses its own soul?" Instead, the U.S. should risk losing its physical life for the sake of other nations and become a "spiritual Israel," a "savior-nation," a Suffering Servant nation whose wounds would heal others and whose demise would create a new world. The world would cherish the memory of a nation that laid down its arms, especially if that nation were the world's wealthiest and most powerful.[58]

No one in power chose what Muste called life. Philosophical opponents like Reinhold Niebuhr saw in his hopes for national conversion a sign of his inability to discern the depths of entrenched, institutional inertia and amorality.

While Muste might have characterized his role more poetically as a voice crying in the wilderness, the end result was the same. No one listened.

Two modes of power competed for ascendancy like two weapons systems seeking a bidder. Brute military and economic force contended against the power of love, the Spirit, and God. As Isaiah observed centuries before, "The Egyptians are human, and not God; their horses are flesh, and not spirit (31:3)," yet nations bet on the losing temporal strength of "horses." Muste found in the Book of Revelation and the hymns of the Church an alternative: the Lamb upon the Throne. He saw the world's salvation in the juxtaposition of the Lamb's weakness with the Throne's power, a recurrent image in his writings: "The Lamb, symbol of meekness, of gentleness, of seeming utter helplessness in the face of evil, of suffering love...is at the heart of all real power and the secret of every final victory." Like the author of Ephesians, Muste knew the necessity of "armor" in battling the principalities and powers, and preferred the "armor of God"--the breastplate of righteousness, the shield of faith, "the equipment of the gospel of peace"--to the weapons of Caesar (Eph 6:11-17).[59]

At the age of fifty-one, when many people have passed the major turning points in their lives, the Marxist-Leninist again became a Christian pacifist. Muste had chosen Gandhi over Lenin, Christ over Churchill, and he followed the path of militant nonviolence for the next thirty years. He wanted to believe that individuals, the Church, even the nations, hardened by centuries of violence and fear, also beyond the point of probable transformation, could experience the same miracle, leave capitalism and communism behind, and choose the way of self-sacrifice and love.

Gandhi wedded the spiritual to the political, personal transformation to social revolution. The Indian leader enacted the dreams of Americans who combined pacifism with the Social Gospel. He erased the caricature of pacifism as passive complicity with evil and opened the world's eyes for a moment's time to the possibilities of nonviolent non-cooperation as a confrontive, proactive tool for political change.

"The Way of Pacifism"

". . .the Spirit of Christ, by which we are guided, is not changeable, so as once to command us from a thing as evil and again to move unto it; and we do certainly know, and so testify to the world, that the spirit of Christ, which leads us into all Truth, will never move us to fight and war against any man with outward weapons, neither for the kingdom of Christ, nor for the kingdoms of this world."
     --George Fox

"May we look upon our treasures, the furniture of our houses, and our garments, and try whether the seeds of war have nourishment in these our possessions."
     --John Woolman.

"Let your life be a counter-friction to stop the machine."
     --Henry David Thoreau.[60]

To become a pacifist during the First World War was outrageous. To march on picket lines in the Lawrence textile strike less than two years after the Russian Revolution--in an air taut with fear of bolshevism--was even more preposterous. Hoping that a minister's presence might moderate police brutality against strikers, Muste led a peaceful procession through town. The police cut off Muste and another leader from the rest of the strikers and forced them down a side street. Police on horseback knocked his companion unconscious but they were careful to beat the pastor only on the body and the legs so that he would retain consciousness. As the horses corralled him forward, a woman yanked him into a barn to try to rescue him. But the police swiftly retrieved him and resumed the systematic beating until they threw him into the back of a waiting patrol wagon.[61]

Management subsequently had machine guns installed and pointed at the houses where the workers' families lived--allegedly to keep the peace, but in reality to intimidate or incite the strikers. Muste urged the strikers, when they passed by, to turn and smile at the machine guns as a sign that they would neither be intimidated nor seduced into a violent confrontation.[62] Their smiles expressed a wry sense of detachment, confidence as much as defiance, and a non-verbal statement that the industrialists did not have ultimate control over the strikers. It paralleled the humor of slave folk stories, of "puttin' on massa," a sense of humor and detachment sometimes invoked by King. Smiling subverted the means of intimidation and undermined the institutional and psychological ground of those in power. At Lawrence, the strategy worked.

As Muste tested the philosophy and methods of nonviolence in the labor movement's confrontational tactics, he began to define for himself the nature, meaning, and relevance of pacifism. Pacifists could not withdraw from the messy business of politics for the sake of an individualistic pseudo-sanctity. Traditional Anglo-Saxon pacifism was a luxury suffering humanity could ill afford. Muste's nonviolence confronted the fundamental causes of violence in order to make war unnecessary or impossible. His experiences at Lawrence taught him that nonviolence did not lead to easy or painless victories. Pacifism led to the Cross. Threats to his life and his beating at the hands of police were down payments on a crown of thorns.

A sardonic Muste lambasted pacifists who, drunk with optimism, believed the Hitlers of the world could be converted "with kindness and gentleness and a smile." Society could not be redeemed without suffering, nor sins remitted without the blood of martyrs. There was a "law of suffering and crucifixion," a "law" that the seed had to fall into the ground so that the grain could grow. "God's weapon and method is the Cross," he said, and the Cross did not eliminate or alleviate tragedy. Those who ignored the pain of social redemption confessed that pacifism functioned only in a non-existent, non-political world. When persons or nations went to war, he said, they had to be prepared to kill. If not so prepared, they were bluffing. A pacifist unwilling to die for the sake of nonviolent social change was also bluffing.[63]

However terrible the cost of each Cross, each one generated redemptive power to transform social problems: "Whenever love that will suffer unto death is manifested, whenever a true Crucifixion takes place, unconquerable power is released into the stream of history." Muste saw in the Cross Thoreau's "counter-friction" to the nations, to nuclear weapons, to spiritual lethargy.[64] Not even during his "detour" did Muste separate the way of pacifism from the way of Israel's Suffering Servant. Quakers wrote of spiritual power flowing into the veins of history, and Muste emphasized that it entered primarily through sacrifice. Each Cross was one more contraction in the birth of the Kingdom.

The relationship of nonviolence to political change had long been debated in Quaker circles. Three centuries earlier, George Fox assured Oliver Cromwell and then Charles II that the Society of Friends had no interest in politics. But in the twentieth century, Muste considered nonviolence a definite threat to the powers-that-be. He knew the lessons of pacifist history: In the seventeenth century, Friends withdrew from society and concentrated on sanctifying their own lives in their own communities; beneath the shadow of the French and Indian War in 1756, most Pennsylvania Quakers interpreted pacifism as a personal credo, not an instrument of policy. Hearing the distant rumblings of a European war in 1939 and

1940, most American pacifists again abandoned nonviolence as a pragmatic political tool.[65] To clear the good name of his Society, Fox said it would never pick up the sword even in the cause of the "kingdom of Christ." Although Muste was driven by hopes for the coming of the Kingdom, he refused to resort to violence even to inch forward toward his promised land. He said, "There is no way to peace; peace is the way."[66]

Writing only months after his "return to pacifism," Muste laid down the foundations of his pacifist creed: "The way of peace is really a seamless garment that must cover the whole of life and must be applied in all its relationships." He built his pacifism on a central affirmation: "God is love, love is of God." He later contrasted Gandhi with the Mahatma's followers: To Gandhi, nonviolence was a way of life; to his followers, a tool with which they could gain political independence from the British Empire. Gandhi's disciples and admirers, once in power, abandoned the Mahatma's teachings and adopted the militaristic politics of the British Empire.[67]

Muste insisted that religious pacifists be "possessed" by their convictions. During a retreat at New York's Finger Lakes in the summer of 1940, he took part in silent worship. When the Spirit moved him, he stood up and said, "If I can't love Hitler, I can't love at all," and he sat down again without elaboration. That was all the Spirit led him to say. If he believed in human unity and that love was the central, binding force at the core of the universe, he could not excommunicate Hitler even as the dictator brutalized Europe.[68]

Pacifism required personal self-examination. John Woolman observed the connection between people's daily way of life and the way of nonviolence, a discovery made independently by Merton. In his crusade against slavery, Woolman convinced his fellow Quakers that the slave system engendered violence. Muste made the same kind of observation: "War is not an accident. It is the logical outcome of a certain way of life. If we want to attack war, we have to attack that way of life." To rid the world of war, people had to rein in their material appetites, as well as society's materialism, militarism, and racism, the midwives of war. Like Merton, Muste found the roots of war in one's personal and interior life as much as in the fabric of society.[69]

Muste always linked personal wealth to international injustice. As he entered his Leninist phase, Muste told a gathering of the FOR that pacifism required personal renunciation of comfort, for material comfort begot violence. Even in the afterglow of his re-conversion, he agreed with Lenin that when pacifists clung to property and prestige, they covertly aided the cause of war. The occasional outbursts of mass violence the world called "war" were merely manifestations of a way of life that infected the culture, its economic and political life, and the spirit of the age. War would not end until uprooted from the things that nurtured it.[70]

The Comradeship had taught Muste that anyone who wanted a nonviolent society in the future had to manifest its values in one's own life in the present. In the language of New Testament scholarship, the "not yet" of God's Kingdom had to be partially realized in the "already."[71]

Muste's co-workers admired his "extreme simplicity" of life. He never changed jobs for financial gain, although his family--often dependent on the generosity of friends--might not have minded had he tried it just once. He tried instead to live up to his own words, "No one can honestly work for the coming of the Kingdom of God without trying to make his life *now* conform to its principles." Pacifism--like carrying one's Cross--was a daily practice. It demanded detachment and freedom from anxiety about social utility and respectability.[72]

Pacifism required political as well as personal discernment. Muste dissociated the FOR from isolationists and war resisters, potential political allies who also opposed American participation in World War II. Isolationists had once

opposed American membership in the League of Nations to free the U.S. to pursue
its own interests; pacifists objected to the League's dependence on the unjust Treaty
of Versailles. While isolationists rejoiced over Munich in 1938, Gandhi said,
"Europe has sold her soul. . . .The peace Europe gained at Munich is a triumph of
violence"; and Muste accused England and France of "giving away what doesn't
belong to you." War resisters isolated war from other social evils and cried out,
"Peace, peace" even if war's absence was built on an infrastructure of injustice (Jer
6:14, 8:11).[73] A generation later, the great majority of protesters and draft evaders
opposed the war in Vietnam because they did not think the cause worth dying for; a
small minority of pacifists objected to killing. Muste discerned the ethical and
theological differences beneath apparent political similarities.

Dorothy Day maintained that "the works of mercy" were always part of true
pacifism, and Muste asserted that the fruits of pacifism had to include visible,
positive forms of ministry to build alternatives to war. As the FOR's Executive
Secretary, Muste challenged pacifists to study and develop ministries in the labor
movement, prison reform, or church reform--concerns other pacifists considered
irrelevant to war--as ways to uncover and dissolve the roots of war. In wartime, he
consistently wrote about the labor movement and domestic racism, and he reminded
social reformers that militarism rode the backs of the poor, diverted national
resources, and derailed social progress.[74]

A true, lasting, and proactive pacifism had to be built on sturdy spiritual
foundations: Spiritual discipline was the handmaid of protest. During World War
II, Muste emphasized the importance of spiritual grounding to members of the
FOR: "Action-oriented worship and worship-centered action are the 'genius' and
essence of the Fellowship." When in 1959 he stepped over the low, barbed-wire
fence at the Mead Missile Base to be arrested, he quoted Isaiah, "In returning and

rest you shall be saved; in quietness and in trust shall be your strength" (30:15). At the age of sixty-six, he fasted during Holy Week in penance for the existence of the H-Bomb.[75]

Muste and Gandhi wanted inner purity to accompany social action. One could not truly seek social revolution without experiencing an "inner revolution," for until people were "born again" they remained addicted to self-justification. "Spiritual revival" had to prepare the way for social programs. Muste, like Gandhi, had to decide whether to wait until everyone in the movement accepted *satyagraha* (truth force) or pursue justice even before their allies became perfect *satyagrahi* (practitioners of satyagraha). Gandhi frequently confounded his allies when he opted for purity over pragmatism and withdrew from political action when his followers abandoned nonviolence. The mixed motives of Muste's allies hurt him less than unhealed human suffering. When forced to choose, Muste tended to lean toward justice over the need for holiness.[76]

Muste's conversion created in him a sensitivity to repentance and an urgent hunger to commune with God. He became an unofficial spiritual guide to the FOR as he urged his flock to meditate for thirty minutes to an hour each day, and to engage in regular Bible study, spiritual reading, solitary and corporate prayer, and non-sacramental confession and communion. No revolution would take place unless the leaders of the movement were "revolutionized." Pacifists and radicals needed to belong to an intimate fellowship where they could practice nonviolence and settle disagreements creatively. Members of the FOR belonged to "cells" or "teams" as part of their spiritual discipline. In cells, they gathered to worship, study, and discern their dependence on God. Cells reinforced individuals against the temptation to despair and reinvigorated their "little faith" so that they could move mountains. In wartime, cells were oases in a pro-war climate. In peacetime, they were incubators for pacifism.[77]

The Comradeship's spiritual discipline had a lasting influence on Muste. Formed to help pacifists live up to the teachings and loving spirit of Christ, it required church attendance, devotional reading, prayer, and Bible study. Members restricted the use of their income, and limited their jobs to peace-creating professions. The Comradeship asked what obedience to the "precepts" of the Sermon on the Mount meant in the present. Like other 1920s pacifists, they sought to order their lives as if the prophets' visions of a new heaven and a new earth had already been enfleshed.[78]

Just as John Woolman wrote of "the humility of Jesus Christ as a pattern for us to walk by," so Muste cautioned his fellow pacifists against any pretense of moral superiority. His friends recalled Muste as one radical who never succumbed to the 1960s tactic of being "more Left than thou." He carefully distinguished between being "right" and considering oneself "righteous." He prescribed humility to heal the pacifist's temptations to self-righteousness and spiritual imperialism, and attested, "[I] stand straightest when I am on my knees." Like the Pharisee in Jesus' parable (Lk 18:10-14), the pacifist who thanked God he was not like the militarist or the soldier committed "spiritual aggression." Pacifists shared responsibility for the conditions that bred World War II. Their sins equalled those of the liar, the thief, and the war-maker. A soldier without moral pretense was nearer the Kingdom of God than the self-righteous non-resister. Muste warned pacifists--as Merton would later--against the inverted, despairing arrogance of equating personal failure with God's defeat.[79]

Muste endured his harshest criticism within pacifist ranks during a World War II debate over camps for conscientious objectors. A step forward from the previous war's imprisonment and torture of C.O.s, the camps still fell far short of the C.O.s' goal of alternative service. Many pacifists wanted the FOR to withdraw its support from the National Service Board for Religious Objectors which worked with the federal government to oversee the camps. Muste personally desired the same course, but the FOR's executive committee voted against him. Some FOR members pulled out of the organization and urged Muste to follow, but he trusted that, in the style of a Quaker meeting, the FOR would come to a new consensus. He also wanted to maintain harmony within the small pacifist community, for if they could not find unity among themselves, there was little hope for the world.[80]

Responding to a vehement, written attack from several camp prisoners, Muste pointed out that even if the FOR withdrew, it would only "superficially" reduce its culpability for the plight of conscientious objectors, just as abandoning politics did not absolve pacifists from complicity in war. Withdrawal smacked of the Anglo-Saxon pacifist's pursuit of a false innocence. Personally, Muste felt "conscripted by God" to stay in the FOR. In conclusion, he paraphrased 1 Corinthians 13: Even if the protesting C.O.s knew the truth, it meant nothing. Even if they were in prison or offered their bodies to be burned, they gained nothing. Without love, all of their sacrifices were empty. Their own borderline self-righteousness presented a greater danger than the conditions against which they protested. Pacifists had to be held together by "our sense of inadequacy, our need of God, the honesty and humility and anguish of our search for truth, our prayer that love may work through us." Even though he shared the dissidents' political perspective, on this occasion he chose good intentions over right actions, inner transformation over outward change, unity and love over truth.[81]

Muste had not turned to pietism, nor even to a rigid pursuit of community holiness over social justice. Personal spiritual balance always led back to action. On the eve of World War II, he asked all FOR members to speak to four people and win one to the organization. He suggested that the FOR form teams of traveling "evangelists for pacifism" to proclaim the good news that individuals and nations could step out of the "death march." In 1950, at the height of the Cold War, Muste wrote of a "new missionary enterprise" to convert communists to pacifism. At other times, he targeted individual Christians or institutional churches to hear the good news of pacifism.[82]

Even to achieve his great dream of converting millions to pacifism, Muste insisted that the proselytizing be non-coercive: No tricks, no pressure to conform, no spiritual brow beating, only assent through "reason, love, and sacrificial suffering." The pacifist ought to convert others to nonviolence as Stephen converted Paul to Christian faith--by giving witness at the blunt end of persecution. When his only son John applied for naval training in 1944, A. J. became embittered toward the Quaker school John had attended because it had not instilled pacifist values, yet he accepted his son's decision. Although he grieved when the children of pacifists turned away from their parents' teaching, he said he would never pressure a young man toward objection if the young man's convictions drew him into the military. During World War II, Muste cautioned imprisoned conscientious objectors that their fast might become moral coercion, a form of violence that attempted to overwhelm another's spirit by the power of one's own. Theodore Roszak observed that Muste taught the meaning of nonviolence by listening; while speaking implies superiority, listening signals respect.[83]

Full-time anarchist and part-time Catholic Worker Ammon Hennacy once made the whimsical quip: Being a pacifist between wars is about as difficult as being a vegetarian between meals. Muste was a pacifist for all seasons. No political atmosphere could be less congenial to nonviolence than that found in a nation on the winning side of a war, an experience that seems to bless violence with a divine sanction. Yet that was when Muste reigned as America's Number One pacifist. In every season and every political climate, he persisted in making one political experiment after another; yet pacifism remained for him more a religious venture than a political one. Pacifism demanded humility, a developed spiritual life, a community of faith, inner nonviolence, and an outward way of life in step with the ways of God's Kingdom. Pacifists bore witness best when they embraced the Cross as a test of fidelity and as an instrument of social redemption.

"Be Not Conformed": The Spiritual Battle With the World

"And be not conformed to this world: but be ye transformed by the renewing of your mind, that ye may prove what is that good, and acceptable, and perfect, will of God."
    --Romans 12:2 (KJV)

"God was the first teacher, in Paradise, and whilst man kept under his teaching he was happy."
    --George Fox

"The more fully our lives are conformable to the will of God, the better it is for us."
    --John Woolman

"The interior voice tells me to go on fighting against the whole world, even though I am alone. It tells me not to fear this world but to advance, having in myself nothing but the fear of God."
    --Mohandas Gandhi.[84]

There is a legend: Outside a nuclear weapons base in the 1950s, A. J. Muste keeps a lonely vigil. He is far from the public eye. Almost no one knows that he is there. Someone asks him: What good does it do to make this witness? He replies: "I don't do this to change the world, I do it to keep the world from changing me."[85]

Although the story is more accurately attributed to Ammon Hennacy, the legend still tells a partial truth about Muste. Quaker tradition had long been concerned with non-conformity. George Fox warned others in the Society of Friends not to be "blending" themselves with the powers of earth. John Woolman feared that by paying taxes to support war Quakers might be "infected with the spirit of the world." God called them not to conform but to be transformed. Muste preached that each faithful person had to conform either to the world or to the ways of love. Like other Quakers, he wanted to live in the world without being "taken over by the world":[86]

> Non-conformity, Holy Disobedience, becomes a virtue, indeed a necessary and indispensable measure of self-preservation, in a day when the impulse to conform, to acquiesce, to go along, is used as an instrument to subject men to totalitarian rule and involve them in permanent war.[87]

Conformity was the primary evil of his time. The world alternately overpowered and seduced people to compromise with the status quo. It quietly spread the assumption that it was normal to conform to the ways of the world, good to get along. But Muste saw conformity as cooperation with a death-dealing, deceitful, and dying way of life. One "conformed" to racist laws, to the draft, to war. When sentenced to one-year's probation in 1959 after an act of civil disobedience, Muste was not sure he could "conform" to his probation for a whole year. At that trial, he stressed the non-conformity of the Boston Tea Party, the Underground Railroad, and the actions of early Christians. War, segregation, immoral laws, and corrupt institutions thrived because people remained silent. Conformity was synonymous with complicity. It wreaked spiritual havoc. King later prescribed "maladjustment" to all forms of social evils, and Merton hinted that society's definition of "sanity" induced conformity. Muste likened the moral effects of conformity to the physical effects of the traditional Chinese practice of foot-binding. To conform was to become deformed.[88]

Every person needed a system of moral self-defense against this covert spiritual assault. When pacifists felt impotent and disheartened during World War II, and Muste feared that the war might initiate a new Dark Age, he encouraged fellow FOR members to stand fast and find in their cells "islands of safety and sanity." He hoped the cells would function like the monasteries of the Middle Ages to keep knowledge, learning, and faith alive, to provide light in darkness and a vision of hope in a time of despair. In the 1950s--the decade of solitary protests-- Muste lent his Amen to Thoreau: "One on the side of God is a majority."[89] There were seasons of hope, but Muste usually ministered in the times of endurance.

Individuals needed friends to withstand the terrible pressure to conform, so Muste co-founded the Central Committee for Conscientious Objectors in 1948 to protect objectors from legal and social persecution. Communities conserved the pacifist's resilience and became reservoirs of strength until a more propitious era arrived when the time to transform society began again.[90]

When men between forty-five and sixty-five were required to register for the draft during World War II, Muste refused. Many pacifists considered the law a bureaucratic trifle and Muste's resistance and subsequent summons to the District Attorney's office a vain symbol, but he wanted to show solidarity with young draft resisters who risked long prison terms. The government, Muste believed, wanted men of all ages to register as "a valuable gesture of conformity," a sign of cooperation with the war effort. To register was an act of idolatry like offering a pinch of incense to Caesar or saying "Heil Hitler."[91]

In 1965, when recently passed legislation made it illegal to destroy draft cards, Muste and Day addressed a meeting in Manhattan's Union Square at which a few young men burned their draft cards. Refusing to cooperate with a subsequent

Grand Jury subpoena, he said that the unjust law "intended to induce conformity in wartime, to discourage dissent, and to intimidate those who cannot in conscience support the war from expressing and acting upon their convictions." The law extended the war in Vietnam, militarized the U.S., and escalated the administration's battle to suppress the war's opponents. It contradicted the legacy of the Nuremberg Trials which mandated that individuals take personal responsibility to disobey unjust orders.[92]

In 1948, Muste stopped paying his income taxes and co-founded Peacemakers, an organization that encouraged draft resistance, tax resistance, and civil disobedience. Leaping quickly from "moral absolutes, commandments of God" to political action, he never paid another cent to the Internal Revenue Service. He began tax resistance partly because he believed that nuclear weapons, created with tax dollars, were "forbidden by the Law and the Gospel." He claimed "Divine Guidance" as his reason for non-payment and, as supporting materials, he sent the IRS copies of Thoreau's "On Civil Disobedience" and the Gospels. The American development of nuclear weapons was an "insane, wicked, and suicidal" policy that would lead to nuclear war. He later included CIA and McCarthy era abuses and the war in Vietnam as reasons for tax resistance. His objections accumulated, but an underlying problem remained: paying taxes meant "committing treason against my own country, Christ, and my religious principles." The government finally brought Muste to trial and won its case, but failed to collect any money since he owned next to nothing and his sole income came from a non-taxable pension.[93]

The legend of Muste at the missile base, while it tells a partial truth, becomes misleading if it reduces non-conformity to self-defense. Just as Day interpreted Catholic Worker protests as "spiritual works of mercy," so her crosstown comrade saw individual witness as the turning point in the spiritual battle with the world. He opposed every "pinch of incense" to Caesar not only for its idolatry but because each pinch created the impression that no one opposed the empire. Each concession to Caesar made it seem less worthwhile to the next person to take a stand against the status quo.[94]

Just as small communities upheld individuals during periods of social hardship, Muste believed that each individual had the responsibility to take bold, personal stands to strengthen the conscientious community. The individual's protest gave courage to the entire body.[95] Only two dozen others in Muste's age group declined to register for the draft; only a handful entered the missile base in 1959; only five burned their draft cards that day in 1965. During the Cuban missile crisis, as most Americans applauded the naval blockade, Muste fasted alone in protest. The power of Muste's life lay in this willingness to stand alone: "He was by no means all things to all men. He owed the wide respect he inspired to the much rarer achievement of being himself to all men."[96]

Non-cooperation carried within it the power to begin a counter-offensive against the world. The individual had the responsibility to edge the world toward conformity with the teachings and spirit of Jesus. While some felt that his solitary actions contradicted his never-ending development of political coalitions, the two were really part of one continuum, one effort to reverse the world's momentum. Muste preferred to act with others, but if no one else was ready, he acted as best he might and encouraged others to join him.[97]

After World War II and again in the 1960s, as Muste's hopes for a more congenial political atmosphere rose, he escalated dramatically his calls for large-scale protests. During the war, he encouraged each pacifist to reach out to a handful of friends; in 1946, he called for thousands to become pacifists, and in *Not By Might*, for millions to become conscientious objectors. He dreamt that a nation, by renouncing war, could become the saving remnant of the world. Early in the 1960s, he complained that there were too few demonstrations, too few protesters, too few people in jail. In preparing for the Spring Mobilization in 1967, he emphasized that the larger the demonstration, the greater the impact on the Johnson administration.[98]

Muste liked to quote General Lewis Hershey, head of the Selective Service System, who referred to conscientious objectors as "termites" and wondered impatiently how long the government would tolerate their existence before exterminating them. The war in Vietnam would cease, Muste said, if more young men burned their draft cards, registered as conscientious objectors, or evaded the draft. Those who fled to Canada were "heroes" like the few who left Nazi Germany rather than serve Hitler.[99]

Muste urged people to resist the world's anti-values and accept pacifism which was "in conformity" with the content of the Bible and Christian prayer. Those who prayed for the coming of the Kingdom had to "conform to its principles" now. The conclusion of *Speak Truth to Power*, a 1955 tract of the American Friends Service Committee to which Muste contributed, bore the stamp of his spirit:

> We call on all men to say "No" to the war machine and to immoral claims of power wherever they exist and whatever the consequences may be. We call on all men to say "Yes" to courageous non-violence, which alone can overcome injustice, persecution, and tyranny.
>
> Such acts of revolutionary love involve putting into action the laws of the Kingdom before the Kingdom has really come. The early Friends realized only too clearly that the Kingdom of God had not come, but they had an inward sense that it *would never come* until somebody believed in its principles enough to try them in actual operation. They resolved to go forward then, and make the experimental trial, and take the consequences.
>
> So we believe and so we advise.[100]

Conformity--a word Muste used with remarkable frequency--was part of a battle with the world which could be won as well as lost. In the 1940s, the FOR's Statement of Purpose spoke of a "desire to follow unswervingly the way of love exemplified by Jesus" and other prophets of love. Muste heard in the Sermon on the Mount a call to the consummation of sanctification, to be "perfect, as your heavenly Father is perfect" (Mt 5:48). Jesus offered a positive conformity in opposition to the world's distorting contortions.[101]

Muste's "holy disobedience" was the flip side of obedience to his Master, Divine Teacher, and Lord. "The method and spirit of Jesus" set "standards" for all of his followers; Christians had to reconcile their lives with "the teaching, example, and spirit of Christ." In the Sermon on the Mount, Jesus delivered a "religious-political manifesto" of nonviolence as basic to Christians as the Communist Manifesto was to Marxists. Positive conformity to Christ excluded loyalty oaths, registering for the draft, and paying income taxes to an immoral government. To take up the sword would "violate the commands" of the Master. What was the crux of discipleship? Obey and imitate Christ.[102]

Typical of the traditions which nurtured him, Muste combined a low Christology--for he says little of Jesus as Son of God or God incarnate--with Jesus' high moral authority. The Quaker tradition's emphasis on teaching is seen in John Woolman's desire to obey the "instructions" of the Father and the voice of Christ, and Caroline Stephen's hope that Friends "*live* the Sermon on the Mount."[103] Muste attributed his understanding of God as "Demand" to his Calvinist heritage, although it fit his adult Quaker faith equally well. He preferred the word "demand" to "judge," for his interest lay in what God required rather than in the ramifications of ignoring the demand. God was the Redeemer and the Everlasting Rock on whom people could depend. In return, God exacted the same kind of dependable behavior.[104]

Muste's was a classical Protestant spirit of the Word-in-scripture refined by the particulars of his Calvinist and Quaker traditions. Jesus, Muste's unexcelled Teacher, was also Jesus-the-saint, a product of saintless Liberal Protestantism. All people of goodwill met the same temptations that confronted Jesus--temptations of worldly power through worldly methods--but Jesus showed the sword to be the way of conformity and Satan, and the Cross the way of life. If people heeded Jesus' words and followed his example, faith as a mustard seed would remove the mountain of war.[105]

In Muste's apocalyptic world-view, questions of authority and obedience were indistinguishable. He cited a common prooftext for civil disobedience: Peter's obstinate commitment to preach in the synagogue and his pledge to obey God over any human authority (Acts 5:29). Muste also dusted off a story from the Book of Daniel: Three young men refused to worship the false god of Babylon and declared they would not kneel before any but the God of Israel. They were thrown into a furnace and left to burn. When the king of Babylon looked in expecting to see them destroyed, they were not consumed by the fire but were joined by a fourth figure with an appearance like a son of the gods. Muste deduced three principles from this story: First, holy obedience inevitably produces non-conformity. Second, when someone breaks the law, he or she can expect to be punished. Finally, God will not abandon the faithful. On the final point, Muste overlooked the parallel between the young men's words and his own feelings about obedience: "If our God whom we serve is able to deliver us from the furnace of blazing fire and out of your hand, O king, let him deliver us. But if not, be it known to you, O king, that we will not serve your gods and we will not worship the golden statue that you have set up" (Dan 3:17-18).[106]

To bend the knee was to adopt the posture of conformity. Those who did not bow before God bowed to their inner "beast" and to dictators like Hitler, Stalin, and Mussolini. World War II's conscientious objectors "incarnated" the timeless morality of the three young men in the furnace. Whenever conscientious objectors refused to enter the military or when protesters burned their draft cards, they withheld Caesar's pinch of incense, refused to bend their knee before false gods, and released spiritual power into history.[107]

When churches and societies conformed to God's unwavering principles, laws, and commandments, they held together in the spirit of Christ and were sanctified, but churches in Muste's lifetime embraced society's values--oppression and violence--and relinquished their redemptive mission. In 1957, at the beginning of the civil rights movement, Muste called the whole Church to imitate the southern black Church, become a revolutionary leaven in the world, and renew its fidelity to Christ.[108]

Objective moral laws were not artificially imposed codes. Muste's conversion convinced him that love was a moral law to be universally obeyed. People could know and do God's Word as the Divine Guidance of the Spirit came to rest in the conscience: "Is there not behind the commandment of stone or of paper a command written on the heart?" Muste combined Quaker nonchalance about systematic theology with its passion for living in conformity to the words of Christ and the leading of the Spirit. He conflated external laws and internal conscience, the indwelling light and the law of God with the Way of the Cross. Whenever someone obeyed God, it gave birth to the new order envisioned by the prophets. When the world obeyed the leading of the Spirit, a new age would dawn.[109]

Muste's tendency to draw on the Bible's apocalyptic writings points again to his radical interpretation of history. Although the story of the three young men does not come from the apocalyptic section of Daniel, it retains that mood: the fear of persecution, the feeling of powerlessness, the hostile atmosphere of a pagan world, the desperate hope for God's saving intervention in an impossible predicament. Muste prized faith undaunted by pain. The English persecution of the Society of Friends did not erode the Quakers' confidence in "the seed of love which is in us, that light of faith which neither inner nor outer storms have put out."[110]

When accused of using extreme tactics, Muste replied that such measures fit the times. He ended *Non-Violence in an Aggressive World* with a reference to the Book of Revelation in which those who have endured the "great tribulation" meet their Lord and their reward (7:9-17). What did it mean to be "faithful in treacherous times?" Being stoned like Stephen to convert the world's Pauls; being thrown into a fiery furnace like the three young men to resist bowing the knee. The Book of Revelation let it be known that eternity remembered every act of silent complicity and every creative witness. The earthly fate of the faithful mattered less than their witness.[111] Perhaps, like the audience of the Book of Daniel, apostolic Christians, and persecuted Quakers, Muste's inability to deflect the world's massive destructive power developed his apocalyptic instinct. His sense of the transcendent comforted and renewed him with the hope that even if he failed, God's final victory would come.

As pacifism declined in 1940, as if in a vision Muste saw a temporal kingdom dying out and God's eternal Kingdom emerging. Why conform to that which is passing away when the future beckons from history's horizon? In his spiritual battle with the passing kingdom, there were many, many times when he had to keep the world from overcoming him, but Muste was not content with holding it at bay. He would persist until the world surrendered unconditionally and conformed to the principles of the coming Kingdom of God.[112]

"Be Ye Perfect":
The Spiritual Battle With Reinhold Niebuhr

"Woe to those who call evil good, and good evil, who put darkness for light and light for darkness."
>   --Isaiah 5:20 (RSV)

"An act of love that fails is just as much a part of the divine life as an act of love that succeeds. For love is measured by its fullness and not by its reception."
>   --Harold Loucks

"Know this: though love is weak and hate is strong,
Yet hate is short, and love is very long."
>   --Kenneth Boulding[113]

In 1929, as Muste's pacifist convictions were eroding, he conferred with then-pacifist Reinhold Niebuhr. They had lived parallel lives: Raised in the Midwest, ordained ministers, they became pacifists during World War I. As they imagined a social order that discouraged war, they became involved in the labor movement and interested in Marx. Muste left his pulpit to enter the labor movement, Niebuhr to teach at Union Theological Seminary. In the 1920s they were colleagues in the FOR; in the 1930s, Niebuhr followed Muste out of pacifism, but unlike his former colleague, he never returned. Thus began a thirty-year spiritual battle for the soul of American Christendom, a skirmish the well-established, well-connected, well-respected Niebuhr practically ignored. While Muste buzzed Niebuhr's theological and ethical positions like an annoying fly, Niebuhr damned Muste with faint interest.[114] Yet Muste persistently tried to engage Niebuhr. If only he could defeat Niebuhr in public debate, he might convert the American Church to pacifism.

In spite of their political and theological antagonism, little personal animosity passed between them. Niebuhr credited Muste--a "perfect innocent"--with avoiding the common pacifist pitfall of bitter self-righteousness. The theologian thought his former co-worker completely "guileless": "I told Muste in 1936, after he had been a pacifist, then a revolutionary, and a pacifist once again, that he had traveled the circle and hadn't learned anything on the journey." Yet Niebuhr's apparent disdain did not keep him from co-sponsoring a fund for the financially marginal Muste family in 1950. After the activist's death, Niebuhr wrote admiringly of Muste's trips to Saigon and Hanoi, yet he ended his complimentary eulogy with a strong backhand: "Perhaps an estimate of rigorous, if inconsistent, idealists is beyond the capacity of mere academic critics, who are obsessed with logical consistency, but who never dared an interview with Ho Chi Minh."[115] Muste exhibited imagination and courage, but Niebuhr, by his own estimate, had been logical and consistent. He had exercised power. He had won.

Muste had had his own "Niebuhr phase." By 1929, he quibbled in Niebuhrian fashion with pacifist concerns, defended the "fundamentally sound" labor movement, and apologized for its sporadic, reactive violence. The reconverted Muste later saw that by valuing political astuteness over integrity he had gained momentum for his step from labor to Leninism, from covert to overt violence. His Niebuhr phase "made me in effect a denier of Christ and only a half-baked revolutionist." So-called political pragmatism, he discovered, was impractical.[116] Their opposing views of ethics, human nature, grace, free will, the relationship of the individual to society, and the role of God in history were so basic--and classic--that Muste and Niebuhr consistently argued past each other.

Their sojourns into the Left of the 1930s encapsulated their dissimilarities in ethics: Niebuhr adapted his religious ethics to meet Marxism half way; Muste disavowed Christian pacifism when he became a Marxist. Niebuhr embraced a both/and view; Muste an either/or position. Already Muste could accuse Niebuhr of being a political chameleon, and Niebuhr could dismiss Muste as a utopian.117

When their debate shifted to *The American Scholar* in the late 1930s, Niebuhr emphasized moral consequences (the classic position of John Stuart Mill's utilitarian ethic) while Muste upheld universal moral principles (the position of Immanuel Kant's deontological ethics). In Muste's mind, Jesus had established an unchangeable principle when he taught that Satan, evil, and violence could not be used to cast themselves out. Niebuhr's willingness to dilute Christian principles in the name of pragmatism placed the theologian against the "love ethic of the New Testament."

Niebuhr argued that Christians had to emphasize the consequences of their actions over constricting, "absolutist" principles such as pacifism. Muste railed against Niebuhr's moral relativism: The Church should declare God's standards of right and wrong even if it had to disregard political expediency. God was the "One who imposes on man an absolute and inexorable obligation to do right at whatever cost."118

While Muste's unbending principles never varied to suit circumstances, Niebuhr's ethics began with present reality (as he perceived it) before he applied principles. Each saw in that distinction a source of strength, yet each system has its flaws. The strength of Muste's obedience-based ethic rests in the certainty of authority and guidance, yet to remember every jot and tittle of the universal law one has to be a scribe. The strength of Niebuhr's consequentialist ethic is its concern for results, yet to foresee the future a person must be a prophet. The advantage of Niebuhr's contextualism is its malleability in fitting the appropriate action to each situation, yet to do always what is loving one must be a saint.

In times of war and Cold War, their argument embodied the traditional disagreement between Just War proponents and pacifists. Pacifism is based on an unchangeable principle that war is wrong in all circumstances. The Just War tradition assumes that differing circumstances make some wars just and others unjust. The Just War criteria emphasize results over principles and trade off war's destructiveness for the benefits of the ensuing peace.

Niebuhr began his moral arguments with a view of the present situation. Like Day, Muste began with a principle from tradition or with a vision of the future, and pitted his politics of "eternity" against Niebuhr's politics of time. Muste insightfully accused Niebuhr of smearing the pacifist as an "absolutist" while the theologian made the present order "eternal and absolute." As Paulo Freire has observed, such an overly generous view of the status quo makes it a "fixed entity...to which men and women, as mere spectators, must adapt."[119] Much of their spiritual quarrel lay in Niebuhr's conventional view of history which assumed something good in every status quo, a stance anathema to Muste's Abrahamic interpretation of history. Niebuhr complained that the activist's dark criticisms of nations and institutions ignored their residual virtues, took away any basis for social improvement, and removed realistic guidance for reform. Muste retorted that violence was the glue holding the status quo together. The theologian, by "providing a pseudo-Christian cover for the sterile sophistication of power-politics," advocated "ethical nihilism."[120]

Biographer Jo Ann Ooiman Robinson tellingly emphasizes Muste's commitment to take an image of the future and make it politically viable. How could one obey God's call to seek the city-to-be? How could one follow Martin Buber's prescription: find the moral principle and bring it to bear on present reality. In effect, Niebuhr repeatedly told Muste that the soil of reality was harder than the activist realized; Muste told his antagonist that in short-changing moral principles,

Niebuhr had no tools with which to alter political reality. Niebuhr believed in reforming the status quo, but Muste recalled that early Christians had not thought their social order worth saving. Why tinker with urban reforms in Babel?[121]

For Muste, timeless Christian principles led to the fulfillment of the Hebrew prophets' visions. For Niebuhr, Muste's bear hug on principles was an obstacle to proximate justice and peace. God's reign could not be established in history, and Niebuhr did not believe in the "relevance of an impossible ideal."[122] Muste's ethical standards seemed to him mere idealistic drivel. Muste decried Niebuhr's tragic vision of history, for biblical prophets spoke of victory and new life.[123]

Here their dispute entered the two-headed issue of human nature and divine grace. Muste joined Niebuhr in criticizing liberal, Anglo-Saxon pacifists inebriated with naive optimism in human nature. Muste confessed that he, too, had been influenced by the optimistic Social Gospel, but his upbringing had given him "too solid a dose of Calvinism not to believe in the corruption of the human spirit."[124]

In Niebuhr's mind, Muste probably played a pacifist Pelagius to his own Augustine, a dangerous advocate of human possibility against an accurate assessment of sin. Muste would have preferred Rufus Jones' pairing of another set of religious figures. Writing of Quaker founder George Fox, Jones said, "He met the Calvinistic theory of a congenital seed of sin in the new-born child by the counter claim that *there is a Seed of God in every soul.*" Fox "met the pessimism of depravity with a rival optimism about human potentiality." Their traditions embodied their views of human nature in the American colonies: Quaker Philadelphia, the city of brotherly love, aimed for holiness; Puritan Boston sought the best community possible given the limits of human nature. Muste demanded perfection. Niebuhr asked for the best results in a bad situation.[125]

The upper limits Niebuhr placed on human nature made no sense to Muste. Why would God call people to "conform" to certain laws if God made people unable to obey them? Muste agreed that, by itself, human sin made hope impossible, but God's grace enabled repentance and restored hope.   He sarcastically summarized Niebuhr's near obsession with sin: "Where grace abounds, sin abounds much more." To the Calvinist-gone-Quaker, grace and repentance made perfection possible.[126]

Niebuhr's dismal view of human nature seemed to Muste to border on the bestial. If individuals were animals, societies could be nothing more than "wolf-packs" ruled by dictators. Muste liked image of humanity found in Psalm 8:

When I look at your heavens, the work of your fingers, the moon
and the stars that you have established; what are human beings that
you are mindful of them, mortals that you care for them? Yet you
have made them a little lower than God, and crowned them with
glory and honor (vs. 3-5).

Muste criticized optimistic pacifists, yet he believed each person to be a creation of spirit and dignity made in God's image.[127]

Muste acknowledged--with some glee--that in certain ways his concept of sin ran deeper than Niebuhr's. Unlike the ethicist, he did not believe it possible for a nation (like the U.S.) or a social class (like the middle class) to make war or set the social agenda for the right reasons. It was Niebuhr's contention, after all, that groups and nations were far too skilled at self-deception to be trusted. Turnabout was fair play: Muste thought Niebuhr amazingly optimistic to trust American decision-makers.[128]

Their debate had less to do with the intransigence of evil than with whose evil they pinpointed. From Muste's perspective, Niebuhr was overly optimistic when it came to America's sins; from Niebuhr's, Muste was too quick to overlook evil in the East. Muste emphasized *our* sin, Niebuhr *their* evil; but Muste insisted that it never worked to say: I'll repent if you do first.[129]

Muste inherited the Quaker sense of love's endurance and ultimate triumph over hatred. In George Fox's vision: "I saw also that there was an ocean of darkness and death, but an infinite ocean of light and love, which flowed over the ocean of darkness. And in that also I saw the infinite love of God."[130] Muste shared John's affirmation that the light shone in a darkness that would not overcome it (1:5). He did not deny evil's expanse but believed Niebuhr ignored the "limitless grace of God" which could transform human nature. Niebuhr dismissed Muste as one of the "children of light," a kindly spirit who blindly believed that nations could rise above self-interest. While virtuous in Niebuhr's estimate, the "children of light" succumbed to "stupidity" by underestimating the power of self-will. Had he known of Muste's visions of light, Niebuhr might have thought that they had blinded him to the reality of darkness.[131]

Muste interpreted his argument with Niebuhr less as a dispute about human nature than as a disagreement about grace. Niebuhr's theology made little room for the Holy Spirit. Grace was primarily a matter of forgiveness in the life to come. For Muste, grace was an enabling power redeeming sin and sanctifying the sinner here and now.[132]

As they debated free will, Muste and Niebuhr echoed Erasmus and Luther. To Muste, Niebuhr's belief in the bondage of the will rendered its adherents impotent. He even suggested that some Christians used Niebuhr's theology to evade responsibility for their actions and rationalize their lack of interest in following Christ. Instead of calling one another to repentance, they reaffirmed their hopeless paralysis. Muste reduced Niebuhr's "realism" to the refrain in Ecclesiastes--"Vanity of vanity, all is vanity"--and reminded the ethicist that the same Bible also said, "Be ye perfect."[133]

Muste claimed that free will came from human nature as created by God and from dependence on God's grace. His own sinfulness had not inhibited his experience of freedom as he changed churches, ideologies, religious beliefs, and vocations. He extrapolated from his re-conversion and second excursion into pacifism that others had the same freedom.[134]

One of Niebuhr's most recognized insights lay in his book, *Moral Man, Immoral Society*: While individuals might be inclined to morality and accept change through persuasion, groups of people were by nature more selfish and required coercion to change. This assumption reduced pacifism to a politically irrelevant matter of personal conscience. When they traded arguments in *The American Scholar* in the 1930s, Niebuhr emphasized that dependence on moral absolutism led to political "disintegration," and Muste replied that non-compliance with moral imperatives caused "inner disintegration": To sacrifice one's conscience on the altar of political pragmatism merely abetted political disintegration. For Muste, individual integrity was the cornerstone of social justice.[135]

Muste attacked Niebuhr's "immoral society" premise from two angles. Remembering that the Hebrew prophets had addressed nations more often than individuals, Muste deduced that God's will *is* intended for groups. Recalling Niebuhr's tendency to apologize for America's sins even while asserting its basic virtues, Muste asked why the theologian called it a sin for an individual to lie or steal or kill when he excused a nation for doing the same? Wasn't the call to repent the identical twin of a call to unilateral disarmament?[136]

Niebuhr's school of thought took on the label of Crisis Realism, and Niebuhr used the title to contrast his position with unrealistic idealists. Muste again agreed with portions of Niebuhr's assessment: Pacifists between the World Wars had been too self-assured about the prospects for a warless world; one cannot simply preach love, ignore economic and political factors, and expect social problems to solve themselves; change cannot come without cost; pacifism does not promise a life without moral ambiguity. Too often pacifists had engaged in superficial political analysis, underestimated the power of evil, and expected simple solutions. [137]

While Muste found it silly to assume that one's enemy is really a "good fellow," he thought it equally half-witted to believe one can use evil to overcome evil. He never conceded "realism" to Niebuhr. In fact, he described the true pacifist--in contrast to the more prevalent variety--as the "supreme realist," and accused his antagonists of "secularist and nationalist sentimentalism." In the 1950s, he charged the "realists" with being "sentimental" when they asserted that the U.S. would never use its nuclear capability. One of his most scathing attacks on Crisis Realism came at the end of the 1930s as some argued that war would usher in an age of justice:

> We have to be romanticists, sentimentalists, capable of flying in the
> face of all the evidence, to believe that another general war, or series
> of wars, under modern conditions and with modern weapons will
> thus prove the gateway to socialism. [138]

While Niebuhr evolved from pacifism, to defending the necessity of class war, to defending the probable need for international wars, Muste attacked the "childish assumption that it might be possible in our day and in our world to have a nice, short, snappy war, or maybe a half dozen of them, and thus achieve peace and social justice." [139]

The critique of pacifism's alleged naivete prompted Muste to remember a story from colonial America when Quakers--unlike their neighbors--pursued peaceful coexistence with nearby Native Americans. When "Indian" raids became more frequent in one colony, most members in the Society of Friends stuck to their principles, but a few started to carry guns to protect their families. Finally, as two gun-toting Friends toiled in their fields, they were ambushed and killed. Their Native American attackers were distraught when they later discovered the identity of their victims, but they blamed the two Quakers: If the farmers had not been wearing guns, they would have recognized them as Quakers and left them unharmed. Muste used the story to insist on the pragmatism of unilateral disarmament.[140]

As each declared himself the winner in the battle for realism, Muste and Niebuhr again collided over their understandings of how Christ and God interacted with history. Niebuhr's Jesus was a non-political non-resister, Muste's the world's Teacher and Prophet, the first-born of a new humanity, the one who overcame evil with nonviolent resistance and gave the world an infallible method for social change. Muste criticized Niebuhr for making Jesus' life and teachings seem impractical, and for reducing the Cross to the pointless, tragic fate of any who would try to build the Kingdom of God with nonviolence. Niebuhr placed the Cross at the "edge of history" even as Muste hammered it into the center. Niebuhr withdrew the Kingdom of God from politics and history even as Muste insisted that the Kingdom of Heaven conflicted daily with the dying kingdoms of earth.[141] By placing hope beyond history, Niebuhr left the real power in the world to Satan. But, Muste averred, God had not abandoned history to dictators and superpowers. God and Christ worked redemptively within history to bring it to its long-awaited fruition.[142]

The pacifist accused the theologian of ignoring Jesus, and being a disciple and servant who pretended to be greater than his teacher and master. Jesus had been "sane--not mad" when he taught the wisdom of giving away coats and putting away swords. Niebuhr used contemporary biblical scholarship to reduce the Sermon on the Mount, a cornerstone of pacifism, to a rhetorical invention of the evangelist Matthew. Whatever its merits, the Sermon was a first century' theological device, not a timeless law. Thus did theological liberalism produce the politically liberal Niebuhr; a conservative instinct towards scripture produced a radical Muste.[143]

An Old Testament archetype reveals the fundamental vocational difference between the two. Niebuhr followed in the tradition of Israel's *sages* who, according to a biblical scholar, took "an open, uncommitted approach" to "the business of the state." The "wise men" believed that their decision-making ought not to be constrained by any simplistic or constricting religious or ethical presuppositions. They were "preoccupied with what is possible." They tried to keep their religious assumptions from affecting their judgment, and thought it a "failure of professional integrity to allow piety to influence their public decisions." They felt compelled "to reckon realistically with political existence and deal faithfully with the world as it was and not as it ought to be." Wisdom lay in treating each and every situation on its own merits.[144]

Like Israel's *prophets*, Muste resisted absolute empiricism in favor of the "revealed authoritative word." The prophets denied that statesmanship was merely a pragmatic art. The political arena, like every other sphere of life, belonged to God. The prophets felt that sages relied on "coarse power" to move history when "it is morality which moves the world and not political shrewdness." Sages sought security in political alliances when it could only be found in obedience to God's Word. In spite of their pretensions to wisdom, they were not "realistic." The prophet Isaiah may have been addressing the sages: "Woe to those who call evil good and good evil, who put darkness for light and light for darkness" (5:20), an appropriate imprecation for Muste to utter against Niebuhr. Sages and prophets, like Niebuhr and Muste, held conflicting understandings of how God worked in the world.[145]

Muste followed the prophets as he sought radical change, obedience to revelation, repentance, compliance with God's Word, and the realization of a totally new order. Niebuhr based his wisdom on human experience, and advocated a morality that began with present circumstances and moved forward, step by pragmatic step. The sages of the Wisdom tradition appreciated the virtues of their culture, even while recognizing its flaws. The prophets identified with the pain of the oppressed and envisioned a different kind of future. If the sage accused the prophet of "utopianism," the prophet lowered the counter-charge of "adaptionism," epithets that became the trademarks in the name-calling between Niebuhr and Muste.

Along with Day, Merton, and (to a lesser degree) King, Muste chose the more marginal vocation, and hoped for a time when his message would be heard. He fought his spiritual battle with Niebuhr on many of Christian theology's traditional battlegrounds: ethics, sin and grace, Christology, the use of scripture, the meaning of free will and history. Their contradictory answers led them to offer conflicting prescriptions and enter competing vocations. Muste yearned for the time when he could be as influential as Niebuhr, not to satisfy vanity, but so that the Christian community could embrace pacifism, fulfill its vocation, and hasten the coming of God's Kingdom.

That day never came.

Prophetic Religion: "The Politics of Repentance"[146]

"Woe to those who go down to Egypt for help and rely on horses, who trust in chariots because they are many and in horsemen because they are very strong, but do not look to the Holy One of Israel or consult the Lord."

--Isaiah 31:1 (RSV)

"Those who say, "I love God," and hate their brothers or sisters, are liars; for those who do not love a brother or sister whom they have seen, cannot love God whom they have not seen."

--1 John 4:20

At his home in Basel, Switzerland, theologian Karl Barth greeted A. J. Muste in March 1955. Not exactly theological allies, each had a common nemesis in Reinhold Niebuhr and his support for American nuclear policy. Barth considered the policy insane yet felt unable to turn the superpowers around. He asked his American guest, "So what shall we do--stand on the street corner and cry 'Madness, madness, madness?'" That was what the Old Testament prophets had done, Muste said. Barth agreed.[147]

The prophets inspired Muste with their "political strategy" of inner communion with God and social passion. They molded his view of the world and modeled his vocation. Caring little for theological distinctions between Judaism and Christianity and nothing at all for theology without love, he labeled his religion "Jewish-Christian prophetism." In *Non-Violence in an Aggressive World,* as elsewhere, he followed the Social Gospel tradition and ranked Jesus as the greatest of the prophets.[148]

While the world detected insanity at the fringes of the political spectrum, Muste saw it at the center. On separate occasions in 1965, Roger LaPorte of the Catholic Worker community and two other anti-war protesters imitated Vietnamese Buddhist monks and immolated themselves as a protest against the war. Muste said: Do not weep for the dead; do not shake your heads at the presumed madness of the suicide victims; grieve over the insane lethargy of the American people who know about the war in Vietnam yet remain quiescent accomplices of murder, for their silence is the greater tragedy. At times, his voice sounded like a shrill unnecessary annoyance, as in the Spring of 1941 when he called for an end to World War II. Yet who was to determine the sane from the insane?[149]

Muste was willing to call madness by name, but he wanted to do more than engage in occasional, futile, loud bursts of monologue. He sought to expose the

self-destructive absurdity in the so-called logic of war and, like the prophets, offer
an unwanted second opinion about political reality. During World War II and the
Cold War, he unmasked the fictions of a "'Messiah vs. devil' theory of
international relations" and war between "angels and devils." He suggested that a
good starting point for a redeemed foreign policy was Jesus' encouragement to
remove first the beam from one's own eye before pointing to the speck in the eye of
another.[150]

Muste saw the crux of World War II as the Allies' defense of a self-serving
status quo against the Axis powers who wanted to steal a piece of the pie. Just as
the prophet Isaiah saw the grim irony in Israel looking to Egypt as its savior, so
Muste pointed out the hypocrisy of the West casting Stalin's Russia as the savior of
civilization, democracy, and Christian faith. The U.S. used the war as a step
toward world domination. Plans for the post-war world were nothing but "bare
faced power politics."[151]

Like Merton two decades later, Muste uncovered self-interest beneath every
political pretense of self-justification. How could World War II be a battle against
German and Japanese racism when American armed forces and American society
were segregated? How could it be a battle for self-determination against foreign
empires in Belgium and Norway while Winston Churchill said, "I have not become
the King's First Minister in order to preside over the liquidation of the British
Empire"? How could it put an end to concentration camps when the U.S. created
its own camps for its citizens of Japanese descent? Until the Philippines, India, and
Eastern Europe were independent, Muste would persist in his belief that the Allies
fought to preserve spheres of influence. Even had he suspended his other
criticisms of the war, he objected to the demand for unconditional surrender which
prolonged the bloodshed. The Allies claimed that military defeat would teach the

Axis powers that it does not pay to make war. In reality, it proved that might makes right.[152]

The Big Three's dreams of a post-war world thinly disguised their desire to re-establish their economic power. Muste found in their visions of a new international order the false peace decried by the prophet Jeremiah which "healed the wound of my people carelessly" (6:14, 8:11); he anticipated a new conflict among the victorious powers.[153] This struggle became known as the Cold War although a plethora of small wars took the place of the one, big war that frightened Americans and Soviets alike. War by proxy became the order of the day, all of it under the lowering umbrella of nuclear destruction that meant "annihilation without representation" to the rest of the world.[154]

While in West Berlin in 1961, Muste likened the division of the world to the time that King Solomon stood in judgment over the two women who each claimed the same child as her own (1 Kings 3:16ff.). When Solomon said he would cut the child in two and give one half to each woman, one of the women said she would rather let the other woman keep the child. Solomon immediately recognized the woman concerned for the child's welfare as its true mother. The U.S. and the USSR both acted as the greedy, desperate woman who cared nothing for the fate of the child and preferred that Korea, China, Vietnam, and Germany be cut in half, and that millions of children starve rather than end the arms race.[155]

While many American liberals viewed the war in Vietnam as an unfortunate aberration in American values and foreign policy, Muste saw it as part of a "pattern," for as early as 1941, he feared a growing American messianism. The war was not an "isolated episode" in history but the logical outgrowth of America's denial of political and military reality, and its inability to repent. After his visit to South Vietnam in 1966, he wrote that the U.S. had driven into a swamp, and the thing to do when one drives into a swamp is to back out of it. But messianism apparently had its own rewards: Vietnamese--on both sides and on no side--and American soldiers paid the price for national arrogance.[156]

The war in Vietnam was the last in a long line of events that Muste saw in a way dramatically different from accepted American points of view. Well before the advent of nuclear weapons he pictured the world on the brink of doom. Often criticized because he could not outline clear political alternatives, he maintained that the threat of extinction itself ought to encourage change:

> It always strikes me as funny when you cry to mankind standing on the edge of a precipice, "Don't take that next step; turn around," to have someone say: "But you aren't offering him a constructive program!"[157]

Wasn't it enough to realize that the first step was to back away from the cliff?

At the brink of doom, Old Testament Israel had an unfortunate tendency to take the wrong turn and go over the cliff. Muste liked quoting Isaiah (31:3): "The Egyptians are men, and not God; and their horses are flesh, and not spirit," and he asked his fellow Christians if the time had not come to cease their reliance on battleships and atomic bombs.[158] As Israel had not faced with faith its concern for security, so the world continued to be plagued by the same problem.

When, as a young minister, he decided to leave his conservative denomination, Muste had an experience of God as "truly present and all-sufficient," an experience the Hebrew prophets tried to communicate to their people so that Israel would not become paralyzed by fear.[159] In a sermon in 1950, Muste presaged Merton when he illuminated a fundamental cause of war in the relationship of fear and security: Nations and individuals seek security to alleviate fear; the U.S. bulged in wealth and power, yet neither ended the fear. In contrast, Jesus' detachment from every form of security--money, ease, pleasure, fame, life and reputation--helped him to overcome his fears on the night before he died. The world could take nothing away from him. Those "attached" to things "can be terrorized, made to conform, sign loyalty oaths, goose step, and stand by silent when freedom is stoned to death." Dictators stood poised but powerless against those whose only fear was to contradict God's will. Perfect security could not cast out fear; in any event, no perfect security could be found. The alternative was for an individual or a nation to imitate Jesus and pray for a blessed fearlessness in the midst of insecurity. Jesus never hinted that his disciples would escape harm, but they could be free from fear. Whenever someone walks in Jesus' footsteps without fear, Muste said, "divine power is released" into the world and "a new creation becomes possible." If a nation learned to live for others instead of itself, if it lived fearlessly in the midst of insecurity instead of creating an illusion of control, "it will have overcome the world. It will walk the earth without fear. It will experience the Resurrection. It will create mankind."[160]

Muste wanted to reveal the reality of naked, omnipresent sin, but nations and peoples deflected their responsibility for the world's ills. He indicted the Western nations as accomplices in the persecution and murder of Germany's Jews in 1938, for they had constructed an unjust peace and thus helped--in effect--to make the guns used to round up the Jews; and "guilty above all are we who call ourselves Christians, believers in peace, pacifists."[161] No one escaped the responsibility for war.

Throughout the years, Muste returned to the parable of the Pharisee and the Publican (also a favorite of Day). He characterized the Pharisee as "a devoted churchman and an ardent patriot" quick to point out flaws in others. The Pharisee nation raised its own image by denigrating others and measured its goodness against its enemies' evil. After Pearl Harbor, Americans quickly denounced "Nazi swine and Fascist dogs and Japanese devils" because, compared to them, the U.S. felt righteous. But after the British and Americans bombed Dresden, Tokyo, Hiroshima, and Nagasaki, Muste called them to recite the Publican's prayer for mercy. The self-righteousness of the Pharisee was itself a "kind of warfare," the "worst sin" imaginable, because it precluded genuine repentance: Even as the U.S. apologized for the last war's atrocities, its leaders planned for the next war's greater barbarism.[162]

Muste followed the example of the Book of Amos. In its canonical form the book plays a trick on its readers: The prophet first condemns the sins of Israel's hostile neighbors (chapters 1-2); only after the book attacks the sins of Israel's enemies--to the glee of its first readers--does it turn with greater vengeance against its own people. The Book of Amos invited its readers to clamor for judgment only to discover themselves judged. Less than a month after Pearl Harbor and again as the Big Three reveled in their military success in 1945, Muste offered them one prescription: Repent. In the late 1950s, while American Christians waited for the communist bloc to convert, the West itself was unwilling to repent.[163] Like Jonah addressing Nineveh, American Christians wanted the East destroyed, not saved. Ironically, of course, Nineveh repents more readily than Israel; perhaps East more quickly than West.

Muste always assumed that "repentance is unilateral business." The flyers distributed during the 1962 San Francisco to Moscow walk at a frenzied peak in the Cold War issued the same invitation to six nations, East and West, to disarm unilaterally. Like Amos, Muste believed in equal opportunity prophecy; he stormed against every nation with the same thunder and offered each the same path to new life. Repentance was neither a one-time event nor an occasional renewal, but a continuous attitude toward oneself and one's life in the world.[164] Muste delivered the message most often to the U.S. because he lived there, because of its enormous impact on the earth's fate, and because its rich blessings gave it special responsibilities to the world.

He believed that when the Hebrew prophets pronounced judgment, in the "same breath" they called for repentance.[165] Unlike King and Merton (and many of the prophets!) who believed there came a time when hope passed, Muste--like Gandhi--never imagined that the moment to choose could end.

Muste's "Jewish-Christian prophetism" offered more than precipice-theology: universal guilt, stark reality, doom-saying, and harsh advice to live fearlessly in the midst of insecurity. It offered visions of the future. In the 1940s and the 1950s Muste envisioned a world government without armies, a new international economic balance, and liberation for the exploited; he foresaw an end of racial segregation, the restoration of civil liberties, and a peace-based domestic economy. He often felt like someone listening to the drinker who resolves to sober up after just one more binge: His adopted nation believed the Cold War would never pass away; the Church--shunning visions of redeemed humanity--succumbed to a parallel pessimism. In an optimistic mood, Muste hoped that the U.S. could see the world differently and imagine alternatives to the Cold War.[166]

Muste's spirit of prophecy assessed the political landscape and called for a pragmatic response: Acknowledge guilt; repent; turn away from death; reinvest trust in God. But the world was too fixed on the Fall just ahead to imagine another option. It had stepped over the moral precipice so many times that it had lost the capacity to gauge the distance to the existential cliff, nor did it realize there might be a connection between the next step and the Fall. Muste and Merton identified the world's so-called order as "madness" and revealed its parade of progress as a dash toward doom. Muste shouted "Stop!" but the world scurried along blind and lame on its tragic death march.

A New Pentecost

"There is a spirit which I feel that delights to do no evil, nor to revenge any wrong, but delights to endure all things, in hope to enjoy its own in the end. . .Its hope is to outlive all wrath and contention."
    --James Nayler

"The only possible way to overcome the world is to carry the forces of the spiritual life into the veins of society until peace and love and righteousness prevail there."
    --Rufus Jones

"Power flows through us, from the Eternal into the rivulets of time."
    --Thomas Kelly[167]

The FOR in the 1940s had a fundamental flaw. It attracted only white-skinned, white-collar members. Muste proposed a remedy: Like the apostles at Pentecost, FOR members had to learn to speak in the language of other races and classes to tear down racial, economic, and national barriers.[168]

Muste inherited the Social Gospel's conviction that the human family was an already existing reality. All people and nations were children of God the Father, and brothers and sisters to one another. He and Day admired Eugene Debs' famous identification with the oppressed: "While there is a lower class, I am in it; while there is a criminal element, I am of it; while there is a soul in prison, I am not free." Yet for most of the world human unity remained an unknown and perhaps undesired prospect. Muste's conviction swam against a strong current of human experience as he placed his hopes in things as yet unseen.[169]

Biblical tradition uses the story of Babel to explain the fragmentation of the world. Once bound by a common language, the world's people were scattered throughout the earth and estranged from one another by their separate languages after the Tower's fall. Most people observed this reality. At Pentecost, when the power of the Holy Spirit enabled a few Christians to speak in the many tongues of the Mediterranean world, it started to reverse the original confusion and launch the reunification of the world. Muste believed this power could transform the world. There was no distinguishing the vocation of Abraham from the goal of Pentecost. They were simply two different ways God worked to reunite the world.

Muste was impatient for the coming of the Kingdom. As Augustine once declared that the human heart is restless until it rests in God, so Muste could not rest until God's will was done on earth as in heaven. He spent much of his life trying to bridge ideological, national, racial, and class barriers. Even among potential political allies, he had to exert enormous effort to unite people. In the 1950s and 1960s, he edited a modest newsletter called *The Correspondent* to reason intellectuals into pacifism. He became a founding editor of *Liberation* which tried to unite socialists, anarchists, Christian pacifists, the labor movement, and advocates of human rights.[170]

When the Fifth Avenue Peace Parade Committee initiated early demonstrations against the Vietnam War, Muste brought together bitter rivals of the Old and New Left with traditional pacifist and religious groups. He overcame the stale-but-bitter aftertaste of his own disillusionment with communism in the 1930s to embrace the principle of "non-exclusion" (that all opponents of the war were welcome at a demonstration). He then mediated between leftists hoisting Vietcong flags and religious pacifists refusing to carry any flag. As Debs identified with the oppressed, so all who worked against oppression could identify with Muste: "He belonged to Presbyterians and Communists, to Catholics and Trotskyists, to Quakers and Anarchists."[171]

In the same decades, Muste took part in a blizzard of activity to keep the human family from obliterating itself. Five annual demonstrations in New York

City against civil defense drills--which encouraged the fantasy of survivable nuclear war--slowly garnered the support of mainstream newspapers which came to ridicule the drills. Muste supported efforts to disrupt American and Soviet nuclear tests and, in the world's first international direct action campaign against nuclear weapons, an attempt to halt French nuclear tests in the Sahara. Following his 1967 trip to Hanoi, he hoped he could play a part in bringing Lyndon Johnson face-to-face with Ho Chi Minh.[172]

The Muste touch was not a Midas touch for nonviolence. Every campaign against nationalism invariably ran into opposition. The Friendship March from New Delhi to Peking sought to ease tensions in the 1962 Sino-Indian border war, but China halted the marchers at its border. Protesters bumped into the same reality when they tried to cross from Ghana into French West Africa to demonstrate against the French nuclear test. The Quebec to Guantanamo walk just a year after the Cuban missile crisis ran into several obstacles. The group's interracial make-up antagonized Georgia officials who arrested and jailed the demonstrators. After other long delays, the walkers waited in Miami and hoped that the State Department would lift its prohibition on travel to Cuba. Without official authorization, a few of the demonstrators launched a boat named *The Spirit of America* toward Cuba, and the authorities impounded the boat. There ensued a court case with the ironic title, The United States of America v. The Spirit of America. The first "trans-curtain" walk from San Francisco to Moscow had hostile encounters with French and Polish officials, but finished its course while distributing flyers in six languages.[173]

Sporadic protests to ease political tensions, reach across borders, and share a new spirit of fruitful coexistence were but preliminary measures. God's world needed an institutionalized way to bring the forces of nonviolence to bear in the midst of armed conflicts. As a proud co-founder, Muste called the birth of the short-lived World Peace Brigade "epoch making." Intended to fulfill Gandhi's vision of a "peace army," it would allow a world peace movement to "operate across geographical, political, and ideological barriers."[174]

In spite of the constant frustrations it caused him, Muste kept hoping that a transformed Church would become an instrument of Pentecost. He hoped that discussions of pacifism by the National Council of Churches (NCC) and World Council of Churches (WCC) meant they were moving closer to nonviolence. He became involved in the Church Peace Mission--a projected six-month experiment that lasted twelve years--which had the two-fold purpose of intensifying the traditional peace churches' commitment to pacifism and challenging mainstream churches to take pacifism seriously. But the same frustrations that drove him out of the Church in the 1930s beleaguered him the rest of his life. In 1942, when the Federal Council of Churches (predecessor to the NCC) prayed for an outpouring of the Spirit after the U.S. won the war, he wondered why they did not pray for an immediate manifestation of the Spirit to end the war. Ten years later he observed no signs of a new Pentecost by or in or through the Church.[175]

Yet it was part of the Christian's vocation to prepare for Pentecost, and Muste suggested that his contemporaries re-examine the example of the post-Easter disciples. The disciples stayed together, waited, and prayed in Jerusalem where Jesus had been defeated and where the opposition remained strongest. So now in the midst of war, institutionalized racism, and personal temptations--where Jesus was still temporarily defeated--God called faithful people to form spiritual communities capable of producing an outpouring of the Spirit. When the Church lived its allegiance to Christ and put its trust in the "Way of the Cross," when it proclaimed a new earth and worked and prayed and suffered together, when it was willing to die for sinners, then the Church could be a channel of grace for the new Pentecost.[176]

Muste, Merton, and King were sure that certain moments in history were pregnant with redemptive possibility. Muste held to the Quaker conviction that the world was still in the apostolic age in which the Spirit moved freely. Just as early Christians and early Quakers carried the forces of eternity into time and heaven to earth, so the Cross-bearing Church could again be a vehicle of divine power. When any individual who *could* kill preferred *being* killed, divine power penetrated history and edged the world toward the new creation. The Spirit could just as easily inflame the Church or a nation.[177]

Muste combined a tentativeness about the precise shape of the future with an irrepressible feeling that the world was about to cross a threshold. The future always impinged on the present. In his internal liturgical calendar, it was always Advent. In his "Statement of Belief" delivered on his sixty-fifth birthday, he spoke of his daily awareness of the goodness of creation. It struck him in faces young and old, in the sky, a tree, in poetry and dance. It was as though he could sense in the present a taste of what the future would be. In the face of omnipresent political divisiveness, he sensed the "burning oneness binding everything." In spite of the sufferings of the world, "I believe nevertheless in the coming of the kingdom of God on earth, in the achievement of the revolution which will bring to pass a brotherly and peaceful human society." This required a miracle, but "that is precisely what I mean to assert."[178]

The Kingdom of God was always at hand. Even as Hitler's armies overran Europe, Muste insisted that the moral structure of the universe prevented dictators from winning ultimate victories. He pondered whether the newborn and newly ferocious Cold War might not soon yield to an era of peace. The demonstration at Red Square at the end of the San Francisco to Moscow Walk seemed to him to enkindle hope like the dove carrying the olive branch to Noah's ark. The chaos was almost over; a new earth about to be born. Christ was "always about to come in power and glory. The divine was always about to break into history." As King had suggested in his telegram on Muste's eightieth birthday, the elder activist had seen the city-to-be, and--whether or not Muste would get there--he would remain impatient until the nations entered it. Interviewed in 1966, when the struggle for racial equality had suffered its embittered and violent turn, while the war in Vietnam escalated and the Cold War seemed set in ice, Muste said he expected that, within a generation of his death, "an essentially warless world will be achieved."[179]

Muste's visions of hope, his experiences of light and "singing peace," his even demeanor, his spiritual equilibrium and his quiet, consistent passion make it easy to forget that his suffering over the war in Vietnam--like all forms of oppression and destruction--tore at his "guts."[180] Muste built his hope for a new Pentecost in the barren wasteland between the world as it is and his vision of what God called it to be. For a man always on the fringes of power, he retained an undying hope that he was about to hit the jackpot. Perhaps, like the biblical Abraham, he was a gambler. Others had a harder time maintaining Muste's delicate spiritual balance: The anti-war movement turned away from his faith in things unseen and foundered when it bumped up against too many billy clubs and inhaled too much tear gas.

His tentative prescriptions for the world's ills make it easy to forget that his life stands less as a set of exclamation points than as a series of question marks pointedly calling for an end to deceit, despair, and war. His life asks questions that touch something deep in the human spirit, something resisted almost as if it came unbidden from the Creator's hand. He asks questions that the world suppresses through violence and dismisses as fantasy; questions that bite into toughened cynicism, the ancient mask of frustrated hope. He poses them on behalf of the world, directing them to the world, and ultimately, to God: Why not a new Pentecost? Why not a new earth?

At Muste's seventy-fifth birthday celebration, someone read one of his favorite poems, "The War God," by Stephen Spender. Written in the consuming Western panic after the Fall of France, Spender posed questions that burned in Muste's heart, questions with which his life still faintly haunts the world:

> Why cannot the one good
> Benevolent feasible
> Final dove, descend?
>
> And the wheat be divided?
> And the soldiers sent home?
> And the barriers torn down?
> And the enemies forgiven?
> And there be no retribution?[181]

NOTES

A.J. MUSTE

1. Nancy Zaroulis and Gerald Sullivan, *Who Spoke Up? American Protest Against the War in Vietnam 1963-1975* (Garden City, New York, 1984), 111; photo of car in *Fellowship* 33:5 (May 1967): 16; Jo Ann Ooiman Robinson, *Abraham Went Out: A Biography of A. J. Muste* (Philadelphia, 1981), 223.

2. Robinson, *Abraham*, 133-34.

3. George Woodcock, "A Moral Man,"*Commentary* 44:14 (October 1967):104; Anon., "A. J. Muste," *Fellowship* 33:3 (March, 1967): 2.

4. Milton Mayer, "The Christer,"*Fellowship*18:1(January 1952): 2; Jo Ann Ooiman Robinson, *A. J. Muste: Pacifist and Prophet: His Relation to the Society of Friends* (Wellingford, Pennsylvania, 1981), 16; see especially *Liberation* 12:6-7 "A. J. Muste Issue," (September-October 1967) and *WIN* 3:4 "A. J. Muste Memorial Issue," (February 24, 1967).

5. Tom Cornell and David McReynolds (untitled) *WIN* 3:4: 8-9.

6. Nat Hentoff, ed., *The Essays of A. J. Muste* (New York, 1967): 149; Anon., "'Grand Old Man' of American Pacifism," *The Christian Century*, 84:8 (Feb. 22, 1967): 230; Anon., "Pacifists Choose New Leader," *The Christian Century*, 57:31 (July 31, 1940): 640; Sidney Lens, "Humanistic Revolutionary," *Liberation*12:6-7 (Sept.-Oct. 1967): 7, 5; Woodcock, "A Moral Man," 105; A. J. Muste, "The Trend--The Historical Imperative of Civilization" in Harrop A. Freeman, ed., *Peace is the Victory,*(New York, 1944), 42; Robinson, *Abraham*, 137.

7. Hentoff, *Essays*, 28.

8. Robinson, *Abraham*, 8.

9. Robinson, *Abraham*, 18.

10. A. J. Muste, "Evanston--After Three Months," *Fellowship* 20:11(Dec. 1954): 12; Hentoff, *Essays*, 45.

11. Peter Brock, *Pacifism in the United States: From the Colonial Era to the First World War* (Princeton, 1968), 479; Peter Brock, *Twentieth Century Pacifism* (New York, 1970), 118, 142-43.

12. Robinson, *Abraham*, 20-22.

13. *Time*, July 10, 1939, 37.

14. Walter Rauschenbusch, *Prayers of the Social Awakening* (Boston, 1910), 108; A. J. Muste, *Gandhi and the H-Bomb: How Nonviolence Can Take the Place of War* (New York, 1950, 1983), 5; Hentoff, *Essays*, 424; Cornell and McReynolds, 9; A. J. Muste, *Not By Might; Christianity: The Way to Human Decency* (New York, 1947), 208; A. J. Muste, "Love and Power in Today's Setting," *The Christian Century* 80:20 (May 15, 1963): 641; Hentoff, *Essays*, 416, 137, 422; A. J. Muste, "They Made It to Moscow," *Liberation* 6:9 (Nov. 1961): 7; Robinson, *Abraham*, 188.

15. Hentoff, *Essays*, 422.

16. Robinson, *Abraham*, 188.

17. Robinson, *Muste,* 14.

18. Murray Kempton, "J. Edgar Hoover and the Industry of Fear," *Liberation* 2: 2 (April, 1957): 8; Robinson, *Abraham*, 101, 179, 167; Zaroulis and Sullivan, *Who Spoke Up?*, 8; Dave Dellinger, "Introduction," *Liberation* 12:6-7: 4.

19. Robinson, *Abraham*, 51; A. J. Muste, "The C.P.L.A. States Its Case," *The World Tomorrow* 16 (Oct. 12, 1933): 570; A. J. Muste, "Where Are We Now?" *Fellowship* 22:1 (Jan. 1956): 20; A. J. Muste, "Prospect for Peace in 1953," *Fellowship* 19:1 (Jan. 1953): 9; Anon., "Tract for the Times," *Liberation* 1:1 (March 1956): 6; A. J. Muste, "Neo-Gandhian India," *The Christian Century* 70:32 (August 12, 1953): 916; A. J. Muste, "Footnote to Cleveland," *The Christian Century* 70:49 (Dec. 9, 1953):1422.

20. Barbara Deming, "'It's a Good Life,'" *Liberation* 12:6-7:60; Barbara Deming, untitled, *WIN* 3:4: 16; Robinson, *Abraham*, 207-8.

21. Walter Rauschenbusch, *Prayers for the Social Awakening* (Boston, 1910), 108.

22. Hentoff, *Essays*, 24, 414-15.

23. John Woolman, *The Journal of John Woolman* and *A Plea for the Poor* (Secaucus, New Jersey, 1975), 126; Hentoff, *Essays*, 415.

24. A. J. Muste, "Pacifism Enters a New Phase," *Fellowship* 26:13 (July 1, 1960): 34.

25. A. J. Muste, "A Meditation on Assurance," *Fellowship* 7:4 (April, 1941): 58; Hentoff, *Essays*, 24, 414; A. J. Muste, "I Believe," *Fellowship* 16:2 (Feb. 1950): 7; A. J. Muste, "Politics on the Other Side of Despair," *Liberation* 7:2 (April, 1962): 9.

26. Hentoff, *Essays*, 375, 415; A. J. Muste, "Utopianism in Christianity," *Fellowship* 16:5 (May 1950): 11; Muste, "I Believe," 7.

27. Muste, "Politics on the Other Side of Despair," 9; Hentoff, *Essays,* 25, 413; A. J. Muste, "What is Left to Do," *Fellowship* 17:7 (July 1951): 16.

28. Robinson, *Abraham*, 166.

29. Sidney Lens, "Humanistic Revolutionary," 6; A. J. Muste, *Not By Might*, 196; A. J. Muste, "Nonviolence--A World Movement," *Liberation* 6:12 (Feb. 1962):16.

30. Robinson, *Abraham*, 84.

31. A. J. Muste, "Love in Action," *Fellowship* 16:6 (June, 1950): 13; A. J. Muste, *Non-Violence in an Aggressive World* (New York, 1940), 186.

32. A. J. Muste, "Some Fellowship Objectives," *Fellowship* 7:10 (October 1941): 165; A. J. Muste, "It Glows in His Heart," *Fellowship* 17:1(January 1951): 5; Muste, *Non-Violence*, 196-97; A. J. Muste, "What is the FOR?," *Fellowship* 22:1 (Jan. 1957): 12.

33. Robinson, *Abraham*, 22; Muste, "Utopianism in Christianity," 11; A. J. Muste, "A Partridge in a Pear Tree," *Sojourners* 13:11 (December 1984): 22.

34. Muste, *Not By Might,* 171, 177; Muste, "Pacifism Enters a New Phase," 34.

35. A. J. Muste, "Fellowship and Class Struggle," in Charles Chatfield, ed., *International War Resistance through World War II* (New York, 1975), 574.

36. A. J. Muste, "The True International," *The Christian Century* 56:21 (May 24, 1939): 668.

37. Hentoff, *Essays*, 133-135, 423; Muste, "The True International," 668.

38. Hentoff, *Essays* , 86, 94; Muste, "Fellowship and Class Struggle," 578; A. J. Muste, "Return to Pacifism," *The Christian Century* 53:49 (December 2, 1936): 1603.

39. Robinson, *Abraham*, 130; Muste, "Fellowship and Class Struggle," 573; Hentoff, *Essays*, 295; Paulo Freire, *A Pedagogy of the Oppressed* (New York, 1970), 13.

40. Muste, "The Trend--The Historical Imperative of Civilization," 40; Muste, *Not By Might*, 140, 208-10, 213; Muste, *Non-Violence in an Aggressive World*, 172.

41. Muste, *Not By Might*, 118, 19; Hentoff, *Essays*, 371.

42. Dorothy Day, *On Pilgrimage: The Sixties* (New York, 1972), 290-292.

43. Henry David Thoreau, "On Civil Disobedience," in *Modern Essays* (Boston, n.d), 12.

44. A. J. Muste, "Pacifism After the War," *Fellowship* 9:12 (Dec. 1943): 203; A. J. Muste, "A Look Around," *Fellowship* 14:5 (May 1948): 5; A. J. Muste, "A Plea to Enlist," *Fellowship* 6:7 (Sept. 1940): 103; A. J. Muste, "Steamer Letter," *Fellowship* 13:7 (July 1947):110.

45. Muste, "A Look Around," 5.

46. A. J. Muste, "Thawing but Unsettled," *Fellowship* 15:7 (July 1949): 23; Muste, "I Believe," 6; A. J. Muste, "The Spiritual Menace of Russian Communism," *Fellowship* 10:6 (June 1944): 105; Muste, "Love in Action," 9, 13.

47. Mayer, "The Christer," 7.

48. Muste, "The True International," 667-668; Robinson, *Abraham*, 63-64.

49. Muste, "Steamer Letter," 109; Robinson, *Abraham* , 63-64.

50. Muste, *Not By Might* , 73.

51. Nat Hentoff, *Peace Agitator: The Story of A. J. Muste* (New York, 1963), 254; A. J. Muste, "A Strategy for the Peace Movement," *Liberation* 7:4 (June 1962): 7; A. J. Muste, *Not By Might*, 43, 52.

52. Charles Chatfield, *For Peace and Justice: Pacifism in America, 1914-1941* (Knoxville, 1971), 303; Muste, *Non-Violence*, 47; Muste, "A Partridge in a Pear Tree," 22; Muste, *Not By Might*, 168; Muste, "Prospect for Peace in 1953," 6.

53. A. J. Muste, "Work for the New Year," *Fellowship* 7:1 (Jan. 1941): 12.

54. Muste, *Non-Violence*, 1, 2, 21, 81; Muste, *Not By Might*, 37, 89; Jo Ann Ooiman Robinson, "The Pharos of the East Side, 1937-1940: Labor Temple Under the Direction of A. J. Muste," *Journal of Presbyterian History* 48:1 (Spring 1970): 32; A. J. Muste, "Pacifism and the Problem of Power," *Fellowship* 16:1 (Jan. 1950): 14; Muste, "Prospect for Peace in 1953," 6; Muste, "A Look Around," 5; A. J. Muste, "The Way of the Cross," *The Christian Century* 55:50 (Dec. 14, 1938): 1543; Muste, *Not By Might*, 119, 129.

55. Hentoff, *Essays,* 14; Muste, *Not By Might,* 2; A. J. Muste, "A New Year--A New Era," *Fellowship* 12:1 (Jan. 1946): 4; A. J. Muste, "'Peace is the Way,'" *Liberation* 10:3 (May 1965): 3.

56. Muste, "A Plea to Enlist," 103.

57. Muste, *Not By Might,* 106, 129.

58. Muste, *Not By Might,* 91, 92, 123.

59. A. J. Muste, "The Pacifist Way of Life," *Fellowship* 7:12 (Dec. 1941): 200; Muste, *Not By Might,* 89-90; Muste, "The Way of the Cross," 1542; Muste, *Non-Violence,* 127.

60. Muste, "The Pacifist Way of Life," 198-200; George Fox, *The Journal of George Fox* (London, 1975), 399-400; Woolman, 241; Thoreau, "On Civil Disobedience," quoted in Hentoff, *Essays,* 290, and Muste, *Not By Might,* 135.

61. Hentoff, *Essays,* 58, 61, 63, 71.

62. Hentoff, *Essays,* 70.

63. Muste, *Not By Might,* 84, 80, 85, 109; Muste, *Non-Violence,* 38; A. J. Muste, "Overcoming Fear," *Fellowship* 16:11 (Nov. 1950): 6-7; A. J. Muste, "Their Church and Ours," *Fellowship* 24:21 (Nov. 1, 1958): 8; Hentoff, *Essays,* 293, 376; Arthur and Vila Weinberg, eds., *Instead of Violence* (Boston, 1963), 106; A. J. Muste, "The Price of Moral Authority," *Fellowship* 18:1 (Jan. 1952): 16; Muste, "I Believe," 5; A. J. Muste, "The Religious Basis of Pacifism," *Fellowship* 5:9 (Nov. 1939): 6; A. J. Muste, "The Way Forward," *Fellowship* 14:1 (Jan. 1948): 4.

64. Hentoff, *Essays,* 294; Muste, *Not By Might,* 127, 85; Muste, "The Way of the Cross," 1541.

65. Brock, *Pacifism,* 141-44; Brock, *Twentieth Century Pacifism,* 150.

66. Muste, "'Peace is the Way,'" 5; Muste, "A Partridge in a Pear Tree," 22; Robinson, "The Pharos of the East Side," 29; Muste, "The Religious Basis of Pacifism," 5; Muste, "The Pacifist Way of Life," 198; Muste, *Gandhi and the H-Bomb,* 11; Muste, *Not By Might,* 217; Muste, *Non-Violence,* 175.

67. Muste, "Return to Pacifism," 1605; Hentoff, *Essays,* 91, 223; Robinson, *Abraham,* 26; A. J. Muste, "The Task Ahead," *Fellowship* 9:7 (July 1943): 129.

68. Mayer, "The Christer," 1; A. J. Muste, *Non-Violence,* 177.

69. Nat Hentoff, "A. J. Muste 1885-1967" *Saturday Review* 50 (April 8, 1967): 35; Nat Hentoff, "A. J. Continuing," *Liberation* 12:6-7: 66.

70. Muste, "Return to Pacifism," 1605; Muste, "Fellowship and Class Struggle," 562; Muste, *Not By Might,* ix, 110, 208; Muste, "The Task Ahead," 129.

71. Lens, "Humanistic Revolutionary," 7.

72. Cornell and McReynolds, 9; Muste, *Not By Might*, 213, 218; Muste, "Fellowship and Class Struggle," 560; Muste, "What is Left to Do?," 16; Muste, "The Price of Moral Authority," 16-17.

73. Muste, "The Task Ahead," 129; A. J. Muste, "The Direction of Growth," *Fellowship* 10:9 (Sept. 1944): 159; Muste, *Non-Violence*, 154; Brock, *Twentieth Century Pacifism*, 99; A. J. Muste, *Nonviolence*, 134.

74. Muste, "The Religious Basis of Pacifism," 5; Muste, *Not By Might*, 218.

75. Muste, "The Direction of Growth," 159; Robinson, *Abraham*, 165; Mayer, "The Christer," 8.

76. Muste, "The Religious Basis of Pacifism," 5; Muste, "The Pacifist Way of Life," 199; Muste, "The Direction of Growth," 159; Muste, "The Way Forward," *Fellowship* 14:1 (Jan. 1948): 8-9; Muste, *Not By Might*, 51, 55, 217; Muste, *Non-Violence*, 193; Robinson, *Abraham*, 176.

77. A. J. Muste, "A Meditation on Assurance," *Fellowship* 7:4 (April 1941): 58; Muste, "The Task Ahead," 129; F.O.R. Spiritual Life Committee, "Thine is the Power," *Fellowship* 18:5 (May 1952): 8; Muste, "The Direction of Growth,"159; Muste, "Steamer Letter," 109-110.

78. Isaiah 65:17, Micah 4:4; Hentoff, *Essays*, 56-57, 85.

79. Woolman, 173; Muste, "The Religious Basis of Pacifism," 5; A. J. Muste, "April 27--A Message to the Fellowship," *Fellowship* 8:5: 75; Muste, *Not By Might*, 108: *Non-Violence*, 178, 126; A. J. Muste, "Letter to the Editor," *Fellowship* 10:8 (August 1944): 147; Robinson, *Abraham*, 160; Muste, "The True International," 667; Muste, "The Pacifist Way of Life," 199; Muste, "Steamer Letter," 109.

80. A. J. Muste, "Fellowship in Discovering Truth," *Fellowship* 10:11 (Nov. 1944): 189; Robinson, *Abraham*, 83.

81. Muste, "Fellowship in Discovering Truth," 189.

82. Robinson, *Abraham*, 25; A. J. Muste, "Today! Speak Out! Bear Your Witness Now" *Fellowship* 5:2 (Feb. 1939): 14; Muste, "Some Fellowship Objectives," 165-166; Muste, "The Task Ahead," 129; Muste, "A New Year--A New Era," 4; Muste, *Not By Might*, 215; Muste, "The Way Forward," 9; Muste, "Love in Action," 12; Muste, "What is Left to Do?," 16.

83. Muste, "Some Fellowship Objectives," 167; Muste *Non-Violence*, 85, 176, 186; A. J. Muste, "The Spirit of the Martyrs," *Fellowship* 6:8 (Oct. 1940): 121; Hentoff, *Essays*, 366; Muste, *Not By Might*, 141-42; Robinson, *Abraham*, 85; A. J. Muste, "Reflections on the Problems of COs in Prison," *Fellowship* 10:1 (Jan. 1944): 14; Muste, "The Religious Basis of Pacifism," 5; Muste, "The Pacifist Way of Life," 199; Theodore Roszak, "A. J.," *Nation* 204:10 (March 6, 1967): 294.

84. Woolman, 103; Thomas Merton, *Gandhi on Non-Violence* (New York, 1965), 19; Douglas Steere, ed., *Quaker Spirituality*, 120.

85. Danny Collum, "Clues to the Future," *Sojourners* 13:11 (Dec. 1984): 3.

86. Steere, *Quaker*, 132, 108, 51; Woolman, 76, 226, 228, 233; Hentoff, *Essays*, 372; Ammon Hennacy, *The Book of Ammon*, (n.p., 1965), x, 299-300; Mel Piehl, *Breaking Bread: The Catholic Worker and the Origin of Catholic Radicalism in America* (Philadelphia, 1982), 213.

87. Hentoff, *Essays*, 372.

88. Robinson, *Abraham*, 109, 167; Dave Dellinger, "Action At Omaha," *Liberation* 4:5 (Summer 1959): 3; Hentoff, *Essays*, 361; Muste, *Not By Might*, 150; Muste, "The Pacifist Way of Life," 198.

89. A. J. Muste, "This Senseless War," *Fellowship* 7:8 (August 1941): 139; Muste, *Non-Violence*, 7; Hentoff, *Essays*, 222; A. J. Muste, "Pacifists Do Not Fight," *The Christian Century* 59:9 (March 4, 1942): 290; *Liberation* 12:6-7: 2.

90. Hentoff, *Peace Agitator*, 123.

91. At the D. A.'s office, Muste had to stand by and witness someone else sign his form for him. Muste, "April 27--A Message to the Fellowship," 75; Robinson, *Abraham*, 80-81.

92. Hentoff, *Essays*, 463.

93. Zaroulis and Sullivan, 370; Anon., "A. J. Muste Takes Tax Refusal Position," *Fellowship* 14:6 (June 1948): 20; Anon., "Muste Refuses Tax Again," *Fellowship* 20:4 (April 1954): 24; Anon., "Muste on Trial for Tax Refusal," *Fellowship* 26:7 (April 1, 1960): 20; Robinson, *Abraham*, 95-96.

94. Hentoff, *Essays*, 373.

95. Hentoff, *Essays*, 372.

96. Anon, "A. J. Muste Fasts; Addresses Crowd of 10,000 at U.N.," *Fellowship* 28:22 (Nov. 15, 1962): 20; Muste, *Not By Might*,151; Woodcock, "A Moral Man," 105.

97. See comments in Robinson, *Abraham*, 177.

98. Muste, "The Way of the Cross," 1543; Muste, "A New Year--A New Era," 4; Muste, *Not By Might*, 133; A. J. Muste, "A Strategy for the Peace Movement," *Liberation* 7:4 (June 1962): 7-8; A. J. Muste, "Mobilize for Peace," *Liberation* 11:11 (Dec. 1966): 23.

99. A. J. Muste, "Pacifism and the Problem of Power, *Fellowship* 16:1 (Jan. 1950): 9; Muste, *Not By Might*, 103; Robinson, *Abraham*, 201, 211; A. J. Muste, "The Vatican Council," *Liberation* 10:10 (Jan. 1966): 37.

100. A. J. Muste, "Pacifism After the War," *Fellowship* 9:12 (Dec. 1943): 203, 205; A Study of International Conflict Prepared for the American Friends Service Committee, *Speak Truth to Power: A Quaker Search for an Alternative to Violence* (n.p., 1955), 70.

101. Muste, "The Direction of Growth," 158; Muste, *Not By Might*, 50.

102. A. J. Muste, "The Reign of Terror," *Fellowship* 4:10 (Dec. 1938): 9; A. J. Muste, "The Roosevelt-Hitler Exchange," *Fellowship* 5:5 (May 1939): 7; Muste, "A Meditation on Assurance," 58; Muste, "What is the FOR?," 9; Muste, *Non-Violence*, 26-28; A. J. Muste, "If I Were in China," *Fellowship* 4:4 (April 1938): 7; A. J. Muste, "'Ye Shall Receive Power': An Easter Meditation," *Fellowship* 10:4 (April 1944): 67; Muste, "Pacifism Enters a New Phase," 34; Muste, *Not By Might*, 134, 80; Robinson, "The Pharos of the East Side," 28.

103. Steere, *Quaker*, 8, 85, 96, 134, 254; Woolman, 175, 194, 200.

104. Muste, "I Believe," 3.

105. Muste, "The Roosevelt-Hitler Exchange," 7; A. J. Muste, "'Let Him Come Down': A Lenten Meditation for Pacifists," *Fellowship* 4:3 (March 1938): 3; Muste, "If I Were in China," 7.

106. A. J. Muste, "Follow the Golden Rule," *Liberation* 3:4 (June 1958): 6; Hentoff, *Essays*, 231, 289; A. J. Muste, "Conscience Against the Atomic Bomb," *Fellowship* 11:12 (Dec. 1945): 209; Muste, *Not By Might* , 151. See discussion in Walter Brueggemann, *Hope Within History* (Atlanta, 1987), 83.

107. Muste, "The Reign of Terror," 9; Muste, *Not By Might*, 52-53, 152; Muste, *Non-Violence*, 6; Muste, "Conscience Against the Atomic Bomb," 208-9.

108. Muste, *Not By Might*, 94, 98; Muste, *Non-Violence*, 189; Muste, "Return to Pacifism," 1605; A. J. Muste, "The Billy Graham Crusade," *Liberation* 2:3 (May 1957): 6; A. J. Muste, "Niebuhr on the Brink of War," *Liberation* 1:12 (Feb. 1957): 10.

109. Muste, *Not By Might*, 94, 56; Muste, *Non-Violence*, 103; Hentoff, *Essays*, 18, 228; A. J. Muste, "World Government--Panacea or Promise?," *Fellowship* 12:10 (Nov. 1946): 179.

110. Hentoff, *Essays*, 424.

111. Robinson, *Abraham*, 165; Muste, *Non-Violence*, 203; Hentoff, *Essays*, 375; Muste, "The Reign of Terror," 9; Muste, "Today! Speak Out! Bear Your Witness Now," 14.

112. Muste, "The Spirit of the Martyrs," 121.

113. Steere, *Quaker*, 47; Kenneth Boulding, *There is a Spirit: The Nayler Sonnets*, (New York, 1945), 3.

114. Hentoff, *Essays*, 137; Robinson, *Abraham*, 145; Laurence Alan Letts, *Peace and the Gospel: A Comparative Study of the Theological and Ethical Foundations of A. J. Muste's Radical Pacifism and Reinhold Niebuhr's 'Christian Realism,'* Ph. D. Dissertation, Yale, 1975, 14.

115. Hentoff, *Peace Agitator*, 13, 181, 41-42; Anon., "A. J. Muste Birthday Celebrated in January," *Fellowship* 16:1 (Jan. 1950): 20; Reinhold Niebuhr, "Christian Revolutionary," *New York Times Book Review* 62:6 (April 16, 196): 6.

116. Muste, "Fellowship and Class Struggle," 574-76; A. J. Muste, "Where 'Crisis Realism' Fails," *Fellowship* 5:4 (April 1939): 4; Muste, "The Task Ahead," 129.

117. Robinson, *Abraham*, 145.

118. Reinhold Niebuhr, "Pacifism Against the Wall," *The American Scholar* 5:2 (Spring 1936): 135; Muste, "Where 'Crisis Realism' Fails," 5; Muste, "Love in Action," 10; Muste, "Fight the Good Fight?," 334.

119. Muste, "Niebuhr on the Brink of War," 9; Reinhold Niebuhr, "Pacifism Against the Wall," 134; Paulo Freire, *Pedagogy of the Oppressed*, 135-36.

120. Reinhold Niebuhr, "Christian Revolutionary," 6; A. J. Muste, "Peace is Indivisible," *Fellowship* 2:8 (Oct. 1936): 6; Niebuhr, "Pacifism Against the Wall," 137; Muste, "Love in Action," 7; Muste, "Niebuhr on the Brink of War," 9.

121. Robinson, *Abraham*, xvii; Muste, "It Glows in His Heart," 6; Muste, "Pacifists Do Not Fight," 289; Muste, "Utopianism in Christianity," 16.

122. G. H. C. Mac Gregor, *The Relevance of an Impossible Ideal* (Nyack, NY, 1941).

123. Niebuhr, "Pacifism Against the Wall,"141; Muste, "Utopianism in Christianity," 13.

124. Niebuhr, "Pacifism Against the Wall," 135; Hentoff, *Essays*, 46, 420.

125. Steere, *Quaker*, 276-277.

126. Muste, "Utopianism in Christianity," 12-13; Hentoff, *Essays*, 312, 313, 318.

127. Muste, "The Way of the Cross," 1543; Muste, *Not By Might*, 52, 40; Muste, *Non-Violence*, 4-5.

128. Letts, 203-4.

129. Letts, 203-4.

130. Fox, 19.

131. Muste, "Utopianism in Christianity," 12; Muste, "It Glows in His Heart," 6; Reinhold Niebuhr, *The Children of Light and The Children of Darkness* (New York, 1944), 9-11, 29-32, 41.

132. Muste, *Not By Might*, 157, 156; Hentoff, *Essays*, 311; Letts, 95ff.

133. Hentoff, *Essays*, 303, 307, 310, 315, 320, 321.

134. Muste, *Not By Might*, 43, 52; Muste, Non-Violence, 4-5.

135. Niebuhr, "Pacifism Against the Wall," 141, 134; Muste, "Fight the Good Fight?," 334.

136. Muste, *Not By Might*, 91, 157.

137. Muste, "Evanston--After Three Months," 14; Muste, "Niebuhr on the Brink of War," 9; Hentoff, *Essays*, 307, 309.

138. Anon., "Muste Testifies Against Rearmament, *Fellowship* 18:8 (Sept. 1953): 22; Muste, "Where 'Crisis Realism' Fails," 5; Muste, "Love in Action," 7; Muste, *Not By Might*, 166; Muste, "Fight the Good Fight?" 340.

139. Muste, "Fight the Good Fight?," 342, 334; Reinhold Niebuhr, "Why I Leave the F.O.R." *The Christian Century* 51:1 (Jan. 3, 1934): 18-19.

140. Muste, *Non-Violence*, 127; Brock, *Pacifism*, 36.

141. Robinson, *Abraham*, 147-48; Niebuhr, "Pacifism Against the Wall," 134-35; Muste, "Where 'Crisis Realism' Fails," 5; Muste, "Utopianism in Christianity," 12.

142. Muste, *Non-Violence*, 36; Muste, "Utopianism in Christianity," 12; Muste, "Where 'Crisis Realism' Fails," 5.

143. *Speak Truth to Power*, passim; Muste, "Where 'Crisis Realism' Fails," 3; Muste, *Not By Might*, 110, 156; Niebuhr, "Christian Revolutionary," 6.

144. William McKane, *Prophets and Wise Men* (Naperville, IL, 1965), 46, 47, 54, 61.

145. McKane 65, 71, 72, 85, 96.

146. The title of a book by fellow FOR member Andre Trocme, *The Politics of Repentance* (New York, 1955).

147. Robinson, *Abraham*, 152-53.

148. Robinson, *A. J. Muste: Pacifist and Prophet*, 17; A. J. Muste, *Non-Violence in an Aggressive World*, 1-2, 193; Robinson, *Abraham,* 162.

149. Zaroulis and Sullivan, 61; A. J. Muste, "Self Immolation," *Liberation* 10:9 (Dec. 1965): 7; A. J. Muste, "USA--Arsenal," *Fellowship* 7:4 (April 1941): 60.

150. Robinson, *Abraham*, 74; A. J. Muste, "Peace and the Power States," *Liberation* 7:8 (Oct. 1962): 17; A. J. Muste, *Non-Violence in an Aggressive World*, 70; A. J. Muste *Not By Might*, 79.

151. A. J. Muste, "This Senseless War," 139-40; A. J. Muste, "Russia in World Affairs," *Fellowship* 10:7 (July 1944): 127.

152. Hentoff, *Essays*, 292; A. J. Muste, "Illusion of Victory," *Fellowship* 8:12 (December 1942): 201; A. J. Muste, "Stalin Pulls the Strings," *Fellowship* 10:3 (March 1944): 37; Muste, "Pacifism After the War," 205; A. J. Muste, "Footnote on Moscow," *Fellowship* 9:12 (December 1943): 213; A. J. Muste, "Twenty-five Years After," *Fellowship* 9:11 (Nov. 1943): 189-190; A. J. Muste, "Dumbarton Oaks or Chaos," *Fellowship* 11:4 (April 1945): 70, 73-84; A. J. Muste, "Three Men at Crimea," *Fellowship* 11:3 (March 1945): 45.

153. A. J. Muste, "The Task Ahead," 128; A. J. Muste, "The San Francisco Charter," *Fellowship* 11:8 (August 1945): 136.

154. A. J. Muste, "Annihilation Without Representation" *Liberation* 5:12 (Feb. 1961): 11.

155. A. J. Muste, "Berlin--Solomon--Kafka" *Liberation* 6:7 (Sept. 1961): 3.

156. Muste, "USA--Arsenal," 60; A. J. Muste, "A Visit to Saigon," *Liberation* 11:3 (Summer 1966): 10; A. J. Muste, "Last Speech," *Liberation* 12:6-7 (Sept.-Oct. 1967): 52.

157. A. J. Muste, "To Teach Peace," *Fellowship* 15:7 (July 1949): 48; Muste, "Nonviolence--A World Movement," 12; Muste, *Not By Might*, 211.

158. Muste, *Not By Might*, 167-68; A. J. Muste, "NOW Is the Appointed Time," *Fellowship* 25:13 (July 1, 1959): 8.

159. Robinson, *Abraham*, 18.

160. Muste, "Overcoming Fear," 4-7; Muste, "The Pacifist Way of Life," 199.

161. A. J. Muste, "The Reign of Terror," *Fellowship* 4:10 (Dec. 1938): 8.

162. Muste, *Not By Might*, 61, 117; Hentoff, *Essays*, 284, 484; Muste, *Gandhi and the H-Bomb*, 7; Muste, "NOW Is the Appointed Time," 8.

163. Hentoff, *Essays*, 286; F.O.R. Executive Committee, "The Course Before Us" *Fellowship* 8:1 (Jan. 1942): 2; Muste, *Non-Violence in an Aggressive World*, 129; Muste, "NOW Is the Appointed Time," 7, 9.

164. Muste, *Not By Might*, 112, 117; Hentoff, *Essays*, 419.

165. Muste, "Steamer Letter," 110.

166. Muste, *Non-Violence in an Aggressive World*, 34; Muste, "Twenty-five Years After," 191; A. J. Muste, "A Pacifist Program--1949" *Fellowship* 15:1 (Jan. 1949): 5-8; Muste, *Not By Might*, 113; Muste, "Utopianism in Christianity," 15; A. J. Muste, "Politics on the Other Side of Despair," *Liberation* 7:2 (April 1962): 8.

167. Steere, ed., 96, 280; Thomas Kelly, *The Eternal Promise* (Richmond, 1988), 34.

168. Muste, "Some Fellowship Objectives," 165; Muste, "The Task Ahead," 128; Muste, "The Way Forward," 5.

169. Muste, *Not By Might*, 59, 63, 70; Muste, *Non-Violence in an Aggressive World*, 130, 167; Hentoff, *Peace Agitator*, 98.

170. Robinson, *Abraham*, 159; Muste, et al., "Tract for the Times," 4.

171. Robinson, *Abraham*, 200, 209; Cornell and McReynolds, 8; A. J. Muste, "Mobilize for Peace," *Liberation* 11:9 (Dec. 1966): 24; A. J. Muste, "Assembly of Unrepresented People: Three Views," *Liberation* 10:7 (Oct. 1965): 27.

172. Robinson, *Abraham*, 159, 163-64, 170, 172, 219; A. J. Muste, "Civil Defense Protest," *Liberation* 6:4-5 (Summer 1961): 3.

173. Robinson, *Abraham*, 182, 185-86; A. J. Muste, "Africa Against the Bomb (II)," *Liberation* 4:11 (Feb. 1960): 11; Muste, "They Made It to Moscow," 8.

174. Robinson, *Abraham*, 176-77, 182-83; Muste, "Nonviolence--A World Movement," 16; A. J. Muste, "The Oxford Conference," *Liberation* 8:1 (March 1963): 25.

175. Muste, "Evanston--After Three Months," 15; Robinson, *Abraham*, 150; A. J. Muste, "'A Just and Durable Peace,'" *Fellowship* 8:4 (April 1942): 62; Muste, "Prospect for Peace in 1953," 7; Hentoff, *Essays*, 419.

176. Robinson, *Abraham*, 148; Muste, *Not By Might*, 172; A. J. Muste, "'Ye Shall Receive Power': An Easter Meditation," 67; Robinson, *A. J. Muste: Pacifist and Prophet*, 21; Muste, "Utopianism in Christianity," 16; A. J. Muste, "Catholic Workers Unite," *Fellowship* 3:6 (June 1937): 5.

177. Steere, ed., 42; Muste, "Overcoming Fear," 7; Muste, "Love and Power in Today's Setting," 640; Arthur and Vila Weinberg, eds., *Instead of Violence*, 105; Muste, "It Glows in His Heart," 2; Muste, *Not By Might*, 173.

178. Muste, "I Believe," 3, 5-6.

179. Muste, *Non-Violence in an Aggressive World*, 176; Muste, "A Plea to Enlist," 104; Muste, "Return to Pacifism," 1606; Muste, "The Way of the Cross," 1541; Muste, *Not By Might*, 180, 195; Muste, "They Made It to Moscow," 9; Hentoff, 415; James Finn, *Protest: Pacifism and Politics* (New York, 1967), 204.

180. Robinson, *Abraham*, 193.

181. *Liberation* 12:6-7 (Sept.-Oct. 1967): 38, 41.

CHAPTER TWO
DOROTHY DAY

She was pregnant with conversion, surprised by joy. With her daughter's birth, her own life was reborn.

If I had written the greatest book, composed the greatest symphony, painted the most beautiful painting or carved the most exquisite figure, I could not have felt more the exalted creator than when they placed my child in my arms. . . .

Such a great feeling of happiness and joy filled me that I was hungry for Someone to thank, to love, even to worship, for so great a good that had been bestowed upon me. . . .

The final object of this love and gratitude was God. No human creature could receive or contain so vast a flood of love and joy as I often felt after the birth of my child. With this came the need to worship, to adore.[1]

Dorothy Day lived as a self-described "sybaritic anchorite," a devotee of luxury and pleasure and a religious recluse. She wandered the beaches near her Staten Island home singing to herself and to her God.[2]

She wanted Tamar Teresa baptized, but the Roman Catholic Church saw complications. Dorothy Day had been divorced, and although she referred to her lover as her common law husband, Foster Batterham rejected every implication of the title. He quickly delighted in the child he had not wanted. The Church, however, remained an unwelcome intruder. It considered him an adulterer; he countered with roughly the same disdainful view of the Church. Day had to choose between the two.

Day had Tamar baptized first. At the moment of her own conditional baptism, she felt no joy, no hope, no conviction. It was a sacrament of duty. As she was baptized, she was "almost groaning in anguish of spirit" for the anticipated loss of Batterham. When the Church sneaked into his house, he escaped out. Birth brought joy; baptism desolation.[3]

Day wrote the obligatory book about her conversion, *From Union Square to Rome*, her transfer of allegiance from secular radicalism's St. Peter's Square to the Church. Yet she thought of herself "as someone who had been looking for God all those years, without really knowing it, and had now *begun* to find Him." Her conversion was "a newly sanctioned continuation of her way of thinking rather than a dramatic turning away from a former viewpoint."[4] Her new life had much in common with her life without Lord or Savior. Her character, interests, values, and tastes remained the same. Her appreciation of nature became a love of God's creation. She transplanted her work for justice and nonviolence into religious soil. She kept coming back to a vocation in journalism.

Born in Brooklyn November 8, 1897, Day moved with her family to Berkeley then Oakland, California, until after the San Francisco earthquake when they moved to Chicago. Her father was a journalist; her mother raised the children. After two indifferent college years at the University of Illinois at Urbana, she rejoined her family in New York City. Two of her brothers followed their father into journalism, but the family patriarch would not hear of his daughter--a woman-- entering the field. In 1916, he conspired with friends in the trade to blackball her, but she confounded his scheme by offering to work at a radical journal for $5 a week.

After her conversion, Day wanted to write only of her experiences of God: the glimpses of the holy that led her from Union Square to Rome, the experiences that sustained her faith. She seemed determined to revise her religious autobiography to share with the prophet Jeremiah the sense of being called from before the womb.

As a youth, she flirted with organized religion. Baptized and confirmed in an Episcopal Church at the age of twelve, she soon engaged in typical adolescent rebellion. In college she latched onto a professor's unoriginal observation that religion was an opiate for the weak. Rejecting the institutional Church, she continued to read the New Testament, John Wesley, and Thomas à Kempis. In retrospect, she was pleased to consider herself, in the words of one of Dostoevsky's characters, "haunted by God." When she would sit next to her friend Eugene O'Neill in a Greenwich Village bar and hear him recite Francis Thompson's "The Hound of Heaven"--the poem Muste used to describe his return to faith--she felt breathlessly pursued by God.

> I fled Him, down the nights and down the days;
> I fled Him, down the arches of the years;
> I fled Him, down the labyrinthine ways
> Of my own mind; and in the mist of tears
> I hid from Him. . . .

As though by some "blind instinct," Day started to slip into the back pew of church during Mass. With the hindsight of the religious neophyte, she saw a religious battle which pitted God against her pride.[5]

Although she had a natural attraction to faith, as a young woman she was much more a convinced radical, and she found these two forces in her life--Union Square and Rome--intractably antagonistic. For reasons she never explained, as a teenager she made a commitment to serve the poor. Her autobiographical accounts vary her resume as a radical: (1) She bounced from socialism to anarchism to the Industrial Workers of the World (IWW); (2) she was a member of the Socialist Party during college, then a member of the IWW, an admirer of communists but never a card-carrying member; or (3) she was a Socialist in college and a Communist in the early 1920s. Even in disarray her radical credentials were authentic.[6]

As a teenager, she read social reformers Charles Dickens, Jack London, and Upton Sinclair. As a young adult she worked for radical publications and interviewed Leon Trotsky. In 1917 she worked for the Anti-Conscription League. She took part in a demonstration outside the White House to urge the courts to treat women suffragists as political prisoners. Arrested and released twice, she was arrested a third time and placed with other protesters in Occoquan, a penitentiary renowned for its brutality. A ten-day hunger strike secured political prisoner status and, a few days later, President Woodrow Wilson pardoned the suffragists. Two months after her release she joined thousands in Madison Square Garden to celebrate the first phase of the Russian Revolution. In the early 1920s, in an indignity that long annoyed her, she was arrested during a police raid on the IWW and mistakenly charged with prostitution.[7]

In her vocational search, she travelled a series of concentric circles. She yearned to write like London or Sinclair whose novels, she believed, encouraged more social change than years of legislation. At college and between jobs, she supported herself doing manual labor. She spent a year training to become a nurse before deciding unequivocally on writing. Yet, the nurse's hour-to-hour familiarity with menial tasks and rudimentary health care became as basic a part of her day-to-day life as her writing. She sold the movie rights to a semi-autobiographical novel and, for a short time, had a job with M.G.M. in Hollywood. A year-long, on-the-rebound marriage merely interrupted an affair that left her emotionally shattered. She wrote for radical publications before Tamar's birth, religious ones afterwards. She moved to Hollywood, New Orleans, and Mexico before resettling in New York City where she worked briefly for the FOR during the late 1920s.[8]

Although she could not have guessed it, her adolescent spirituality, her radicalism, and her early writing career prepared her to become co-founder of the Catholic Worker movement. A few years after Tamar's birth in 1927, Tamar's mother became the mother of a community.

Trying to understand the Catholic Worker without a grasp of Day has been compared to studying the FBI without considering J. Edgar Hoover.[9] It is equally difficult to understand Day without a sense of the movement. Daily existence meant living "without rules, regulations, memberships, committees or endowment." The Worker ignored organizational techniques. Part lay Benedictine social service group, part university, and part work camp, the community was an "extraordinary combination of anarchy and dictatorship," an "anarchist abbey." Day said that Catholic Worker anarchism meant living by the teachings of Jesus and following Augustine's admonition to "love God and do as you will." After the first New York "house of hospitality" opened, independent houses sprang up in over thirty American cities; one opened in England. At the New York house, Day was the reluctant "abbess" or "abbot," an autocratic anarchist, the tough Mother Superior of the movement. Like the apostle Paul, she traveled, established new communities, and wrote letters to teach, give pastoral guidance, and spread the good news of the Catholic Worker. Day's relationship to the new communities also resembled Teresa of Avila's with the foundations she established in Spain for ecclesiastical and spiritual renewal.[10]

The distribution of the first issue of *The Catholic Worker* on May Day in 1933 launched the movement. High unemployment made it easy to recruit volunteers to hand out the paper. Six years later, at the age of forty-two, having survived many tense moments within the Catholic Worker family, Day described herself as "the grandmother of the revolution." The paper lost subscribers when it supported strikes and child labor legislation, and when Day clarified its pacifist stance during World War II. The Church hierarchy intervened to correct her when, in 1940, *The Catholic Worker* urged Catholics to become conscientious objectors. She was criticized because the Worker refused funds from Church and State to assist its ministry; the movement relied on individual gifts as a witness to co-founder Peter Maurin's belief in personal responsibility. She grieved because volunteers and guests were unable to live by the Worker's creed of freedom and responsibility. She found it hard to tolerate self-righteous co-workers. As the movement's court jester, Stanley Vishnewski, said, "The Catholic Worker is made up of saints and martyrs. You have to be a martyr to put up with the saints." [11]

The history of the movement can be divided into five periods. (1) During the Depression, the Catholic Worker focused primarily on labor and unemployment. It developed the monthly paper, houses of hospitality, and its first farming communes. The paper became a prominent voice against anti-Semitism and took a pacifist position on the Spanish Civil War--a "holy war" that divided American Leftists from American Catholics. (2) World War II brought employment in the military and war-related industries, deflated the ranks of the Worker, and caused the closure of several houses. The movement split when, in conscious disregard of war-fever, Day espoused pacifism. The emptying of the houses gave her time for spiritual reflection. Maurin's declining health and his death in 1949 left the movement entirely in Day's hands. (3) The nuclear age and the arrival of Ammon Hennacy at the Worker reunited Day with her roots in direct political action and civil disobedience. In the 1950s, in collaboration with Muste, five annual protests against New York City's civil defense drills (and four trips to jail for

Hennacy and Day) led the city to suspend the drills. (4) The 1960s saw the Vietnam War, protests against the draft, and Day working more frequently with Muste. She attended the Second Vatican Council in Rome, and flew to India and the Soviet Union. (5) Her health in decline, in the 1970s she handed the loose reins of her anarchistic movement to others; she died in 1980.

By most political reckonings the movement was never large. The circulation of *The Catholic Worker* never exceeded 200,000 and for much of its history it labored at less than half of that. Yet Day and the Worker won the honor coveted by many twentieth-century American radicals: J. Edgar Hoover considered the movement subversive, and on three occasions recommended charges of sedition against Day who had become grandmother to many radical groups.

Day had no interest in Muste's kind of experimentation, yet the number of publications and organizations born of the Catholic Worker would have pleased her Quaker colleague. *The Catholic Worker* not only nudged the liberal Catholic press towards more radical positions, publications emerged from the Worker like a set of Eves from Adam's rib. The community gave birth to peace groups in both the 1930s and the 1960s. In the 1930s, Catholic Worker graduates moved on to Catholic labor organizations and a Catholic Union of the Unemployed (similar to the Communist and Musteite unemployed councils). Day met weekly with the Baroness Catherine de Hueck Doherty whose sister movement in Harlem-- Friendship House--touched the life of Thomas Merton. Perhaps the Worker's most influential alumnus was socialist Michael Harrington, whose book, *The Other America*, became a foundation for 1960s liberalism's ill-executed war on poverty.[12]

Day lived with various contradictions. She relished good food and adored classical music, yet chose a life that separated her from both. She demonstrated in 1917 so that women could vote, then boycotted the ballot box for sixty-three years. Her gruff exterior invited harsh exchanges, yet she was easily wounded by criticism, and slow to forgive any slight. Admired for her saintliness, she often felt herself a failure. Popularity brought more invitations for public speaking, which she rarely enjoyed. At the height of her popularity in the 1960s, she experienced a spiritual and emotional depression.

Day's sole consolation in later years was her grandchildren. Unlike Muste, her health failed her and she became increasingly withdrawn. Muste nurtured organizations like a doting grandfather; Day expressed indifference to the Catholic Worker's fate. Muste's flexibility and ability to listen gained the trust of young people; Day's rigorous nature fossilized to rigidity. Church reforms offended her. She abhorred the sexual revolution. She did not embrace old age gracefully. A little boy at the Rochester House of Hospitality had been excited all day because people kept saying "Dorothy Day is coming...and now she's here and she's just an old woman." In response, Day prayed for "holy indifference."[13]

Day gave Tamar Teresa her middle name for Teresa of Avila, the Spanish mystic. While in the maternity ward, a woman gave Day a medal of "Little Therese" of Lisieux. The two saints shaped Day's self-awareness for life. Taken with the earthiness of Teresa of Avila, she at first preferred the powerful Spaniard to the meek French child. Yet Day came to prefer the "little flower" and the "little way," a better fit for the Catholic Worker's small-scale witness.

Day, who has been remembered with the masculine "abbot" as well as the feminine "abbess," more closely resembled the rough Spanish mystic who told her nuns to "be strong men." Yet she wrote a sentimental hagiography, *Therese*, about the French girl with the bubblingly sweet, adolescently romantic spirit. Perhaps Day, the repentant sinner, was attracted to her opposite in Therese, the pure soul. Perhaps Day yearned for her own vanished purity. Yet, to look more deeply, Teresa seems a spiritual mother to Day, and *Therese* reveals Day's motherly affection for the French girl who died in her early twenties--an age when Day flirted with Church and men with equal facility. She seemed to see in Therese those sweet traits some mothers desire in their daughters.[14]

Day stood between the two saints; daughter of great Teresa and mother of little Therese. The mother's love gave Day the greater joy.

A Word Made Flesh

"The world would be better off
if people tried to become better.
And people would become better
if they stopped trying to become better off.
For when everybody tries to become better off,
nobody is better off.
But when everybody tries to become better,
everybody is better off.
Everybody would be rich
if nobody tried to become richer.
And nobody would be poor
if everybody tried to be the poorest.
And everybody would be what he ought to be
if everybody tried to be
what he wants the other fellow to be."

--Peter Maurin[15]

In her twenties, Day was a political radical, a Greenwich Village bohemian, a religious skeptic who befriended leftists, artists, and writers. Yet she nurtured a secret piety. Tamar's birth drove her from Union Square to Rome. The radical was now a Roman Catholic; and in the American milieu of that time, the two could not become one.

In 1932, freelancing for the liberal Catholic magazine *Commonweal*, Day covered a hunger march sponsored by the Unemployed Councils and the Communist Party. As she watched them enter Washington on the last leg of their trek from New York, she felt joy and pride for the marchers, and bitterness that her newborn Catholic faith separated her from them. *They* were the ones who, like the Son of Man, had no place to lay their heads; *they* were his beloved friends, close to his heart in their work for justice. Since becoming a Catholic, her work for others seemed "puny." She felt self-absorbed, self-indulgent, sinfully withdrawn into an individualistic, salvation-for-one piety that provided some inner peace but left her disconnected from the world. Neither atheistic radicalism nor religious quietism quenched her spiritual thirst.[16]

It was the Feast of the Immaculate Conception, and after the demonstration, Day went to the national shrine at the Catholic University. "On the brink of losing my faith," she felt that she had to be either Catholic or radical. She prayed "with tears and with anguish" for an avenue to open up so that she could use her gifts for the workers and the poor.[17] The prayer began a transformation as marked as motherhood. The birth brought her faith to full term; the answer to her prayer ordained her for ministry.

Returning to New York after the march, Day found a man waiting for her. At first, she found him annoying. In his thick French accent, he spoke without pause in an endless monologue until she was exhausted. Eventually, she realized that God had "brought" Peter Maurin into her life to give her a vocation, to begin the Catholic Worker movement, and to knit together Union Square and Rome.[18]

Maurin did not converse. He indoctrinated. He presented Day with a program, an ideology, a view of history, and a spirituality. His was the Word by which she then lived, the Word she altered as she enfleshed it. His program had four points: (1) round-table discussions for cross-fertilization between workers and scholars (Muste's pentecostal bridge), (2) houses of hospitality to practice the traditional "Works of Mercy"--feeding the hungry, clothing the naked, sheltering the homeless, (3) farming communes to break the death-grip of industrial capitalism and bring people back to the land, and (4) a newspaper to publicize the movement's work. The program united Day's fragmented life. Maurin connected Church traditions to contemporary social problems. He proposed a new social order built without violence. A Catholic labor paper linked her faith to social commitment and to journalism.[19]

To Maurin, this movement followed the example of apostolic Christians in the Roman Empire and Irish monks in Medieval Europe by subverting the dominant culture through personal witness. Like the early apostles and Irish monks, the new movement would be a "community witness of faith and charity in the midst of a decadent and dying milieu," and would transform culture from below.[20]

Maurin taught in "easy essays" sounding "like advertising jingles composed in an abbey." His firm roots in Church history and theology did not keep him from borrowing freely from secular radicals, comparing and contrasting their methods and goals with his. Lenin said that revolution required a theory of revolution; Maurin furnished a Catholic theory for social revolution. To describe the goal of social change, he borrowed the IWW's phrase: "A society in which it is easier for people to be good," for when people are good, he added, they are happy. A planned Catholic Worker Labor School, modeled partly on Muste's Brookwood school, and "agronomic universities" (farming communes with educational facilities) shared Brookwood's commitment to bring historical perspective to contemporary social problems.[21]

Maurin's critiques struck a resonant chord in Day: "Liberals cannot be liberators" because they lack commitment; Catholics feared Bolshevik revolution because the Church offered no Christian revolution; Communists claimed to be the arch-foes of capitalism, but they were really spiritual kin:

> The bourgeois capitalist
> tries to keep
> what he has,
> and tries to get
> what the other fellow has.
> The Bolshevist Socialist
> tries to get
> what the bourgeois capitalist has.
> The Bolshevist Socialist
> is the son
> of the bourgeois capitalist,
> and the son
> is too much
> like his father.
> All the sins of the father
> are found in the son.

Communists spoke of a "popular front," so Maurin called for an "unpopular front" of "Humanists, who try to be human to man; Theists, who believe that God wants us to be our brother's keeper; Christians, who believe in the Sermon on the Mount as well as the Ten Commandments; Catholics, who believe in the Thomistic Doctrine of the Common Good."[22] Maurin would collaborate with any allies to create his envisioned Christian society. His even-handed, open-ended round-table discussions engaged other ideologies in the hope that he could convert them through reasoned debate.

Maurin preferred personal to governmental responsibility, an agrarian village economy over putting the worker in charge of the means of production. His lack of interest in the Depression's labor movement and class conflict, which astounded Day and mystified others, may have been rooted in his peasant upbringing. His emphasis on decentralization made his program appear both radical and reactionary. Who then believed that the labor movement merely accommodated capitalism? Who believed that farming communes could solve unemployment? His vision of a decentralized, agrarian economy and his emphasis on personal responsibility resembled the nostalgia of the turn-of-the-century English "distributists" and conflicted with Muste.[23] Intrigued by Muste, Maurin invited him to speak at various symposia in the late 1930s. Yet Maurin had a different way of interpreting the intensifying class conflict.

> When the little shots
> are not satisfied
> to remain little shots
> and try to become
> big shots,
> then the big shots
> are not satisfied
> to remain big shots
> and try to become
> bigger shots.
> And when the big shots
> become bigger shots
> then the little shots
> become littler shots.
> And when the little shots
> become littler shots
> because the big shots
> become bigger shots
> then the little shots
> get mad at the big shots.
> And when the little shots
> get mad at the big shots
> because the big shots
> by becoming bigger shots
> make the little shots
> littler shots
> they shoot the big shots

full of little shots.

Maurin's farming communes were an alternative to class warfare.[24]

While Protestant and secular allies believed in variations on a theme of progress and historical determinism, the modern era looked no better to Maurin than the past. History had reached a fundamentally tragic turning point centuries before when societies began to value currency over labor, and became acquisitive instead of functional economies. The twentieth century was an age of chaos, a Dark Age lacking any sense of the sacred. Maurin remembered that, in their own Dark Age, Irish monks practiced personal charity and voluntary poverty, and emphasized round-table discussions, houses of hospitality, farming colonies, and "Agronomic Universities." Just as Protestants Muste and King idealized early Christianity, Maurin romanticized Christians in early Medieval Europe.[25]

Born in France in 1877 and raised in a large peasant family, Maurin emigrated to Canada in 1909 and to the U.S. in 1911 where he worked odd jobs. He stopped going to church for ten years because, in his own mind, he had stopped living as a good Catholic. At the time he met Day, he taught French and asked people to pay him what the lessons were worth. He visited New York City a few days at a time and went to Union Square to indoctrinate people. He owned nothing, and carried his library in the pockets of his only suit. Day described him as a modern Francis of Assisi, yet even in moments of hagiographical excess, she knew his uninterruptable speech and inattentiveness to bathing often made him unpleasant company.

Familiar with European Catholic social thought, Maurin was influenced by his youthful involvement in France with Le Sillon, a reformist Catholic movement that bore a striking resemblance to the program he founded thirty years later in Manhattan. Le Sillon distributed a newspaper on the street to publicize its work (cooperatives and hospices) and its beliefs (pacifism). Each of its members was to be absorbed with the thought of Christ, make Christ's presence known to others, and strive to conform the social order to Christlike principles.[26]

Stories of Maurin's humility and passion for justice fill the Catholic Worker's lore. People reading his essays in *The Catholic Worker* would invite him to speaking engagements, rarely prepared for his unkempt appearance. When he arrived at the house of hospitality in Buffalo, they rudely told him to go away until they opened the soup line. Invited to the home of a Columbia professor, the professor's wife, who had not met Maurin, mistook him for the plumber and led him to the basement where he waited patiently until the professor, upon returning home, rescued him. Organizers of a suburban women's club phoned the Worker office wondering about the whereabouts of their speaker. When Day suggested that Maurin was probably at the train station, they replied that the only person there was "an old tramp"; it was Maurin. While staying in a Chicago "flophouse," a prostitute knocked on Maurin's door and asked if he wanted to have a "good time." He invited her in for his idea of a good time--indoctrinating her in the Catholic Worker program. It is not known if either party paid for the other's services.[27]

Day respected Maurin's commitment to Church teachings, the sacraments, and scripture. She admired his thought, patience, humility, voluntary poverty, detachment, and passion. She likened him to a Benedictine, to St. Francis, and John the Baptist. He embodied Paul's fool who confounded the wise, the weak one overcoming the strong (1 Cor 1:18f). Maurin's "anarchism" meant washing feet and practicing the way of love instead of the way of empire. Yet he embarrassed Day with his physical appearance and evangelical fervor. When asked why he gave no thought to his appearance, he replied simply, "So as not to arouse envy." He pursued doctor, plumber, landlord, and grocery clerk, gesticulating with his finger in the air as he made each "point."[28]

Like Muste, Maurin saw moral coercion as a form of violence, so when a fight broke out at the farming commune breakfast table over an egg, he vowed not to eat eggs nor drink milk for the rest of the summer. Out of respect for personal dignity, no one at a house or farm was ever forced to work. Just the same, when Maurin went out to work on the farm he suggestively carried extra tools. Most of the time nobody followed. When a stroke stripped him of the only possession he treasured--his mind--he lived a quiet, mournful, five years with a new form of physical poverty. No longer able to speak, he attended Mass each day. His body stiff, his mind seemingly oblivious to his surroundings, he always forced himself to kneel at the Sanctus.[29]

Maurin found his first disciple in Day, yet differences in spirit and temperament complicated their mentor-disciple relationship. Day filled the first issue of *The Catholic Worker* with denunciations of the status quo and news of protests, and Maurin was incensed. He accused her of patching up the status quo. He wanted a paper dedicated to "annunciation" of the light ahead. But Day always admired the exile disguised as a priest in Ignazio Silone's novel *Bread and Wine*; when Italy invades Ethiopia, he chalks "No" on public buildings to protest.

> When he is asked what good such a puny dissent does, and why he is risking his life, which is so precious to others, by such a futile gesture, he replies that as long as one man says "No!" the unanimity of consent is broken.[30]

Maurin shared Muste's focus on the future-to-be; Day shared Muste's appreciation of the individual protest against conformity.

Together, Maurin and Day split the vocation of Jeremiah: She tore down as he built up (Jer 1:10). He wanted to call the paper "The Catholic Radical" or "The Catholic Agronomist" to lead people toward the land. She called it *The Catholic Worker*, associating it with the labor movement and class partisanship. After their disagreement over the paper's content, Maurin resigned as an editor to become a contributor.

When controversy arose over the paper's pacifism, Maurin wanted Day to soft-pedal the issue, but the editor stood firm. When conflict tore at the community from within, Maurin wanted to walk away and start over again, but Day was immovable. When he announced new programs, she pronounced them impractical; and he gave in. He seemed to her too intellectual, too optimistic, too unrealistic. Still, at times he won her over. Her opinion of the labor movement evolved towards his. He won her over to a lay movement guided by the clergy but unencumbered by the hierarchy.

That he emphasized the farming communes and she the houses of hospitality was more than a conflict between agri-peasant and urban-worker backgrounds. The houses emphasized the present and the works of mercy so close to her nurse's heart; the farming communes announced the future. The visionary wanted to take a communal leap into the future while the nurse met the practical day-to-day needs of individuals.[31]

If Day was the professed mother, grandmother, and abbess of a far-flung family, she quickly deflected credit to Maurin as its catalyst and theoretician. With his oft-repeated, playful quip upon giving into Day, Maurin analyzed their relationship differently: "Man proposes, woman disposes." Yet the true nature of their intricate relationship lay deeper. In the late 1960s, Day described leaders like Cesar Chavez of the United Farm Workers as "the word made flesh," the people who put "flesh on the dry bones of principles and ideals. . . .There must be the *idea*, the theory of the personalist and communitarian revolution, but the idea must be clothed in flesh and blood." Maurin's message--his spirit and vision--was the idea, the Word. The power to make his Word incarnate as a living community came through Day: "In collaboration with Peter Maurin, she conceived it and brought it to term."[32] Without Day, Maurin might never have found a disciple. Without her as mother and midwife, the movement would have died stillborn in his mind.

The Mystical Body

"Why do the Members of Christ tear one another? Why do we rise up against our own Body?"

--Clement of Alexandria[33]

Deeply engrossed in the seamen's strike of 1937, the Catholic Worker, for the only time in its history, opened a special soup line specifically for the strikers. Always financially precarious, it plunged more deeply into debt.

On her way to the Seamen's Defense Committee headquarters, Day was saying her rosary while waiting for a traffic light to change.

> The recitation was more or less automatic, when suddenly like a bright light, like a joyful thought, the words Our Father pierced my heart. To all those who were about me, to all the passersby, to the longshoremen idling about the corner, black and white, to the striking seamen I was going to see, I was akin, for we were all children of a common Father, all creatures of one Creator, and Catholic or Protestant, Jew or Christian, Communist or non-Communist, were bound together by this tie. We cannot escape the recognition of the fact that we are all brothers. Whether or not a man believes in Jesus Christ, His incarnation, His life here with us, His crucifixion and resurrection; whether or not a man believes in God, the fact remains that we are all the children of one Father.[34]

This illumination--so similar to Merton's later experience in Louisville--confirmed her in her commitment to end human strife.

For Day, the main purpose of *The Catholic Worker* was to bring the doctrine of the Mystical Body of Christ to the person on the street. Christ's Mystical Body was broader than the Roman Catholic Church. The Mystical Body transcended all ecclesiastical and ideological barriers and united the living to the dead. Day liked to cite Aquinas (although she sometimes attributed the statement to Augustine) that all people are "members or potential members" of Christ's Body. She wanted the communion she felt with others while kneeling at the altar rail to exist within the struggling Catholic Worker community, between labor and management, in the middle of the Spanish Civil War. If people could recognize that Christ lived in all, and all were one in Christ, there would be no war.[35]

In her pre-Christian days with the Anti-Conscription League, she opposed the American entry into World War I but--like Reinhold Niebuhr later--still believed in class war. Later, she spoke of the Fatherhood of God and the Brotherhood of Man, a vocabulary she shared with the Social Gospel and liberal Protestantism. Every war, all violence, was unchristian. All people belonged to the Mystical Body; all shared equal dignity as God's children; all were created in God's image and likeness; God loved them all.[36]

The Catholic Worker declared itself neutral during the Spanish Civil War. Pro-Franco Catholics and anti-Franco leftists, crusaders all, attacked the newspaper from opposite sides. Day infuriated each side by praying for both because all were at least potential members of the Mystical Body. People should love their enemies, not out of fear, but because God loved them, and because "our enemies are the galley slaves that row us into heaven."[37]

Again opposing both sides in an unholy Korean War, at Christmas in 1950, Day wrote a "Message of Love."

> We are on the side of the poor. . . .Who are the poor? They are our soldiers in Korea fighting in zero [degree] weather, thousands of them suffering and tortured and dying. . . .They are the Koreans themselves, north and south, who have been bombed out, burnt out in the rain of fire from heaven.

Forty thousand American bombs fell on a city of 45,000, killing "men, women, and children, the old and the sick and the cripples. The innocent, the noncombatant." When napalm killed a thousand Korean soldiers, Day prayed, "God have mercy on them all and those who killed them as well as those who died!" Christmas was a time to see Christ in everyone, "when love came down to the mire, to teach us that love."[38]

Day found it hard to love capitalists and bureaucrats--the enemies of the poor. Her natural inclination to side with the oppressed collided with her belief in the all-inclusive Mystical Body. Events in the 1930s often tested her beliefs. Shortly after she visited soup kitchens and headquarters where a strike in Chicago forced plants to close, police shot down hundreds of workers, killing ten, in what was called the Memorial Day Massacre. In her ensuing article in *The Catholic Worker*, she asked rhetorically whom to blame for shooting people while they walked a peaceful picket line: the police? Tom Girdler of the Republic Steel Company? Other industrialists? The press? The clergy? Anyone who had not worked or protested for labor? She leapt into a written prayer:

> One more sin, suffering Christ, worker Yourself, for You to bear. In the garden of Gethsemane, You bore the sins of all the world--You took them on Yourself, the sins of those police, the sins of the Girdlers and the Schwabs, of the Graces of this world. In committing them, whether ignorantly or of their own free will, they piled them on Your shoulders, bowed to the ground with the weight of the guilt of the world, which You assumed because You loved each of us so much. You took them on Yourself, and You died to save us all. . . .
>
> And the sufferings of those strikers' wives and children are completing Your suffering today.
>
> Have pity on us all, Jesus of Gethsemane--on Tom Girdler, those police, the souls of the strikers, as well as on all of us who have not worked enough for "a new heaven and a new earth wherein justice dwelleth."[39]

"Jesus of Gethsemane" suffered and died for all, innocent victims and guilty murderers. Without diluting her loyalty to the workers, her prayer transcended sides even while taking one. In her grief she whispered an announcement.

The lessons Day absorbed among the workers helped her to understand the Mystical Body. Christians who denied Christ's presence in the poor drove her to communism. Oddly, Communism's commitment to human solidarity edged her back toward God. The workers' solidarity and the IWW slogan--an injury to one is an injury to all--proclaimed the unity of the Mystical Body. The Left revealed to her the true nature of the poor. Even individual communists pointed her back toward the Church: Knowing of her spiritual quest, a communist friend gave Day her first rosary; another gave her a statue of the Virgin Mary.[40]

Christians rejected the poor. They denied God when they ignored those in need (Mt 25:40). They lied when they said they loved God while disregarding their sisters and brothers (1 Jn 4:20). Their faith was dead, for when someone in need approached, Christians turned them away with empty words (James 2:15ff.). Her experience with communism "helped me to find God in His poor, in His abandoned ones, as I had not found Him in Christian churches." She learned of Christian love and human unity outside the Church.[41]

Maurin helped her to discover the correlation of the material and the spiritual, the lesson of the eucharist. Day came to see earth inseparable from heaven, as body is from soul. There were no divisions in Christ. Nothing separated the Catholic from the Communist, the unbaptized, or the God-hater.[42]

Long after her conversion, conservatives reviled Day as "Moscow Mary," a communist in Catholic clothing. She accepted the slander with equanimity: they would brand anyone who threatened money and property. She prayed for her old leftist friends. She trusted that, in reaching out to Good, Truth, and Love, they held their arms out to God. Day prayed for convicted spies Julius and Ethel

Rosenberg, and urged superpatriot Cardinal Spellman to intercede on their behalf. After their executions, she noted that the Psalms read as they walked to their deaths were the same ones Spellman read every week. The Psalms joined alleged traitors to patriotic cardinals.[43]

Day visited Cuba shortly after Castro came to power and returned using the Parable of the Two Sons (which Muste had found apt thirty years before) to define the political situation: the one who passively prays for the poor is less pleasing to God than the one who cares for them. She also alluded to the story in which the religious establishment interrogated the healed blind man to prove Jesus a sinner (Jn 9). When asked, the Cuban people said: Whether Castro is a sinner we do not know, but now there will be schools and land and bread. In 1962, the year of the American Missile Crisis, she wrote that the Body of Christ included Cuba, China, the Soviet Union and all professing Marxist-Leninists.[44]

Having prayed for peace during the Spanish Civil War, Day later prayed for guerilla Che Guevara. At the Kremlin she prayed for journalist John Reed. She prayed for Lenin at his tomb, perhaps echoing her words written two decades before: "May Lenin too find a place of refreshment, light, and peace." On another trip she prayed at the grave of Karl Marx:

> Perhaps if we thought of how Karl Marx was called 'Papa Marx' by all the children on the street, if we knew and remembered how he told fairy stories to his children, how he suffered hunger and poverty and pain, how he sat by the body of his dead child and had no money for coffin or funeral, perhaps such thoughts as these would make us love him and his followers.[45]

Having used personal anecdotes to humanize the Bowery's downtrodden for her readers, she used them again to pry away the demons from Marx's name. Ironically, Merton wrote of the personal lives of Holocaust bureaucrats to accentuate the insidiousness of evil. Day wanted fellow Christians to ponder Charles Péguy's question: "What would God say if some of us came to Him without the others?"[46] She tried to soften the encrusted shell of projected evil from the saints of communism so that Christians could find their common humanity.

Weary from the daily grind of anarchistic community living and the daily news of World War II, Day began a one year retreat, but gave up after six months: God intended people to live in community.[47] As conflict evoked her thoughts on the Mystical Body, imprisonment engendered her most powerful writings on community. In a passage she later criticized as adolescent melodrama--perhaps because it imitated Eugene Debs--she wrote of her 1917 experience in jail: "I was that mother whose child had been raped and slain. I was the mother who had borne the monster who had done it. I was even that monster, feeling in my own heart every abomination." In another jail forty years later, guards did not issue clothing to Day or her co-defendants and refused to let them go to chapel in their "wrappers." Prostitutes, drug addicts, forgers, and thieves gathered underwear, shoes, socks, and dresses so that the women could go to Mass: "Being with others, sharing with others, makes the Cross so much easier." She saw evidence of transcendence whenever the oppressed sought community; and she grieved for the alienated, isolated futures of fellow inmates.[48]

The Catholic Worker community shared in the traditional corporal and spiritual Works of Mercy: Feeding the hungry, giving drink to the thirsty, clothing the naked, ransoming the captive, harboring the homeless, visiting the sick, and burying the dead; admonishing the sinner, instructing the ignorant, counseling the doubtful, comforting the sorrowful, bearing wrongs patiently, forgiving all injuries, and praying for the living and the dead. The Worker was to be the grain of sand around which a pearl would form, a new society taking shape within the shell of the old.[49]

As a model of Christian relations, however, it was a dismal failure. Stanley Vishnewski described the New York house of hospitality as "a house of hostility" and joked, "Happy must be those leaders who die before they see the accomplishments of their followers." Instead of cultivating cooperation between scholars and workers, farming communes started a "war." Day described those who agreed with her as Catholic Workers; those who disagreed were "readers" of *The Catholic Worker*: "It is a fluid situation." Maurin wanted to create a Christian community so that people could say of them, "See how they love each other." Although grateful for sporadic sounds of harmony, Day observed, "Nobody can say that about us."[50]

Intentional communities, every new society formed within the shell of the old--Israel, the apostolic Church, the monastic movement, sectarian Protestant groups--always suffer internal friction. The Catholic Worker lived with several unresolved tensions. Its members tried to be both Catholic and radical, oriented to service and social change, moral purists and institutional pragmatists. Its policy of absolute non-discrimination--accepting all residents until the house was full--wrecked any thoughts of a peaceable kingdom. But the Worker community was not meant to be utopian.[51] In uniting diverse ideas and people, it was but a microcosm of the Mystical Body that united sinners in the communion of saints.

Day revealed her conventional piety in her writings on the movement's spiritual superstructure. She counted nuns' prayers a "power house" for the Worker's ministry, a notion that would have chilled the mature Merton. She entrusted the fate of the movement to Teresa, Therese, and, most often, the calloused, working hands of St. Joseph. When the community moved to a new house, they erected a statue of St. Joseph to "oversee" them. When debts became too large, they would "picket" St. Joseph with prayers and candles. In prayer and print, Day gently reminded St. Joseph of a plumber's bill, and a $4000 debt to be paid.[52] In Day's cosmology, heaven existed, in part, to help with work on earth.

Day shared Muste's affection for the verse from 2 Peter:

"We wait for new heavens and a new earth in which righteousness dwells" (3:13, RSV)--for her, the final realization of the Mystical Body; for him, the city-to-be. She asked a Mustean question: Can we accomplish heaven on earth? and saw that some things would be left undone. Change was like a child forming slowly in a womb: It takes a long time but is worth the wait. Perhaps Muste's hope was more imminent because he worshiped in a Church with an empty cross and a Risen Christ; when Day worshiped, she saw a suffering Christ on a crucifix. The new earth accentuated historical hope; the new heaven a hope transcending history. Muste found more room in his heart for the new earth; Day had equal room for both.[53]

Had Day been a visual artist, the drawings and woodcuts in *The Catholic Worker* showing Christ in the soup line, eating with the unemployed, and working as a carpenter would have been hers. This same feel for the divine presence endowed her with a sacramental sense of life.[54]

Channels of Grace

"[Jesus said] I have left Myself in the midst of you, so that what you cannot do for Me, you can do for those around you...and what you do to them I count as done to Me."

--Catherine of Siena

"Pagan Greeks used to say
that the poor
'are the ambassadors
of the gods.'
To become poor
is to become
an Ambassador of God."

--Peter Maurin[55]

The Catholic Worker's first internal crisis came in its infancy when the Campion Propaganda Committee, a caucus within the New York and Boston houses, wanted to model the Worker after more efficient Catholic Action groups in Europe and Quebec. The Campions planned to expand parish fundraising efforts, an idea antithetical to Maurin's prescribed dependence on personal charity. Causing even greater friction between caucus and co-founders was the Campions' desire to cut expenses on the soup kitchen to concentrate on the newspaper. As Day analyzed the situation: The Campions favored scholars over workers, the paper over food and shelter, writing about ministry over doing it. The most sensitive of the multiplying sore points was the Campions' wish to improve morale and effectiveness by weeding out undeserving "bums" and retaining only the worthy poor. As tensions became severe in mid-1935, Maurin wanted to avoid a confrontation, leave with Day, and start over. But Day refused to back down. A plot to oust her as editor fizzled, and the Campions left in 1936.[56]

The Catholic Worker had set a precedent: individuals over efficiency, ungrateful clientele over up-and-coming leaders. The farming communes never became self-sufficient because Maurin's non-coercive spirit prevailed. No one was forced to work, so few did. A saying developed: "In the Catholic Worker the gold is expelled and the dross remains."[57]

The Campions distinguished between the poor who cooperated, sought jobs, and gave thanks, and those who did not. Even before Day heard Maurin put it into words, she embraced the poor as "ambassadors of God." Through his unique catechism, the poor became for her sacraments of God, the Holy Family in disguise, channels of grace.[58]

Day's rejection of the Campions and her view of the poor grew out of the sacraments, the mainstay of her spiritual sustenance. She renewed the joy of childbirth in daily Mass, and on Saturdays attended the service of Benediction where, Teresa said, the humanity of Christ was "disguised" and approachable in the tabernacle's bread.[59] Day likened feeding the hungry to the eucharist. As Jesus was not recognized on the road to Emmaus until he broke bread, so she prayed that "in knowing the least of His children, we are knowing Him." The Worker fed the physical hunger of the poor. Day wanted to bring the masses to mass to feed their spiritual hunger. She tried to introduce them to Christ first in the soup kitchen, then in church; first in bread and soup, then in bread and wine. The Worker refused to proselytize the vulnerable in coercive or manipulative ways. As it was with work, so it was with worship. With regular opportunities for worship, the Worker led by example.[60]

An early member of the community, who assiduously avoided church and scorned the "sluggish drones" around the soup kitchen, was dying. While in the cancer ward he decided to be baptized. In Day's presence, a priest administered the sacrament with a singular lack of conviction or dignity, reciting the Latin prayers "in a garbled monotone" and performing the rite by rote. Annoyed with the priest, she experienced grace even in the empty rite. Reflecting on this baptism, she compared the sacraments to an interpersonal ritual: "And just as a husband may embrace his wife casually as he leaves for work in the morning, and kiss her absent-mindedly in his comings and goings, still that kiss on occasion turns to rapture, a burning fire of tenderness and love."[61] Though a priest may go through the motions, the sacraments retain their objective value and, every once in a while, spark the fires of love.

Day deeply appreciated the "sacramentality of life." Through the "sacrament of duty," even life's daily drudgery could be a channel of grace. While an adolescent, Day knew a woman in a Chicago tenement who prayed each day after washing the breakfast dishes; in doing so the woman's "life was shot through with glory." As a grandmother working in her daughter's farmhouse, Day recognized sacredness in the children and the countryside. Even when the busyness of farm and family life precluded time for prayer and study, she found in housework an opportunity for spiritual union with God. Every time of eating and drinking was "a communion," every Thursday a reminder of the Last Supper. As she washed and teased wool for a comforter, she thought about the sacramentality of things. In her introduction of *Houses of Hospitality*, she said that when she wrote of her work, of children playing and ordinary people on the street, she wrote of God, for "God enters into them all." Her intuition as a child told her that when she held the Bible she touched something holy. In her youth in the Episcopal Church, she felt drawn to the Te Deum and Benedicite in worship: "O all ye works of the Lord, bless ye the Lord." Now she found holiness in all things. She wrote richly detailed descriptions of persons, places, and things, treasuring the sacramental uniqueness of each one. From the Catholic Worker house she revelled in a neighbor's yard and gloried wherever a tree grew on the Lower East Side.[62]

In January 1941, while newspapers filled headlines with the national budget's billions of dollars for war, *The Catholic Worker* headline proclaimed the birth of a baby boy at its Mott Street house. This single child was worth more than all the other headlines. Christ was born of Mary for the sake of this child, and for this child's sake Christ had died. The budget had its billions of dollars, but this one child was of infinite worth.[63]

Day's sacramentality framed her political ideas. Because work is holy, she could not abide seeing laborers--God's co-creators--treated as chattels. It was hard for farmworkers to know that they were created in God's image and likeness, and filled with God's glory, when they were treated as animals.[64] Even private property, the bugaboo of Day's secular radical past, possessed a sacramental quality. She accepted Maurin's reading of Roman Catholic tradition that each person needed a little private property, and quoted St. Gertrude, "All property, the more common it becomes, the more heavenly it becomes." The Catholic Worker never opposed private property; it proposed that property was best used when shared.[65]

Jewish writings were filled with the sacramentality of life. To be a Jew was to be sacramental. Day shared Maurin's special affinity for the Jewish people, her affection going back to friends in college and early radical days in New York. Maurin said that Christians should love Jews for being part of Jesus' race. In the 1930s, *The Catholic Worker* became the earliest opponent of anti-semitism in the American press. Maurin insisted that the U.S. welcome Jews fleeing from persecution, and that Christians protect them in the shadow of the Cross.[66]

Protestants Muste and King related to the human Jesus, the teacher, the example. Day related to the Incarnate One, known through his teachings and life to be divine as well as human. Muste and King might have characterized Jesus as the teacher who told the story of the Good Samaritan, or see Christ as the compassionate, helpful Samaritan. Day followed her tradition in seeing Christ beaten and left in the ditch to suffer, the one in need of compassion. The low-Christology Protestants set Jesus apart from his family. Day saw her divine Christ as part of the Holy Family, Joseph and Mary as extensions of Jesus' identification with burdened people. They performed manual labor, became refugees in Egypt, and lived simply. Joseph was an ordinary carpenter, and Mary knew every woman's household drudgery. Their example eased Day's burdens: "Hardships to offer up. Going to bed at night with the foul smell of unwashed bodies in my nostrils. Lack of privacy. But Christ was born in a stable and a stable is apt to be unclean and odorous. If the Blessed Mother could endure it, why not I?"[67] In contrast to Therese's "Queen of Heaven," Day's Mariology was incarnational.[68]

Jesus also knew human needs and indignities. Day liked Francois Mauriac's saying that Jesus was so ordinary that it took the kiss of Judas to single him out. Jesus was born in a stable and spent years in exile. He was the carpenter who worked with his hands, the wanderer who lived in the fields. He called common fishermen to follow him. He was acquainted with migrant workers; he told parables about the proletariat. He needed food, shelter, and a warm fire. He received hospitality from Peter's mother-in-law, Matthew the tax collector, the people of Samaria, and from Mary, Martha, and Lazarus. He told the story of the rich man going to hell while poor Lazarus went to heaven. He treasured a special love for the poor and the lost, and gave an example of militant action against materialism and corruption when he cleansed the Jerusalem temple.[69] The men of the Bowery were his lost sheep. The depraved and the lost were Jesus himself masked in his most hidden disguise. As the paper's art work revealed, Jesus waited in bread lines among the destitute. He left himself in the Blessed Sacrament, wherever two or three were gathered in His Name, and in the poor. It was not two thousand years too late to show hospitality to Jesus. Day saw Christ's hands and feet in the poor. She began to love the poor by loving Christ in them until she loved them because they were "going through their long-continuing crucifixion."[70]

Because they attracted the "wounded ones," houses of hospitality became "concentration camps of displaced people." Writing an article through her tears, Day said: "Surely we are, here in our community, made up of poor lost ones, the abandoned ones, the sick, the crazed and the solitary human beings whom Christ so loved and in whom I see, with a terrible anguish, the body of his death." Eyes of love saw nothing of the poor but Christ in them.

> If everyone were holy and handsome, with "alter Christus" shining in neon lighting from them, it would be easy to see Christ in everyone. If Mary had appeared in Bethlehem clothed, as St. John says, with the sun, a crown of twelve stars on her head, and the

moon under her feet, then people would have fought to make room
for her.

But that was not God's way. It required faith and will to see and love. Many
ignored Jesus, but humble shepherds, Wise Men, and the women at the Cross
compensated for the neglect.[71] With Merton, Day sensed that people on society's
margins seemed more able to detect Christ's presence in the poor and in the world.

Christ "made heaven hinge on the way we act toward Him in His disguise
of commonplace, frail, ordinary humanity." Day's vision of judgment came from
Matthew 25:31-46, but she did not always wait for God's final wrath against those
blind to Christ in the poor. After giving a talk to the Four Arts Club in Palm Beach,
Florida, she heard responses that revealed as great a gulf between herself and her
listeners as the abyss between Lazarus and the Rich Man.

"Miss Day, I hope you can convey to your readers and
listeners, that we would give our very souls to help the poor, if we
saw any constructive way of doing it. . . .The workers come to my
husband's mill and beg him with tears in their eyes to save them
from unions. I hope you don't mind my saying so, but I think you
are all wrong when it comes to unions."

They all were deeply moved, they told me, by the picture of
conditions in Arkansas and the steel districts and the coal mining
districts, but "You can't do anything with them, you know, these
poor people. It seems to me the best remedy is birth control and
sterilization."

We are told always to keep a just attitude toward the rich,
and we try. But as I thought of our breakfast line, our crowded
house with people sleeping on the floor, when I thought of cold
tenement apartments around us, and the lean gaunt faces of the men
who come to us for help, desperation in their eyes, it was
impossible not to hate, with a hearty hatred and with a strong anger,
the injustices of this world.

St. Thomas says that anger is not a sin, provided there is no
undue desire for revenge. . .But when we meet people who deny
Christ in His poor, we feel, "Here are atheists indeed."[72]

Day's "atheists" did not deny the existence of God; they denied that Christ was present in every human being, that the poor were channels of grace, that Christ was hungry, thirsty, naked, in prison. Day tried to nurture a merciful attitude toward the rich (in truth, her "just" attitude fed her rage). She tried not to condemn, but Christ's suffering in the poor pierced her own heart.

Suffering was the common denominator binding Christ to the poor, for Christ's whole life was a "Passion." In 1964, Day wrote of Christ crucified in the suffering of African-Americans; in 1965, of Jesus martyred in Vietnam. Christ shared the pain of victims of the Ku Klux Klan and the Korean War.

> He would have suffered all the desolation and the loneliness and the utter desertion that anyone has ever suffered in all ages. He suffered not only the despair of one but of countless millions. The accumulated woe of all the world, through all the centuries, He took upon Himself. Every sin that was ever committed, that ever was to be committed, He endured the guilt of it. In His humanity, He was the I.W.W. who was tortured and lynched out in Centralia and Everett, and He likewise bore the guilt of the mob who perpetrated the horror on their victim. There was never a Negro fleeing from a maniacal mob whose fear and agony and suffering Christ did not feel. He Himself, in the person of the least of His children, has been hanged, tortured, afflicted to death itself, and He has at the same time been the one who has borne the guilt of the evil done.[73]

It was harder to see Christ in the calloused women of the Four Arts Club, the perpetrators of the Memorial Day Massacre, or a lynch mob than to see Christ in the faces of the destitute. Day wondered whether anyone had even begun to be a Christian. It was easy to love people in the abstract; loving flesh and blood was another matter.[74]

The Four Arts Club conversations infuriated Day because they added to the greatest burden of the poor--the scorn and contempt of others, sealed with an assumption of superiority. Because prison officials looked at people as criminals, they found criminals. The Campions spoke for others in calling the poor "worthless" and in blaming poverty on prodigal lives. Those who loved humanity abstractly and knew the statistics of poverty but who did not know "any particular poor person" merely degraded the poor. Society had stolen the names and identities of the oppressed. Newspapers devoted more attention to the sufferings of animals than to the problems of the dispossessed. Given the chance, social workers would have classified Lazarus as a "mental case."[75]

As a secular journalist and as a nurse, Day did not linger on every tragedy. In each vocation, the tortured lives passed quickly and continuously by like disfigured faces on a grotesque merry-go-round. The combination of the Worker's hands-on ministry with the publication of the newspaper--the nurse's action with the writer's reflection--helped her to articulate horror and empathy. Living among the destitute, she rode the tragic carousel with them.

The Parable of the Prodigal Son taught her that God sided with the "unworthy poor," and that she must take the same side. The Worker's bread lines sought to nurture human dignity; its writings to restore self-respect. In her writings, she named the guests, told their histories, described their identities and feelings; each one an individual, no one a statistic. She practiced what theologian Paul Tillich called "Holy Waste." A well-dressed woman donated a diamond ring on a visit to the Worker. Later that afternoon, Day gave it to a bereft old woman. When a staff member argued that it would have been better stewardship to sell the ring and use the money to help many in need, Day replied simply that the gift might renew the woman's dignity. The woman could sell it for rent or a vacation, or wear it for pleasure. Day's prodigality recalls the woman of Bethany who anointed Jesus with the jar of expensive ointment. His disciples argued against her lavishness, but he praised her gratuitousness. Day poured out the same extravagance, over the same objections, on an ordinary woman.[76]

In spite of her use of "romantic realism" and the religious significance she granted the oppressed, Day did not idealize them. Only in her secular past did she approach a quixotic view when she considered the poor a collective Messiah. As a Christian writer, she adopted a more subtle posture.[77] Day's "beloved poor" were rarely models of good behavior. The new society being built in the farming communes was misshapen. In 1969, she told of the grief brought to the New York house by a prostitute and an alcoholic priest. The young volunteers' sexual ethics--or lack thereof--dismayed her. The poor themselves stole books, statues, crucifixes, and tapestries. In one of the more "despicable acts" she remembered, someone stole the suit off a corpse. Without excusing the crimes, Day offered perspective. The coat stolen out of a closet had hung as a silent siren's song before the needy; it would not have been stolen had it been given away. The empty cash box should not have been left out as a temptation. She expected everything and nothing from people because they were both angels and "dust." She soon learned not to expect gratitude from the poor, yet she believed the poor quicker than the rich to feed the hungry, cloth the naked, and give shelter to the homeless. Like Muste and King, she believed that redemption moved from the bottom of society upwards. Like Merton, she saw redemption gently creeping inward from the margins of society.[78]

The poor were created in the image and likeness of God. They were temples of the Holy Spirit, Christ in the midst of the city, ambassadors of God, and channels of grace. Psalm 8 announced that they were little lower than angels, and Day knew from personal experience just how much lower that might be. Maurin said that houses of hospitality were intended "to give to the rich the opportunity to serve the poor," and in doing the works of mercy, they found their salvation through another sacrament. When people heard Francis of Assisi speak of Lady Poverty, they assumed that poverty was an ugly, old hag. Maurin insisted that she was young and beautiful. Americans, like the rich man at the feast, needed to become Lazarus at the gate. They had to embrace Lady Poverty to improve the lot of the dispossessed and find their own salvation.[79]

Members of the Catholic Worker fed "ambassadors of God" and squinted to see Christ in the prostitute, the alcoholic, the mentally ill, the racist, the thief, the murderer, and the rich. Day's words and deeds re-humanized the poor; and through them, she received grace.[80]

With her intuitive sensitivity to the sacramental, Day saw each person, place, and thing transfigured as though the presence of Christ were condensed and squeezed into bread and wine, people, trees, and wool.

Seeing the poor as channels of grace, she found in voluntary poverty a response of faith.

"Precarity"

"The coat that hangs in your closet belongs to the poor."

   --St. Jerome.

"The less you have of Caesar's the less you have to give to Caesar."

   --St. Hilary.[81]

There were no rules at a house of hospitality, but the desire to create order did not abate with the 1936 exodus of the Campions. Volunteers tried to impose stability on the chaos. Someone put up a sign saying that everyone should get up by 9:00 a.m. and make their beds. The sign violated the personalist principles of the Worker, and Day tore it down. Rules attacked personal freedom; they coerced; they were unacceptable. Staff members were to lead by example only. Someone installed locks on the pantry and closet while Day was away on a trip. She disapproved: People should be free to take clothes and food, and dress and feed themselves. The Catholic Worker had to be a society free of locks. The never-ending petty thievery led a wag to re-word the classic Marxist vision as a motto for the Catholic Worker: "From each according to his agility, to each according to his greed."[82]

Day saw many people wanting to lead the oppressed, but the Worker tried to be *with* them; it wanted "the workers and the guests to be indistinguishable." Stanley Vishnewski said the only difference between workers and guests was that workers looked "miserable and worried." Day accomplished the feat when she went to a social service agency as an advocate for a guest and was mistaken for a client. In such moments, she felt that she shared the contempt heaped on the poor.[83]

Her imprisonment after the civil defense protest in 1957 gave her another chance to become indistinguishable from society's human debris. She shared the common embarrassment of having to strip naked before her captors and suffered through the humiliation and discomfort of being searched for drugs "in the crudest ways." Only in jail did she believe she experienced destitution. Only after these arrests did Catholic Workers visit prisoners, the lone Work of Mercy they had not routinely practiced.[84]

Unlike the other prisoners, the protesters had given up their freedom voluntarily. As Day put it, the demonstrators offered to lose their lives in order to save them; to give up part of their lives--to say "no"--because they were "against things as they are." They stood against the capitalist-industrialist system and idolatrous nationalism, against racism and conscription, against war and taxation for war. The commitment to stand against large-scale injustice drew the Catholic Worker to individual responsibility and personal ministry.[85]

Day coined the term "precarity" to describe a way of life that included voluntary poverty. The spiritual foundations of precarity were the admonitions in the Sermon on the Mount to be as free from anxiety about physical needs as the lilies of the field. America's war economy gave a pragmatic reason for voluntary poverty: Participating in the economy meant preparing for war. Like Muste and Merton, Day knew that personal comfort could cause thousands of deaths: "Detachment gives peace. Attachment gives war." The Epistle of James hinted at withdrawal from the economy when it asked, "Those conflicts and disputes among you, where do they come from? Do they not come from your cravings that are at war within you" (4:1)? Day used voluntary poverty to disengage from the mechanisms of violence.[86]

Day called poverty "my vocation," and felt, with Muste, that if fear made a person insecure, one had to fight the fear, not begin a futile search for security. People had no right to security until all were safe, no right to a bed when others lacked shelter, no right to food when others were hungry. Possessions separated Christians from their neighbors and failed to provide individual security. Security came in minimizing individual needs and living near the bottom of the economic ladder. Voluntary poverty paved the way toward community security. Going to jail--purposeful insecurity--was a form of voluntary poverty because one shared the sufferings of others and saw the world in a new way.[87]

Day made a critical distinction between poverty and destitution. A person who chose to live without money in the slums was not destitute. Involuntary poverty made a daily crisis of physical survival and defiled the human spirit. The voluntarily poor and the destitute could become so similar as to fool an untrained eye, yet a gap remained.[88] Muste observed people grouped according to their experience of humiliation, a different kind of *haves* and *have nots*. Solidarity with the destitute meant narrowing the gap, like the asymptote of mathematics in which a straight line and a curve always approach but never meet. Practicing voluntary poverty was like riding a parabola closer to a straight line that could never be reached. Giving up possessions was a gateway into a new life. As Merton divested himself of possessions and discovered more difficult forms of poverty, so Day and her co-Workers found that voluntary poverty meant losing privacy and free time, abandoning pretenses to power, and placing trust in Providence.

For the Church, voluntary poverty meant relinquishing impersonal programs and social services. Day called the work of the Manhattan Municipal Lodging House, with its 1700 bed shelter, the "collectivization of misery." She wanted the Church to renounce what Charles Dickens had called "telescopic philanthropy." Maurin compared twentieth-century Christians unfavorably with their first-century counterparts: In the apostolic age, people said of Christians, "See how they love each other"; in the secular age, "See how they pass the buck." Voluntary poverty required the revival of personal responsibility. Without voluntary poverty, talk of world peace and the Christian's spiritual weapons meant nothing. The Worker tried to re-establish a different way of being the Church: "All that we give is given to us to give. Nothing is ours."[89]

Day made no claims to innovation. The saints stressed voluntary poverty; Francis of Assisi was its most famous practitioner. "Our Blessed Mother" had to spin and weave to clothe Joseph and Jesus; she never knew security. Joseph--the "workman saint"--experienced unemployment as he struggled to meet his family's needs. Jesus grew up in obscurity and found no place to rest his head. His suffering, hunger, thirst, and hard toil modeled voluntary poverty. Christians were to rejoice because they shared his poverty, sufferings, and way of the Cross, which led to joy, fulfillment, and victory.[90]

Daily life at the Worker was in a state of permanent crisis. Other institutions referred alcoholics and the mentally ill to the house of hospitality. Circumstances forced the New York house to move every few years. Disdaining pragmatic advice, Day insisted that *The Catholic Worker* survive issue to issue without budget or endowment. Like Francis of Assisi, they should give everything away and then beg. They were not a business, but a movement dependent on gifts of money, food, furniture, blankets, and clothing. The Catholic Worker never incorporated as a non-profit organization: it did not believe in paying taxes for war, nor in giving donors a tax-deduction (so that they could derive the full spiritual value of self-sacrificial giving!). Staff members had only their own desks, except for Maurin who shunned even this concession. For many of them, the supreme sacrifice came when they allowed their books to become part of the common library. And when the Worker inevitably fell into debt, it was again time to put bills beneath a statue of St. Joseph until they got paid.[91]

Based on estimates of five years' income, in 1972 the IRS presented the Catholic Worker with a bill for over $296,000. Day did not submit it to St. Joseph. She scorned the IRS and, since the Worker had never paid taxes, wondered in print what the amount would be if it were audited back to 1933. Presented with a summons by the IRS, she was singularly uncooperative. A young IRS staff person, impatient with her lengthy homiletical discourses, issued a thinly veiled threat when he asked her to estimate her personal income (for she paid no personal income taxes either). She answered, "I'll tell you what. You estimate my income for the past ten years, and you estimate what I owe, and I won't pay it! How's that?" An outpouring of community support--*The New York Times* asked if the IRS did not have better things to do--convinced the government to drop its case.[92]

The practice of "precarity" transcended voluntary poverty and included taking controversial stands. Neutral during the Spanish Civil War and, a generation later, cautiously hopeful about the first fruits of Castro's Cuba, the Worker sided with the poor and revolution even though it put Day on the same side with the Church's persecutors.

Those not already alienated by the Worker's policies dropped their subscriptions in greater numbers over Day's zealous World War II pacifism. A landlord who had given them gratis use of a building in Harlem evicted them. Day's past secular, selective pacifism, which made a distinction between international wars and class wars, helped her recognize the same inconsistency in post-Pearl Harbor Americans who were class-war pacifists but eager to fight enemies overseas. In her editorial after Pearl Harbor, she described an incident in Missouri the previous month in which a black man had been shot, dragged by a mob behind a car, soaked in kerosene, and set afire. The mob left his body in the street until a garbage truck took it away. She asked whether African-Americans ought to take up arms to avenge this cruel injustice as the U.S. government used Pearl Harbor to justify war against Japan. Of course, white America would have been shocked if black Americans were anything but patient and nonviolent.[93]

The most infuriating insult came from those who discounted Day's pacifism as "sentimental."

> Let those who talk of softness, of sentimentality, come to live with us in cold, unheated houses in the slums. Let them come to live with the criminal, the unbalanced, the drunken, the degraded, the perverted. . . .Let them live with rats, with vermin, bedbugs, roaches, lice. . . .Let their flesh be mortified by cold, by dirt, by vermin; let their eyes be mortified by the sight of bodily excretions, diseased limbs, eyes, noses, mouths. Let their noses be mortified by the smells of sewage, decay, and rotten flesh....Let their ears be mortified by harsh and screaming voices, by the constant coming and going of people living herded together with no privacy. Let their taste be mortified by the constant eating of insufficient food cooked in huge quantities for hundreds of people...the smell of such cooking is often foul. Then when they have lived with these comrades, with these sights and sounds, let our critics talk of sentimentality.[94]

Had *this* life shielded her from harsh realities? She responded as did Merton when activist friends accused him of hiding from real life in the monastery: If it's so easy, try it!

Day's pre-Worker way of life was ready-made to fit the pattern of the movement. She took her first job as a New York journalist for $5 a week. Other than the royalties from her pre-conversion novel with which she bought her Staten Island beach house, profits from her writings went into the Catholic Worker coffers. She wore clothes donated to the Worker and rarely had much privacy for Tamar or herself. She indulged herself by owning a few books. Perhaps the greatest material sacrifice--and act of faith--the journalist ever made was when she sold her typewriter to help finance the second issue of *The Catholic Worker*.[95]

Her career led her down a precarious path. Her work at *The Masses* ended during World War I when the government accused its editor of treason and closed it down. She went to an anti-war demonstration in Baltimore during World War I and had two ribs broken by a policeman who could barely see through his own blood dripping into his eyes. Her imprisonment with the women's suffrage movement was the first of almost a dozen times behind bars. She could not have been sanguine about accepting the persuasive charms of Ammon Hennacy who convinced her to protest against civil defense drills. Over two decades had gone by since her last arrest and she had grown accustomed to being called a communist, but the judge at their trial perversely denounced the protesters as "murderers" for their pacifist stance. In the 1950s, as she kept watch outside Georgia's integrated Koinonia community, the car in which she sat was hit by a shotgun blast, presumably an assault by the harassing Ku Klux Klan.[96]

Her concern about the oppression of farmworkers began in the 1930s and led her to write about the need for people to share the farmworkers' fate. Cesar Chavez visited the New York house several times and, in 1973, Day invited her final arrest at a demonstration in California. The threat of violence hung over that picket line as it had when the Catholic Worker picketed the German ship "Bremen" in the 1930s to protest Nazi anti-semitism.[97]

"Precarity" did not erupt sporadically. Hers was a daily encounter with filthy toilets, smelly bodies, and lice. Early in the movement's history, she woke up in the middle of the night terrorized by her responsibilities. Frightening confrontations were an ever-present possibility at a house of hospitality: Once as she gave an ominous, grumbling man her bowl of soup, he growled threateningly at her. As the rest of the room feared violence and cowered in silence, she recalled Paul's admonition to overcome evil with good: she broke bread, gave it to him, and invited him to come again. He left and returned the next day offering bags of vegetables to put into the soup. She was no more romantic about voluntary poverty than she was about the poor. Precarity meant living in chaos and calling it joy.[98]

In her first few years at the Catholic Worker, Day developed a view of ministry similar to John of the Cross' understanding of the "dark night of the soul." One could pray or engage in ministry in pursuit of sweet and consoling experiences. One might even be tempted through spiritual gluttony to crave opportunities to help others because it felt better to give than to receive. But after awhile, ministry turns to drudgery, consolations dissipate and then disappear. One enters a time of disorientation and disillusionment, a night time which eradicates all sense of direction and certainty. Yet the place of discouragement is also the place of God's mysterious presence. Day found that she did not act any more from a hunger for immediate spiritual reward, but rather for the sake of the action itself and because the act served God. She could love people for Christ's sake, increase her love for God, and desire only to love and serve God in the dark night of her activist's soul.

Teresa of Avila described life as a "night spent in an uncomfortable inn." Day must have felt that she applied Teresa's words all too literally. Like Maurin, she realized that most Christians preferred detachment to poverty, and thought the latter something unpleasant to avoid. But Day saw "simplicity" as a bourgeois compromise. Precarity could not be learned by reason. It had to be embraced through faith.[99]

Day heard the poverty of Christ and Francis praised "in song and story. But its reality is little known. It is a garden enclosed, a secret beauty." The city-dweller revelled in every tree in Manhattan, and considered the farming communes foretastes of heaven.[100] Christian tradition remembers both the unspoiled Garden of Eden and the suffering in the Garden of Gethsemane. The subtle beauty, the secret serenity, and the redemptive suffering all came together in voluntary poverty. The two gardens, and the uncomfortable inn, were one.

Day shared the painful joy of precarious living: King spurned material success and physical security, Merton popularity, Muste stability. As Day unearthed the secret beauty of precarity, so pain and joy converged again in penance.

Penance

"I conceived a great desire and prayed our Lord God that he would grant me in the course of my life three wounds, that is, the wound of contrition, the wound of compassion, and the wound of longing with my will for God."

--Julian of Norwich[101]

Day usually looked to Julian of Norwich for comfort, but she might well have identified with Julian's three wounds. Each wound had a particular role: "By contrition we are made clean, by compassion we are made ready, and by true longing for God we are made worthy."102 Day's compassion was as old as her youthful commitment to dedicate her life to the poor. Her longing for God led to a leap of grief away from her lover and into the Church. Her muscular conscience naturally attuned her to contrition. Like Therese whom she admired and King whom she never met, she was guilt-prone. While Muste frequented the Parable of the Pharisee and the Publican to corral self-righteousness, Day identified with the publican's awareness of sin and hunger for forgiveness. Yet she knew that identifying with sinners might tempt those too quick to count themselves publicans to lazily avoid the pharisee's healthy moral rigor.103

When someone asked Day if she had visions, she brusquely jolted the inquirer who wanted to idolize her as she sentimentalized Therese. In one version of the story, she answered: "Visions of unpaid bills"; in another, "Hell no." Those who called the Catholic Workers "saints" merely gave themselves easy absolution by assuming they were unregenerable sinners.104

When the paper's editor objected to one of Day's arbitrary decisions, the Worker's hierarch told him that he worked for *The Catholic Worker*; if he desired to work for "the Quaker Worker," he could go elsewhere. Asked to hold her temper in the heat of a fierce argument, she replied, "I hold more temper in one minute than you will in your entire life." Under arrest in 1917, she kicked her guards' shins and bit the prison warden's hand.   She confessed that she failed to maintain a charitable attitude toward Senator Joseph McCarthy, probably an understatement for the usually overzealous penitent. As Mexico's secular government suppressed religion in the 1930s, and Day contemplated a civilization offering silk stockings and refrigerators in place of God's love, she began "to long for a good class war, with the civilizers lined up to be liquidated." Prone to anger and rudeness, she felt her health problems in later years made her a chronic complainer: "I should keep a pebble in my mouth for silence." It comforted her to know of Teresa of Avila's temper, for--by her own admission--the Spaniard's spiritual daughter was "stiff-necked."[105]

She found a quote from William Blake in the foreword of Merton's *Contemplative Prayer*: "We are put on earth for a little space that we may learn to bear the beams of love." It reminded Day of a "strange incident":

> Suddenly I remembered coming home from a meeting in Brooklyn many years ago, sitting in an uncomfortable bus seat facing a few poor people. One of them, a downcast, ragged man, suddenly epitomized for me the desolation, the hopelessness of the destitute, and I began to weep. I had been struck by one of those "beams of love," wounded by it in a most particular way. It was my own condition that I was weeping about--my own hardness of heart, my own sinfulness.[106]

She was "wounded" by compassion and contrition at the same moment. The experience makes the other bookend to her joyful realization of solidarity with the workers on the way to the Seamen's Defense Committee headquarters. The memory of the bus ride revealed the distances between herself and the destitute, between compassion and her own hard heart.

Day quilted incidents together in an unattractive self-portrait. She discovered, as did Merton, ample material in herself to require a lifetime of self-examination. Her frequent internal explorations uncovered a multitude of sins.

> This afternoon, glimpses of my own ugliness, vanity, pride, cruelty, contempt of others, levity, jeering, carping. Too sensitive to criticism, showing self-seeking love. . . .

> I am constantly humiliated at my own imperfections and at my halting progress. . . .

> Here is my examination at the beginning of Advent, at the beginning of a new year. Lack of charity, criticism of superiors, of neighbors, of friends and enemies. Idle talk, impatience, lack of self-control and mortification towards self, and of love towards others. Pride and presumption. . . .Self will, desire not to be

corrected, to have one's own way. The desire in turn to correct
others, impatience in thought and speech.[107]

Her biographers patched the same traits together more charitably, still
describing her as "thin-skinned," dominating, and inclined to bruise others'
feelings. One Lent she begged a former staff member's forgiveness for her
overbearing criticisms. She prayed to become less domineering. She admitted
being arrogant, justifying herself, failing as a mother: "We are in spite of all we try
to do, unprofitable servants." So drawn to the saints, she heard a priest friend say,
"One could go to hell imitating the imperfections of the saints." She may have
wondered if she was the "one."[108]

Day diagnosed Therese's adolescent guilt as neurotic, yet mirrored it in her
own life. She wrote of the vanity of Eve in each woman, each woman's desire for
power, to seduce and drag another down, "the monster, the tempter" within each
person. Yet her penchant for guilt masked a powerful ambivalence toward sin.
Looking back, she noticed that she had homogenized her conversion story, *From
Union Square to Rome*, omitting her hedonism, abortion, divorce, and child's
illegitimacy.[109]

The "abbess" recognized herself as a hard taskmaster. She found it hard to
hate the sin and love the sinner, easy to play the pharisee, easy to elevate herself
above others when the Sermon on the Mount suggested that she should compare
herself only to her perfect God. Like Merton, for a time after her conversion, she
"became disgustingly, proudly pious." Trying to avoid spiritual complacency by
counting her daily moral compromises, she still felt herself reaching out "like an
octopus" to seek her own comfort, ease, and refreshment.[110]

Day's keen sensitivity to sin led her past ordinary moral considerations.
Under most circumstances, many Christians would be satisfied to turn the other
cheek. She rebelled against the "sanctimoniousness" of inviting someone else to

sin in order to grow in grace: "One would all but rather be a sinner than a saint at the expense of the sinner." She could not turn the other cheek if it did not redeem the person doing the slapping. All had to become saints together.[111]

Her self-examinations brought pain and shame. She feared she could not bear to see herself with God's clarity. Her spiritual weakness made her ministry difficult; had she been stronger, she would have been "happy." Were she more patient and loving, the Catholic Worker would inspire more to conversion. Unable to be with an early member of the Worker community as he died, she felt guilty for months. She shied away from penance and also thirsted for more, sometimes almost too eager to torment herself, sometimes willing to moderate the process: It was fine, she thought, to make preparation for death part of her monthly day of recollection, but not if she tried to recall every sin in living memory. Excessively rigid--if not frigid--in her rejection of sixties' sexual mores, in her failing years she may still have been fighting to forgive herself for her youthful hedonism.[112]

When a beautiful, young actress was arrested with Day at the civil defense protest in 1957, some non-political women prisoners jeered and shouted that they wanted to "have" the actress in their cells. Fearing physical or sexual assault on her friend, Day "demanded" that she be put in the same cell to protect her. She later regretted her reasonable fears, quick condemnation of fellow inmates (those society too easily scorned), and inability to trust that her friend might win others to nonviolence by the strength of her convictions. Again, the abbess turned her fierce judgment on herself.[113]

If Day imitated Therese in having an aggressive conscience, she also experienced with her the relief of absolution. Therese pleaded with people not to be discouraged by their faults but to place their full confidence in God's mercy. Day did both. At the end of her meditation on her 1957 imprisonment, she referred to Julian of Norwich and reminded herself that Christ "has already repaired the greatest evil that ever happened or ever could happen." She urged herself to trust Christ to forgive her sins and failures. She found occasional solace in remembering that Christ had lost His temper: "When I forget *His* humanity, I forget my own, too, and then I'm in the devil's hands."[114]

Another illumination revealed the tenuous relationship between God's mercy and human sin.

> One time I was travelling and far from home and lonely, and I awoke in the night almost on the verge of weeping with a sense of futility, of being unloved and unwanted. And suddenly the thought came to me, of my importance as a daughter of God, daughter of a King, and I felt a sureness of God's love and at the same time a conviction that one of the greatest injustices, if one can put it that way, which one can do to God is to distrust His love, not realize His love. God so loved me that He gave His only begotten son. "If a mother will forget her children, never will I forget thee." Such tenderness. And with such complete ingratitude we forget the Father and His love![115]

God's love and human ingratitude interacted in a continuous circle of judgment and mercy.

The sacrament of penance was part of the rhythm of her rule of life. Absolution bathed her with a sense of relief. In her maternal care for her children, "Holy Mother Church" provided penance and the eucharist to reassure, forgive, sustain, and nourish them. Day might have applied her words about retreats to her experience of penance: "Thank God there are such oases as these where one can gather strength and fortitude for the combat, the strong conflict which goes on in one's own soul." After she heard a sermon comparing penance to an appearance in court, Day contrasted that court with another one: "What a strange court, indeed, when over and over, repeating our offenses again and again, we are forgiven; where everyone is forgiven! How different from *The Trial* of Kafka, where men are tried, found guilty and sentenced."[116]

She missed the greater irony. In Kafka's novel, K. never finds out why he is arrested, sentenced, or condemned. Seemingly innocent, his universe conspires to destroy him. To Day, only a guilty verdict seemed possible for herself and her race, but God contrived to find them innocent. K.'s universe was senselessly malevolent, Day's unexpectedly blessed.

A frequent visitor to the confessional, Day knew that forgiveness prepared the way for reconciliation. She admonished herself not to be harsh with those dependent on the Worker. In the house of hospitality, she once became so angry with two women's constant fighting that she "almost wanted to beat them both." One night, as she imagined the two women "in the hands of our Blessed Mother," she wept before falling asleep. The image amused her, and her transformed attitude calmed the women. On this occasion, she tried to be a reconciler *among* the poor, but more often she felt the need to be forgiven *by* the poor. Even voluntary poverty gave her three meals a day, a place to sleep, and meaningful work. As Muste's pacifist shared responsibility for war, Day shared responsibility for destitution.117

Believing she had to come closer to Christ before bringing others to the Lord, Day scrupulously examined herself for the stumbling blocks she might lay before others, for even the best of human love contained a seed of self-seeking. After receiving communion, she prayed to "the Blessed Mother": "Here He is in my heart; I believe, help thou mine unbelief; Adore Him, thank Him and love Him for me. He is your Son; His honor is in your hands. Do not let me dishonor Him." The anarchist and advocate of nonviolent revolution saw her greatest challenge in designing a new order within herself through "a revolution of the heart." She had to seek the lowest place, wash the feet of others, and burn with the love that led Jesus to the cross. The pacifist wrote, "There must be a disarmament of the heart." Following Gandhi, she demanded a consistency of spiritual rigor and political action.118

Day also turned her jabbing style of self-examination against her nation and her world. Like Merton, she called an unrepentant people to the confessional. Like Muste, she dismissed Niebuhrian distinctions between the spiritual lives of individuals and nations. She agreed with her Quaker comrade that pacifists bore partial blame for World War II. She shared Merton's disdain for delusions of innocence. No one escaped guilt for the actions of one's nation. All took part in economic exploitation and war. All Americans had been guilty of the Memorial Day Massacre. Sin caused the Korean War. All Americans were at fault for bombing North Vietnam; even if the U.S. withdrew its troops from Vietnam, it would start a war elsewhere. Garment industry mills produced blankets and parachutes for the military. In wartime, teachers urged students to bring scrap metal to school. Those serious about prayers for peace ought to do penance, increase almsgiving, and fast to feed the hungry. Union workers in steel plants and factories ought to quit jobs connected to the military. A spirit of penance would create massive economic dislocation and thousands of personal crises.[119]

Day objected to the Soviet arms buildup, but she operated on the principle that one first had to remove the beam from one's own eye, so her calls to repentance, like those of King and Merton, focused almost exclusively on the U.S. When criticized for uncovering signs of goodness in Castro's Cuba, she countered that life in an American skid row prepared her to find good in the midst of evil. She lambasted "atheistic capitalism" and "atheistic materialism" for manipulating God to bolster greed. When Jesus said that there would always be poor people in the world, he had not intended that there be so many. The ingenuity of human sin made poverty proliferate. In a lengthy article in 1954, she wrote incisively that American support of French colonialism in Vietnam defended not Christianity or freedom, but investments. The U.S. was like the rich man at the feast. It valued the works of war more than the works of mercy.[120]

Specific sins sharpened the wrath of her pen: World War II's internment camps of Japanese-Americans were "a bit of Germany on the West Coast"; bracero camps for farmworkers "the nearest thing to the Russian slave labor camps we can boast of." But no incident so infuriated her as the bombings of Hiroshima and Nagasaki. Jesus pronounced his verdict on the bomb when he said, "Inasmuch as ye have done it unto one of the least of these My brethren, ye have done it unto me." She was appalled that a Roman Catholic institution, Notre Dame, had even a minor role in preparing the bomb. She called the scientists "murderers," but saved a special tribute for President Harry Truman.

> Mr. Truman was jubilant. President Truman. True man; what a strange name, come to think of it. We refer to Jesus Christ as true God and true Man. Truman is a true man of his time in that he was jubilant. He was not a son of God, brother of Christ, brother of the Japanese, jubilating as he did. He went from table to table on the cruiser which was bringing him home from the Big Three conference, telling the great news; "jubilant" the newspapers said. *Jubilate Deo*. We have killed 318,000 Japanese.[121]

As a "true man of his time," Truman was an Adam figure, a focus for sin and repentance. If Christ, the second Adam, set people free from sin, Truman was a third Adam returning the world to bondage. And in their false jubilation the people followed.

Day called the nation to feel the same wound of contrition that ached in her own heart. In its protest against the civil defense drills, the Catholic Worker stood against "the entire militarism of the state." Its leaflet read, "In the name of Jesus who is God, who is Love, we will not obey this order to pretend, to evacuate, to hide...we will not be drilled into fear. . . .We do not have faith in God if we depend upon the Atom Bomb."[122]

Demonstrations against civil defense drills and the war in Vietnam were forms of public penance. A draft resister in prison did penance for the sins of others. People offered to do penance when they volunteered to share the prison sentences of the Milwaukee Fourteen who burned draft records with napalm. Roger LaPorte, briefly a Catholic Worker, erred in immolating himself to protest against the war in Vietnam. Yet, while his suicide was a "sad and terrible act," he intended to lay down his life for his brothers and sisters in Vietnam. Like two other self-annihilating protesters, LaPorte showed his willingness "to endure the sufferings that we as a nation are inflicting upon a small country and its people." His suicide was tragic, but not evil like editorials boasting that the war added "extra zip" to the American economy. The Catholic Worker named a farm after LaPorte, and Day honored his intention to do penance without supporting his act.[123]

LaPorte's self-immolation is too dramatic a metaphor for Day's stringent penitence but, overcome by her own sins as LaPorte had been overwhelmed by those of his nation, she sometimes neared spiritual despair. Her deep wound of contrition brought her into a merciful circle of self-examination and grace. She invited others--individuals, groups, and the U.S.--into that same circle. The same passion that fueled her stance against militarism launched interior crusades against spiritual enemies. She said "No" as loudly to herself as she did to others.

The "Little Way"

"The Sermon on the Mount
will be called practical
when Christians make up their mind
to practice it."

> --Peter Maurin.

"He who attempts to set up God's Kingdom in his heart, furthers it in the world."

> --John Henry Newman[124]

Maurin and Day founded the Catholic Worker on a four-point program: houses of hospitality to practice the works of mercy, round-table discussions to promote the clarification of thought, farming communes to signal the future direction of civilization, and a newspaper to publicize their work. They did not plan the soup line.

During the Depression, a man from the Bowery living at the Worker distributed clothing until he ran out. He then seated his unhappy supplicants, poured them hot coffee, and ladled out bowls of soup. The good news of free coffee and hot soup spread through the streets until a line stretched around the block: a new ministry had begun. As Day put it: "we" started an organization to build a new social order; "God" invited the poor.[125]

There were sporadic tensions between announcing a new order and doing the corporal works of mercy. The Campions were not alone in wanting to de-emphasize the hands-on ministry. Maurin promoted farming communes over houses of hospitality, future vision over present ministry. But the mother and former nursing student was also the abbot. The works of mercy took precedence.

Day transformed Therese of Lisieux's "little way" into a political philosophy, a principle of spiritual development, a restatement of Maurin's personalist philosophy, and a tool to interpret the Catholic Worker. Day's childhood desire to become a saint turned, in her early Roman Catholic years, to an attraction to "spectacular saints" she found it "impossible" to imitate. She shared Teresa of Avila's scorn for those who did God's will "like hens with their feet tied." But by the 1940s, Therese's picture adorned the wall over the foot of her bed. First hearing of Therese in the maternity ward, Day came to call her "the greatest saint of our time." As Muste believed in the individual conscience, so Day believed the little way contained a power equivalent to the atom.[126]

Day felt her spiritual progress move at the pace of Teresa's hens. When Elizabeth of Hungary gave a leper her bed, went away, and returned to tend him, she saw Christ. When Francis of Assisi got off his horse and kissed a leper, he looked back and saw Christ. Day had kissed two lepers in her life: a woman's face had been eaten away by cancer so Day kissed her where her nose and eye had been; a toothless prostitute returned her kiss in a "loathsome" way. Day received no comfort. She did not see Christ. Yearning for large, plain signs, she received small, obscure ones. Wanting to make one great leap forward, her Lord demanded "as many small steps as we can manage." Seeking a spiritual war to end all spiritual wars, she found "the battleground of the spiritual life is in the small things."[127]

As she entered the Roman Catholic Church, Day repeated the brief, "wonderful prayer" of the man asking Jesus to exorcise the demons possessing his son: "I believe, Lord, help thou my unbelief." Living between assurance and healing, and praying with the possessed and dispossessed, she often felt the prayer's comfort.[128]

Therese believed that by cultivating peace in her heart she could "increase the sum total of love in the world" without ever leaving the convent. Day sounded like Merton when she wrote that "the most effective action" she could take was to disarm her heart and conform her life to the folly of the Cross.[129]

Day's meditations on the mystery of suffering sometimes made her cry. During a stay in jail, she contemplated evils against which social reform and political revolution were powerless. Only Therese's way--sanctity, fidelity and constancy--could overcome evil. While Muste built coalitions and King pressured politicians, Merton and Day practiced a more solitary witness. In calling her history of the Catholic Worker *Loaves and Fishes*, she described its method and a modest style of hope that allowed her to share Muste's detachment from immediate, tangible success. She was content with lightening the sum total of human misery. Therese said that Jesus demanded self-surrender and gratitude more than great deeds. Daily self-denial was more demanding than the occasional grand gesture or outward show of sacrifice.[130]

Maurin's philosophy of personal responsibility permeated the Catholic Worker: Because Jesus said, "Inasmuch as you have done it to the least of these, you have done it to me," Christians should welcome guests into their homes, and parishes open houses of hospitality on their property. Day's Jesus refused to join a movement to overthrow an oppressive, foreign regime. He acted, and urged others to act, out of personal responsibility. Day believed with Muste that each individual stood at a critical juncture in an on-going spiritual battle. She quoted Pope John XXIII favorably when in 1963 he spoke to a group of peace-seeking pilgrims, "The beginnings of peace are in your own hearts, in your own families, schoolrooms, offices, parishes, and neighborhoods." Only by taking personal responsibility could Christians end destitution.[131]

Paradoxically, Day preached both "the little way" (which allows one to remain in one's station) and "precarity" (which demands severe disruption). Because Jesus was ignored by the powerful, Day encouraged the ordinary and powerless. Anyone working in handicrafts, food production, construction, or factories producing items for human needs performed works of mercy and contributed to peace. The little way alleviated a sense of futility and democratized the work for the Kingdom because even the poor could increase the sum total of love. Everyone could perform the works of mercy; anyone could work for peace.[132]

In 1950, the Catholic Worker gave out 460,000 meals and 18,250 nights' lodgings. If Day wanted to impress the world, she said, she would multiply the figures by eighteen years. But God does not count meals. God sees individuals, each with a name, waking up early each morning. God sees each person serving and eating, giving and given shelter. God does not care about statistics; neither did Day.[133]

A woman threatened by unjust institutionalization stood by as Day faced a crucial point in editing an issue of *The Catholic Worker*. The editor left the editing behind.[134] One woman counted more than thousands of readers and the seeds they could plant to further the movement. Day had to care for the individual or lose the basis of the revolution. The paper was the first work to be neglected; ministry to the individual took priority.

The Catholic Worker movement was a "permanent revolution," and the goal of each house of hospitality "to work out a theory of love."

> When they marched in picket lines, demonstrated at embassies, organized unions, or helped integrate all-white facilities in the South, the Workers insisted that they were not engaging in politics but performing one of the works of mercy--"enlightening the ignorant."

When Workers sang Christmas carols at the Women's House of Detention, they incarnated their political philosophy. In 1972, the Catholic Worker distributed leaflets outside IBM on Wall Street hoping to touch the consciences of people "participating in the hideous and cowardly war we are waging in Vietnam." Day saw protests performing other spiritual works of mercy: "rebuking the sinner" and "counseling the doubtful." Historian Mel Piehl noted that early anti-Vietnam War protesters, mostly religious pacifists, never controlled the anti-war movement, especially after it became more powerful and less idealistic.[135] Of course, Day would not have cared; but both of them may have missed the point: the Catholic Worker, the FOR, and other tiny groups were midwives to the movement. It was a small, easily forgotten role--another aspect of the Worker's vocation Day found spiritually commendable.

At times, the Catholic Worker dreamed like Muste and King: of people reading their paper on every continent; of the multiplication of houses and farming communes. In the 1930s, when discouraged Catholic Workers saw twenty people at round-table discussions, Day reassured them that Lenin started with twenty in Paris. She sounded a Mustean note in 1951 when she called for an army of conscientious objectors. Far more often, however, she urged each person to act responsibly. Others could base their actions on the conviction that they could solve the world's puzzles and live in "a bright, sunny future," but future dreams did not motivate Day as much as today's achievements.136

Even before she planted herself on the Lower East Side with the Catholic Worker, Day focused on life's daily grind. With political and religious controversy swirling all around her in the 1930s in Mexico, she wrote of the humdrum life of the poor. Ammon Hennacy resurrected her interest in demonstrations in the 1950s. She took part with Muste on the Committee for Nonviolent Action (CNVA), and participated in draft card burnings in 1962, 1964, and 1965. Still, the main work was local: St. Francis' first job was to clean up a church; St. Benedict taught a two-fold rule of life around work and prayer. Hennacy's joke notwithstanding, pacifism could be practiced between wars: the racist guest tested one's nonviolence; McCarthy era "martyrdom" meant losing a job for refusing to take a loyalty oath; among the 1960s' Left, it meant turning the other cheek when branded irrelevant, the decade's ultimate curse.137

Day and the Worker faced the temptation to focus on large-scale issues, but "the heart of our work" was in "the daily pastoral responsibilities: making the soup and serving it, trying to help someone get to the hospital who otherwise might not get there, because he's confused, because she's not aware she even needs to go there." Day entitled her history of the movement *Loaves and Fishes* because she saw the Kingdom of God breaking in with each healing, every exorcism, each exchange of bread, every act of kindness. Muste and King anticipated the final banquet; Day appreciated the daily foretastes.[138]

Cleaning floors, doing dishes, and raising children could show that someone was increasing in love. Like Teresa of Avila, Day believed that "the Lord walks among the pots and pans" even as in Eden. When Day took care of her grandchildren, her humble work reminded her of Mary and the saints. Saying a prayer and waving to prisoners as one walked past the Women's House of Detention increased the love of God and might plant a seed of faith. The ten just men who saved Sodom were like those engaged in small-scale actions throughout salvation history.[139]

Catholic Worker and liberal Protestant had different views of hope. The Worker shared the liberal Protestant's "high" view of human nature--created in the image of God and ennobled by Christ's incarnation. But the movement bore the imprint of Day's perpetual penitence. Her sensitivity to sin and evil marked the distance from her little way to Muste's new Pentecost and kept her from sharing his undying hope that the Kingdom of God could be established on earth. To God a thousand years was like a day, so two-day old Christianity might be ripe for transformation, yet world history contained more continuity than change. Day hoped that as the lives of saints touched her, so the Catholic Worker might enter the stream of tradition and touch people living centuries in the future.[140]

Critics questioned the Worker's effectiveness. A self-effacing Worker could have easily joked that it was a good thing its revolution was permanent; it would have to be. Without coercion, little got done. The rule about having no rules handicapped the theory of love. People had to convert to create a Christian social order, yet only a Christian social order encouraged people to convert. Instead of trying to cut a Gordian knot, the Catholic Worker emulated the IWW in combining its long-range program with a soup kitchen and lodging.[141] In Muste's terminology, the Worker tried to live as if the Kingdom had already come; in Day's, it developed like a fetus in the womb.

Some accused Day of being oblivious to success. A student critic complained that the Worker had no impact on 99% of the problems and people in the U.S. But Day stressed fidelity. As the parable's shepherd leaves 99% of the sheep to save the one percent, so Day put thousands of readers aside for the person in need. Many of those the Worker tried to help had "no chance" of rehabilitation or reintegration into society. When a social worker asked Day how long people were allowed to stay at the house of hospitality, she answered, "Forever": "They live with us, they die with us and we give them a Christian burial. We pray for them after they are dead." Strangers became guests, and then family. All the Catholic Worker could do was "throw our pebble in the pond and be confident that its ever-widening circle will reach around the world." Just as God fed the multitudes with the child's loaves and fish, so God could multiply their humble offerings. When Workers distributed bundles of the paper on the streets, they were "scattering seeds" like a parable's sower. The harvest could be generations or centuries away.[142] Hope lay in the sower getting up each day to reproduce the small, sturdy act without anxiety about results.

Day seemed defiantly comfortable with failure; certain kinds of success might be a sign of moral ruin. Jesus' failure--his crucifixion--created a new world. Day joined Muste in believing that the failures of faithful disciples had the same re-creative power. The answer to futility was to engage in one action at a time.[143]

Many Catholics branded Day a Jansenist because she democratized sanctification and the counsels of perfection. Christ had not limited his demands to a cloistered elite of nuns and monks, an ordained elite of priests and bishops, nor a bourgeois elite among the laity. If God had not called the saints to do the ordinary, and the ordinary to become saints, the saints would be very few. Day attributed a

saying to Paul that people were saved "by little and by little." In 1946, she changed
the name of her column to "On Pilgrimage" because everyone was a pilgrim on the
way: "It is in our everyday lives that God judges us, not in the positions we take
on issues, the statements we sign, the political parties we join, the causes we
advocate." Judgment came down to the little things: feeding the hungry, loving
one's enemy, forgiving others as one has been forgiven.[144]

A dream posed the question of judgment on her ministry and the quest of
the Catholic Worker:

> The other night I had a dream. I am fifty, but I thought I had a little
> baby and was nursing it. And then I was amazed that I had not only
> the one but a little Negro baby to foster. I felt my aging breasts to
> see if there was milk there for this other one, and I had great joy that
> I could nurse a foster child of those most numerous of the oppressed
> in our own country.

Once awake, she found her dream presumptuous for an "empty cistern."[145]

Its disdain for programs and lack of interest in swaying the powerful made
even sympathizers ask what the Worker offered. Its creed of personal
responsibility ran counter to prevailing liberal, reformist thinking and planning.
Could the little way really overcome evil and nourish so many?

Words Written on the Heart

"Your decrees are my delight, they are my counselors."

--Psalm 119:24

"I will put my law within them, and I will write it on their hearts;
and I will be their God, and they shall be my people."

--Jeremiah 31:33

In the wake of Pearl Harbor, Day editorialized, "We are still pacifists. Our manifesto is the Sermon on the Mount." Even in January 1942, the words of Jesus were unbendable, and overwhelmed all other considerations.146

Day's editorial unleashed a storm of angry letters, canceled subscriptions, and the second great rift within the Catholic Worker movement. Houses of hospitality in other cities did not endorse nonviolence. Discussion of pacifism was forbidden in Buffalo and St. Louis Worker communities to keep household peace. The Chicago Catholic Worker, whose newspaper had matched the quality of its New York sibling, openly opposed Day's stance. Houses in Seattle, Los Angeles, and Pittsburgh decided to sell the Chicago paper instead of Day's. When bundles of the New York paper arrived in Los Angeles, Workers burned them.

Eighteen months before, Day sent a letter to all the houses saying they could disagree with her pacifism, but they had to distribute her paper or disassociate themselves from the movement and forfeit use of the Catholic Worker name. Its recipients considered the epistle an anachronistic violation of anarchist principles. Day met with the editor of the Chicago paper, but the rift remained. More because of rising employment than the rift, several houses closed. Others dropped the Worker name and continued as local charities. The thirty houses dwindled to sixteen by the end of 1942 and to ten by the end of 1944. Like the seeds of a sower, the movement had blossomed thirtyfold in the soil of the Depression. The words engraved on Day's heart now scorched it like the sun.147

Her prior writings had given co-Workers sufficient warning of her pacifism, but the Depression kept her colleagues from understanding how central nonviolence was to Day. The Spanish Civil War, after all, was fought over there. To her, being a Christian meant following the teachings of Jesus here, taking His words and example "as the most important message in the entire world."148

Roman Catholic piety placed Church authority over scripture, and some of Day's Catholic friends made fun of her "Protestant" streak. Yet, she treasured the Bible, and believed she would wither without it. The breviary of Matins and Vespers guided her through the Psalms, which gave her solace in and out of prison. In the 1970s, biblical quotations coated the walls of the Worker's basement. The Bible had carried her through painful times; it could do the same for others.[149]

The Word in scripture gave straightforward spiritual direction. Paul instructed people to let their abundance supply the want of others. His admonition to abstain from things that led others to stumble (1 Cor 10) applied to alcohol, a chronic malady among the destitute. Were Jesus present in the flesh during the Spanish Civil War, he would say to Roman Catholics: "Put up thy sword." In the 1930s, when Day wanted to persuade ten white women to let a black woman live with them in the New York house, she reminded them that, since Jesus washed the feet of his disciples, they ought to serve one another regardless of race. At a demonstration with the United Farmworkers in 1973, she promised police that, when she returned the next day, she would read them the Sermon on the Mount. She sometimes rattled off a series of Jesus' teachings at a moment's notice. In her defiant editorial following Pearl Harbor, she took a potshot at the rest of the Christian press when she wrote, "We will print the words of Christ."[150]

In spite of her so-called Protestant leanings, Day had many specifically Roman Catholic words written on her heart. The words of the saints tumbled easily into most of her articles. Brother Lawrence guided her in the practice of the presence of God; St. Ignatius advised her to work as though everything depended on her and pray as though all depended on God. Maurin--whose vocation was to make papal "encyclicals click"--helped her to become a walking reader's digest of contemporary Catholic writing. Day found encyclicals refreshing because they integrated Christian tradition with contemporary issues and challenged the laity.[151]

Although Day made a distinction between "commandment" and "counsel," critics chastised the Worker for treating the counsels of perfection as norms for the laity. Day countered that some Christians acted as if Jesus had come to dispense advice.[152] While Muste and King combined a low Christology with an exalted view of Jesus' authority as a teacher, Day avoided the ironic pitfall of many who-- with a high Christology--ignore Jesus' teachings. For Day, Jesus' divinity reinforced the power of his words.

In the words of Jesus, the prophets, the saints, the popes, and contemporary writers, Day read messages from a demanding God. She commended the Catholic Worker to people "trying literally to follow the Gospel." Salvation depended on undoing the works of war. The Sermon on the Mount "ordered" people to be perfect. Jesus "commanded" people to feed the hungry, clothe the naked, and visit the sick.[153]

The Worker used only the Gospel's "tactics" and the "techniques of Christ" to raise money. In 1960, New York City paid the Catholic Worker $3700 because interest had accrued on Worker property the city bought when it forced the Worker to move. Day returned the money. She might have been returning a diamond ring to the unworthy rich, but canon law and the teachings of the Early Church opposed usury; in the Middle Ages, lending money with interest was a sin "classed with sodomy." Tradition, as she interpreted it, could not err. The Worker could not participate in a system it did not believe in. The words were written; her path was clear.[154]

In her obituary for Muste, Day recalled his childhood memorization of Psalm 119. She remarked parenthetically that the 176 verse love song to God's laws, commandments, and statutes was her favorite psalm. If this was more than a momentary fancy, she placed herself in a small group! Sharing Muste's conviction that "all are called to be saints," she thirsted for guidance, discipline, and structure to help her on her pilgrimage. She found in Old Testament laws their original purpose as signposts to keep her from straying from the way to life.[155]

Part of the Church's vocation was to bear Jesus' words from one generation to another. Yet Day's Church too often hid them like a light under a bushel basket. As a result, many Roman Catholics were woefully ignorant of both scripture and tradition. The Church not only failed to spread the Word; it failed to heed it herself.

Holy Harlot Church

"The Church is the Cross on which Christ was crucified; one could not separate Christ from His cross."

> --Romano Guardini[156]

In 1949, gravediggers went on strike against the Archdiocese of New York. Archconservative Cardinal Spellman smeared strikers as communist-inspired and ordered seminarians to act as scabs. Calling herself "the obedient but angry daughter of Holy Church," Day wrote and asked him to reconsider his position, and she joined the strikers on their picket line. Spellman acknowledged neither the letter nor her presence on the picket line. The strike failed within a month.[157]

An insistent daughter of the Church, Day visited Rome during Vatican II as part of a delegation for peace. The group went to thank Pope John XXIII for his statement on peace, to pledge themselves to work for peace, and "to ask, too, a more radical condemnation on the instruments of modern warfare."[158] Even in fundamental agreement, she offered constructive criticism to the Pope.

As a convert, Day adopted the Church much as Ruth had adopted her mother-in-law Naomi: "Do not press me to leave you or to turn back from following you! Where you go, I will go; where you lodge, I will lodge; your people shall be my people, and your God my God" (Ruth 1:16). Ruth's beautiful words may hide Day's greater personal sacrifice: she left a living husband to attach herself to this new mother.

Day received the spiritual care of the Church with gratitude as her early confessors guided her with grace, compassion, and the experienced skill of generations. She wondered how others searched for God without scripture's strength and the Church's wisdom. She practiced customary forms of piety, accepted traditional dogma, and believed the Church infallible in doctrinal matters. She used the rosary, believed the presence of the Blessed Sacrament held off evil powers, and venerated statues of Joseph and Mary. She felt it impossible to live faithfully without daily mass, weekly confession, and the service of Benediction each Saturday. She hoped that Tamar's infant baptism would bring order to her daughter's life--which had not existed in her own--and keep Tamar from "floundering" into hedonism. Whenever the Catholic Worker searched for land for a new farming commune, her first question was always how far it was to the nearest church.[159]

In later years, she staunchly upheld the Church's teaching on divorce, birth control, and abortion, apparently without any sense of personal irony. She disliked folk masses, opposed women's ordination, and disapproved of clergy discarding traditional garb for Hawaiian shirts. While others addressed the Berrigans by their first names, she called them Father Dan and Father Phil. When an activist priest, suspended by his bishop, wrote from prison to say he had given up on the Church, Day promised to "scold" the *priest!*[160]

A traditionalist himself, Maurin designed a Benedictine daily schedule for the farming communes: 5-7 work, 7-9 Mass, 9-10 breakfast, 10-11 lecture or discussion, 11-2 rest or study, 2-3 lecture or discussion, 3-4 cold lunch, 4-5 lesson in handicrafts, 5-8 work, 8-9 dinner, 9-5 sleep. He found as few followers in keeping the schedule as when he loaded himself down with extra gardening tools to encourage work.[161]

In spite of her conservatism, Day quickly became an anomaly within the hierarchical Church. She asked subversive questions: Who should the Christian obey when Church teachings and Christ's words conflicted with bishops' political pronouncements? When the "princes of the church" publicly blessed the war in Vietnam, she countered with Jesus' words and example.[162] With Merton, Muste, and King, she turned to Christ's authority to reform the Church. Muste's conservative religious spirit produced a radical political stance; Day's traditionalism advocated both social change and ecclesiastical reform.

The Roman Catholic Church had seen millions of people outwardly eager to confess past sins and enter the Church, only to see their backs when their initial fervor subsided. The routine entrance and quick exit made it seem that each narthex had a revolving door. The Church may not have known the whole story of Day's past, but an illegitimate child and a common law marriage warranted suspicion.

As she approached baptism, Day was more reticent about the Church's past than her own. The Church sided with the powerful, and Day feared that baptism would betray her commitment to justice. The nun whose rote religious instruction prepared Day for baptism lived in a convent on land given by Charles Schwab. Schwab, once the head of Bethlehem Steel, had broken strikes, refused to recognize unions, and enriched himself with money that properly belonged to workers. In accepting his money, the Church practiced hypocrisy, allied itself with capitalistic materialism, and made of religion an opiate.[163]

Day compared herself to one of Dostoevsky's characters who felt "tormented" by God. She had been teased by traces of the holy and guided by the scattered faithful. Yet, she violently reproached herself as a satiated bovine intoxicated by her own expanding womb and led passively toward baptism. She tried to accept on face value that the presence of the poor in Roman Catholic churches made it the Church of the poor. But baptism did not brainwash her: her God still preferred the unchurched unemployed to middle-class churchgoers.164

When Day measured her obedience to bishops against her loyalty to the Church's teachings, she favored labor over the hierarchy, the poor over the Church. Although a pacifist, she preferred violence on behalf of the destitute to indifferent inaction. When priests prayed and sang with lettuce strikers in California, and their conservative bishops transferred them all over the Western Hemisphere, Day spoke tongue-in-cheek: "If young priests want to see the world, they have only to speak out on the agricultural conflict."165

Going through its own adolescent identity crisis in the U.S. in the 1930s, Roman Catholicism struggled for acceptability by wedding Catholicism to Americanism. The Church in the U.S. rarely addressed social problems and habitually sided with the wealthy. The Catholic Worker went the opposite way. At the peak of the work of the House Committee on Unamerican Activities, Day stated the alternative baldly in a headline: "We Are Un-American; We Are Catholics." J. Edgar Hoover had suspected as much.166

In her twenties, Day abhorred the hypocrisy of professing Christians. Like Muste, she was attracted to the dedication and self-sacrifice of secular radicals: "I did not see [any Christian] taking off his coat and giving it to the poor. I didn't see anyone having a banquet and calling in the lame, the halt, and the blind." She could not comprehend faith without works: how could Christians see a person in need and say only, "Go in peace, be warmed and filled" (James 2:16)? She half-hoped that God would vomit out the lukewarm (Rev 3:16). Individual Christians had to choose: accept personal responsibility for the welfare of others or repeat the words of Cain, the first murderer, who asked if he was his brother's keeper. In her old age, she felt sickened when Catholics--made "one flesh" in the Mystical Body of

Christ--used their religious affiliation as an ornament, and continued as members of the John Birch Society, as bigots and racists. The infidelity of individual Christians had repelled her and remained a stumbling block to others.[167]

Disturbed by the hypocrisy of the laity, Day was outraged by the failures of the clergy and the hierarchy. She liked to tell the story of the Catholic Workers who, when a man shouted that their cardinal slept with his housekeeper every night, replied that it revealed how democratic he was! Far more upsetting to her were the clergy's posh residences. The poor were supposed to be "the first children of the Church," yet it spent less on the needy than on church furnishings. Buildings were sacraments of the church's indifference to the oppressed:

> Would Jesus sit in some big, fancy, air-conditioned room near the banks and the department stores where the rich store their millions . . .? Would He let Himself be driven in big black limousines, while thousands and thousands of people who believe in Him and His Church are at the edge of starvation? Would he tolerate big mansions and fancy estates and luxurious traveling, while people come to church barefooted and ragged and hungry and sick, children all over the world? In my mind, there is only one answer to questions like those: no![168]

The clergy were like the incompetent shepherds described by the prophets (Jer 23:1-2, Ezek 34:1-10). They did not feed their sheep with God's Word nor direct them to serve Christ in the world. The "Protestant" in Day attacked her clergy for limiting themselves to a sacramental role.[169] Before she met Maurin, she resented the Church for letting her engage in spiritual reading without calling her to social action. As nothing in Muste's upbringing or theological training linked Christian faith with pacifism, nothing in Day's experience--until she met Maurin--connected faith and social change.

Day's docile acceptance of Church doctrine and mores did not preclude a radical contribution to the life of the Church. A female in a male institution and mother in a celibate society, she emphasized lay ministry in an ordained world. The Catholic Worker sought to develop a "lay apostolate." She wanted *The Catholic Worker* to promote a nonviolent ecclesiastical revolution, creating a new church within the shell of the old. In "the age of the laity," she encouraged people to enter into economics and politics in ways closed to the clergy. God sent Christ into the world; the Church sent the laity.[170]

Day said she steered clear of theologizing to avoid thinking about things she did not understand. She stayed steadfastly loyal to the Church's teachings and limited most of her direct rebukes of the hierarchy to private communications. The political anarchist accepted her hierarchical Church. She considered in-fighting over Church reforms a diversion from her real work of battling injustice. She encouraged lay people displeased with the hierarchy's inaction to engage in direct action. Yet, she was never satisfied herself. In spite of her deep admiration for them, Day even questioned the saints. Why did they only remedy evil instead of preventing it? Why did they not try to heal twisted and twisting social structures?[171]

In spite of her cynicism, as a young adult Day still believed in God, read the New Testament, and admired Tolstoy's priest- and institution-less, interior and ethical Christianity. As a Catholic, she believed that a truly Christian Medieval Church would have allowed Muslims to overrun Europe and conquered the conquerors with the Sermon on the Mount. A truly Christian modern Church would follow the same strategy. In 1936, she asked American Catholics to encourage Spanish Catholics to practice Christlike nonviolence so that the world could play the centurion at the Cross and call them "sons of God." Instead American Catholics echoed the crowd addressing Christ: If you are the Son of God, come down from the cross.[172]

Like Teresa of Avila's foundations in Spain, and Francis of Assisi's brotherhood, Day's lay movement sought to reinvigorate the Church. The saint of Assisi and Day were kindred spirits: each reverenced the eucharist and creation, and saw Christ poor and crucified. They remained loyal to the hierarchy while subverting it from within. Even in the Church, redemption came from the bottom up.

Maurin was such a devout Catholic that Day was stunned when he told her to pray for the Church as though it was a terrible sinner. Only later did she realize that it was *because* he was so dedicated that he felt that way.[173] It helped her in her own struggle to know that one as loyal as Maurin could share her discomfort with the Church.

Day also found guidance and solace in the story of Hosea, whom God commanded to marry the temple prostitute so that, in experiencing his wife's profligate, idolatrous infidelity, he would know how God felt about Israel. Now Christ suffered through the infidelity of his Bride, the Church. Like Hosea, Christ remained the cuckolded spouse trying to win the Church back with nothing but love.   Thus did Day remain a faithful daughter in spite of the Church's unfaithfulness: "Though she is a harlot at times, she is our Mother."[174]

The Church still offered many blessings, including its basic strategy against war: "The plan for peace is in the Scriptures, the church, the confessional, the altar rail." In benevolent moments, Day hoped that the Church, like an infant, would soon grow up. She was heartened at the Second Vatican Council to see barriers lowered between clergy and laity, and bishops--more accessible away from their episcopal palaces-- spending as long in confession as overly scrupulous nuns.[175]

Romano Guardini said that the Church is the Cross of Christ, and Day lived, as he suggested, in "permanent dissatisfaction" with the Church. When the Church spent exorbitant amounts of money to build convents while families lived in overcrowded conditions, when its only good news to the poor promised rewards after death, when it did not seem to care about feeding, clothing, or housing Christ, Day wondered if its long pollution by materialism had not made it become like Job's so-called comforters.176

> When I see the church taking the side of the powerful and forgetting the weak, and when I see bishops living in luxury and the poor being ignored or thrown crumbs, I know that Jesus is being insulted, as He once was, and sent to his death, as He once was.177

The Church was not only Christ's Cross; it was His crucifier. The Church was less; and it offered more:

> To be in church isn't to be calmed down, as some people say they get when they are at Mass. I'm worked up. I'm excited by being so close to Jesus, but the closer I get, the more I worry about what He wants of us, what He would have us do before we die.178

Whatever the Church's infidelities, Christ worked through it. Whatever the harlot's sins, the way to heaven lay within church walls.

All the Way to Heaven

"We praise thee, O God; we acknowledge thee to be the Lord. All the earth doth worship thee, the Father everlasting. To thee all Angels cry aloud, the Heavens and all the Powers therein. To thee Cherubim and Seraphim continually do cry: Holy, holy, holy, Lord God of Sabaoth; Heaven and earth are full of the majesty of thy glory."

> --Te Deum

"And this has always been a comfort to me, that I chose Jesus by his grace to be my heaven in all this time of suffering and of sorrow."

> --Julian of Norwich

"All the way to Heaven is Heaven."

--Catherine of Siena.[179]

A pregnant Day strode Staten Island beaches and returned to the joyful praise of the Te Deum, which she had loved as a teenager. Pregnancy surprised her. A series of gynecological problems followed her abortion. She thought herself barren, perhaps believing it a divine punishment.

The first of the Bible's stories of surprising births came when Sarah conceived when her age and history made it impossible. Sarah and Abraham named their child Isaac, meaning "laughter." Day named her child Tamar (unaware of the fates of her biblical namesakes), but Tamar's birth brought laughter.

In 1917 in Occoquan prison, Day had turned to God in despair, but when the agony faded, she turned away again. Now pregnant years later, filled with appreciation of creation and her role as a co-creator, she committed her life to God. Hers was not a death-bed conversion, but a maternity ward conversion. Her love and joy compelling her to pray, her physical condition preventing her from kneeling, she walked on the beach praising the only One who could contain all her thanks.[180]

Day's younger brother, born when she was fourteen, became her first love because their mother's heavy household workload made Day the boy's "mother" figure. When Day left home for college she felt as though she had been torn away from her own child.[181] Tamar's birth fulfilled her desire for motherhood and blissfully united her with women of all classes, as birth brought a kind of solidarity with others she had not imagined.[182]

Day's adolescent idea of heaven had been a place of "fields and meadows, sweet with flowers and songs and melodies unutterable, in which the laughing gull and the waves on the shore" sang and thundered ecstatically. To the wounded of class warfare, the farming communes were bits of Paradise on earth. She remembered that Dostoevsky said the world would be saved by beauty. Surveying poverty, hunger, and war in 1940, she wrote:

> But we would be contributing to the misery and desperation of the world if we failed to rejoice in the sun, moon, and the stars, in the rivers which surround this island on which we live, in the cool breezes of the bay, in what food we have. . . .183

Batterham, a biologist, had opened up her appreciation of creation and--after her affair, abortion, marriage, and divorce--fulfilled her desire for intimacy. The contentment she felt in their Staten Island cottage made her sense the possibility of something greater. She let God find her in this time of profound personal joy.184

She could not thank God enough. When saying the Lord's Prayer, she started over again to end on a note of praise. Gratitude became a hallmark of her spiritual life. She felt naturally thankful for those in solidarity with the poor; with an act of will, she found in unpleasant people a reason for thanksgiving. A violent man who lived on a farming commune for several years greeted guests with curmudgeon-like anger, yet she gave thanks for his presence because he tested her faith and opened her to introspection.185

Day's omnipresent use of Catherine of Siena's saying, "all the way to heaven is heaven," made a peculiar mantra for the often angry, penitential, and dictatorial journalist. It was not always easy to be joyful, yet she submitted to the "duty of delight." Abundant life began now. Her sacramental sense of life made heaven a part of her daily existence.186

There were many openings into heaven: Heaven, she said, begins at baptism; retreats help people make their lives "a beginning of heaven": the eucharist provided a foretaste of heaven. Yet her high expectations sometimes betrayed her. She wanted to recognize her daily work as a part of heaven, but it often seemed like hell. When work overwhelmed her, she found "relief" in the mass and herself upheld by her blessings. The eucharist enabled her to be more patient and kind when she went back to work so that she could spread heaven to others. Without prayer, work was grim; with it, she discovered joy all around her. Living for awhile with her daughter, son-in-law and their children on their farm, Day liked to make up verses for the Benedicite:

> All ye works of the Lord, bless ye the Lord. Oh ye ice and snow, oh ye cold and wind, oh ye winter and summer, oh ye trees in the woods, oh ye fire in the stove, oh ye Beckie and Susie and Eric, bless ye the Lord! Praise Him and exalt Him above all forever.

She composed variations on the canticle to include anyone who came to the Catholic Worker, and to cows, goats, and chickens.[187]

She quoted Fr. Zossima, the monastic saint of *The Brothers Karamazov*: "Love in action is a harsh and dreadful thing compared with love in dreams...Active love is labor and fortitude" almost lacking in mirth or pleasure. Teresa of Avila prayed for deliverance from "frowning saints"; little Therese said, "all is grace"; and Julian of Norwich wrote, "all will be well, and all will be well, and all manner of things will be well."[188] By any measure, Day led a harsh life in the midst of oppression, accepting powerlessness, living in vulnerability, continually re-discovering that the wretched of the earth often make wretched companions. But she had known joy, experienced a great miracle, tasted eternal life. Like Muste, she had known a deep, singing peace. She felt the presence of heaven on earth in human love, in creation, and in the confluence of the two in the birth of Tamar. She felt it on the farm, at the seashore, in her work, through the poor, at the altar, in the confessional. All the way to heaven was not heavenly, but it was heaven.

In Love with God

"The Lord does not look so much at the magnitude of anything we do as at the love with which we do it. . . .The good of the soul does not exist in thinking much but in loving much."

--Teresa of Avila

"Our hearts were made for Thee, O Lord, and find no rest until they rest in Thee."

--Augustine

"Where there is no love, put love, and there you will find love."

--John of the Cross

"What, do you wish to know your Lord's meaning in this thing? Know it well, love was his meaning. Who reveals it to you? Love. What did he reveal to you? Love. Why does he reveal it to you? For love."

--Julian of Norwich[189]

Even in her most personal writings, Day set out to write about the things that brought her to God and kept her with God. Her "long loneliness" was a "spiritual hunger" chronically unfulfilled. Her collegiate ideological rejection of religion temporarily limited her "glimpses" of God, but as a New York secular radical, enticed by Eugene O'Neill to read Augustine's *Confessions*, she slipped into churches during mass. The Hound of Heaven was after her; the courtship with God was on.[190] King meditated on the meaning of love, and Merton wrote of moments of intimacy with God, but the mystical tradition's romantic, erotic language flowed more naturally from Day.

Describing her first communion at the age of eleven, Therese of Lisieux wrote, "What comfort it brought to me, that first kiss our lord imprinted on my soul! A lover's kiss; I knew that I was loved, and I, in my turn, told him that I loved him, and was giving myself to him for all eternity." She wanted "to make God loved," to love Christ "more than He has ever been loved." When she entered the Order, she composed an invitation to the "spiritual marriage" of "Jesus, King of Kings and Lord of Lords with Little Therese Martin." He was her betrothed, her spouse, her "Prince Charming," her first and only love. She ended her autobiography with a prayer: "I want to be the prey of Your love. I hope that one day You will swoop down on me, carry me off to the furnace of love, and plunge me into its burning depths so that I can be its ecstatic victim for all eternity."[191]

While Therese wrote in terms of adolescent fantasy, Teresa of Avila described a consummated spiritual intimacy:

> I would see beside me, on my left hand, an angel in bodily form
> . . . . In his hands I saw a long golden spear and at the end of the
> iron tip I seemed to see a point of fire. With this he seemed to pierce
> my heart several times so that it penetrated to my entrails. When he
> drew it out, I thought he was drawing them out with it and he left
> me completely afire with a great love for God. The pain was so
> sharp that it made me utter several moans; and so excessive was the
> sweetness caused me by this intense pain that one can never wish to
> lose it, nor will one's soul be content with anything less than
> God.[192]

For Day, the mystic was "in love with God," prayer "like falling in love," retreats times to be "in love": "The love of God can become so overwhelming that it wishes to do everything for the Beloved, to endure hunger, cold, sleeplessness in an ecstasy of zeal and enthusiasm." Sexual intimacy was a sample of Heaven and the enjoyment of God. She read in *The Cloud of Unknowing* of the soul stretching itself toward God and felt her own soul yearning and reaching out.[193]

Jesus had been so tender and loving with women that Day sometimes felt closer to Him than to the air she breathed. All the way to heaven was heaven, Catherine said, "because Jesus is the way." As a young woman, when Day heard of God, it had been like "hearing of someone you love and who loves you." Being in love was a sample of God's love: Her love for Batterham helped her to understand divine love.194

She wrote of leaving the house of hospitality to sit for an hour in the presence of the Blessed Sacrament as though she were sneaking off for an affair. Emotionally overwhelmed in prison, she took out her rosary and "felt a sense of such closeness to God. Such a sense of His love, such love for his creatures."195

In her ecstasy for her beloved, Day would sacrifice anything. A previous lover made her give up her unborn child. Forced to choose between the man she loved and God, she chose God. She would have Tamar baptized "cost what it may." She paid the cost in her "infidelity," her self-confessed "adultery" against Batterham for the sake of her love for God. Love incarnate was harsh and dreadful, demanding actions, counting costs.196

Day knew the Commandments true in calling God a jealous lover. Jesus told his disciples to hate their loved ones if their family hindered their relationship with God. Day compared herself to Abraham who had to choose God over his beloved Isaac (Gen 22:2). Muste's Abraham risked his own life; Day's Abraham did not sacrifice Isaac, but she had to kill her joy-filled life with the one she loved.197

Day actually gave up two lovers for God, for she loved her life in the radical movement. She loved the way of life--the personal sacrifices, the late nights, the endless discussions. In falling in love with God she was going over to the opposition, the Church, the oppressors as part of her "painful and tortured, yet joyful process of conversion." She felt disloyal twice over.198

When in love you begin to see others through the eyes of your beloved. When in love with God, your first duty is to praise God by loving the whole Mystical Body of Christ. Therese started by loving God alone and found that her heart grew to love--with an affection she thought impossible--those whom God loved.[199]

Day's spiritual director and the Catholic Worker's retreat leader said, "You love God as much as the one you love the least." Combined with the judgment in Matthew 25, these words had terrible significance for Day who worked with the "least of these" every day: "Love makes all things easy. . .But it is hard to love, from a human standpoint and from the divine standpoint, in a two room apartment."[200]

Identifying herself as a "Martha," the nurse tending to every nagging need, Day wanted to be more of a "Mary," the mystic and lover.[201] She could not claim Christ or God as her first love. She was more like Augustine, who realized that his relationship with God was the one he had longed for all along, a love better than all of the vices and virtues he had tried. Day was more like the earthy, hard-edged Teresa than romantic Therese. Teresa openly complained to God of life's discomforts and the trials of their relationship; Therese never experienced the fits and starts of even the shortest relationship. Yet Day yearned for a lost innocence and a purity of affection she could not attain.

Day knew both the pain and ecstasy of divine loving and divine love. God gave her a miraculous birth. God answered her prayer and sent one wise man bearing a peculiar gift, a vocation to give birth to a movement. God gave her a sacramental sensitivity to people and things. God engraved words on her heart to guide and comfort her on her pilgrimage to heaven. But she made sacrifices to make it work, giving up human love and entering a rigorous life without physical comfort or emotional security.

Before Therese entered the convent, Day noted, she was God's child; once inside the cloister, she became God's spouse and used the erotic language of the Song of Songs to interpret her love for God. One's relationship with God could take many forms: shepherd and sheep, master and servant, parent and child: "We may stand at times in the relationship of servant, and at other times in that of son, as far as our feelings go and in our present state. But the relationship we hope to attain to, is that of the love of the Canticle of Canticles." The love of bride and bridegroom--equals and intimates--was the tie that sustained her throughout her long loneliness: "I loved, in other words, and like all women in love, I wanted to be united to my love."[202]

NOTES

DOROTHY DAY

1. Dorothy Day, *Therese* (Springfield, IL, 1960), v, vi; Dorothy Day, *The Long Loneliness* (San Francisco, 1952), 139.

2. Dorothy Day, *From Union Square to Rome* (New York, 1938), 123; Day, *The Long Loneliness*, 133.

3. Day, *From Union Square to Rome*, 17, 141-42.

4. Robert Coles, *Dorothy Day: A Radical Devotion* (Reading, MA, 1987), 56, 59.

5. Day, *From Union Square to Rome*, 34; Day, *The Long Loneliness*, 11, 43, 84, 85, 81.

6. Day, *The Long Loneliness*, 38, 62, 115; Day, *From Union Square to Rome*, 68, 146; Dorothy Day, *Loaves and Fishes* (San Francisco, 1963, 1983), 8.

7. Day, *From Union Square to Rome*, 34, 78, 81-86, 99-107; Day, *The Long Loneliness*, 64, 66.

202

8. Day, *The Long Loneliness*, 160-61, 93, 156; Day, *From Union Square to Rome*, 43, 63, 110; William D. Miller, *Dorothy Day: A Biography* (San Francisco, 1982), 154.

9. Mel Piehl, *Breaking Bread: The Catholic Worker and the Origin of Catholic Radicalism in America* (Philadelphia, 1982), x, 77.

10. Peter Maurin, *Easy Essays* (Chicago, 1977), Foreword; Robert Ellsberg, ed., *By Little and By Little: The Selected Writings of Dorothy Day* (New York, 1983), xxxvii, 354, 357; Day, *Loaves and Fishes*, 39-40, 133; James Forest, *Love is the Measure: A Biography of Dorothy Day* (New York, 1986), 209; Piehl, 109-10; John C. Cort, "My Life at the Catholic Worker" *Commonweal* 107:12 (June 20, 1980): 364, 367; Dorothy Day, *On Pilgrimage: The Sixties* (New York, 1972), 282.

11. Day, *Loaves and Fishes*, 24, 60, 87; Day, *The Long Loneliness*, 186, 236; Dorothy Day, *Houses of Hospitality* (New York, 1939), 92, 170, 172, 261, 262; Piehl, 108.

12. Ellsberg, ed., xxx; Piehl, 162, 167, 169, 173, 200, 227, 236; Nancy L. Roberts, *Dorothy Day and the Catholic Worker* (Albany, NY, 1984), 171; Stanley Vishnewski, *Wings of the Dawn* (New York, n.d.), 168-74, 145, 147, 149, 153.

13. Ellsberg, ed.,148, xxxviii, 360; Day, *Houses of Hospitality*, 171, 172, 174; William D. Miller, ed., *All is Grace: The Spirituality of Dorothy Day* (Garden City, NY, 1987), 155.

14. E. Allison Peers, *Mother of Carmel: A Portrait of Teresa of Avila* (Wilton, CT, 1944), 3, 84, 213; Therese of Lisieux, *The Story of a Soul* (New York, 1957), 49, 57, 113.

15. Maurin, *Easy Essays*, 37.

16. Day, *Houses of Hospitality*, viii; Day, *The Long Loneliness*, 165-66.

17. Day, *The Long Loneliness*, 166; Coles, 11.

18. Coles, 73; Ellsberg, ed., 149; Day, *Loaves and Fishes*, 13; Day, *Houses of Hospitality*, v; Miller, 374.

19. Maurin, 36; Day, *Houses of Hospitality*, xxvii, xxxv.

20. Marc Ellis, *Peter Maurin: Prophet in the Twentieth Century* (New York, 1981), 63.

21. Day, *Loaves and Fishes*, 7; Day, *The Long Loneliness*, 170; Vishnewski, 35; Piehl, 119; Ellsberg, ed., xxv, 175.

22. Maurin, 61, 22, 115, 146.

23. Piehl, 51; Day, *Houses of Hospitality*, 225; Stanley Vishnewski, ed., *Meditations* (New York, 1970), 70.

24. Ellis, 117; Maurin, 49.

25. Miller, ed., 28; Ellsberg, ed., 293, xxv; Maurin, 182, 205, 17, 59, 66; Piehl, 116.

26. Piehl, 66, 96; Ellis, 28.

27. Dorothy Day, *On Pilgrimage* (New York, 1948), 83-85; Ellsberg, ed., 127; Piehl, 58.

28. Ellsberg, ed., 71, 123, 126, 314, xxiv; Day, *The Long Loneliness*, 279; Day, *Houses of Hospitality*, 251, 269, xxviii.

29. Ellsberg, ed., 124; Vishnewski, ed., *Meditations*, p. 71; Vishnewski, *Wings of the Dawn*, 190, 192; Day, *The Long Loneliness*, 274, 275; Ellis, 165.

30. Day, *Loaves and Fishes*, 110; Day, *Houses of Hospitality*, 269; Day, *The Long Loneliness*, 11; Ellsberg, ed., xxvii; Day, *On Pilgrimage: The Sixties*, 328.

31. Day, *Houses of Hospitality*, 42; Day, *Loaves and Fishes*, 21, 27; Day, *The Long Loneliness*, 174, 180, 181, 195; Miller, 254; Piehl, 60; Ellis, 47, 137, 138; Day, *On Pilgrimage*, 77; Maurin, 107; Ellsberg, ed., 242, 253.

32. Maurin was playing on the old saying, "Man proposes. God disposes." Day, *Loaves and Fishes*, 138; Miller, ed., *All is Grace*, 63; Day, *On Pilgrimage: The Sixties*, 355; Debra Campbell, "The Catholic Earth Mother: Dorothy Day and Women's Power in the Church" *Crosscurrents* 34 (Fall 1984): 280.

33. Piehl, 86.

34. Day, *Houses of Hospitality*, 179-80; Miller, *Dorothy Day*, 306-7.

35. Vishnewski, *Wings of the Dawn*, 58; Day, *On Pilgrimage*, 78; Piehl, 86; Miller, ed., *All is Grace*, 146; Day, *The Long Loneliness*, 87; Day, *Houses of Hospitality*, 149; also Maurin, 186.

36. Day, *The Long Loneliness*, 87; Day, *Houses of Hospitality*, 187; Ellsberg, ed., 91, 275, 335.

37. Miller, *Dorothy Day*, 314-15; Ellsberg, ed., 322; Miller, ed., *All is Grace*, 87.

38. Dorothy Day, "Message of Love," *The Catholic Worker* 17:6 (Dec. 1950): 1-2.

39. Schwab and Grace were other industrialists. Day, *The Long Loneliness*, 211; Ellsberg, ed., 246; Day, *Houses of Hospitality*, 208.

40. Day, *From Union Square to Rome*, 10, 109, 140; Ellsberg, ed., 160, 180, 244, 345; Day, *The Long Loneliness*, 108, 147; Day, *On Pilgrimage*, 75.

41. Day, *From Union Square to Rome*, 147, 148; Day, *Houses of Hospitality*, 258; Ellsberg, ed., 271.

42. Miller, ed., *All is Grace*, 22; Day, *On Pilgrimage*, 125, 78.

43. Ellsberg, ed., 145, 147, 276.

44. Ellsberg, ed., 303; Day, *On Pilgrimage: The Sixties*, 94.

45. Day, *On Pilgrimage: The Sixties*, 319; Miller, *Dorothy Day*, 83, 473-74; Forest, 176; Day, *On Pilgrimage*, 53, 54.

46. Day, *Houses of Hospitality*, 223; Day, *On Pilgrimage: The Sixties*, 116.

47. Miller, ed., *All is Grace*, 106.

48. Day, *From Union Square to Rome*, 6; Ellsberg, ed., 292, 174; Miller, ed., *All is Grace*, 109; Day, *Loaves and Fishes*, 166.

49. Ellsberg, ed., 98, 85; Maurin, 209.

50. Day, *Loaves and Fishes*, 38, 51, 131, 57, 213; Maurin, 110; Vishnewski, *Wings of the Dawn*, 205.

51. Bill Moyers' Journal, "Still a Rebel," 1973.

52. Day, *Houses of Hospitality*, 224, 131, 140, 190, 202, 216, 240, 242.

53. Day, *Houses of Hospitality*, 255; Ellsberg, ed., 91; Day, *From Union Square to Rome*, 35.

54. Roberts, 56.

55. Day, *Loaves and Fishes*, 176; Day, *On Pilgrimage: The Sixties*, 124; Ellsberg, ed., 291, 310; Maurin, 123.

56. Piehl, 124; Day, *Houses of Hospitality*, 53-54, 99.

57. William D. Miller, *A Harsh and Dreadful Love: Dorothy Day and the Catholic Worker Movement* (New York, 1973), 247; Piehl, 130; Day, *On Pilgrimage: The Sixties*, 186.

58. Day, *Houses of Hospitality*, 53; Ellsberg, ed., 144.

59. Miller, ed., *All is Grace*, 81; Day, *Houses of Hospitality*, 65; Day, *From Union Square to Rome*, 160.

60. Day, *Houses of Hospitality*, 190; Ellsberg, ed., 81.

61. Day, *The Long Loneliness*, 199-200.

62. Miller, ed., *All is Grace*, 60; Day, *The Long Loneliness*, 191, 91, 20, 28; Day, *On Pilgrimage*, 9, 41, 10; Day, *From Union Square to Rome*, 25; Day, *Therese*, 74; Ellsberg, ed., 355, 326; Day, *Houses of Hospitality*, 2; Day, *On Pilgrimage: The Sixties*, 88.

63. Ellsberg, ed., 157.

64. Ellsberg, ed., 250, 83, 248, 241; Day, *Houses of Hospitality*, 142, 227.

65. Ellsberg, ed., 250; Day, *Houses of Hospitality*, 100.

66. Forest, 189; Miller, *Dorothy Day*, 317; Maurin, 178-79; Roberts, *Dorothy Day and the Catholic Worker*, 122-23.

67. Day, *On Pilgrimage*, 16; Day, *Houses of Hospitality*, 201-2, 78.

68. Therese of Lisieux, *The Story of a Soul*, 46, 76.

69. Day, *From Union Square to Rome*, 10; Day, *Houses of Hospitality*, 259; Day, *Loaves and Fishes*, 129; Day, *On Pilgrimage*, 97; Ellsberg, ed., 338, 92, 113, 95, 146, 344; Day, *The Long Loneliness*, 204-5; Vishnewski, ed., *Meditations*, 68.

70. Ellsberg, ed., p. 112, 101, 329, 94; Day, *On Pilgrimage*, 123, 52; Day, *Loaves and Fishes*, 171; Day, *On Pilgrimage: The Sixties*, 168.

71. Day, *On Pilgrimage: The Sixties*, 71, 170, 171; Day, *Houses of Hospitality*, 87-88; Ellsberg, ed., 300, 330, 96-97.

72. Day, *On Pilgrimage: The Sixties*, 196; Ellsberg, ed., 97; Day, *Houses of Hospitality*, 203.

73. Day, *On Pilgrimage: The Sixties*, 192, 236, 238; Coles, 117; Miller, *Dorothy Day*, 204; Ellsberg, ed., 273; Day, *Houses of Hospitality*, 250.

74. Ellsberg, ed., 323; Day, *Houses of Hospitality*, 136; Vishnewski, ed., *Meditations*, 96.

75. Miller, ed., *All is Grace*, 134; Ellsberg, ed., 287, 114; Day, *Houses of Hospitality*, 97, 15-16; Day, *The Long Loneliness*, 38, 215; Coles, 98.

76. Day, *The Long Loneliness*, 92; Day, *On Pilgrimage: The Sixties*, 330; Vishnewski, ed., *Meditations*, 61; Ellsberg, ed., xli; Day, *Loaves and Fishes*, 61, 71; Forest, 90-91.

77. Piehl, 11; Day, *The Long Loneliness*, 46; Day, *From Union Square to Rome*, 48, 61.

78. Day, *Loaves and Fishes*, 47, 202; Miller, ed., *All is Grace*, 161, 109; Day, *Houses of Hospitality*, 234; Vishnewski, *Wings of the Dawn*, 41, 100.

79. Day, *The Long Loneliness*, 10; Maurin, 9, 103, 167, 123, 124; Ellsberg, ed., 114; Day, *On Pilgrimage: The Sixties*, 288.

80. Day, *Houses of Hospitality*, 236.

81. Day, *Houses of Hospitality*, xxvi; Vishnewski, ed., *Meditations*, 40; Day, *On Pilgrimage*, 157; Ellsberg, ed., 99; Ammon Hennacy, *The Book of Ammon* (n.p., 1965), 393.

82. Day, *Houses of Hospitality*, 23; Vishnewski, *Wings of the Dawn*, 104, 157, 206.

83. Coles, 103, 111; Marc Ellis, *A Year at the Catholic Worker* (New York, 1978), 58; Vishnewski, *Wings of the Dawn*, 201; Ellsberg, ed., 106; Day, *Houses of Hospitality*, 60; Day, *On Pilgrimage: The Sixties*, 199.

84. Ellsberg, ed., 288, 279, 284; Day, *Loaves and Fishes*, 172, 167, 160.

85. Ellsberg, ed., 280.

86. Ellsberg, ed., 108, 111, 298; Vishnewski, ed., *Meditations*, 63; Miller, ed., *All is Grace*, 148; Day, *Loaves and Fishes*, 82; Day, *On Pilgrimage*, 166.

87. Day, *On Pilgrimage: The Sixties*, 30; Ellsberg, ed., 109, 330, 70; Day, *On Pilgrimage*, 166; Day, *Houses of Hospitality*, 110, 111; Day, *Loaves and Fishes*, 82.

88. Ellsberg, ed., 111, 304, 313; Day, *Houses of Hospitality*, 273; Day, *Loaves and Fishes*, 78; Day, *On Pilgrimage*, 16, 127; Day, *On Pilgrimage: The Sixties*, 273.

89. Ellsberg, ed., 107, 313; Day, *Houses of Hospitality*, 19, 98; Coles, 155-56; Maurin, 110-11; Day, *On Pilgrimage*, 82.

90. Day, *Loaves and Fishes*, 80; Miller, ed., *All is Grace*, 139; Ellsberg, ed., 61, 80, 83, 52; Day, *On Pilgrimage*, 169; Day, *On Pilgrimage: The Sixties*, 329.

91. Forest, 110; Day, *Loaves and Fishes*, 49, 181; Day, *Houses of Hospitality*, 190, 25, 117, 118, 159; Ellsberg, ed., 324; Vishnewski, 75; Day, *On Pilgrimage: The Sixties*, 52.

92. Ellsberg, ed., 311-315; Forest, 179-80.

93. Ellsberg, ed., 299, 264; Day, *Houses of Hospitality*, 115.

94. Ellsberg, ed., 263-64.

95. Ellsberg, ed., 313; Coles, 133; Roberts, 40.

96. Day, *From Union Square to Rome*, 77, 86, 80; Ellsberg, ed., 352, 278; Day, *Loaves and Fishes*, 106; Day, *On Pilgrimage*, 130; Forest, 143.

97. Ellsberg, ed., 248, 253-57; Miller, ed., *All is Grace*, 188, 180;

98. Day, *Houses of Hospitality*, 71; Vishnewski. 65, 113; Coles, 123-25.

99. Day, *On Pilgrimage*, 110, 175, 86; Ellsberg, ed., 71, 109.

100. Day, *On Pilgrimage*, 86.

101. Julian of Norwich, *Showings* (New York, 1978), 127.

102. Julian of Norwich, 245.

103. Day, *On Pilgrimage: The Sixties*, 186.

104. Day, *The Long Loneliness*, 188; Ammon Hennacy, 319; Sally Cuneen, "Dorothy Day: The Storyteller as Human Model," *Crosscurrents* 34 (Fall 1984): 290.

105. Roberts, 105; Ellsberg, ed., xxxvi; Miller, *Dorothy Day*, 95, 456; Miller, ed., *All is Grace*, 146; Day, *Houses of Hospitality*, 202-3, 89, 131.

106. Ellsberg, ed., 181.

107. Miller, ed., *All is Grace*, 113; Day, *Houses of Hospitality*, 79; Day, *On Pilgrimage*, 174.

108. Miller, *Dorothy Day*, 103, 376, 463; Piehl, 81; Forest, 181, 106; Miller, ed., *All is Grace*, 2; Day, *Houses of Hospitality*, 125; Day, *The Long Loneliness*, 141; Day, *On Pilgrimage: The Sixties*, 56.

109. Day, *Therese*, 78, 82, 98, 81; Day, *The Long Loneliness*, 10; Therese of Lisieux, *The Story of a Soul*, 57.

110. Ellsberg, ed., 291; Day, *Loaves and Fishes*, 176, 80; Day, *On Pilgrimage*, 58; Day, *The Long Loneliness*, 20; Day, *From Union Square to Rome*, 27.

111. Ellsberg, 131, 317; Day, *Loaves and Fishes*, 58; Day, *On Pilgrimage*, 174.

112. Miller, ed., *All is Grace*, 4, 79; Ellsberg, ed.,183; Day, *The Long Loneliness*, 216; Coles, 23; Day, *Houses of Hospitality*, 130, 134; Day, *On Pilgrimage*, 125.

113. Ellsberg, ed., 290-93 or Day, *Loaves and Fishes*, 174-78.

114. Day, *Therese*, xii, 167; Day, *Loaves and Fishes*, 178; Ellsberg, ed., 193, 105; Coles, 118.

115. Day, *On Pilgrimage*, 120.

116. Day, *Loaves and Fishes*, 214-15; Ellsberg, ed., 169; Day, *On Pilgrimage*, 120, 37.

117. Day, *Houses of Hospitality*, 96-97, 188; Ellsberg, ed., 80.

118. Miller, ed., *All is Grace*, 56; Day, *Houses of Hospitality*, 255; Ellsberg, ed., 159; Day, *Loaves and Fishes*, 210; Forest, 100.

119. Miller, ed., *All is Grace*, 148; Ellsberg, ed., 262, 266, 273; Day, *Houses of Hospitality*, 207-8; Day, *The Long Loneliness*, 264; Day, *On Pilgrimage: The Sixties*, 277, 317, 308.

120. Roberts, 154, 158; Ellsberg, ed., 306, 301, 337; Day, *Loaves and Fishes*, 70; Day, *On Pilgrimage: The Sixties*, 97.

121. Miller, *Dorothy Day*, 352; Day, *Loaves and Fishes*, 190; Ellsberg, ed., 266-69.

122. Day, *Loaves and Fishes*, 161; Hennacy, 287.

123. Dorothy Day, "Where Are the Poor? They are in Prisons, Too" *The Catholic Worker* 22:1 (July-August 1955): 1, 8; Anonymous, "By Personal Protest" *The Catholic Worker* 23:1 (July-August 1956): 2; Anonymous, "C.W. Editors Arrested in Air Raid Drill" *The Catholic Worker* 23:1 (July-August 1956): 1, 8; Dorothy Day "On Pilgrimage" *The Catholic Worker* 24:1 (July-August 1957): 2-3; Ellsberg, ed., 179-80, 165-68; Day, *On Pilgrimage: The Sixties*, 316.

124. Maurin, 180; Ellsberg, ed., 335; Day, *On Pilgrimage: The Sixties*, 258.

125. Ellsberg, ed., 112, 341; Day, *On Pilgrimage: The Sixties*, 377.

126. Day, *From Union Square to Rome*, 26; Day, *Loaves and Fishes*, 123; Day, *Houses of Hospitality*, 74; Day, *On Pilgrimage*, 164; Day, *Therese*, v, 35, 175; Peers, 203; A. J. Muste, "Conscience Against the Atomic Bomb" *Fellowship* 11:12 (Dec. 1945): 208-9.

127. Ellsberg, ed., 95, 110; Day, *Loaves and Fishes*, 79-80; Miller, ed., *All is Grace*, 4, 67, 114; Coles, 112.

128. Day, *From Union Square to Rome*, passim; Day, *On Pilgrimage*, 18, 39, 164; Ellsberg, ed., 159, 173, 175, 181; Day, *On Pilgrimage: The Sixties*, 68, 200.

129. Ellsberg, ed., 335, 339, 345.

130. Day, *On Pilgrimage: The Sixties*, 340, 260, 270, 273, 60, 258; Ellsberg, ed., 285; Miller, *Dorothy Day*, 431; Therese of Lisieux, 50.

131. Day, *Houses of Hospitality*, 236; Day, *On Pilgrimage*, 80; Day, *On Pilgrimage: The Sixties*, 361, 259.

132. Ellsberg, ed., 180; Day, *Houses of Hospitality*, 237; Day, *On Pilgrimage: The Sixties*, 258.

133. Ellsberg, ed., 104.

134. Day, *Houses of Hospitality*, 179.

135. Day, *The Long Loneliness*, 186, 181, 220; Day, *On Pilgrimage*, 161, 130; Ellsberg, ed., 145, 317; Piehl, 142, 242; Vishnewski, ed., *Meditations*, 71.

136. Vishnewski, ed., *Meditations*, 117; Ellsberg, ed., 105; Day, *Houses of Hospitality*, 77; Coles, 104.

137. Only late in life did she report that her political writings had been turned down by publishers; see Bill Moyers' Journal, "Still a Rebel," 1973; Piehl, 23, 214, 216, 230, 232; Ellsberg, ed., 105; Day, *On Pilgrimage*, 45-46; Day, *Loaves and Fishes*, 35.

138. Coles, 102; Ellsberg, ed., 339; Day, *On Pilgrimage: The Sixties*, 377.

139. Day, *On Pilgrimage*, 16, 41; 19. Miller, ed., *All is Grace*, 85, 98; Peers, 214; Ellsberg, ed., 286-87; Day, *On Pilgrimage*, 96.

140. Piehl, 73; Ellsberg, ed., 335; Coles, 109.

141. Day, *The Long Loneliness*, 185.

142. Coles, 93, 97; Miller, *Dorothy Day*, 283; Ellsberg, ed., 98, 354, 92, 99; Vishnewski, ed., *Meditations*, 93; Day, *Houses of Hospitality*, 268; Day, *Loaves and Fishes*, 169, 211; Miller, ed., *All is Grace*, 68;

143. Ellsberg, ed., 243; Coles, 134.

144. Jansenism was an ill-fated seventeenth- and eighteenth-century French movement whose moral rigorism bordered on pharisaic perfectionism. Miller, ed., *All is Grace*, 102; Ellsberg, ed., 105; Miller, *Dorothy Day*, 379; Vishnewski, ed., *Meditations*, 99; Coles, 101.

145. Ellsberg, ed., 101.

146. Ellsberg, ed., 262.

147. Piehl, 155-58, 196-97; Roberts, 133; James Finn, *Protest: Pacifism and Politics* (New York, 1967), 375.

148. Coles, 79.

149. Coles, 125, 129; Miller, ed., *All is Grace*, 63, 69-70; Ellis, *A Year at the Catholic Worker*, 80; Ellsberg, ed., 315-16; Day, *The Long Loneliness*, 80; Day, *On Pilgrimage*, 24, 27.

150. Ellsberg, ed. 78, 254, 336, 261; Day, *Houses of Hospitality*, 47, 109; Day, *Loaves and Fishes*, 88; Day, *The Long Loneliness*, 261.

151. Day, *On Pilgrimage*, 41; Day, *Loaves and Fishes*, 32; Day, *The Long Loneliness*, 194; Day, *Houses of Hospitality*, 75, 184.

152. Day, *Houses of Hospitality*, 266-67; Day, *The Long Loneliness*, 140; Day, *On Pilgrimage: The Sixties*, 81, 154.

153. Day, *Loaves and Fishes*, 87; Day, *On Pilgrimage*, 166; Vishnewski, ed., *Meditations*, 69; Day, *On Pilgrimage: The Sixties*, 16.

154. Day, *Houses of Hospitality*, 26; Ellsberg, ed., 294-95; Day, *On Pilgrimage: The Sixties*, 380.

155. Dorothy Day, "A. J.," *Commonweal* 86: 1, (March 24, 1967): 14.

156. Coles, 51, 66. He says she used it eleven times in his tapes; Ellsberg, ed., 300; Day, *The Long Loneliness*, 150; Day, *On Pilgrimage: The Sixties*, 71.

157. Hennacy, 142; Miller, *Dorothy Day*, 404-5; Herbert W. Rogers, "The Obedient but Angry Daughter of Holy Church" *America* 127:15 (Nov. 11. 197): 390.

158. Day, *On Pilgrimage: The Sixties*, 137.

159. Day, *From Union Square to Rome*, 155, 145; Day, *Loaves and Fishes*, 122, 118; Vishnewski, ed., *Meditations*, 89; Miller, ed., *All is Grace*, 83; Vishnewski, *Wings of the Dawn*, 44, 79; Day, *The Long Loneliness*, 136.

160. Ellsberg, ed., 348; Roberts, 92; Miller, ed., *All is Grace*, 185, 191, 176; Ellsberg, ed., 347.

161. Ellis, *Peter Maurin*, 129.

162. Day, *On Pilgrimage: The Sixties*, 289.

163. Day, *The Long Loneliness*, 144, 149; Day, *From Union Square to Rome*, 138; Ellsberg, ed., 34; Miller, *Dorothy Day*, 189.

164. Day, *From Union Square to Rome*, 1, 7-8, 15, 18, 19, 40, 88, 93, 138; Day, *Loaves and Fishes*, 12; Day, *The Long Loneliness*, 107, 143.

165. Day, *On Pilgrimage: The Sixties*, 19, 217.

166. Piehl, xi; Ellsberg, ed., 270.

167. Ellsberg, ed., 339, 82, 303, 311; Day, *From Union Square to Rome*, 38; Day, *The Long Loneliness*, 39, 285, 63; Coles, 59; Day, *On Pilgrimage: The Sixties*, 297.

168. Day, *Houses of Hospitality*, 90; Coles, 67-68, 76; Day, *On Pilgrimage: The Sixties*, 214; Ellsberg, ed., 99.

169. Day, *The Long Loneliness*, 223; Vishnewski, ed., *Meditations*, 84.

170. Ellsberg, ed., 145, 169, 170; Day, *Houses of Hospitality*, 155; Day, *The Long Loneliness*, 210.

171. Day, *The Long Loneliness*, 45; Day, *From Union Square to Rome*, 47; Day, *From Union Square to Rome*, 169; Coles, 82; Piehl, 92.

172. Day, *From Union Square to Rome*, 36, 40, 42, 81, 133; Miller, ed., *All is Grace*, 150; Ellsberg, ed., 78.

173. Coles, 59.

174. Ellsberg, ed., 339; Roberts, 26; Vishnewski, ed., *Meditations*, 90-91; Day, *On Pilgrimage: The Sixties*, 290.

175. Miller, ed., *All is Grace*, 148; Ellsberg, ed., 331; Day, *On Pilgrimage: The Sixties*, 250.

176. Day, *The Long Loneliness*, 150; Ellsberg, ed., 307, 301; Coles, 69; Day, *On Pilgrimage: The Sixties*, 101; Day, *Houses of Hospitality*, 184.

177. Coles, 58.

178. Coles, 77.

179. *The Book of Common Prayer*, 52-53; her citations of the Te Deum are in Day, *From Union Square to Rome*, 32, 122; Day, *The Long Loneliness*, 133; Day, *On Pilgrimage*, 2, 75; the words of Catherine of Siena are from Miller, ed., *All is Grace*, 100; Ellsberg, ed., 104, 250, 302; Day, *On Pilgrimage*, 17, 88, 97, 102; Day, *Therese*, 121; Day, *On Pilgrimage: The Sixties*, 77, 95, 124, 165, 308.

180. Miller, *Dorothy Day*, 181; Day, *The Long Loneliness*, 141, 133, 135, 132; Ellsberg, ed., 345; Day, *From Union Square to Rome*, 121-22, 127; Day, *On Pilgrimage*, 75.

181. Day, *The Long Loneliness*, 30-31, 40-42; Day, *From Union Square to Rome*, 37, 128; Day, *The Long Loneliness*, 136, 139.

182. Day, *The Long Loneliness*, 137.

183. Day, *On Pilgrimage: The Sixties*, 333, 52; Miller, ed., *All is Grace*, 62; Ellsberg, ed., 356, 361, 94; Day, *The Long Loneliness*, 29; Day, *Loaves and Fishes*, 198; Day, *Houses of Hospitality*, 212.

184. Day, *From Union Square to Rome*, 111, 10; Day, *The Long Loneliness*, 116, 134.

185. Day, *From Union Square to Rome*, 121-23; Day, *The Long Loneliness*, 133; Day, *Houses of Hospitality*, 204; Day, *Loaves and Fishes*, 57.

186. Day, *The Long Loneliness*, 285.

187. Day, *On Pilgrimage*, 116, 99, 162, 102, 2; Ellsberg, ed., 325, 250; Day, *Houses of Hospitality*, 2, 121; Day, *Loaves and Fishes*, 200.

188. Fyodor Dostoevsky, *The Brothers Karamazov* (Signet, n.d.), 62; Peers, 111; Day, *Therese*, 175; Miller, ed., *All is Grace*, 198; Day, *On Pilgrimage*, 22.

189. Teresa of Avila, *The Interior Castle* (Garden City, NY, 1961), 233; Day, *On Pilgrimage*, 116, 52; Day, *Houses of Hospitality*, 135; Ellsberg, ed., 287, 352; Day, *Loaves and Fishes*, 38; Day, *The Long Loneliness*, 225, 252; Julian of Norwich, 342.

190. Miller, ed., *All is Grace*, 14; Day, *The Long Loneliness*, 94; Coles, 62; Day, *From Union Square to Rome*, 89.

191. Day, *Therese*, 84, 130, 131; Ellsberg, ed., 273; Therese of Lisieux, 54, 102, 45, 64, 95, 147, 155, 156, 158.

192. Teresa of Avila, *The Life of Teresa of Jesus* (Garden City, NY, 1960) 274-75.

193. Ellsberg, ed., 183; Day, *From Union Square to Rome*, 11, 171-72; Day, *The Long Loneliness*, 250; Day, *On Pilgrimage*, 12.

194. Day, *On Pilgrimage*, 39; Vishnewski, ed., *Meditations*, 89; Day, *From Union Square to Rome*, 27, 151; Miller, ed., *All is Grace*, 97; Ellsberg, ed., 179; Day, *On Pilgrimage: The Sixties*, 200.

195. Vishnewski, ed., *Meditations*, 97; Miller, ed., *All is Grace*, 109.

196. Miller, *Dorothy Day*, 139; Day, *Houses of Hospitality*, 136; Vishnewski, ed., *Meditations*, 91; Coles, 50; Day, *From Union Square to Rome*, 127, 128; Day, *The Long Loneliness*, 137, 140.

197. Ellsberg, ed., 170; Day, *On Pilgrimage*, 50, 158; Day, *Therese*, 88; Day, *The Long Loneliness*, 239, 256.

198. Day, *The Long Loneliness*, 149; Day, *On Pilgrimage: The Sixties*, 304.

199. Miller, ed., *All is Grace*, 58, 69-70; Ellsberg, ed., 114; Day, *Therese*, 134.

200. Day, *On Pilgrimage*, 102; Miller, ed., *All is Grace*, 95; Ellsberg, ed., 301; Day, *On Pilgrimage*, 166; Forest, 116; Day, *On Pilgrimage: The Sixties*, 75.

201. Miller, ed., *All is Grace*, 128.

202. Day, *Therese*, 134; Day, *On Pilgrimage*, 156; Day, *On Pilgrimage: The Sixties*, 383; Coles, 61.

CHAPTER THREE
MARTIN LUTHER KING, JR.

Nothing in his life had prepared him for this moment. Growing up in a middle-class, Atlanta family had made Martin Luther King, Jr. a natural voice for the aspirations of the liberal, Southern black bourgeoisie. He believed in the ballot, in education, and in integration. He joined young W.E.B. DuBois in the post-Reconstruction dream that education and voting rights could deliver racial equality. King followed in the footsteps of his father and maternal grandfather who had worked with the NAACP when integration was considered dangerously radical.[1] Trained to preach or teach, he had used his verbal skills to dismantle Southern segregation and to articulate the hopes of the oppressed. But now he was in the North, in urban America, in Chicago.

The enemy was more slippery here, elusively disguising itself as an ally. Here racism wore masks. People knew they were oppressed, but the constellation of forces arrayed to casually press them down was murky, harder to identify. The black movement in Chicago had cloned itself into two clumsy offspring: the middle-class wanted to move into all-white neighborhoods; ghetto dwellers, who had no realistic chance of integrating a white neighborhood, wanted to improve their communities. Lineage, training, and experience had taught King to fight clearly defined segregation. He had not been prepared to battle poverty, subtle prejudice, and systemic injustice.

It was 1966. Negotiations between the city of Chicago and local African-American leaders were on the verge of breaking down. City administrators demanded that all demonstrations be stopped as a pre-condition to a final agreement. They wanted to trade a set of non-concessions for an end to the embarrassing conflict; beads for an island. In the negotiating room, black leaders spoke angrily. Outside in the streets, the atmosphere suggested yet another urban riot. Many blacks openly rebelled against their leaders' nonviolent tactics. Some were as angry with Martin Luther King as they were with Mayor Richard Daley. In the negotiating room, King responded to the city's proposals:

> I am tired of demonstrating. I am tired of the threat of death. I want to live. I don't want to be a martyr. And there are moments when I doubt if I am going to make it through. I am tired of getting hit, tired of being beaten, tired of going to jail. But the important thing is not how tired I am; the important thing is to get rid of the conditions that lead us to march. . . .

> We don't have much. We don't have much money. We don't really have much education, and we don't have much political power. We have only our bodies and you are asking us to give up the one thing that we have when you say, "don't march."[2]

The protesters' critics, he said, should equally condemn those pelting marchers with rocks and bottles and, above all, condemn the demeaning social conditions that produced the protests. The dialogue should continue so that the great city of Chicago could "be a greater city." At a mass meeting that night, King again expressed his feelings: "I'm tired of marching. . .I don't march because I like it, I march because I must."[3]

Eleven years before, when King first took part in a civil rights campaign in Montgomery, he said: "We are here this evening to say to those who have mistreated us so long that we are tired--tired of being segregated and humiliated; tired of being kicked about by the brutal feet of oppression."[4] Speaking to garbage workers in 1968 in Memphis, he stressed the same theme:

> You have assembled for more than thirty days now, to say, "We are tired. We are tired of being at the bottom. . . .We are tired of having to live in dilapidated, substandard housing. We are tired of working our hands off and laboring every day and not even making a wage adequate with the daily basic necessities of life. We are tired of our men being emasculated, so that our wives and daughters have to go out and work in the white ladies' kitchens."[5]

Physical exhaustion became King's frequent companion. He often spoke of being tired--for himself personally and for African-Americans collectively. He loved to quote the Montgomery woman who, during the bus boycott, said "My feets is tired, but my soul is rested." He preached about the Exodus from bondage, the Red Sea in which evil drowned, the mountaintop from which he had seen the Promised Land, but he rarely named the Wilderness where people were tired of walking without rest or relief, tired of unfulfilled promises, tired and frustrated and bitter.

In Chicago, King's feet were tired and his soul was not rested. In the civil rights movement's folklore he had become a black Moses, but the ironic similarities were overlooked: He had not been anxious to lead; and people turned easily against him. King confessed later that when he received his Ph.D. from Boston University and became the pastor at Montgomery's Dexter Avenue Baptist Church, he had no inkling of what was to come.

He felt "catapulted" into his role in the Southern Christian Leadership Conference (SCLC). Interviewed in 1964 after the announcement that he had won the Nobel Peace Prize, King said, "History has thrust me into this position." His friend Andrew Young said King was "pushed," "trapped," and "shamed" into the civil rights hierarchy; and only in 1963 did he finally accept that "he wasn't going to be able to escape." King did not find the movement; the movement found him. As James Baldwin observed, "Once he had accepted the place they had prepared for him, their struggle became absolutely indistinguishable from his own, and took over and controlled his life." He shared their exhaustion. He walked because they had to walk.[6]

The way of nonviolence also found King. In seminary and graduate school, he sought an intellectual synthesis for the optimistic Social Gospel of Walter Rauschenbusch and the pessimistic Crisis Realism of Reinhold Niebuhr. When A. J. Muste visited his seminary, King heatedly debated him, arguing that nonviolence was impractical. When first involved in the Montgomery bus boycott, King knew almost nothing about Gandhi. One of Muste's colleagues, Bayard Rustin, took a leave of absence from the Fellowship of Reconciliation to go to Montgomery and enroll King in an informal introduction to Gandhian thought. Rustin met an inexperienced pastor not yet committed to nonviolence: There were guards outside of King's house and a gun inside. King later admitted that only when he was refused a gun permit did he reconsider the advisability of owning a gun. In 1968 he wrote that he had been more afraid with a gun at home than without it. Rustin found an eager convert in King who soon observed that, while most revolutions combined hope and hate, Gandhi combined hope and love.[7]

Commentators divide King's campaigns and marches between successes and failures: Montgomery, success; Albany, failure; Birmingham, success; the March on Washington, success; Alabama voter registration, failure; St. Augustine, failure; Selma, success; Chicago, failure; the Meredith March, failure; speaking out against Vietnam, counterproductive but perhaps noble; plans for the Poor People's Campaign, a projected failure. His shift from racial injustice to economic problems marked a descent from success. His career has been divided geographically--South and North--as he reversed the direction and method of Sherman's March.

The birth of the SCLC in the sweet afterglow of the Montgomery boycott threw it into the political arena with other black groups. The most venerated organization, the National Association for the Advancement of Colored People (NAACP), was still basking in its greatest victory: the Supreme Court's 1954 decision to desegregate public schools. The momentum from that determination encouraged other civil rights efforts, and engulfed King. As the NAACP worked within the legal system, so the National Urban League worked within existing economic structures to help blacks enter the mainstream and get a piece of the American pie. The Congress of Racial Equality (CORE), godchild of the FOR, was oriented to direct action. Although most of its early work for integration took place in the North, CORE pioneered Freedom Rides in 1947 which inspired the more famous rides of 1960-61.[8] In 1960, with the blessing of the SCLC, the Student Nonviolent Coordinating Committee (SNCC) formed, began its grassroots work for Southern voter registration, and later gave rise to calls for Black Power.

King's bumpy ride from Montgomery to Memphis took place within the context of these jostling groups. The NAACP and the Urban League worked within the status quo to foster racial equality. SNCC, CORE, and the SCLC were more confrontational, yet they, too, clashed. CORE and the SCLC applied their direct actions tactics differently. SNCC worked for months in Southern communities to build up local organizations and social momentum until someone invited the more media-attractive SCLC which often waltzed away with credit for progress and funding for future projects.

King's personal life often crumbled under the intense pressure of his public career. Coretta Scott, whom he married while in graduate school, chafed at his chauvinism, and at being left to raise their four children while he was often away. Her promiscuous husband became intimate with long-term lovers and engaged in regular one-night stands. He said he felt guilty about being away from his children, yet he expressed no remorse for his infidelity. Perhaps because of his discomfort with being alone, he often stayed up much of the night with friends and co-workers. Unlike Gandhi, his prison sentences tormented him; he found solitary confinement almost unendurable.[9]

Ralph Abernathy served as his pastor, confidant, and "spiritual brother," but King needed more. Periodic hospitalizations for exhaustion were the only breaks in his torturous schedule. He took little time for spiritual renewal. Only in the hospital did he find enough time to read and think. A resolution made after his 1959 trip to India to follow Gandhi into a more meditative way of life bent under the pressure of his schedule. He feared losing his perspective and creativity, but seemed enslaved by his commitment to alleviate suffering.[10]

King knew he needed time for a retreat, and friends encouraged him to go to the monastery at Gethsemani, Kentucky to spend time with Merton, but other demands intruded. On the rare Tuesdays when he was not out of town, he tried to keep the day for reading, silence, and meditation. Imagining what he would do with a free week, he said he wanted spiritual refreshment, time to reflect "on the *meaning* of the movement," time gratuitously given to Merton and aggressively carved out by Day. Often drained physically, emotionally, and spiritually, King suffered manic swings in mood and spirit.[11]

Overworked and depressed, he considered changing vocations. Although he co-pastored Atlanta's Ebenezer Baptist Church with his father, the SCLC--with its speaking tours that made him complain he had degenerated into a fundraiser--

was his main work. At different times throughout his twelve year career he longed to remove himself from the public eye, to become a full-time pastor, or to return to "the world of ideas" at a seminary or a university. When awarded the Nobel Peace Prize, he spoke of "the temptation of wanting to retreat to a more quiet and serene life." He entertained the idea of teaching for a year at Union Theological Seminary or accepting a prominent New York pulpit. Yet he always backed away from concrete offers. When racial equality was realized, he thought, he could again become a pastor. As liberal alliances shattered in 1968, he was approached to run for president as the nominee of a third political party--an idea that never tempted him. He turned down an offer to receive $100,000 a year as a lecturer. Even when he took a one or two month leave of absence, he worked with ghostwriters to finish his books. He contemplated taking a year's sabbatical in Africa or Switzerland.[12]

When King's family visited the 1964 New York World's Fair, they were given VIP treatment. When his young son asked why they did not have to wait in line like everyone else, King felt embarrassed. He found privilege awkward; he wanted to be a man of the people. Even during the Depression, he had not felt poverty firsthand, yet he conversed easily with janitors, porters, and pool hall hustlers. As a young man, he liked fine suits. His attendance at Morehouse College was de rigueur for the Southern black bourgeoisie. His parents' pleasure with his graduation from Crozer Theological Seminary manifested itself in a new car.[13]

Coretta noted India's affect on his way of life:
Martin returned from India more devoted than ever to Gandhian ideals and simplicity of living. . . .He felt, as in India, that much of the corruption in our society stems from the desire to acquire material things--houses and land and cars.

It took a few years for the post-India Martin to yield to Coretta and buy a home--he found it ostentatious, others modest. Even though she asked that $20,000 of the

$54,000 Nobel Prize be put aside for their children's education, he gave it all to "the cause." Supporters established a fund for the children's schooling.[14]

King received a salary from Ebenezer, one dollar a year from the SCLC, and income from his speaking and writing. He directed all royalties from his writing to Morehouse College. His speaking engagements raised about $200,000 a year for the SCLC and supplemented his total income to about $10,000 a year. He considered a vow of poverty. At the start of the Chicago campaign in 1966, he moved his family into a small, inner-city apartment. The immediate negative change in their children's behavior, however, squelched the idea and the Kings moved the children back to Atlanta.[15]

King had sought solidarity with the poor. Like Day, he drew closer, but could never truly know destitution. To be destitute is to be violently stripped of identity and integrity as well as possessions, to be deprived of the freedom to take one's children out of a denigrating situation and depart at a convenient time. Francis of Assisi embraced voluntary poverty when he took off his clothing and handed over his privilege. There is no such pristine undressing for the destitute. Involuntary poverty bites into muscle and bone, fouls mind and spirit. King recoiled from voluntary poverty for the sake of his children--the opposite of Day's decision--and adopted Muste's more modest simplicity. And although he never shared the well-known holes in the soles of Muste's shoes, King understood with him the binding connection between possessions and oppression.

A turning point in King's career came in 1965 when the Watts Riots followed the Selma March. Selma climaxed the struggle for the legal integration of public bathrooms, public transportation, and the American political system; Watts represented the urban, economic crisis. A nightclub comedian had once joked that if those sitting-in at Greensboro lunch counters in 1960 had been served, some could not have paid, and after King's visit to Watts, he told Bayard Rustin, "I worked to get these people the right to eat hamburgers, and now I've got to do something. . .to help them get the money to buy [them]." Aware of poverty yet still looking through middle-class eyes, in 1965 he began--first in rhetoric, then in action--to address economic injustice.16

Now he pointed out the limitations of legal desegregation. True integration required massive government spending and political power for the disenfranchised. King wanted a Bill of Rights for the Disadvantaged. He wanted the U.S. to know that civil rights victories had been won mostly for middle-class African-Americans, that the Chicago campaign was a pilot project for the North, that the Memphis garbage workers' strike set the stage for the 1968 Poor People's March on Washington.17 The mountaintop experiences of 1963-65--Birmingham, Washington, the Nobel Prize, and Selma--had passed. Opposition mounted. Racists still called him "Martin Lucifer Coon." SNCC militants sarcastically referred to him as "De Lawd." White liberals had become impatient with what they perceived as black ingratitude. By opposing the war in Vietnam, King segregated himself from the Johnson administration, funding sources, and mainstream black leadership. As the Black Power movement began in earnest, more blacks renounced nonviolence as passe and naive. Others--black and white, left and right --agreed that time had passed King by. He had learned of the Nobel Prize while recuperating from exhaustion in the hospital, but there were no more mountaintops to relieve the frustrations of the Wilderness--the last three years of his life offered no honors or victories, only declining acclaim and developing despair.

Day always resisted the suggestion that she was a saint, an exception to be admired instead of an example--however flawed--to emulate. As King became posthumously a national and liberal hero, there began a process to turn him into a kind of African-American gentle-Jesus, to domesticate him into a house slave. Only the content of the SCLC's acceptable Southern campaigns is remembered.

The national folklore forgot his increasing militancy, his turn to economic issues, his expanding condemnations of the U.S. Liberals celebrate his hopes and victories, but overlook his anguish and defeats. As Muste has been ignored, so collective memory has chosen selective amnesia about King. Secular canonizations have pulled King's teeth, torn out his vocal cords, and buried his hopes.

A "Hopeful Imagination" [18]

"O, don't you want to go to that gospel feast
That promised land where all is peace."

>   --"Deep River"

"Shout the glad tiding o'er Egypt's dark sea
Jehovah has triumphed, his people are free."

>   --Freedman's Hymn

"Where there is no vision the people perish."

>   --Proverbs 29:18 (KJV)[19]

Throughout the Southern campaigns, King made distinctions: Obey a just law consistent with God's will; disobey an unjust law until it conformed to God's will. He had always distinguished between administration of the law and the principle of law, between Southern and federal courts. He had never before defied a federal judge.

In 1965, a federal judge ordered voting rights demonstrators to halt their attempts to march out of Selma. Attorney General Nicholas Katzenbach telephoned King to convince him to postpone the march. Struggling against inner uncertainty and political pressure, King responded: "Mr. Attorney General, you have not been a black man in America for three hundred years." The march would proceed.20

Every African-American bore the scars of three centuries of degradation. The sins visited upon their parents worked their weary way beneath their skin to steal away their consciousness of their rightful place before God and white neighbor. Not even sympathetic whites could understand.

Four years earlier, Attorney General Robert Kennedy phoned King to dissuade him from joining Freedom Riders, and to persuade him to influence a temporary halt in the Freedom Rides. A younger, more restrained King replied, "It's difficult to understand the position of oppressed people." The rides would continue.21

In between those confrontations, King responded to the insinuations of Southern moderates in his "Letter from Birmingham Jail." Like Kennedy, the moderates deemed the campaign in their city "ill-timed." King's jail cell gave him time for a fuller answer:

> I guess it is easy for those who have never felt the stinging darts of segregation to say, "Wait." But when you have seen vicious mobs lynch your mothers and fathers at will and drown your sisters and brothers at whim; when you have seen hate-filled policemen curse, kick, brutalize and even kill your black brothers and sisters with impunity; when you see the vast majority of your twenty million Negro brothers smothering in an airtight cage of poverty in the midst of an affluent society. . .then you will understand why we find it difficult to wait.22

The physical, psychological, and spiritual oppression had lasted 340 years. In effect, King told Attorneys General and white clergy: You do not understand because you are not black. Muste had noted the abyss dividing peoples who had been humiliated from those who had not, a chasm that separated a King from a Kennedy. In this division lay the explanation of *Why We Can't Wait.*

King's people were "born into want and deprivation," lived in the "basement" of Lyndon Johnson's Great Society, and sang slave songs because they were still in bondage. "The central quality in the Negro's life," he said, "is pain," and this "womb of intolerable conditions and unendurable situations" gave birth to a nonviolent revolution for racial equality.[23] Deprivation was fertile soil for imagining a future radically different from the present. King nurtured a "hopeful imagination" and enabled a "public processing of pain."[24]

In the African-American experience, religion had comforted generations of the oppressed: "By imagining their lives in the context of a different future they gained hope in the present." Many spirituals are marvelously ambiguous about whether their announced future will occur in heaven or on earth, and interpreters disagree whether Canaan alluded to heaven or to the North. Following the interpretation of his boyhood idol, Frederick Douglass, who said that Canaan was a code word for the North, King considered the spirituals' "heaven" a veiled reference to freedom in Canada. At times, black preachers have humorously chided each other for making heaven so attractive that they accelerate their congregation's mortality rate! The scholarly controversy about the this-worldly/other-worldly orientation of the spirituals temporarily recedes behind their "unvoiced longing toward a truer world." The same hunger for justice fueled both this- and other-worldly interpretations of the spirituals even among the slaves. Each interpretation, in its own way, announced the end of the unjust status quo.[25]

> Two generations before King, W.E.B. DuBois reflected:
> One ever feels his twoness--an American, a Negro; two souls, two thoughts, two unreconciled strivings; two warring ideals in one dark body, whose dogged strength alone keeps it from being torn asunder.[26]

In his later years, DuBois shed his American soul in favor of the African one, a move Malcolm X demanded as necessary to mental health, a divorce King never fully contemplated.

King offered hope by painting verbal murals of a future made implausible but necessary by current social conditions. In his "Letter from Birmingham Jail" and "I Have a Dream" speech, when what DuBois termed American and Negro souls cohabited peacefully within King, he allowed European-American, African-American, and personal dreams to mingle together.

To King, the nonviolent revolution--Montgomery bus strike, lunch counter sit-ins, Freedom Rides, Birmingham boycott, and Selma March--edged America toward fulfilling its dream.[27] In his Birmingham Jail letter he responded to Protestant, Catholic, and Jewish critics with the ideas of Paul Tillich and Reinhold Niebuhr, Augustine and Aquinas, and Martin Buber. He placed himself in the spiritual lineage of Socrates, Jesus, Paul, Amos, Abraham Lincoln, and Thomas Jefferson to show that the civil rights movement united the aspirations of Western Civilization and the calling of Christian faith.[28]

In 1965, King looked proleptically into the future:
After the March [from Selma] to Montgomery, there was a delay at the airport and several thousand demonstrators waited more than five hours, crowding together on the seats, the floors and the stairways of the terminal building. As I stood with them and saw white and Negro, nuns and priests, ministers and rabbis, labor organizers, lawyers, doctors, housemaids and shopworkers brimming with vitality and enjoying a rare comradeship, I knew I was seeing a microcosm of the mankind of the future in this moment.[29]

At a 1959 rally, he had glimpsed in his integrated audience "the face of the future." Marking the end of the Montgomery bus boycott by riding with a white minister (and member of the FOR), King may have felt that he was entering a new world.[30]

King's American dream promised equal opportunity, economic parity, and just distribution of privilege and property; a land without racial prejudice, a people living in mutual respect and in service to humanity.[31] Facing 250,000 people in front of the Lincoln Memorial in August 1963, King engineered white and black dreams to flow together in a confluence of hope. He identified his vision as "a dream deeply rooted in the American dream that one day this nation will rise up and live out the true meaning of its creed--we hold these truths to be self-evident, that all men are created equal." The end of racism would fulfill this dream. At the end of his speech, he juxtaposed two songs together: "My Country 'tis of Thee" and "Free at Last." The first provided the refrain for much of his remaining speech. "Let freedom ring," he said, from Stone Mountain of Georgia, Lookout Mountain of Tennessee, and "every hill and molehill of Mississippi." Let the American dream ring in the South. And when this patriotic song was given its deepest meaning, people could turn to a black spiritual and sing together, "Free at last, free at last; thank God Almighty, we are free at last."[32] "Free at last" gave historical perspective to the civil rights struggle as an extension of "the incomplete revolution of the Civil War." The movement shared its desire for freedom with ante-bellum slave revolts and contemporary Asian and African independence movements.[33]

Education and class separated King from many of his listeners, but the wounds of racism bound them together. Knowing that Southern blacks had to play an updated version of "puttin' on massa," he told a congregation, "The next time the white man asks you what you think of segregation, you tell him, Mr. Charlie, I think it's wrong and I wish you'd do something about it by nine o'clock tomorrow morning!" The congregation laughed and King smiled as they recognized the impossibility of such direct talk. Yet it is precisely the prophet's task to "construct poetic scenarios of alternative reality," and in imagining that kind of speech--and the end of masters--all together tasted the freedom they wanted and knew they would have.34

King's personal hopes integrated easily into the American dream because his class expected to enter society's mainstream on the wings of the NAACP and the Urban League. Remove segregation, inferior education, and disenfranchisement, and his vision at the Montgomery airport, he believed, would be fulfilled.

King's personal humiliations shaped his hopes. While in high school, in a moment he remembered as the angriest of his life, he and his teacher were forced to give their bus seats to white passengers. So the Montgomery bus boycott became an apt vehicle with which to remove shame from his future. The childhood experience, shared universally in the South, of having a white playmate abandon his friendship at a certain age, fed his "I Have a Dream" vision of children of different races playing together. When, in his "Letter from Birmingham Jail," he wrote, "You seek to explain to your six-year-old daughter why she can't go to the public amusement park that has just been advertised on television, and see tears welling up in her little eyes when she is told that Funtown is closed to colored children. . .," it was his daughter Yolanda asking about Funtown in Atlanta. The father of four shared with generations of black parents the frustration of trying to build self-respect in their children while society conspired to break it down.35

As the 1960s lunged into chaos, King began to speak of "deferred dreams." But his dreams had not been shelved as much as re-shaped by new perceptions. Idle industries and empty stomachs now stoked his vision as much as racial inequality. He dreamed of the death of colonialism, exploitation, and poverty. No longer did he look to other civil rights movers and shakers to bring change from the top down: "The deep rumbling of discontent that we hear today is the thunder of disinherited masses" moving toward their goal like "a tidal wave." In a sermon given the Sunday before his murder, he described the proposed Poor People's

Campaign in a previously unused, biblically militant metaphor. The poor were the "David of truth set out against the Goliath of injustice, the Goliath of neglect, the Goliath of refusing to deal with the problems." For the U.S. to become great, it would first be hit and slain by a stone from a moral slingshot.[36]

The story, of course, is full of suggestive possibilities. David has only one weapon; Goliath many. David wears so vulnerably little while Goliath's armor is weighed in shekels--literally in money. After Goliath intimidates all of the other Israelites, David still trusts that God will overcome his adversary (1 Sam 17). King's poor would no longer seek to convert the government Goliath by absorbing blows. Although barely equipped, they would defeat the wealthy and powerful with politically effective nonviolence. King had latched on to a primal story of "a much larger struggle of the marginal against the tyrants." He was engaging a people's hope that the marginal can overcome the powerful. Like David, he was promising victory before the battle, and basking in the biblical confidence that God casts down the mighty.[37]

King believed he shared with ante-bellum slaves a faith in the goodness and justice of God: "Our God is Able," he preached. The future, they believed, would be different from the present. As slaves in Gabriel's Rebellion in 1800 compared themselves to the Israelites, so King likened his people to the slaves God brought out of Egypt through the Red Sea to the Promised Land.[38] In the spirituals, DuBois found "a faith in the ultimate justice of things." The slave songs had an "obsession" for freedom, justice, and judgment. The experience of human suffering met a belief in God's power and justice and created a faith in change because a good and able God could not possibly maintain the status quo.[39]

King shared these assumptions: that God moved history toward justice, that the finite powers-that-be faced the infinite power of God. The "saddest thought" for Frederick Douglass was not that he was a slave, but that he might be a "slave for life." Hope was the alternative to horror at the thought that the status quo would never end; hope was a consequence of despair. And as dreams receded into the future, the complex relationship of faith and denial tempted King to claim premature political victory. Yet, as he knew, the real victory for African-Americans--a sense of dignity and destiny--had already been won.[40]

The spiritual dichotomy of present and future is far older than the African-American religious tradition, as ancient as Abraham and Sarah, as distant as bondage in Egypt and exile in Babylon, as old as the stirring words of Second Isaiah, as fresh as the parables of Jesus, as poignant as the visions of John of Patmos. The appropriation of that tradition worked uniquely well in King's words.

There was a crisis in the Birmingham campaign. The SCLC--which had pledged to bail people out of jail--was out of money. King had promised to get arrested, but the SCLC needed his fundraising skills. In Albany, the campaign's morale faltered when he failed to go to jail. Now, at a crucial meeting in a hotel room on Good Friday morning, he listened to all of the pros and cons. He left to be alone in his room, recalled the three hundred people in jail, and considered his community's expectations. And his mind leapt to a vision of twenty million black people "who dreamed that someday they might be able to cross the Red Sea of injustice and find their way to the promised land of integration and freedom." He would be arrested.[41]

King has been rightly criticized for his weaknesses as an organizer and administrator, for the failure of his actions to match his powerful rhetoric.[42] His gift was to give voice to pain and hope. His "poetic imagination" inspired social change by planting seeds in other people's hearts, for the act of imagining is, itself, subversive and redemptive. He appealed to old memories, biblical memories, slave memories, to jar people into discerning reality in a new way. As Day's voluntary poverty allowed her to name and unmask the powers of oppression, so King's privileged economic background may have prepared him for this, for those who work closely with the destitute might better articulate dreams because the poor themselves are in too much pain.[43] Yet at the same time, King seemed to recognize the counterfeit nature of pretending to be a voice for the voiceless, because someone with a voice cannot share the perspective of the voiceless. No one with power can speak for the powerless without distorting their message. No one with money can speak for the impoverished without imposing a money-colored perspective. No man can speak for a woman, no white for a black, no Kennedy for a King, no preacher with a Boston University Ph.D. for a non-literate Mississippi sharecropper or Chicago ghetto-dweller.

Richard Wright remembered working in the basement of a Chicago hospital where he assisted a doctor in slitting the vocal cords of dogs brought from the city pound for experiments. They cut the vocal cords so that the dog's howls would not disturb the hospital's patients. After their surgery, "when the dogs came to, they would lift their heads to the ceiling and gape in a soundless wail. The sight became lodged in my imagination as a symbol of silent suffering." The hospital also kept its four black employees in the basement

> as though we were close kin to the animals we tended, huddled
> together down in the underworld corridors of the hospital, separated
> by a vast psychological distance from the significant processes of
> the rest of the hospital--just as America had kept us locked in the
> dark underworld of American life for three hundred years.[44]

King described urban riots as "the language of the unheard." The rioters' rage was just another soundless wail that was not supposed to disturb domestic tranquillity. King struggled to give voice to the griefs and yearnings of the unheard while straining to understand their lives that so differed from his own. His vocation became that of a translator performing Muste's pentecostal task of bridging racial and economic boundaries. He tried to hear the penetrating insights in the cries of searing, blinding, and tongue-numbing pain and translate them for a comfortable, powerful audience. He was also like a pastor trying to discern his people's feelings more clearly than their deafening daily trauma allowed. He was like someone at the scene of a crime trying to speak for the victims. As James Baldwin said, King was "our *witness.*"45

God did not create King's hopeful imagination ex nihilo. His early preaching was highly theoretical and filled with Greek words; he had not yet shaken the dust of seminary and graduate school off of his feet. At that point in their respective careers, Ralph Abernathy interpreted the relevance of King's philosophical discourses "for tomorrow morning." Yet even then, King often created a dramatic tone in his sermons as he detailed problems elaborately before solving them. As in his "I Have a Dream" speech, he loved using rhetorical images of midnight and dawn to contrast the present with the future:

> Now is the time to rise from the dark and desolate valley of segregation to the sunlit path of racial justice; now is the time to lift our nation from the quicksands of racial injustice to the solid rock of brotherhood.

The image of a long night transformed into dawn made the transition from status quo to coming justice seem automatic.46

King was a bard singing songs to nonviolent warriors going to battle as he preached about crises to be resolved, midnights turning to dawn. But his middle-class upbringing had not prepared him to contend with naked evil, and his developing understanding of hope would depend on his discovery of evil's complexity. Long before James Earl Ray fired the shot that took his life, the powers of evil targeted his voice, his dreams, and his hope.

"The Kingdom of Evil"

"Power concedes nothing without a demand. It never did and it never will."

--Frederick Douglass.

"The Pharaohs are on both sides of the blood-red waters."

--Henry Highland Garnet (1843)[47]

King liked to trace his evolving understanding of collective evil to Reinhold Niebuhr. Until confronted by Niebuhr's thought, he had embraced liberal Protestantism which, in H. R. Niebuhr's classic critique, believed that "a God without wrath brought men without sin into a kingdom without judgment through the ministrations of Christ without a Cross."[48] King tried to fashion a Hegelian synthesis from Walter Rauschenbusch and Reinhold Niebuhr but, in truth, he stood closer to the former than he imagined.

Two of Rauschenbusch's books--*Christianity and the Social Crisis* (1907) and *A Theology for the Social Gospel* (1917)--chronicle his developing concern about evil. The first book ended with Muste-like mixed messages about human perfection.

> We know well that there is no perfection for man in this life: there is only growth toward perfection...We shall never have a perfect social life, yet we must seek it with faith...The kingdom of God is always but coming. . . .

> Perhaps these nineteen centuries of Christian influence have been a long preliminary stage of growth, and now the flower and fruit are almost here. If at this juncture we can rally sufficient religious faith and moral strength to snap the bonds of evil and turn the present unparalleled harmonious development of a true social life, the generations yet unborn will mark this as that great day of the Lord for which the ages waited. . . .[49]

In 1917, tempered by a World War and social decay, and caring less for results than for integrity, Rauschenbusch called Christians to battle for the Kingdom of God against "the Kingdom of Evil." "The bonds of evil" were not so easily snapped. The day that had seemed so tantalizingly close had drifted into an indefinite future.[50]

In spite of his self-diagnosed Niebuhrian streak, King tended to show all the symptoms of a typical Social Gospeller. He believed with them that ignorance as much as sin was the root of evil, the cause of American slavery and Christ's crucifixion. While sin is overcome by grace and faith, the solution to ignorant blindness is enlightened education. In such a theology, Christ saves less with his death than in being a revealer of truth.[51]

Although he denied it, King began his ministry with a belief in the inevitable progress of justice and a Mustean faith in a realizable eschatology. In speeches and sermons, he returned repeatedly to the same three citations: Thomas Carlyle: "No lie can live forever"; William Cullen Bryant: "Truth crushed to earth will rise again"; and James Russell Lowell: "Truth forever on the scaffold, wrong forever on the throne, yet that scaffold sways the future."[52] Even after his career began its publicly discerned descent, he told SCLC insiders that he looked forward to the day in the near future when they could say, "We have overcome." In *Where Do We Go From Here?*, a late effort, he wrote of a new world, for "when slaves unite, the Red Seas of history open and the Egypts of slavery crumble." Even "A Testament of Hope," the posthumously published late interview with King, ended with millennial suggestions of a burgeoning Christian era. In his Northern years, King said he had underestimated the power and complexity of evil in his Southern career. Now the movement's ultimate goal seemed to be "a receding point never to be reached."[53] Muste survived his disappointments by inaugurating new experiments. The weight of disillusionment pushed King downward into depression.

Necessity dictated that Muste create different strategies for different seasons: there were times to overcome and times to keep from being overcome. King was part of a visible, oppressed group trying to raise itself up. The powers of evil raged at him both as a leader and as an African-American. He had to discern how to overcome and not be overcome at the same instant.

King did not inherit his divided soul from Rauschenbusch and Niebuhr. Their spirits collided in the African-American tradition and within King before he ever knew of either one. He had to follow "Rauschenbusch"--and with him, Muste--because the Social Gospel expressed the spirituals' convictions that a just God would not tolerate an endless stream of human suffering. His oft-used quotations encapsulated the hopeful message arising from the agony of the oppressed. Yet King also had to follow "Niebuhr" because African-Americans experienced the intransigence of collective evil on a level about which the white theologian could only speculate. In the spirituals, blacks sang in their own words the message of Niebuhr, Muste, and Rauschenbusch, words of sorrow and hope. The two readings of the spirituals correspond to Muste's belief that God's grace can create a new earth, and Niebuhr's that pain can only be transcended in heaven. King could not create a Rauschenbusch-Niebuhr synthesis any more than he could resolve the tension between faith in a just God and the continuous existence of evil.

Successive SCLC campaigns forced King to wrestle with his inbred optimism. He often conflated sin with ignorance, evil with moral blindness. In describing economic conditions, he paired sets of terms--haves and have nots, privileged and underprivileged, oppressors and oppressed. A worldview of privileged haves and underprivileged have nots assumes that a social order has arisen naturally or by uncontrollable forces. It is a no-fault world in which some are more fortunate than others. The language that speaks of oppressors and oppressed--biblical language--assumes adversarial relationships in the world.

Through no accident of chance, providence, or historical determinism, one group actively keeps another group down. King used the terms interchangeably without any awareness of the difference between the two worldviews.[54] In his last collection of sermons, *The Trumpet of Conscience*, his rhetoric sounded Marxist as he wrote of the deprived, the dispossessed, and the exploited. Yet he again wrote of the "privileged."[55]

King called slums the handiwork of a vicious system created by white society, and said urban riots derived from the inner city's prison-like conditions. Yet his social critique reverted to bourgeois fatalism, and a laissez faire God--as though social decay dropped from heaven--when he described the Watts Riot as a "class revolt of the underprivileged against the privileged."[56]

Whether he learned the lesson from Reinhold Niebuhr or Frederick Douglass, King came to realize that the powers-that-be would not give up their position easily. In the Southern struggles, the federal government had often assisted the cause of civil rights. By 1967, he knew that blacks would have to "compel unwilling authorities to yield to the mandates of justice."[57] He considered using massive civil disobedience in the Poor People's Campaign. He had seen Goliath and knew that he needed a David to defeat injustice.

King had evolved between the 1963 and 1968 events in Washington. The text SNCC speaker John Lewis had prepared for his speech at the 1963 March made white religious and political leaders nervous. It used loaded words like "masses" and "revolution," took an antagonistic position toward the federal government, and said proposed civil rights legislation was "too little and too late." It questioned the integrity of political leaders who remained allied with the forces of exploitation, and bluntly asked, "Which side is the federal government on?" The oppressed, it said, could not count on Washington to bestow legislative blessings. People had to create sources of power outside existing structures. Lewis predicted that the masses could bring meaningful social change with a Sherman's March through the South to "burn Jim Crow to the ground--nonviolently." King joined a moderating chorus urging Lewis to tone down his language. For the sake of unity, the SNCC contingent compromised.[58]

In 1967 and 1968, as SNCC evolved toward Black Power and black moderates remained enamored of reformism, King echoed Lewis' original text. Now King wanted to know whose side the administration was on and spoke of the masses taking matters into their own hands. As early as 1963, King had used paramilitary language, describing the civil rights struggle as a "nonviolent army."

> We did not hesitate to call our movements an army. But it was a special kind of army, with no supplies but its sincerity, no uniform but its determination, no arsenal except its faith, no currency but its conscience. It was an army that would move but not maul. It was an army that would sing but not slay. It was an army to storm bastions of hatred, to lay siege to the fortress of segregation, to surround symbols of discrimination.[59]

Now he sounded the call for a David to overthrow Goliath--nonviolently.

With time, the SCLC became more sophisticated at measuring its opponents and gauging its tactics. In early campaigns, King identified the enemy as the "Satan of segregation," a natural target following the Supreme Court's 1954 rejection of separate-but-equal schools. He spoke confidently of a system that would die within ten years. But he also sensed that the battle would be more complex, for legal separatism had an "inseparable twin" named "discrimination." Later he saw segregation as a symptom of racism deeply rooted in the American psyche. After Chicago whites showered marchers with violence, King said, "I've been in many demonstrations all across the south, but I can say that I have never seen--even in Mississippi and Alabama--mobs as hostile and hate-filled as I've seen in Chicago." More worrisome than open violence, "deep prejudices...exist in hidden and subtle and covert disguises." Echoing the sentiments of free blacks in the ante-bellum

North, he said, "Egypt still exists in Chicago but the Pharaohs are more sophisticated and subtle." The South's glaring segregation had been "easier to get at." In Los Angeles, Chicago, and New York, mayors promised freedom but withheld the means to attain it. Racism was alive and well in the North.60

The Montgomery protest targeted buses, sit-ins lunch counters, Freedom Rides inter-state transportation, the Birmingham campaign specific businesses. The SCLC failed in Albany and Chicago because it did not attack evil one piece at a time. Confident with past successes, King called for the desegregation of all of Albany's public facilities--lunch counters, libraries, bowling alleys, movie theaters, and parks. Months of protests forced only the integration of the public library, but authorities had its chairs removed to prevent interracial seating. After Albany, the SCLC decided to specify its targets. Its "Birmingham Manifesto" contained broader demands than in Albany, but in Birmingham the SCLC bypassed city officials by targeting downtown businesses. The SCLC made almost the same demands in St. Augustine, but failed to muster economic pressure before the white community overwhelmed it in torrential violence. In Chicago, the SCLC tried to serve two constituencies, battling both "the violence of segregation" and "the violence of poverty." Arriving in Chicago, King pinpointed the campaign's primary goal as "the unconditional surrender of forces" maintaining slums. But some local leaders wanted educational reforms; others integrated housing in middle-class neighborhoods. Imitating Martin Luther, the Reformer's black namesake pasted his own ninety-five theses at Chicago's City Hall. A document for everybody, the broad list of demands dissipated the movement's energy, and the SCLC habitually drifted into the old familiar battleground of integration to salvage a small victory in a large conflict. Instead of improving living conditions for the many stuck in the inner city, the SCLC paved the way for the few who could afford to flee into surrounding white neighborhoods.61

From 1955-65, King preached racial integration as the fulfillment of the American dream. In Montgomery, in 1957, he announced that integrated schools would deliver "full equality" for blacks; at the Lincoln Memorial that year, he repeated the refrain, "Give us the ballot" to transform the South.[62]

The South had obvious demons, and King had provincially assumed that the race problem was geographically bound. He discovered that the ballot had no magic, that legislation which helped in the South did nothing in the North. Urban riots gave him a new way of interpreting the U.S. and imagining social progress. Laws declared rights but could not deliver them. Legal equality alone could not solve America's problems as long as poverty and the war in Vietnam persisted. It was easier to integrate buses and lunch counters than to transform slums. The civil rights movement, he admitted, had always been too middle-class.[63]

King liked to group evils as "twins" or "triplets" to underscore an interlocking quality of corruption. He associated racial and economic injustice; racism, materialism, and militarism; and racism, economic exploitation, and war. Identifying evils was a first step toward change. Observing social tragedies held in a "web" of injustice helped him to see the difficulty of combating any single target alone.[64]

He personified evil in his sermon "The Death of Evil Upon the Seashore" in a way that equated the death of Egyptians at the Red Sea with the death of evil. This allegorization let him explain his faith in God's ultimate triumph. He often portrayed evil as an octopus or a monster: in the same sermon, he spoke of the "prehensile tentacles" of evil. As Muste reminded war resisters to work for justice and social reformers to seek peace, so King identified racism and poverty as two tentacles of evil; neither could be defeated until both were attacked.[65]

The most feared disease of his time was cancer, and King often invoked images of disease to describe evil. He adopted a popular 1960s practice--and followed in the footsteps of the Social Gospel--when he used the metaphor of the U.S. as a "sick society," "infected" with racism, a "sickness unto death." President Eisenhower had tried to remove racial injustice with a pair of tweezers instead of a surgeon's knife. President Kennedy's assassination was part of a "contagion," "a plague afflicting the South." The war in Vietnam was "a symptom of a far deeper malady within the American spirit." King called hatred, egotism, sin and unemployment cancers, and spoke of the "disease of fear," "the cataracts of sin," and "the virus of pride."[66]

By applying health terminology to the body politic and appealing to primal fears of unpredictable contagion, King tried to create a consensus against social evils. His language sent an ominous message about the nation's health. In speaking of cancer, he gave the impression that only a concerted effort could defeat evil.

The whole analogy of sickness and health was part of his theology of redemption. King's faith in a just God and his era's confidence that the medical profession would progressively control illness combined in a belief that society could be healed. He used the same general approach in Chicago as he had in Birmingham. Expose the evil; destroy the cancer. Chicago's civic leadership, like Birmingham's religious leadership, blamed the doctor for the diagnosis. Condemning the demonstrators was easier than addressing the problems. King insisted that Chicago's cancer was "curable." Demonstrations opened infected areas to healing like bringing a boil to the surface to lance it. Medical science had leapt forward to relegate several illnesses to history books. So King hoped that the civil rights movement could X-ray society, reveal the full extent of racism, and surgically extract it.[67]

In philosophical moments, King reflected that God allowed evil; in passionate moments, he rebelled against every form of evil and equated poverty

with cannibalism. He acknowledged, "Evil is stark, grim, and colossally real."[68]
He became more sophisticated in his analysis of evil; but all the while, the weight of
evil pressed almost unbearably on him. There always seemed to be more of it than
he first recognized. One surgery was not enough; nor were several. Each time he
looked, the diseases seemed more life-threatening for the U.S. and for himself.

Like Merton, King was aware of a war within himself. He did not share
Day's daily ritual of combing her soul for sins nor did he imitate Muste's detailed
self-examinations. Yet, like them, he recognized his need for an inner revolution
against evil. He called his internal battle a "civil war,"[69] a pregnant image for an
African-American; for in the Civil War, one force enslaved, another liberated.

King used conflicting interpretations of time and providence. The spirituals
sang his creed: Something in the make-up of the universe made the coming of
justice inevitable. Yet, he also insisted time did not heal all wounds; it was either
neutral or favored the status quo. He made no effort to synthesize the two
propositions; each served its own purpose. The oppressed could trust that time was
on their side; those demanding patience from the oppressed could not count on time
alone to end injustice.

At the moment the Montgomery bus boycott faced defeat, a Supreme Court
decision forbade segregated seating on public transportation, and King exclaimed,
"The universe is on the side of justice." Looking back at the Selma March that led
to the Voting Rights Bill, he wrote that Selma's sheriff had "stumbled against the
future." Along with his favorite litany of Carlyle, Bryant, and Lowell, he repeated
that "the arc of the moral universe, although long, bends toward justice." He
repeatedly reaffirmed his faith: "There is something in the very structure of the
cosmos that will ultimately bring about fulfillment and the triumph of that which is
right." He believed, with Muste, that universal moral laws favored the struggle for
justice.[70] His hopes stirred other hearts for, as Baldwin noted, King and the

movement had become one flesh. When he addressed the movement's lack of faith, hope, or love, he whispered inwardly to his own fears, frustrations, and desolation.[71]

King promised "there *will* be a victory" over evil. Evil could succeed temporarily, but it always contained within itself the seeds of its own destruction. He pronounced colonialism and imperialism dead; Asian and African independence movements and the civil rights movement were part of "Providence"; "the Negro's forward march can no longer be stopped"; the elimination of poverty was a practical possibility: "I believe in the future because I believe in God." His frustrations in the North merely dented his hope.[72] In his last book, *Where Do We Go From Here?*, he allowed that "in any social revolution there are times when the tail winds of triumph and fulfillment favor us, and other times when strong head winds of disappointment and setbacks beat against us relentlessly." His revised judgment revealed that "the line of progress is never straight"; it "encounters obstacles and the path bends." There were inevitable delays and detours. The movement had to treasure even the small victories that did not deliver the final, great day.[73]

Conversely, when anyone urged the movement to wait or hinted that protesters would best get to their destination by slowing down, King called time neutral. Both early in his career and late in his life, he argued that social progress was not automatic. He supported the hopes of the oppressed but disdained the disingenuous patience of those who could afford to wait. Those who said "Wait!" did not care whether social change ever came.[74]

James Baldwin wrote that King "had looked on evil a long, hard, lonely time," and after Chicago King wrote that the movement--stunned by the depth of evil--had "entered a time of temptation to despair." The civil rights neophyte in Montgomery had only begun to experience such temptations. By the mid-1960s he had revised his premature predictions of "the death of evil." The twins and triplets had multiplied into legions. He uncovered diseases, but found few cures; and the diseases, not content to await their demise, came after him.[75]

In 1963 and again in 1966, King saw African-Americans living "on a lonely island of poverty in the midst of a vast ocean of material prosperity." But in 1967, he asserted that developed nations "cannot remain secure islands of prosperity in a seething sea of poverty." Vast suburbs did not surround a pocket of inner city despair like an ocean around an island; the majority of the world encompassed a small, white minority. King now saw the U.S. in the context of the world, prosperity in the context of poverty, hope in relationship to evil.[76]

The Kingdom of Evil was not a last pocket of resistance pitted against the overwhelming power of God, a tiny island in trepidation of an imminent tidal wave. Evil was not a Southern problem. It was a symptom of a virus infecting the nation and seeking to poison the spirit of the one diagnosing it.

When There is No Dawn

"Weeping may linger for the night,
but joy comes with the morning."

> --Psalm 30:5

"How long, O Lord? Will you forget me forever?
How long will you hide your face from me?
How long must I bear pain in my soul,
and have sorrow in my heart all day long?"

> --Psalm 13:1-2

"Great God dost thou from heav'n above
View all mankind with equal love?
Why dost thou hide thy face from slaves,

Confin'd by fate to serve the knaves?
When will Jehovah hear our cries,
When will the sons of freedom rise,
When will for us a Moses stand,
And free us from a Pharaoh's land."

--"The Negro's Complaint," Thomas Cooper (c. 1775-c. 1811).

"My brudder, how long
My brudder, how long
My brudder, how long
'Fore we done sufferin' here?
It won't be long
It won't be long
It won't be long
'Fore de Lord will call us home."

--"We'll Soon Be Free"[77]

Demonstrations in Selma evoked two powerful speeches. Calling the bloodshed "an American tragedy," two murders and hundreds of bloody beatings led President Lyndon Johnson to announce that he was presenting a Voting Rights Bill to Congress. In making his case to the nation, he repeatedly used the movement's invocation: "We shall overcome." As King watched the televised speech with co-workers in the living room of recently slain Jimmie Lee Jackson, tears welled up in his eyes as he was overcome with emotion. Johnson's speech was the most powerful endorsement the White House ever gave the civil rights movement. Midnight seemed ready to give way to dawn.[78]

At the end of the triumphant march from Selma to Montgomery, King stood on the state capital's steps just two blocks from the church parsonage where he had lived ten years before during the bus boycott. He told the crowd of 25,000 that, as they marched against segregated housing, schools, and ballot boxes, segregation lay on its deathbed and the American dream neared realization. Even so, he allowed that, in 1965, the South would still experience "a season of suffering." Then he discerned a question in the crowd's heart and answered it with a refrain from an 1865 spiritual sung as Union troops liberated slaves:

> I know you are asking today, "How long will it take?" I come to say to you this afternoon however difficult the moment, however frustrating the hour, it will not be long, because truth pressed to earth will rise again.
>
> How long? Not long, because no lie can live forever.
>
> How long? Not long, because you still reap what you sow.
>
> How long? Not long. Because the arc of the moral universe is long but it bends toward justice.
>
> How long? Not long, 'cause mine eyes have seen the glory of the coming of the Lord, trampling out the vintage where the grapes of wrath are stored. He has loosed the fateful lightning of his terrible swift sword. His truth is marching on.
>
> He has sounded forth the trumpets that shall never call retreat. He is lifting up the hearts of man before His judgment seat. Oh, be swift, my soul, to answer Him. Be jubilant, my feet. Our God is marching on.[79]

Rarely do words converge with an event in a perfect marriage of human imagination and historical moment. He had used the theme before in Albany: The approaching freedom of 1865 coming on horseback and with cannon had almost arrived in 1965 beneath the marching feet of the children and grandchildren of slaves.

That night members of the Ku Klux Klan shot and killed Viola Gregg Liuzzo, a white volunteer from Detroit, and the "season of suffering" continued.[80]

Hope was both a political strategy and a spiritual necessity. The promise of victory had to be repeated to convince a people accustomed to bottomless defeat that their actions could change their lives, their communities, their nation. The "How long? Not long" litany had been built on the foundations of African-American religion, the faith of oppressed slaves and sharecroppers. The sufferers could easily have asked "Why?" "Why" seeks an explanation. "How long" seeks action. Slaves asked "how long" because they trusted in the goodness, justice, and power of God to deliver them from their present condition. Confidence in the radical disjunction of present and future left room for only one question, the question of timing. And, as in the Psalms, the question can also be a taunt against God: Are you deaf? Listen! Are you asleep? Wake up! King's "how long," born out of years of trial on the edge of freedom, was spiritual cousin to Muste's "when" borrowed from Stephen Spender on the edge of war.

The words spoken from the steps of the capital building culminated the Southern civil rights struggle. King pronounced segregation dead on the eve of the Watts Riot. One season of suffering had almost ended; another was already under way.

King had referred to his dream before the March on Washington in 1963. After Selma and a few Northern failures, he looked back at that speech as a light at the beginning of a gloomy, endless tunnel.

I must confess to you today that not long after talking about that dream I started seeing it turn into a nightmare. I remember the first time I saw that dream turn into a nightmare, just a few weeks after I had talked about it. It was when four beautiful, unoffending, innocent Negro girls were murdered in a church in Birmingham, Alabama. I watched that dream turn into a nightmare as I moved through the ghettos of the nation and saw my black brothers and sisters perishing on a lonely island of poverty in the midst of a vast ocean of material prosperity, and saw the nation doing nothing to grapple with the Negroes' problem of poverty. I saw that dream turn into a nightmare as I watched my black brothers and sisters in the midst of anger and understandable outrage, in the midst of their hurt, in the midst of their disappointment, turn to misguided riots to try to solve that problem. I saw that dream turn into a nightmare as I watched the war in Vietnam escalating, and as I saw so-called military advisers, 16,000 strong, turn into fighting soldiers until today over 500,000 American boys are fighting on Asian soil.[81]

King reassessed his hopes. He remembered his own earlier sermon that spoke of nearing a destination without reaching it, of the Kingdom of God breaking in sporadically. His re-molded dream included the deeper issues he had discovered in his parallel journeys North and into the Kingdom of Evil. In the context of the parable of the powerless widow and the powerful judge (a variation on David and Goliath), King reiterated his earlier words, "Our determined refusal not to be stopped will eventually open the door to fulfillment" (Lk 18:2-5). Hope had come to mean that blacks would not be stopped by white indifference. Asked when the U.S. would finally be integrated, he replied: By the end of the twentieth century.[82] King and Muste were both confident that God would make their vision a reality, but King came to believe that it would take longer than he had first thought.

Because his were not the only hopes to be deflated, King's public image was severely wounded. Members of the Black Power movement in Chicago booed him at a mass meeting. At first feeling his work and sacrifices unappreciated, and himself betrayed, he realized that his own promises of quick change had caused the disappointment. They rejected his hopes as false: if "not long" was wrong, perhaps it would be not-at-all.[83]

King found the roots of his optimism in his protected childhood, the roots of his pessimism in his experiences of racism. His self-confessed "unwarranted optimism" made him despondent when early negotiations in the Montgomery bus boycott collapsed. The ensuing years separated hope from optimism like wheat from chaff. He tried to accept "finite disappointment" while clinging to "infinite hope."[84] Perhaps his faith had depended too much on signs and wonders.

At the turn of the century, DuBois described the faces of two Southern African-Americans as the extremes of the black problem: "Careless ignorance and laziness here, fierce hate and vindictiveness there." Sixty years later, the same two attitudes prevailed everywhere. King considered hope the only alternative to urban rage and dismissed advocacy of violence as a sign of despair. He tried to empathize with the rioters' frustration, but he thought their actions futile. Impatient with the apathetic, he grieved for the hopeless. His own sense of hope had endured tribulations and been transfigured from simple optimism into "the final refusal to give up." King still saw hope opposing despair. Merton's understanding that the two almost merged together might have been closer to King's experience than King's own embattled comprehension could grasp. Just as King tried to speak for those made mute by their suffering, perhaps the activist's pain made it impossible for him to articulate his experience as clearly as the monk.[85]

The terrible intertwining of hope and evil in King's life placed him uncomfortably close to the most famous of innocent sufferers--Job. The Book of Job positions its uneasy protagonist between belief in an orderly cosmos and the experience of tragedy. Formerly an advocate of a moral order, Job's encounter with chaos contradicts and undermines his rigid faith even as his "comforters" besiege him with dogmatic affirmations: "Who that was innocent ever perished? Or where were the upright cut off? . . .Does God pervert justice? Or does the Almighty pervert the right?" (4:7, 8:3).

King's life did not proceed neatly from blessing to curse, nor from dogmatic assertions to a faith fitting experience. He never completely abandoned his convictions about the "predestined structure" of the universe, the "doctrine of the omnipotence of God," or the belief that "unarmed truth and unconditional love will have the final word in reality." But the "benign Intelligence" steering the universe toward love did not help him when his spirit fell from the mountaintop into the Wilderness.[86]

Biographer David Garrow pictures King in an existential abyss after 1965 because his political norms had disappeared. Northern blacks were less conversant in the religious language that propelled the civil rights movement; they had no commitment to nonviolence. White liberals believed that the battle was over; they were impatient for a return to normalcy. The federal government had swiftly passed over the war on poverty to the war in Vietnam. As it became increasingly harder to identify the movement's obstacles and goals, King slid into an emotional pit.

His advisers feared that the 1968 Poor People's Campaign would be another Albany or Chicago, a campaign without well-defined goals or a nonviolent consensus, a series of demonstrations without a nonviolent army. They wanted King to abort the campaign. He hoped that success in Memphis could change their minds.

King was experiencing what Day intuited as the activist's "dark night of the soul." The disappearance of familiar political terrain brought spiritual desolation. Having lost all consolations (the prizes and successes), seeing his ideas of spiritual cause and effect come to naught, having reasonable expectations of spiritual comforts destroyed, knowing that midnight might not give way to dawn he became anxious and depressed. Unlike the traditional contemplative in the "dark night" (and unlike Job), King could have removed himself from the agonizing chaos. Without a dawn, he groped forward in the darkness guided more by commitment than insight. Without the infrastructure of universal laws of progress or the consolations of spiritual grace, he entered more fully into the mysteries of risk and hope, evil and love. King's assassination led Merton to wonder, "Is the Christian message of love a pitiful delusion? Or must one just 'love' in an impossible situation?"[87] The unresolvable question pursued King in death even as it did in life.

God's righteousness and justice were the foundation of King's early beliefs (Ps 97:2). Job came to acknowledge the difference between living faith and static dogmatism. King knew only that "I can't lose hope. I can't lose hope because when you lose hope, you die." He was caught between hope rooted in experience and hope rooted in a structured universe that exists only at the eschaton. The orderly universe, like hope, was both a strategy and a necessity. In both personal and social chaos, King may have needed that universe in order to counter his people's fears and his own doubts. He may have been caught between experience and need. Job and his opponents quarreled within King. Struggling daily against hopelessness, he recalled that to be black was to "hope against hope."[88]

Both the story of Job and the experience of the "dark night" destroy all certainties and consolations, and replace them with a powerful direct experience of God. Like Job, King had a powerful experience of God's presence. Unlike Job, that experience came at the beginning of his public career. He would speak of it often, clinging to the memory as if holding on to the only real and lasting source of hope in the world.

God is With Us

"O thou great companion of our souls, do thou go with us today and comfort us by the sense of thy presence in the hours of spiritual isolation."

   --Walter Rauschenbusch

"My God is a rock in a weary land,
Shelter in a time of storm."

   --Spiritual

"Sometimes I feel discouraged
And think my work's in vain
But then the Holy Spirit
Revives my soul again.
There is a Balm in Gilead
To make the wounded whole,
There is a Balm in Gilead
To heal the sin-sick soul."

--"Balm in Gilead"[89]

Biographer David Garrow describes it as the most important night in King's life. At home in their Montgomery parsonage in 1956, Coretta had gone to sleep. When he answered the phone, someone barked a death threat that brought down the cumulative weight of danger on his shoulders. He sat in his kitchen not touching his cup of hot coffee. He had nothing left inside himself to strengthen and encourage others. He could not face the situation alone. Afraid, he prayed.

> At that moment I experienced the presence of the Divine as I had
> never experienced Him before. It seemed as though I could hear the
> quiet assurance of an inner voice saying: "Stand up for
> righteousness, stand up for truth; and God will be at your side
> forever." Almost at once my fears began to go.[90]

In sermons and books, King re-told the story with different details but the same point: "And lo I will be with you, even until the end of the world...I heard the voice of Jesus saying still to fight on. He promised never to leave me, never to leave me alone. . . ."[91] In his later speeches, the refrain "never alone" took the place of "free at last," marking a decisive shift from the expectation of a nearby Promised Land to a dull, persistent treading through an almost endless Wilderness.[92]

The "inner voice" King heard in his kitchen had much the same effect as Muste's "inner voice" in St. Sulpice Church twenty years before. Muste was groping with his disillusionment with the Left's moral corruption, King with his fears of reactionary violence. Each voice left its beneficiary with a sense of serenity, still at work at the center of the maelstrom, now renewed on his vocational path.

By interpreting the event solely as King's most significant experience of God's comfort, Garrow ignores the content of the inner voice's message to King and falls into the trap that has captured conventional piety's interpretation of God speaking quietly to Elijah as he hid in a cave (1 Kings 19:9f). The voice tells Elijah to leave his sanctuary and return to the place of ministry, vulnerability, and risk. King's inner voice told him to "stand up" and "fight on." With the comfort came more exposure to violence; with the anguish, the peace of God.

Later, being driven from the Montgomery city jail, King feared that he would be lynched, and again he prayed silently for strength. Once when the loneliness of prison broke him down, he cried, felt ashamed of himself, and asked God for the power to endure.[93] When his house was bombed, he credited this earlier night's inner voice for giving him the inner calm he needed to face splintered wood and shattered glass. In that kitchen God had become profoundly real to him. Thereafter, he often spoke of "cosmic companionship," "cosmic sustenance."[94]

Howard Thurman wrote that slaves latched onto the question, "Is there no balm in Gilead?" (Jer 8:22) and "straightened the question mark in Jeremiah's sentence into an exclamation point."[95] In his kitchen King learned that there *is* healing for the sorrowful, the discouraged, the doubtful. He had been nourished by the hopeful collective imagination of his people.

God did not comfort King because of a privileged, privatized relationship that set him apart from the rest of the movement. King experienced God's presence in and through the movement. On the lonesome road to justice, "God walks with us." God worked with the movement to struggle against evil and uphold its members' strength. In a phrase echoing Muste's new pentecost, King said that, by letting God "pour his triumphant, divine energy" into their souls, people could become God's instruments. God would lead them "out of a bewildering Egypt, through a bleak and desolate wilderness, toward a bright and glittering promised land." He trusted the woman who, on a dreary night in 1956, told him "God's gonna take care of you."[96]

King believed in a God both tough and tender, a God of justice and love, wrath and grace, a God with two arms: One representing justice, the other forgiveness. He valued God's power, but above all, God was a loving Father, "a Heart." God gave people second chances; God loved, cared, understood; God poured out soothing compassion on the helpless and the outcast. While Day held up the praxis of charity, each insignificant interaction, one's daily life and temperament as the stuff of God's judgment, King said: "God does not judge us by the separate incidents or the separate mistakes that we make, but by the total bent of our lives." King wanted to be judged, not for his peccadilloes, but according to the main direction of his life.[97]

Like Day, Muste, and Merton, King found political ramifications in common Christian convictions. King's adopted Personalist philosophy was congenial with his Christian view that people are created in God's image, and that personal human worth derives from being made in that image. If God is present in each person, then segregation, which deprives a person of worth, contradicts God's purpose. Philosophy and faith joined to make a political statement: each abuse of a black person violated a creature of infinite worth.[98]

To describe the common bond of humanity, Muste spoke of the Brotherhood of Man, Day of the Mystical Body of Christ, and King cited John Donne:

> No man is an island entire of itself; every man is a piece of a
> continent, a part of the main. . .any man's death diminishes me,

because I am involved in mankind, and therefore never send to know for whom the bell tolls; it tolls for thee.

All people, King insisted, are "children of God": "We are caught in an inescapable network of mutuality; tied in a single garment of destiny."[99]

Revelations of God's love and God's image made King commit himself to all people. When black separatists and Black Muslims questioned whether God really cared for the "white devil," King answered that God was not interested in freedom limited only to the black, brown, and yellow. The same faith, and experiences of God's presence, sustained him. Life without God, he said, was meaningless; faith in God could move one from despair to hope.[100] Paul told of praying fervently for an end to a traumatic experience. The pain remained even as God informed him, "My grace is sufficient" (2 Cor 12:9). King felt some of his prayers answered. He heard a voice saying, "Do not be afraid." On a terrifying night at the beginning of an oft-threatened public life, the presence of a loving God was sufficient.

Jesus: Teacher and Pattern

"When Jesus saw the crowds, he went up the mountain; and after he sat down, his disciples came to him. Then he began to speak, and taught them. . . ."

--Matthew 5:1-2

"We are not Christians because we profess Thy name and celebrate the ceremonies and idly reiterate the prayers of the church, but only in so far as we really comprehend and follow the Christ spirit...For the sake of righteousness and of our cause we must bow to persecution and reviling, and again and again turn the stricken cheek to the striker; and above all the cause of our neighbor must be to us dearer than our own cause. This is Christianity. God help us all to be Christians."

--W.E.B. DuBois

"If you love him why not serve him
If you love him why not serve him
If you love him why not serve him
Soldier of the Cross."

    --Spiritual[101]

The Commitment Card in the Birmingham demonstrations listed Ten Commandments for each marcher. The first said: "Meditate daily on the teachings and life of Jesus." The second reiterated the ultimate goal of reconciliation. The third read: "Walk and talk in the manner of love, for God is love." As a preacher to the civil rights movement, King constantly connected spiritual roots to daily actions. In making Jesus' life and teachings their top priorities, the SCLC's spirit walked with King's. As Maurin designed a Benedictine rule of life for Catholic Worker farming communes and Muste a spiritual discipline for FOR members, so King and the SCLC guided their movement with these commandments.[102]

In his public life, in both planned actions and unplanned reactions, King tried to show a consistent regard for Jesus' teachings. Two crises in Montgomery reveal the way Jesus' teachings touched him. He recalled that, hurrying to his bombed home to find his wife and daughter safe, he spoke from his porch to an angry crowd in a vengeful mood:

> Remember the words of Jesus: "He who lives by the sword will perish by the sword." I then urged them to leave peacefully. "We must love our white brothers," I said, "no matter what they do to us. We must make them know that we love them. Jesus still cries out in words that echo across the centuries: 'Love your enemies; bless them that curse you; pray for them that despitefully use you.'" This is what we must live by. . . .[103]

Whether these were King's actual words or simply the way he remembered them, he wanted Jesus' teachings to guide the movement.

Internal dissension racked the Montgomery Improvement Association when the recording secretary, Rev. U. J. Fields, publicly accused other MIA leaders of misusing funds for personal use. Called a "black Judas," Fields admitted to King that he had lied because of clashing egos, and they arranged to have Fields retract his accusation at a mass meeting. In introducing Fields, King spoke first of the weakness of human nature. Then he "spoke the words of Christ: 'Let him who is without sin cast the first stone.'" Finally he recited the Parable of the Prodigal Son and asked the audience if they were going to be like the unforgiving elder brother or the forgiving father.[104]

All preachers invoke Jesus' teachings, but King gave them special prominence. His Jesus was the teacher and example of the Social Gospel and liberal Protestantism, the Jesus heeded so literally by Muste and Day. Rarely did King refer to Jesus as "Lord," even more rarely as "Savior," unusual omissions in the African-American religious tradition. He said little of the crucifixion, less of the incarnation or the resurrection. Like Muste, he focused primarily on Jesus' life.

In his sermon, "Transformed Nonconformist," King quickly listed six situations in which Jesus' words offered moral guidance. Like Muste and Day, he considered love of enemies a "command." As they found a "manifesto" in the Sermon on the Mount, King found one in Jesus' quote from Isaiah:

> The Spirit of the Lord is upon me, because he has anointed me to preach the gospel to the poor; he has sent me to heal the brokenhearted, to preach deliverance to the captives, and recovering of sight to the blind, to set at liberty them that are bruised, to preach the acceptable year of the Lord (Lk 4:18-19; Is 61:1-2).

King hoped that the criteria for his own judgment would be drawn from the Judgment of the Nations (Mt 25:31f). In the adolescence of his nonviolence in Montgomery, he wrote that Jesus provided the spirit for the movement and Gandhi the method, that Gandhi had applied Jesus' "love ethic" to social change.[105]

Love was at the heart of God and the core of Jesus' teachings. The Greek words with which he confounded his early congregation were often the three Greek words for love--*philia, eros,* and *agape.* Agape was God's other-regarding, other-serving love already residing in the human heart, a love that made no distinctions between friend and enemy. "Christian love," the regulating ideal behind all of Jesus' words, directed the movement. Unarmed love was the most powerful force in the world. If some found this idealistic, he insisted with Muste that Jesus was a "practical realist."[106]	When King paraphrased 1 Corinthians 13, he played Merton's role as spiritual director to activists.

> You may give your goods to feed the poor, you may bestow great gifts to charity, and you may tower high in philanthropy, but if you have not love, your charity means nothing. You may give your body to be burned, and die the death of a martyr, and your spilled blood may be a symbol of honour for generations yet unborn, and thousands may praise you as one of history's supreme heroes; but even so, if you have not love, your blood is spilled in vain.[107]

In guiding others, King used words resonant with meaning for his own eulogy.

For King, love was less a response to grace than a demand born of God's love for others, less a form of thanksgiving than a way to become a child of God (Mt 5:9). People were "potential sons of God" who, when they loved their enemies, knew God and shared God's holiness. Through the Christian "imperative," the "law of love," one became intimate with God.[108]

Christ "came to this world to show us the way," and God helped one "live in line with that high calling, that great destiny." King stood in the tradition of the black preacher Richard Allen who, in 1794, in telling his people to love their enemies, called Jesus "the great pattern of humanity."[109] King also stood in the line of liberal Protestantism and the Social Gospel which raised the Christian's emulation of Christ to the central tenet of its faith.

In a society that demanded compliance and branded King an "extremist," King's Jesus was "the world's most dedicated nonconformist" and a radical. "Conformity and respectability" could not be reconciled with the way of Christ.110 In a society that used the norms of psychology as social control to pressure those who challenged its conception of reality, King's Jesus was "maladjusted." King bracketed his list of extremists--Amos, Paul, John Bunyan, Thomas Jefferson, Abraham Lincoln--with Jesus, who went to extremes to proclaim love, who was crucified between extremists for immorality, and whom he called "an extremist for love."111

Moral people had to be "maladjusted" and "extremists." Jesus' example prohibited King from accepting discrimination, mob rule, violence, militarism, economic injustice, and religious bigotry. Christians had to be "dissatisfied" with the social order. The salvation of civilization depended on the maladjusted.112

In his 1968 sermon, "The Drum Major Instinct," King described Jesus:
He was thirty-three when the tide of public opinion turned against him. They called him a rabble-rouser. They called him a troublemaker. They said he was an agitator. He practiced civil disobedience; he broke injunctions. And so he was turned over to his enemies, and went through the mockery of a trial.113

As King moved purposefully away from respectability and was increasingly vilified, he found his life running parallel with Jesus' life, and he re-interpreted Jesus as a civil rights radical.

The spiritual genealogy of Muste's heroes differed from King's, yet both warned against conformity. King's words about maladjustment also hint at Merton's criticism of the concept of "sanity" in a violent society. While Merton addressed the issue's shadow side by describing amoral sanity, King promoted the positive value of nonconformist renunciation.

King evaluated churches--white and black--according to their fidelity to Christ's teachings and their actions toward the civil rights movement. Jesus laid an "imperative demand" on Christians to live differently from others. In a page torn out of Muste's ecclesiology, King wanted the churches to nurture the "creative maladjustment" of "transformed nonconformists" who could redeem the world.[114]

King had a gloomy view of Church history. Seduced by wealth and position, the Church after Constantine had diluted the demands of the Gospel. Overly enamored of heaven, it had sanctioned slavery, segregation, exploitation, and war, and fulfilled Marx's critique by becoming an opiate of the people. Sixteenth-century reformers, pessimistic about human nature, had convinced Christians to wait passively for God to change the world. The Church in the U.S. had become like the Russian Church prior to the 1917 Revolution, a force against social change. With typical Protestant sentimentality, King exalted the Early Church as a model for regeneration and urged his contemporaries to recapture their spirit. Early Christians were "nonconformists" molded by the demands of the Gospel. They heard and lived the teachings of Jesus, and knew they were a "colony of heaven" on earth.[115]

King wanted the Church to be the "voice of moral and spiritual authority on earth," the conscience of the State, a source of hope and social action. Even before becoming involved in the bus boycott, his Montgomery church published a biweekly newsletter to inform church members about social and political issues, and emphasized voter registration and the NAACP. The Church should shape, not be shaped by, public opinion. It ought to be an anvil or a hammer. It ought to be a thermostat instead of a thermometer, a voice instead of an echo, a headlight instead of a taillight. It ought to obey God, not "man." Yet its people prostrated themselves before the false gods of nationalism and materialism; the Church

ignored cries for freedom in Africa and the American South and silently acquiesced
to the arms race.[116]

God's judgment hovered over the Church as never before. The Church had
become a social club. Preachers who should, like Amos and Jesus, decry injustice
acquired earthly possessions while preaching only about heaven. Black churches
soothed the poor with emotional release and the bourgeoisie with class divisions.
Black clergy were more concerned about the size of their cars than their service to
the community. Yet King's greatest disappointment came from most white,
Southern clergy who ignored or opposed the civil rights movement The Kingdom
of Evil had prospered within the Church's doors. The Church needed to
acknowledge its guilt and become a true servant. It would be judged according to
its obedience to Jesus and its work to "speed the day" of freedom.[117]

Following a long Protestant tradition, King found within the institutional
church an invisible saving remnant, the *ekklesia*, an "inner spiritual church," a
redemptive force that was the hope of the world. He uncovered hope in the black
churches that served justice, and compared their faithfulness to that of the
"Christians in the catacombs" who, like themselves, weathered persecutions.
When a bomb killed four girls in a Birmingham church, King found it significant
that the bomb also "blew the face of Jesus Christ from a stained-glass window." A
Church true to Jesus would surely share his sufferings.[118]

King counted on the Church as an instrument of social change and spiritual
grace. As Muste had the FOR, so King had a religious institution--the SCLC--to
call home. His discouragement with the Church never descended to Muste's mid-
life detour, nor did waves of ambivalence tempt him to distance himself from it as
did the senior Muste. In spite of his dissatisfaction which grew in the large gap
between Jesus' example and the Church's works, the Church remained King's
shelter. Even so, Jesus remained planted as a wild seed within otherwise carefully

tended buildings. Jesus was the Church's chief critic, its prophet calling his people to repent. He was the plumbline with which King measured the Church's fidelity.

King's understanding of the Cross both confirms and refutes H. R. Niebuhr's critique of liberal Protestantism. In King's Christology, Jesus saves by revealing God's will. King did not preach Christianity without a Cross, but the Cross he preached challenged each disciple to follow Jesus more than it praised Christ's sacrifice to reconcile God with the world. In King's life, the Cross did less to reveal God's unconditional love than to create new conditions for salvation.

One of the few teachings King did not take as seriously as Merton, Muste, or Day was Jesus' injunction to the rich young man to sell all he had and give it to the poor. Merton and Day took parallel vows of poverty. The IRS found nothing of Muste's to harvest. But King--following a middle-class interpretation--saw this story as specific spiritual counsel given to a particular person in unique circumstances. As Rauschenbusch noted, each Christian has a canon within a canon, specific words and stories that shape one's religious and social outlook, and King kept this passage safely outside of his personal, internal Bible. While Muste lived simply, and Day practiced voluntary poverty, King quibbled and went halfway--in Day's book--to detachment.

King's wife and colleagues remember him as a "guilt-ridden man." One of his favorite songs was "I Want to be More and More Like Jesus," a hymn of the heart leading to inevitable disappointment. He once said, "All who honor themselves with the claim of being 'Christians' *should* compare themselves to Jesus." Only by making incessant demands on himself, imitating Jesus, and loving his enemies did he believe he could become a child of God. "Christ's chief legacy to his disciples," he said, was a sense of inner peace in the midst of turmoil, yet Christ's legacy to King was to make the long race of faith seem endlessly uphill.[119]

Muste thought of God as "Demand." King attributed demands to the Second Person of the Trinity, an unusual trait in American piety, which tends to envision a distant Creator and a gentle Jesus. King split God's qualities between the two Persons: The Father was the love-giver, dispensing mercy and grace; Jesus the love-requirer, demanding justice and faith. King's Jesus--extremist, nonconformist, teacher and saint--drove him to a demanding form of righteousness as Jesus' words and example were always rolling back to the bottom of a mountain made huge in King's own Myth of Sisyphus.

A Conditional Covenant

"We hold these truths to be self-evident, that all men are created equal, that they are endowed by their Creator with certain inalienable rights, that among these are life, liberty, and the pursuit of happiness."

--Declaration of Independence

"We bake de bread,
Dey gib us de crust.
We sif de meal,
Dey gib us de huss.
We peel de meat,
Dey gib us de skin.
And dat's de way
Dey take us in."

--Slave Song

"Rich Man, Dives, lived so well,
When he died he found a home in hell."

--"Got A Home in That Rock"[120]

On a Sunday afternoon not long before President Johnson's speech brought tears to King's eyes, Alabama state troopers and local possemen cleared the Pettus Bridge of marchers trying to leave Selma for Montgomery. King's sweet tears contrasted with the marchers' burning tears as they fled gassed, beaten, panicked, and bloody, chased into Selma's streets by men on horseback. That night ABC interrupted its Sunday Night Movie to show graphic film of troopers pummeling marchers with nightsticks. ABC then resumed its showing of *Judgment at Nuremberg.*[121]

Sandwiched by the movie about the German people's failure to withstand Nazi race hatred, racial violence in Alabama received a new perspective. As much as Americans wanted to judge twentieth-century Western Civilization's version of evil incarnate, that judgment remained lodged like a camel in the eye of a needle. Germany was not the only nation to be indicted for racism. The judgment at Nuremberg had become a commentary on the U.S.

If Johnson's speech days later marked the pinnacle of White House cooperation with the civil rights movement, continuing FBI investigations into King's life marked the relationship's descent into tragic absurdity. With the ambivalent complicity of John and Robert Kennedy, J. Edgar Hoover probed King's connections with communists and, for lack of politically incriminating evidence, investigated King's extramarital encounters. In 1964, the FBI sent a tape recording of alleged infidelities to King's home and a note hinting that suicide was his only logical course of action. While the FBI scrutinized his political associations and private life, King conducted his own spiritual examination of the nation. Like Muste and Merton, King observed a national self-destructiveness that left it unknowingly on the verge of spiritual suicide.[122]

Any nation spending more on its military than on social welfare, King declared, was "approaching spiritual doom." If the U.S. discovered its soul poisoned, part of the autopsy would read "Vietnam." He pronounced it "fatal" to pursue "gradualism" in racial and social justice. In Mustean fashion, he gave the U.S. a choice between racial justice and "domestic suicide."[123]

For King as for the black liberal tradition, God judged the U.S. according to the way it lived up to its own creed as stated in the Declaration of Independence and the Constitution. Segregated from these inclusive ideals, Southern blacks viewed them as outsiders. King still believed in an American covenant; the U.S. would live up to its creed or perish.[124]

The Declaration of Independence, King contended, contained more intent than reality, for the Founding Fathers excluded slaves, women, and the property-less from voting. Since 1776, the U.S. had been "schizophrenic" about race: It proclaimed democracy, but practiced slavery, segregation, and injustice. In the midst of wealth, it relegated many to poverty. According to Matthew's story of the Judgment of the Nations, the U.S. would be found wanting.[125]

King's view of history was like that of the Old Testament Deuteronomic historian. The covenants with Moses and David dominated Israel's memory. The Davidic covenant promised unconditional love to his descendants: Any king who failed to obey God would be punished, "but I will not take my steadfast love from him" (2 Sam 7:15). In the Mosaic tradition, if Israel were unfaithful, God could break the stone-made covenant. The Deuteronomic historian interpreted Israel's history through the prism of the conditional Mosaic covenant: Because Israel and Judah had sinned, they were destroyed and exiled. King applied the same theo-history to every nation: "Over the bleached bones and jumbled residues of numerous civilizations are written the pathetic words: 'Too late.'" The same fate stared the U.S. in the face.[126]

King had spiritual antecedents in the Social Gospel movement and the African-American religious tradition. Black tradition enforced a conditional covenant on white America in the song of Dives and Lazarus, in preaching and writing, and in folk stories. In one story, a Jim Crow preacher told a black congregation that heaven would be segregated. After the sermon, an old black deacon, who was not allowed to preach, prayed that if they did not like blacks all over heaven, whites were free to go elsewhere. In another story, a master tells his slave of a nightmare in which the master was taken to "Nigger Heaven," a place where garbage lined muddy streets, and broken-down houses were crowded with dirty inhabitants. His slave replies that he had a parallel dream of visiting a white heaven where, inside the pearly gates, the streets were silver and gold, filled with milk and honey, "but dey wuzn't uh soul in de whole place." In a third story, a master tells his slave that--when they have both died--he will reward the slave by burying him in the same vault next to his master. The slave graciously demurs: he does not want the devil to grab *his* body by mistake.[127]

King invited his hearers to share this barely suppressed laughter that had been snapping spiritual chains for generations. When he kiddingly chided a Southern black congregation to tell their white employers to end segregation, he not only raised again the silent laughter at the pretensions of Pharaoh's power and white control, he also hinted that--to offer redemption--they had to make their secret laughter public.

Writing a generation before the Emancipation Proclamation, black writer David Walker warned white Americans more directly: "Unless you speedily alter your course, *you* and your *Country* are gone!!!!!!" A black preacher's sermon about 1900 contained a similar caveat:

> The individual race, or nation which does wrong, which sets at defiance God's great law, especially God's great law of love, of brotherhood, will be sure, sooner or later, to pay the penalty. We reap as we sow. With what measure we mete, it shall be measured to us again.[128]

Belief in Jesus' words and confidence in God's justice made the African-American religious tradition certain that those who practiced slavery and oppression could not escape judgment forever.

Many of King's admonitions paralleled forms of prophetic speech. The Hebrew prophets often emulated Israel's legal language with a series of accusations leading inevitably to a pronounced punishment: because you have turned against God and committed injustice, therefore you will be punished. Less frequently, the prophets used a Deuteronomic if/then form: if you turn away from God, you will be cursed; if you turn back to God, you will be blessed. King regularly employed this second form: If you act without compassion toward Vietnam you will be "dragged down shameful corridors" of history; if the race problem is not solved, you are on the road to self-destruction, but if it is solved, the American dream will be fulfilled; if the federal government does not provide hope for blacks, there will soon come the worst racial holocaust in the nation's history; if you do not obey God, God will break the backbone of your power; if you do not use your power to help the helpless, you are writing your own obituary. The oracles of the Hebrew prophets use a simple and awful arithmetic--actions have consequences. Rarely did King pronounce judgment or imply that it was "too late," but he urgently demanded repentance.129

King allegorized two parables to illustrate America's dilemma before God. In the Parable of the Rich Man and Lazarus (Lk 16:19ff.), he likened the rich man to the capitalist system. Like the rich man, capitalism had been indifferent to the gulf between rich and poor, unmoved by compassion for the needy at its doorstep. The rich man "went to hell because he allowed his brother to become invisible. . . And this can happen to America." These sentiments in King's last Sunday morning sermon may have carried over into the sermon he planned, but did not live to preach, the following week: "Why America May Go To Hell."130

In King's telling of the parable, Western Civilization and the U.S. played the role of the Prodigal Son. After they have misspent their treasures, God the loving Father calls to them.

> I can hear a voice crying out today saying to Western Civilization: "You have strayed away to the far country of colonialism and imperialism. You have trampled over one billion six hundred million of your colored brothers in Africa and Asia. But, O Western Civilization, if you will come to yourself, rise up, and come back home, I will take you in. . . ."[131]

> It seems that I can hear a voice saying to America: "You started out right. You wrote in your Declaration of Independence that 'all men are created equal and are endowed by their Creator with certain inalienable rights. Among these are life, liberty, and the pursuit of happiness.' But, America, you strayed away from that sublime principle. You left the house of your great heritage and strayed away into a far country of segregation and discrimination. You have trampled over sixteen million of your brothers. You have deprived them of the basic goods of life. You have taken from them their self-respect and their sense of dignity. You have treated them as if they were things rather than persons. . .If you will come to yourself and rise up and decide to come back home, I will take you in. . . ."

Unlike the father in Jesus' parable, King's God offered conditional, if/then promises. But it was not quite too late for the U.S. to return home and avoid "national suicide."[132]

Like Muste and Merton, King offered choices between chaos and community. And like Merton, he believed that there were moments or moods in history brimming with redemptive possibility which--if missed--quickly disappeared beneath a static status quo. Johnson's speech and King's tears only briefly narrowed the gap between administration and movement. In recounting the violence in Selma, Johnson mentioned the death of a Northern, white Unitarian minister and omitted the name of the young black Selma resident in whose home

King watched the speech. But God had not rendered a final sentence. Americans could still choose between dream or nightmare, to live together as family or perish together as fools. Redemptive moments like the Selma March could still save the U.S. from itself, but with the hour late and the clock of destiny ticking, "the time," King said, "is NOW."133

King's perspective had changed. When he first addressed a mass meeting in 1955 he called American democracy the "greatest form of government on earth." In his initial speech against the war in Vietnam in 1967, he called the American government "the greatest purveyor of violence in the world today." He had counted on the national conscience, a great, decent majority of white moderates and liberals. He found the ingenuous silence of Southern moderates more heartbreaking than the obstructionism of the White Citizen's Councils or the spasmodic fury of the Ku Klux Klan. He believed the hottest places in Dante's hell were reserved for neutrals.134 As the SCLC moved North, so did disillusionment. Northern whites had only consented to Southern reforms because they were disgusted by openly brutal racism. Offended by segregation's indecency, neither white moderates, white liberals, nor White House residents cared about racial equality. They preferred order to justice. King's early view of Southern white moderates became his later verdict on the federal government. The so-called "white backlash" of the mid-1960s was merely another expression of the norm of racism in American history, for the U.S. was unconsciously "enmeshed in evil."135

Like Merton, King used the classic figure of the Holocaust--Adolf Eichmann--to urge the U.S. to face its responsibility and complicity. He came close to a Mertonesque analysis of urban violence and American foreign policy when he said, "Riots are caused by nice, gentle, timid white moderates who are more concerned about order than justice" and "by a national administration more concerned about winning the war in Vietnam than the war against poverty right here at home."136 In the wake of the Detroit riots, King sent an angry telegram to President Johnson bemoaning Congress' failure to pass legislation to ease urban suffering:

> The suicidal and irrational acts which plague our streets daily are being sowed and watered by the irrational, irrelevant, and equally suicidal debate and delay in Congress. This is an example of moral degradation. This hypocrisy and confusion seeping through the fabric of society can ultimately destroy from within the very positive values of our nation which no enemy could destroy from without.137

As his understanding of the nation changed, he refined his view of how African-Americans might fit into white America. He had no reservations in 1955: America could become Canaan, the Promised Land of freedom. But, with time, he began to wonder if the U.S. was not more akin to Egypt or Babylon than to Zion.

In the black political spectrum, King's interpretation of the U.S. stood somewhere near the middle. The NAACP, Urban League, and CORE sought acceptance into the mainstream of a reformed American life. SNCC, Black Power advocates, Black Muslims, and black separatists believed white society to be inherently detrimental to black health. Initially, the SCLC had sought the reformist path, but King came to see blacks in America like Israelites in Babylon. He adopted Jeremiah's advice to the exiles: Seek the welfare of that city, for its welfare will be your own, but retain your own identity and cling to the only true God (29:4-7). The Black Moses realized that the Promised Land was also a place of paradox.

Social integration and exile remained unresolved in King's developing view of the African-Americans' place in America. Even as inner cities burned, he said that blacks should seek economic gratification and total integration into American life. In a presentation to the SCLC, he called for both a quick entrance into society's mainstream and for the restructuring of capitalist society, hoping perhaps that the two developments could reinforce each other. Blacks had to reject existing values, retain their identity in exile, become an oasis in a spiritual wasteland and, with creative dissent, guide the U.S. to a higher destiny. Paraphrasing Jesus' conversation with Nicodemus, King said to his country, "Your whole structure needs to be changed." The U.S. needed to be born again.138

King knew he would have trouble prodding middle-class blacks to seek more than simple integration. Moses had found it difficult to convince some slaves to leave Egypt; the exilic prophets had to persuade some Israelites that Jerusalem's hardships were better than Babylon's luxuries. The black bourgeoisie still sang slave songs because the work of the Emancipation Proclamation was incomplete. The early part of King's "I Have a Dream" speech could easily have been re-titled "Exile in His Own Land," a refrain he used to describe the status of African-Americans.139

His early confidence in the U.S. had not blinded King to the African-American's exile. Yet even as he more astutely discerned the evils intrinsic in American society, he clung to an ideal of integration, hoping against hope that Babylon could be transformed. He never entertained the "back to Africa" ideal of an earlier generation, or a separate North American black state favored by his militant comrades. In his way of life, he tried to avoid the temptation of becoming too comfortable in Babylon. His stabs at simplicity and financial risk coexisted with the accoutrements of fame and prestige. He maintained the freedom to wear overalls in Birmingham for arrest and formal attire in Oslo to receive the Nobel Prize.

If the U.S. slouched next to a plumbline of justice, if its covenant was conditional, if it urgently needed to repent, then blacks like King had to find a way to live in America that was different from the way whites had lived there for hundreds of years.

Saving Souls

"You may be a white man,
White as drifting snow
If your soul ain't been converted,
To Hell you're sure to go."

　　--Spiritual

"Why will you die, O house of Israel? For I have no pleasure in the death of anyone, says the Lord God. Turn, then, and live."

　　--Ezekiel 18:31b-32

"Righteousness and peace will kiss each other."
　　--Psalm 85:10 [140]

Chicago 1966. A march in Marquette Park. King planned to lead 600 marchers while over 1000 policemen kept white mobs at a safe distance. Moments after King stepped out of a car, a flying rock hit him in the head and knocked him to one knee. As aides surrounded their dazed leader to protect him, the white crowd kept raining rocks and bricks and bottles on them. Thirty of this day's marchers had been injured, but King was determined to walk again regardless of the danger: "I have to do this--to expose myself--to bring this hate into the open." [141] In the South, the midnight lynchings had to be revealed in broad daylight, the beating of children recorded on film; in the North, de facto segregation, like a quiet day in an all-white park, had to be exposed.

Chicago's civil authorities accused King and the civil rights movement of causing trouble. The old dialogue that had been heard in Montgomery, Albany, St. Augustine, Birmingham, and Selma, during Freedom Rides, at lunch counters, and on marches, was resumed. All that had changed was the accent. At issue was the nature of evil and the redemptive value of nonviolence. Mayor Daley wanted negotiations to end the protests. King reminded city authorities that negotiations were meant to reform their segregated city, that the demonstrators were receiving blows, not inflicting them.

According to King, practitioners of nonviolence were like diagnosticians revealing already existing evil beneath layers of denial. City leaders called Montgomery peaceful and quiet, but King considered it a "pagan peace." Southern whites contended that their system was just, workable, and fully acceptable to most blacks; Northern mayors insisted that blacks were upwardly mobile. Jesus' "love ethic," in the form of protests, confronted the South's segregation and rural poverty, the North's urban discrimination and destitution, and uncovered a barely submerged sneer beneath the surface of civility. Nonviolent confrontations evoked brutality from the simple and verbal abuse from the subtle. Nonviolence was a light shining in darkness, and the darkness did not apprehend or appreciate the invading light. King's strategy for overcoming evil with redemptive love meant bringing the evil to the surface so it could be treated.142

The Birmingham marchers' Ten Commandments typified the movement's catechism: they sought reconciliation with, not victory over, whites. Demonstrators were to "refrain from the violence of fist, tongue, or heart," and remember the words of Jesus on the Cross: "Father, forgive them; for they know not what they do." They needed to learn the lesson of the Cross, that only goodness and love can defeat evil and hate. While violence marred many campaigns, King found it remarkable that blacks controlled so much of their pent-up rage. Not as zealous as Gandhi, who ended campaigns when passions boiled over, violence sometimes led King to back off temporarily. In Albany, he called for a day of penance for black violence yet, like Muste, he would not postpone action until the movement reached spiritual perfection; laws oppressed and humiliated, the status quo itself killed and maimed. The movement needed to reveal the South's false peace, the North's apathy, the presidents' indifference.[143]

King, however, was far less sanguine about revealing tensions within the SCLC's staff-full of competitively large egos, nor did he ever reverse the SCLC's tendency to seek premature reconciliations--as if they could cover up unresolved tensions--in their campaigns. Pointing to Albany, St. Augustine, Chicago, and even Birmingham, critics cited their habit of settling for insubstantial paper victories.[144]

The door to peaceful change, King said, had a double lock; blacks held one key and whites the other. Whites had to try to understand the suffering they had inflicted on blacks and accept guilt. He hoped black nonviolence could "awaken moral shame" among whites so that their confessed guilt could lead to redemption. King happily pointed to a few outstanding Southern whites who had already stretched their imaginations across an abyss to understand the oppressed.[145]

Although the idea got no further for King than it did for Muste, the civil rights leader suggested the creation of a nonviolent, justice-seeking domestic army, resurrecting the idea for the 1968 Poor People's March. He had known from the beginning that the "double lock" on the door of justice would first have to be opened from the black side--the outside. A nonviolent army was part of the search for the right key.[146]

After enlisting as a disciple of Gandhi, King believed that redemptive suffering would play a role in the American nonviolent movement. He recalled the Beatitude about "those who suffer for righteousness' sake" (Mt 5:10). Consciously paraphrasing Gandhi, he repeated a magnificent paean to the power and durability of nonviolence:

> We shall match your capacity to inflict suffering by our capacity to
> endure suffering. We shall meet your physical force with soul
> force. Do to us what you will, and we shall continue to love you.

We cannot in all good conscience obey your unjust laws, because non-cooperation with evil is as much a moral obligation as is co-operation with good. Throw us in jail, and we shall still love you. Send your hooded perpetrators of violence into our community at the midnight hour and beat us and leave us half dead, and we shall still love you. But be ye assured that we will wear you down by our capacity to suffer. One day we shall win freedom, but not only for ourselves. We shall so appeal to your heart and conscience that we shall win *you* in the process, and our victory will be a double victory.147

Certain dynamics made unearned suffering redemptive. Victims received the same random blows they already endured, but their willing acceptance was energized with the purpose of ending their humiliation. In standing up for freedom, they had already broken their own chains which--like the double lock on freedom's door--had required their brutalized complicity. Even unsuccessful demonstrators in Albany, like the slaves who swapped dreams, prayers, and jokes with their masters, had already freed themselves. Imitating the crucified Jesus, they bore their own crosses and so completed the cycle of grace and faith. King sensed with Day that the oppressed--subconsciously trained by years of denigration--tend to become self-destructive. Nonviolent self-affirmation reversed the trend and pointed them toward triumph.

Directed, unearned suffering also carried seeds of redemption for those who carried out or witnessed the violence because it revealed the hidden, contorted hatred in all its malevolence. Nonviolence sought conversion. King tried to shame whites into finding something vulnerable, human, and conscientious within themselves. Muste and King believed that nonviolence led to reconciliation as though there were some mysterious system of cause and effect branded into the soul of the universe.

King repeated the chorus: unearned suffering redeems. At the funeral of the four girls killed by a bomb in their Birmingham church, King tried to comfort the families and the congregation: "the innocent blood of these little girls may well serve as the redemptive force that will bring new light to this dark city." He called his own suffering--the bombing of his home and his days in the Montgomery jail--redemptive.[148] Physical death might be necessary to prevent psychological death. Black parents might have to die to free the children of both races. Their ordeals were opportunities to "transfigure" themselves and society. When King spoke of a redemptive cross, he referred to the crosses borne in imitation of Christ which redeemed those who bore them, those for whom they carried them, and--potentially--those who nailed them to their crosses.[149]

As years passed, King learned a peculiar lesson about redemptive suffering. In the clarity of the Southern campaigns, when he felt assured of progress, he made confident statements about the positive value of suffering. As the forces of evil multiplied, he said less. He grew silent as it became less clear to him that his own pain had the power to redeem. As he entered more deeply into the mystery of suffering he became, like Job, less interested in discussing it. As his own agony intensified, his orderly ideas of suffering-as-cause and redemption-as-effect disappeared.

As King picked up his own cross, he plunged into the depths of suffering with Jesus at Gethsemane and Golgotha. The opening words of Psalm 22--"My God, my God, why have you forsaken me?" spoken by Jesus in the act of redemptive dying--reveal the mystery in all of its contradictions. The Gospels joined Psalm 22 in holding forsaken pain and assuring vindication in tension. King's experience seemed to reflect Jesus' words: If your suffering is truly redemptive, you may be uncertain that it will accomplish its purpose, yet you are called to risk all in faith.

King was murdered the day before Good Friday, Day reflected, and poured out his blood for blacks and whites alike.[150] Distance and perspective helped her to see what King could not know for sure. The often divergent Gospels of Mark and John converge to proclaim that the road to glory does not merely pass through suffering servanthood. It peaks and ends there. Yet, personal pain makes faith in its healing value almost impossible. The events that stripped King of his optimism also stole his confidence that suffering was reliably redemptive.

Just as Rauschenbusch was ostracized for his neutrality during World War I, King antagonized former allies by publicly opposing the war in Vietnam. The psalmist spoke of a moment when righteousness would kiss peace (Ps 85:10), but few were happy when King tried to wed the civil rights and peace movements. The usually supportive *Washington Post* said that by speaking out against the war, "He has diminished his usefulness to his cause, to his country and to his people." King argued with fellow civil rights leaders who supported the war out of misplaced patriotism or narrow pragmatism. The White House, Congress, and white liberals rescinded political, moral, and financial support. The only allies King gained in following militant critics of the war, aside from the fragile peace movement, were inner city blacks.[151]

In 1965 King made some initial statements against the Vietnam War, but angry White House opposition, lack of interest in civil rights ranks, and token tolerance within the SCLC, made him quickly and quietly retreat. In his first book, he quoted Thoreau that even one person's abandonment of slavery would end the system; now King tested his convictions about the power of the individual conscience. By 1967 he was ready to protest again, speaking in Los Angeles, preaching at New York's Riverside Church, and addressing Muste's posthumous parade--the Spring Mobilization against the war in Vietnam.[152]

American policy-makers, he said, were misreading history, "destroying the soul of our nation," and sending people mixed messages about violence. Violence was praiseworthy when it defended "freedom" in Vietnam, but immoral when it combatted injustice in American cities. King did not miss the racist implications in the killing of thousands of non-white people. He also saw the Asian war defeating Lyndon Johnson's "war on poverty" by drawing off money and manpower like a "demoniacal destructive suction tube." And he echoed the complaints of black leader A. Philip Randolph and A. J. Muste in World Wars I and II: Why should the poor die for a country that did not give them the opportunity to live a decent life? Why should blacks fight to guarantee rights to people in Asia that could not be found in Georgia or Harlem? Why, in Asia, could whites and blacks kill and die together when, in the U.S., they could not attend the same schools or live on the same block?[153]

Never had King been forced to work harder to justify his views. In assaulting racism, he divided the white community. Opposing the war in Vietnam, he appeared unpatriotic. The fragmented white community--racists and liberals alike--rallied tightly together around the flag.

Photographs of the war in an issue of *Ramparts* shook King out of his self-restraint; he could no longer "segregate" his convictions and keep his opinions out of the traditionally white neighborhood of foreign affairs. As a minister, he felt "mandated" to seek peace. His opposition to the war might harm the SCLC financially; it might be bad politics; it might be unpopular, inexpedient, and tactically stupid, yet he could no longer violate his conscience.[154]

Used to absorbing the hatred of enemies, King now endured the loss of friends and allies, a different kind of pain, abuse, and vulnerability. The staggering number of death threats hurt him less than the slow ebbing away of his liberal/white, moderate/black coalition. No stone hurt him more than the ones thrown at him by those he had counted as friends. Politically, he was becoming marginal, a painful loss for one accustomed to wielding tremendous influence. Day rested content for forty-seven years with the small-scale anarchy of the Catholic Worker. Muste searched relentlessly for an experiment and a miraculous new pentecost to produce massive social change and propel him from the margins of power to its capital. In mid-ministry, King emptied himself of power in order to serve his conscience.

Yet his opposition to the war was perfectly consonant with his early ideals. The 1957 SCLC slogan embodied the goal of the civil rights movement: to "save the soul of America." African-Americans were "the conscience of America," goading the nation until it repented. Early on, King equated integration with redemption. Later, it meant revolutionizing American values. But the spiritual overtones and the direction of redemption remained consistent.[155] Day saw the destitute as sacramental channels of God's grace. Muste shared her conviction that redemption never trickled down. Merton envisioned the power of grace moving into society through cracks in its outer walls. Whether King worked with the victims of segregation or of poverty, he saw the power of redemption rising up like steam.

African-Americans had long identified with Old Testament Israel's Exodus and Promised Land. They had also adopted Israel's vocation to be a blessing to other peoples. In history, this sense of calling occasionally led to missionary activity in Africa, but more often to a mission to redeem white America. King touched on this sense of purpose at the end of his first address at a mass meeting in Montgomery. Future historians, he said, would look back and say, "There lived a great people--a black people--who injected new meaning and dignity into the veins of civilization." In his famous Birmingham letter, he told condescending white clergy that, in their city, blacks were the heroes. On his other flank, he argued with militants favorably quoting Franz Fanon, who had advocated violent revolution as the only psychologically healthy way to keep blacks from internalizing violence. King used Fanon to refute his opponents, for Fanon did not want Africa to be a "reflection" of Europe. African-Americans had to be different from white America. Nonconformity meant nonviolence that "seeks to break the chain reaction of evil." Black violence merely mirrored the deadliest germ of white civilization. The only way to be free from violence was to willingly absorb it. To fulfill their special destiny, blacks had to choose an apparent absurdity. King quoted James Baldwin who, in a letter to his nephew, wrote, "The really terrible thing, old buddy, is that *you* must accept *them*." Only black love could cast out white fear.[156]

As King became more concerned with economic justice, the players in the drama of redemption changed; from black and white to poor and rich. Young blacks made an historic contribution to the movement when they "took off their Brooks Brothers ethic and put on overalls." Changed clothes altered allegiances. When King, who normally wore suits, left the meeting at the Gaston Hotel in Birmingham primed for arrest, he had changed into overalls, a sacramental act in a changing consciousness. If King remained too patriotic and integrationist for his militant critics, at the time of his death he was still younger than Gandhi when the latter abandoned the look of the British barrister for Indian cloth and supported the British Empire during World War II. Two intertwined souls unravel slowly even in a mahatma. King had insisted that America could not be free until its black minority was free. Now, he added, the salvation of the black middle-class depended on the well-being of the black masses.[157]

King told and re-told the Parable of the Good Samaritan as a story of personal responsibility. Individual charity was as important as abstract justice, although the Samaritan's altruism could also transform the Jericho road to prevent future troubles. Sometimes he described black reaching into the ditch to help black, sometimes white lifting black out of poverty. On the eve of his assassination, he identified the Samaritan as "a man of another race." With this re-telling of the story, he grasped the subversive intent of the original story-teller: an outcast, good-for-nothing Samaritan could be "good." Now King had said something equally preposterous. He placed his listeners in the same imaginary ditch with those who first heard Jesus and challenged them to see someone of "another race" coming to help: angry blacks would accept aid from willing whites; whites, who could not fathom their desperate need to be rescued, would accept the black race as their redeemer. King's telling of the parable finally coincided with the movement's original theology. Blacks were not only equal to whites. They were the only ones who could retrieve white America from its moral ditch and restore it to health. Hope rested in the hands of the helpless.[158]

Black redeemed white; poor redeemed middle-class. Blacks, by carrying their own crosses, straightened their own backs so that no other burdens could be laid on them without their consent. Legislation could not deliver psychological freedom. The enslaved had buried their own psychology of servitude and signed their "own emancipation proclamation." Even Albany's political failure contained spiritual freedom. Not yet a political reality, freedom, like the Kingdom of God, was already realized in mind and spirit.[159]

Two strands in the African-American religious tradition wove their way into King's utterances. In one strand, he called on white America to live up to its professed creed promising freedom to all. In this view, blacks had to wait for whites to act. Yet, what sense did it make to stand weeping in the Wilderness and wait for the Promised Land to come to you? In the other strand, blacks seized the initiative in accepting their peculiar vocation to redeem their oppressors. The double lock had two keys and the lock that kept blacks out imprisoned whites within. King did not assert the proximity of God's Kingdom on earth as did liberal double lock had two keys and the lock that kept blacks out imprisoned whites within. King did not assert the proximity of God's Kingdom on earth as did liberal Protestantism, yet he followed the Social Gospel in adopting a kind of Jewish millenarian messianism that believed human actions could "speed the day" when "the beloved community" would be established.[160]

As a preacher and pastor, King's concern with saving souls did not manifest itself in an individualistic style. Like Rauschenbusch, he believed that redemption gave the individual eternal life and the world the Kingdom of God.[161] For Day, political demonstrations were "works of mercy"; for King, they fell under the rubric of redemption.

The Cords of Death

"The cords of death encompassed me; the torrents of perdition assailed me; the cords of Sheol entangled me; the snares of death confronted me."

--Psalm 18:4-5

"When you pass through the waters, I will be with you; and through the rivers, they shall not overwhelm you; when you walk through fire you shall not be burned, and the flame shall not consume you. For I am the Lord your God, the Holy One of Israel, your Savior."

--Isaiah 43:2-3

"I must walk my lonesome valley
I got to walk it for myself
Nobody else can walk it for me
I got to walk it for myself."

--"I Must Walk My Lonesome Valley"

"We shall walk through the valley of the shadow of death,
We shall walk through the valley in peace,
If Jesus Himself shall be our leader,

We shall walk through the valley in peace."

--Spiritual

"Precious Lord, take my hand,
Lead me on, let me stand,
I am tired, I am weak, I am worn.
Through the storm, through the night
Lead me on to the light,
Take my hand, precious Lord,
Lead me home."

--"Take My Hand, Precious Lord," Thomas A. Dorsey[162]

In September 1962, as King addressed the SCLC convention in Birmingham, a young white man--a member of the Nazi Party--arose from the audience, walked up on the stage, and punched him in the face. King did nothing to defend himself, and his assailant delivered more blows. Finally several people pulled the attacker away. King did not file charges. Speaking to an audience four months later in Chicago, he spotted the same man in the crowd apparently stalking him from city to city.[163]

As he sat in a Harlem department store signing copies of *Stride Toward Freedom*, an emotionally unstable black woman stabbed him with a letter opener. He sat completely still for several minutes until taken to a hospital. Had the deceptively painless wound penetrated a fraction of an inch to the side, it would have killed him. A scar in the shape of a cross covered his heart where the weapon had punctured his chest.[164]

Before the 1963 Birmingham campaign, King warned his co-workers that some of them might not survive the year. He foresaw that he might be killed in Selma. He lived; three others died. After John F. Kennedy's assassination, King predicted the same fate for himself. When a mid-1960s conversation with a film producer turned to making a movie about King's life, the producer facetiously asked him how the movie would end. He said, "It ends with me getting killed." Telling the story, the producer added, "He was smiling but he wasn't joking."[165]

His home in Montgomery was bombed. His motel room and his brother's home were bombed in the city blacks punned "Bombingham." There was a bomb threat at a university, another on an airplane, yet another on the flight that carried him to Memphis the day before he was shot.[166] Each day prepared him for the assassin's bullet that tore the flesh from his face and throat.

Hardly a day went by without a mailed or phoned death threat. The Ku Klux Klan vowed to kill him. A cross was burned on his lawn at home. There were rumors of conspiracies in Florida and Mississippi. A fire gutted the cottage where he had been staying in St. Augustine. He received special protection in Washington, D.C. Two wealthy, reactionary men in the St. Louis area made standing offers of $20,000 to $50,000 to have him killed.[167]

The 1966 Meredith March detoured to Philadelphia, Mississippi to join a rally commemorating the 1964 murders of three young civil rights workers. Heckled by hostile whites, King remarked, "I believe in my heart that the murderers are somewhere around me at this moment." A voice from the crowd said, "You're damn right, they're right here behind you right now." Violence stalked and numbed him. Death was never far away.[168]

In an unusual public display of emotion, King told a gathering in Montgomery at the start of his career: "If anyone has to die, let it be me." Eleven years before he mentioned the "mountain top" in Memphis, he spoke of it in Montgomery. His vision of the coming of freedom gave him the strength to go on.[169]

King smiled at the movie producer when speaking of his death. Even after that day in Mississippi's city-of-brotherly-love, when he heard the voice behind him and yielded to the "inevitability of death," he laughed with friends as he told how he and Ralph Abernathy knelt to pray. King confessed with a chuckle, "And brother, I sure did not want to close my eyes when we prayed." Abernathy had prayed aloud and, as a grinning King told his friends, "Ralph said he prayed with his [eyes] open!"[170]

He suffered depressions and wild mood swings under the duress of violent hatred, yet he also joked about death, poked fun at the FBI's attempts to hound him, and preached amusing eulogies about his living colleagues to make them laugh. As slave stories jabbed at their masters and kept the oppressed spiritually free, so King's mock eulogies announced his freedom from the final power of death.

After receiving the Nobel Peace Prize, he spoke of being on a mountain: not the one overlooking the Promised Land, but the mount of the Transfiguration where, though tempted by a more serene life, he knew he had to "go back to the valley." As often as he trekked up a mountain, he had to return to the Wilderness. To have walked his lonesome valley without qualms would have required denial. His faith, conviction, and courage meant going on in spite of his fear, enduring with over three centuries of African-Americans the daily psychological assaults, the daily threats, the daily shadow of murder. His life manifested the power of resurrection as, in spite of his fears, he refused to be overcome by the entangling cords of death.[171]

When Day wrote of "precarity," when Muste said that any pacifist unwilling to die for justice was bluffing, when Gandhi said, "He who perished sword in hand is no doubt brave, but he who faces death without raising his little finger and without flinching is braver," they could have been describing King's life.[172] Muste observed people and nations trying to alleviate their fears by seeking security, but the only way to security was to alleviate fear. King rebuffed the more far-fetched attempts at physical security. Muste spoke forthrightly about the Cross of nonviolence, and King hung on it. Published photographs of Day and Muste tend to show them in their venerable old age, an age King never had the luxury to experience. Day and Muste lived precariously, gave up security and risked the Cross, but King bore the special weight of white rage against the black race: he hung as perpetual effigy.

Christians speak rhetorically about dying daily. King was murdered daily. He never closed his eyes to the imminence of death. But social and political persecution bothered him as much as the threat of physical violence; the loss of supporters over his stand on Vietnam may have cut even closer to his heart than the sharp letter opener in his chest.

The first wave of death threats washed over him in Montgomery when he heard that inner voice reassure him that God would not forsake him. Announcing the Birmingham campaign, King referred to Isaiah,

> God has told me that he wants freedom for us...I'm not going to run from the responsibility. It may mean going through the floods and going through the waters, but I'm going if it means that. It may mean going through the storms and through the winds, but I'm going if it means that. It may mean going to jail, but I'm going if it means that. It may even mean physical death, but if it means that I will die standing up for the freedom of my people. . . .

Applause drenched his closing words. [173]

Death confronted him, preceded him, followed him, and encompassed him --but it did not overwhelm him. He persisted because of what he had seen from the mountaintop, what he had heard when the cords of death were all around. Under the threat of death, he sat in his kitchen like Elijah in his cave. And like Elijah, when the still, small voice came to him, it not only comforted him, it called him back to his vocation, to being murdered daily, to walking on toward the Promised Land he would never reach, to striding through his own Gethsemane toward his own Golgotha without any final assurance that his life or death would have any redemptive purpose. He felt God's presence with him in that moment at the start of his public ministry and he prayed for that reassuring presence again as he spent the rest of his short life fearing no evil as he walked through the valley of the shadow of death.

NOTES

MARTIN LUTHER KING, JR.

1. W.E.B. DuBois, *The Souls of Black Folk* (New York, 1903, 1969), 48-49, 52; Stephen B. Oates, *Let the Trumpet Sound: The Life of Martin Luther King, Jr.* (New York, 1982), 7.

2. David J. Garrow, *Bearing the Cross: Martin Luther King, Jr. and the Southern Christian Leadership Conference* (New York, 1986), 512-13.

3. Garrow, 515.

4. Oates, 70.

5. Oates, 470.

6. Garrow, 355, 125, 76, 171; Martin Luther King, Jr., *Why We Can't Wait* (New York, 1963), 90. Howell Raines, *My Soul is Rested* (New York, 1977), 425, 426; James Baldwin, "The Highroad to Destiny," in C. Eric Lincoln, ed., *Martin Luther King, Jr.: A Profile* (New York, 1984), 96.

7. Garrow, 41; Raines, 53; Martin Luther King, Jr., *Stride Toward Freedom: The Montgomery Story* (San Francisco, 1958), 101, 140; James M. Washington, ed., *A Testament of Hope: The Essential Writings of Martin Luther King, Jr.* (San Francisco, 1986), 323; Martin Luther King, Jr., *Where Do We Go From Here?*, (New York, 1968), 51.

8. Nat Hentoff, *Peace Agitator: The Story of A. J. Muste*, 109, and Jo Ann Ooiman Robinson, *Abraham Went Out: A Biography of A. J. Muste*, 113.

9. Garrow, 236, 375, 604.

10. Oates, 183, 144; Garrow, 366.

11. Garrow, 125, 134; Washington, ed., 372; Oates, 127, 140, 169.

12. Garrow, 322, 164, 219, 341, 578, 365, 352, 557-8, 428, 540, 603; Washington, ed., 375; Raines, 427; Oates, 205.

13. Garrow, 345, 604, 33, 36, 44, 45; King, *Where Do We Go From Here?*, 188.

14. William D. Watley, *Roots of Resistance: The Nonviolent Ethic of Martin Luther King, Jr.* (Valley Forge, PA, 1985), 59; Garrow, 114, 198, 357; David J. Garrow, *The FBI and Martin Luther King, Jr.* (New York, 1981), 217; David Halberstam, "When 'Civil Rights' and 'Peace' Join Forces," in C. Eric Lincoln, ed., 203.

15. Garrow, *Bearing the Cross*, 459; Washington, ed., 371; King, *Where Do We Go From Here?*, 135-6.

16. Oates, 303; Garrow, *Bearing the Cross*, 439; Martin Luther King, Jr., *The Measure of a Man* (Philadelphia, 1959), 5.

17. Washington, ed., 67, 104, 118, 354; King, *Why We Can't Wait*, 137; Garrow, *Bearing the Cross*, 443.

18. Walter Brueggemann, *Hopeful Imagination* (Philadelphia, 1986).

19. Langston Hughes and Arna Bontemps, eds., *The Book of Negro Folklore* (New York, 1958), 297; Albert Raboteau, *Slave Religion: The "Invisible Institution" in the Antebellum South* (Oxford, 1978), 319.

20. Garrow, *Bearing the Cross*, 402.

21. Garrow, *Bearing the Cross*, 159-60; Oates, 217.

22. Washington, ed., 292-3.

23. King, *Where Do We Go From Here?*, 21, 122; King, *Why We Can't Wait*, 23, 61, 131-32.

24. Walter Brueggemann, *Hope Within History* (Atlanta, 1987), 16, 87; Marguerite K. Rivage-Seul, "Peace Education: Imagination and the Pedagogy of the Oppressed" *Harvard Educational Review* 57:2 (May 1987): passim.

25. Raboteau, 218, 247; Hughes and Bontemps, eds., 153; DuBois, 212, 267.

26. DuBois, 45

27. Washington, ed.,105, 206, 208, 219, 221, 286, 375; King, *Where Do We Go From Here?*, 98-99; King, *Why We Can't Wait*, 94.

28. Washington, ed., 292-93.

29. King, *Where Do We Go From Here?*, 10.

30. Washington, ed., 21; Oates, 106.

31. Washington, ed., 206, 208.

32. Washington, ed., 217-20.

33. Washington, ed., 207, 216, 97; King, *Stride Toward Freedom*, 191.

34. James Baldwin, 97; Brueggemann, *Hopeful Imagination*, 95.

35. Washington, ed., 343, 219, 342; Garrow, *Bearing the Cross*, 35, 33; Oates, 181-82.

36. King, *Where Do We Go From Here?*, 30, 198; Martin Luther King, Jr., *The Trumpet of Conscience* (New York, 1967), 77; Washington, ed., 277.

37. Walter Brueggemann, *David's Truth* (Philadelphia, 1985), 31.

38. Martin Luther King, Jr., *Strength to Love* (Philadelphia, 1963, 1981), 65, 106-114; Washington, ed., 286; King, *Where Do We Go From Here?*, 199; Garrow, *Bearing the Cross*, 621; Raboteau, 147.

39. DuBois, 261, 274; Raboteau, 218, 311; James Cone, *The Spirituals and the Blues: An Interpretation* (New York, 1972), 72, 95; John Lovell, Jr., "The Social Implications of the Negro Spiritual," in Bernard Katz, ed., *The Social Implications of Early Negro Music in the United States* (New York, 1969), 134-35.

40. See Raboteau, for a discussion, 211-88; King, *The Trumpet of Conscience*, 3; King, *Stride Toward Freedom*, 64; Frederick Douglass, *Life and Times of Frederick Douglass* (New York, 1971), 92.

41. King, *Why We Can't Wait*, 72-73; Washington, ed., 228.

42. Garrow, *Bearing the Cross*, 201-2; David L. Lewis, *King: A Biography* (Urbana, IL, 1970, 1978), 107, 314; Reese Cleghorn, "Crowned with Crises," in Lincoln, ed., 121; August Meier, "The Conservative Militant," in Lincoln, ed., 152; Louis Lomax, "When 'Nonviolence' Meets 'Black Power,'" in Lincoln, ed., 163.

43. Brueggemann, *Hopeful Imagination*, 25, 96, 98; Brueggemann, *Hope Within History*, 39, 86.

44. Richard Wright, *American Hunger* (New York, 1977), 48, 59.

45. Oates, 377; King, *Where Do We Go From Here?*, 133; James Baldwin, *The Evidence of Things Not Seen* (New York, 1985), 89.

46. Raines, 54; King, *The Measure of a Man*, 33; King, *Strength to Love*, 66, 146; King, *Stride Toward Freedom*, 48, 172; Washington, ed., 197, 222, 224, 226, 218; King, *The Trumpet of Conscience*, 77.

47. John J. Ansbro, *Martin Luther King, Jr.: The Making of a Mind* (New York, 1982), 162; Gayraud S.Wilmore, *Black Religion and Black Radicalism* (Garden City, NY, 1973), 131.

48. Sydney E. Ahlstrom, *A Religious History of the American People* (Garden City, NY 1975), vol. 2, 249.

49. King, *Stride Toward Freedom*, 98-100; Walter Rauschenbusch, *Christianity and the Social Crisis* (New York, 1907), 420-22.

50. Walter Rauschenbusch, *A Theology for the Social Gospel* (New York, 1917), 276-77.

51. King, *Strength to Love*, 40, 41; King, *Where Do We Go From Here?*, 219; Garrow, *Bearing the Cross*, 416.

52. Washington, ed., 52, 207, 277; King, *Stride Toward Freedom*, 77, 111.

53. Washington, ed., 252, 328, 313; King, *Where Do We Go From Here?*, 146, 215; Garrow, *Bearing the Cross*, 569.

54. Garrow, *Bearing the Cross*, 598; King, *Stride Toward Freedom*, 40, 93, 97, 171, 212; King, *Why We Can't Wait*, 80; Washington, ed., 44, 86.

55. King, *The Trumpet of Conscience*, 17, 62.

56. King, *The Trumpet of Conscience*, 8, 9, 14; Garrow, *Bearing the Cross*, 440.

57. King, *The Trumpet of Conscience*, 14.

58. Garrow, *Bearing the Cross*, 281-83.

59. King, *Strength to Love*, 78; Washington, ed., 86, 374; King, *Where Do We Go From Here?*, 22, 106, 151, 62; Garrow, *Bearing the Cross*, 492.

60. Lewis, 180; King, *Why We Can't Wait*, 109; King, *Strength to Love*, 82, 33; Garrow, *Bearing the Cross*, 199, 352, 358; King, *The Trumpet of Conscience*, 6; Washington, ed., 358; Oates, 413, 380.

61. Washington, ed., 344; King, *Where Do We Go From Here?*, 189; Garrow, *Bearing the Cross*, 217-18, 226, 458; Oates, 194-95, 199, 211, 216, 297, 380, 387, 393, 407, 415, 417.

62. Garrow, *Bearing the Cross*, 83, 77; Washington, ed., 197-98.

63. King, *The Trumpet of Conscience*, 6; King, *Where Do We Go From Here?*, 40, 52, 180, 196; Garrow, *Bearing the Cross*, 466, 537, 540.

64. King, *Stride Toward Freedom*, 90; Washington, ed. 240, 250, 357; Garrow, *Bearing the Cross*, 216.

65. King, *Strength to Love*, 76-85; Washington, ed., 271.

66. King, *Where Do We Go From Here?*, 39, 74, 79, 81, 107, 109, 116; King, *Why We Can't Wait*, 143, 144; King, *Strength to Love*, 51, 69, 134, 125, 132; Washington, ed., 203, 70, 71, 240; King, *The Trumpet of Conscience*, 32; compare to the use of Rauschenbusch, *A Theology for the Social Gospel*, 57, 84.

67. Washington, ed., 383, 387; Garrow, *Bearing the Cross*, 512-13; King, *Strength to Love*, 138; King, *Why We Can't Wait*, 119, 121, 151.

68. King, *Strength to Love*, 76, 90; King, *Where Do We Go From Here?*, 194.

69. Garrow, *Bearing the Cross*, 101.

70. Garrow, *Bearing the Cross*, 80, 290; King, *Where Do We Go From Here?*, 1, 210; King, *Stride Toward Freedom*, 171, 106; Washington, ed., 52, 88, 207, 252, 277, 9, 13, 14; King, *Strength to Love*, 101, 110.

71. Baldwin, "The Highroad to Destiny," 96.

72. King, *Strength to Love*, 80, 109, 110; Washington, ed., 83, 200; King, *Where Do We Go From Here?*, 19, 167; Garrow, *Bearing the Cross*, 101.

73. King, *Where Do We Go From Here?*, 55, 14.

74. King, *Stride Toward Freedom*, 197; Washington, ed., 270; King, *Where Do We Go From Here?*, 151; King, *Why We Can't Wait*, 86.

75. Baldwin, "The Highroad to Destiny," 104; King, *The Trumpet of Conscience*, 48.

76. I owe this insight to Mary Sawyer, "Legacy of a Dream," in Lincoln, ed., 267; Washington, ed., 217; Oates, 389; King, *Why We Can't Wait*, 23; King, *The Trumpet of Conscience*, 17.

77. John Lovell, Jr., *Black Song: The Forge and the Flame* (New York, 1972), 106-7; Thomas Higginson, "Negro Spirituals," *Atlantic Monthly* 19:116 (June 1867): 692; Herbert Aptheker, ed., W.E.B. DuBois, *Prayers for a Dark People* (Amherst, 1980), 3.

78. Garrow, *Bearing the Cross*, 408; Oates, 354-55.

79. Garrow, *Bearing the Cross*, 412-13; Washington, ed., 228-30; Oates, 90.

80. King, *Strength to Love*, 95; Garrow, *Bearing the Cross*, 455, 600; King, *The Trumpet of Conscience*, 76.

81. King, *The Trumpet of Conscience*, 76; King, *Where Do We Go From Here?*, 53.

82. King, *Strength to Love*, 83, 93; King, *The Trumpet of Conscience*, 77; King, *Where Do We Go From Here?*, 54; Washington, ed., 375.

83. King, *Where Do We Go From Here?*, 52; Garrow, *Bearing the Cross*, 537, 598; King was also booed in Harlem, Oates, 306, 406.

84. Garrow, *Bearing the Cross*, 42, 45; King, *Stride Toward Freedom*, 113; King, *Where Do We Go From Here?*, 53.

85. DuBois, *The Souls of Black Folk*, 157; King, *Where Do We Go From Here?*, 54; Robert E. Daggy, ed., *The Hidden Ground of Love* (New York, 1985), 156.

86. King, *Strength to Love*, 90, 106, 124; Washington, ed., 226.

87. John Howard Griffin, *Follow the Ecstasy* (Fort Worth, 1983), 192.

88. Garrow, *Bearing the Cross*, 596; King, *Where Do We Go From Here?*, 134.

89. Walter Rauschenbusch, *Prayers of the Social Awakening* (Boston, Chicago, 1909), 29; Christa Dixon, *Negro Spirituals* (n.p., 1967), 193; John W. Work, *American Negro Songs and Spirituals* (New York, 1970), 128.

90. Garrow, *Bearing the Cross*, 57, 58, 89; King, *Stride Toward Freedom*, 134-35.

91. King, *Strength to Love*, 113.

92. Garrow, *Bearing the Cross*, 608; Garrow, *The FBI and Martin Luther King, Jr.*, 218.

93. King, *Stride Toward Freedom*, 128; Garrow, *Bearing the Cross*, 148.

94. King, *Stride Toward Freedom*, 136, 106; Garrow, *Bearing the Cross*, 35, 174; King, *Strength to Love*, 124; King, *The Trumpet of Conscience*, 75; Washington, ed., 9, 14.

95. Howard Thurman, *Deep River: Reflections on the Religious Insight of Certain of the Negro Spirituals* (New York, 1955), 56.

96. King, *Strength to Love*, 110, 15, 83, 84, 114, 135, 136, 126; King, *Stride Toward Freedom*, 136, 138; Washington, ed., 200.

97. King, *Strength to Love*, 15, 97, 106, 132; Washington, ed., 234; Garrow, *Bearing the Cross*, 587.

98. King, *Strength to Love*, 82; King, *The Trumpet of Conscience*, 72; Washington, ed., 119; King, *Where Do We Go From Here?*, 113-14, 210.

99. Merton entitled one of his books with Donne's opening phrase. Washington, ed., 210, 269, 122; King, *Why We Can't Wait*, 77; King, *Strength to Love*, 70, 34; King, *Where Do We Go From Here?*, 206.

100. Washington, ed., 215; King, *The Measure of a Man*, 32-33.

101. DuBois, *Prayers for a Dark People*, 63; Dixon, 141.

102. King, *Why We Can't Wait*, 63-64; compare with the FOR in *Fellowship* 18:5 (May 1952): 8.

103. King, *Stride Toward Freedom*, 137-38, 179.

104. King, *Stride Toward Freedom*, 153-57.

105. King, *Strength to Love*, 18-19, 47, 100; Washington, ed., 267; King, *Stride Toward Freedom*, 85, 97; see Raboteau, 312.

106. King, *The Trumpet of Conscience*, 73; King, *Stride Toward Freedom*, 104-5, 74, 84, 62; King, *Strength to Love*, 146, 48.

107. King, *Strength to Love*, 145.

108. King, *Strength to Love*, 50, 53, 98.

109. King, *The Measure of a Man*, 18; King, *The Trumpet of Conscience*, 76; King, *Strength to Love*, 37; James H. Smylie, "On Jesus, Pharaohs, and the Chosen People: Martin Luther King as Biblical Interpreter and Humanist" *Interpretation* 24:1 (January 1970): 77.

110. King, *Strength to Love*, 18; Garrow, *Bearing the Cross*, 532.

111. King, *Strength to Love*, 57, 17-25; King, *Why We Can't Wait*, 88, 89; Washington, ed., 356.

112. Washington, ed., 14-15, 89-90, 216, 251; King, *Strength to Love*, 24.

113. Washington, ed., 266.

114. King, *Strength to Love*, 19, 23, 24.

115. King, *Strength to Love*, 21, 22, 101, 130, 62, 103; Washington, ed., 349.

116. King, *Where Do We Go From Here?*, 112, 113, 189; King, *Strength to Love*, 62, 19, 102, 23, 61; Washington, ed., 407; King, *Why We Can't Wait*, 91.

117. Washington, ed., 346, 344; King, *Why We Can't Wait*, 92; King, *Strength to Love*, 62; King, *Where Do We Go From Here?*, 42, 147, 113.

118. Washington, ed., 345, 347; King, *Why We Can't Wait*, 92.

119. King, *Strength to Love*, 68, 50, 111; Garrow, *The FBI and Martin Luther King*, 216; Lewis, 254, 14; Washington, ed., 356.

120. Hughes and Bontemps, 87; Work, 169, and James Weldon Johnson, *The Book of American Negro Spirituals* (New York, 1925), 97.

121. Garrow, *Bearing the Cross*, 399; Oates, 349; Charles E. Fager, *Selma, 1965: The March that Changed the South* (Boston, 1974), 98.

122. See Garrow, *The FBI and Martin Luther King*, passim.

123. King, *The Trumpet of Conscience*, 33; Washington, ed., 241, 234, 218; anon., "King Speaks for Peace," *The Christian Century* (April 29, 1967), 492; King, *Stride Toward Freedom*, 196.

124. DuBois, *The Souls of Black Folk*, 52, 95.

125. King, *The Trumpet of Conscience*, 55; Washington, ed., 217, 315, 91, 203; King, *Strength to Love*, 37; King, *Stride Toward Freedom*, 190; King, *The Measure of a Man*, 17.

126. Washington, ed., 275, 243; King, *Where Do We Go From Here?*, 207, 222.

127. Hughes and Bontemps, 156-57, 71; Raboteau, 292.

128. Wilmore, 57, 102.

129. King, *The Trumpet of Conscience*, 34; Washington, ed., 377; Garrow, *Bearing the Cross*, 292; James Cone, "The Theology of Martin Luther King, Jr." *Union Seminary Quarterly Review*: 40: 4 (1986): 32, 33; King, *Where Do We Go From Here?*, 203, 206.

130. King, *Strength to Love*, 102; Washington, ed., 274; King, *Where Do We Go From Here?*, 217; Garrow, *Bearing the Cross*, 622; Lewis, 386.

131. King, *The Measure of a Man*, 14-16.

132. King, *Where Do We Go From Here?*, 98-99.

133. King, *Where Do We Go From Here?*, 223, 200; Washington, ed., 228, 209, 199, 167, 218; King, *Why We Can't Wait*, 86, 128.

134. David J. Garrow, "The Intellectual Development of Martin Luther King, Jr.: Influences and Commentaries" *Union Seminary Quarterly Review* 40:4 (1986): 14; Washington, ed., 233, 199, 270, 355; Garrow, *Bearing the Cross*, 12, 4, 382; King, *Where Do We Go From Here?*, 41; King, *Why We Can't Wait*, 50, 84, 86, 119; Ansbro, 259.

135. King, *The Trumpet of Conscience*, 6; King, *Where Do We Go From Here?*, 80, 81, 97, 51; Garrow, *Bearing the Cross*, 532.

136. King, *Where Do We Go From Here?*, 100; Garrow, *Bearing the Cross*, 572.

137. Oates, 445.

138. Washington, ed., 58, 249, 350, 250, 251; Garrow, *Bearing the Cross*, 323; King, *Where Do We Go From Here?*, 157.

139. King, *Strength to Love*, 14; Brueggemann, *Hopeful Imagination*, 111; Washington, ed., 348, 217, 219.

140. John Lovell, Jr., *Black Song: The Forge and the Flame*, 337.

141. Garrow, *Bearing the Cross*, 499-500.

142. King, *Stride Toward Freedom*, 40, 51, 69, 70, 104, 193; King, *Strength to Love*, 19; Washington, ed., 350, 383; King, *Where Do We Go From Here?*, 29, 32, 39, 97, 106, 107, 212; King, *Why We Can't Wait*, 85; Garrow, *Bearing the Cross*, 512-13, 536.

143. King, *Why We Can't Wait*, 64; King, *Strength to Love*, 39, 43; Garrow, *Bearing the Cross*, 209; Oates, 196.

144. Garrow, *Bearing the Cross*, 463-64; Lewis, passim.

145. King, *Where Do We Go From Here?*, 25, 80, 98, 119, 122; King, *Stride Toward Freedom*, 102; King, *Why We Can't Wait*, 89.

146. King, *The Trumpet of Conscience*, 60; King, *Why We Can't Wait*, 38, 39, 62; Garrow, *Bearing the Cross*, 194, 222.

147. King, *Strength to Love*, 144, 54; King, *Stride Toward Freedom*, 217; King, *The Trumpet of Conscience*, 74-75.

148. King, *Stride Toward Freedom*, 103, 179; Washington, ed., 219, 222, 41; Garrow, *Bearing the Cross*, 149.

149. King, *Stride Toward Freedom*, 216; Washington, ed.,207; King, *Strength to Love*, 92, 25; King, *Where Do We Go From Here?*, 54; Garrow, *Bearing the Cross*, 290.

150. Dorothy Day, *On Pilgrimage: The Sixties*, 336.

151. Paul M. Minus, *Walter Rauschenbusch: American Reformer* (New York, 1988), 180-81; Garrow, *Bearing the Cross*, 553, 546, 470; Ansbro, 236.

152. Garrow, *Bearing the Cross*, 394, 445; Washington, ed., 231; King, *Stride Toward Freedom*, 218.

153. King, *The Trumpet of Conscience*, 25-31, 23, 24; Garrow, *Bearing the Cross*, 543; "King Speaks for Peace," 492; Washington, ed., 233; Oates, 120, 401.

154. Garrow, *Bearing the Cross*, 543, 453, 550, 554; Washington, ed., 408, 276.

155. Ansbro, 259; Garrow, *Bearing the Cross*, 160, 593; Frederick Downing, "Martin Luther King, Jr. as Public Theologian" *Theology Today* 44:1 (April 1987): 27, 29; King, *The Trumpet of Conscience*, 25, 62; Washington, ed., 105.

156. Wilmore, 171; King, *Stride Toward Freedom*, 63; King, *Why We Can't Wait*, 94; King, *Where Do We Go From Here?*, 69-70, 72, 63-77.

157. King, *The Trumpet of Conscience*, 46; Washington, ed., 233, 354; Baldwin, "The Highroad to Destiny," 109; King, *Where Do We Go From Here?*, 156

158. King, *The Measure of a Man*, 25-27; King, *Strength to Love*, 26-35; Washington, ed., 241, 284; King, *Where Do We Go From Here?*, 218.

159. Washington, ed., 286, 344, 246; King, *Where Do We Go From Here?*, 50; King, *Why We Can't Wait*, 111.

160. King, *Strength to Love*, 105; Washington, ed., 220, 242, 25; King, *Where Do We Go From Here?*, 221; Garrow, *Bearing the Cross*, 81.

161. Minus, 81.

162. Work, 108; Lovell, *Black Song*, 309; Hughes and Bontemps, 320.

163. Garrow, *Bearing the Cross*, 221, 232.

164. Garrow, *Bearing the Cross*, 109-10;

165. Garrow, *Bearing the Cross*, 229, 365, 307, 469.

166. King, *Why We Can't Wait*, 106; Garrow, *Bearing the Cross*, 311, 135, 619.

167. Washington, ed., 355; Garrow, *Bearing the Cross*, 328-29, 341, 392-95, 135; Oates, 455.

168. Garrow, *Bearing the Cross*, 483; Oates, 404

169. King, *Stride Toward Freedom*, 178; Garrow, *Bearing the Cross*, 89, 621.

170. Oates, 404.

171. Oates, 334, 322, 338.

172. Peter Brock, *Twentieth Century Pacifism* (New York, 1970), 73.

173. Garrow, *Bearing the Cross*, 302.

CHAPTER FOUR

THOMAS MERTON

In Louisville, at the corner of Fourth and Walnut, in the center of the shopping district, I was suddenly overwhelmed with the realization that I loved all those people, that they were mine and I theirs, that we could not be alien to one another even though we were total strangers. It was like waking from a dream of separateness, of spurious self-isolation in a special world, the world of renunciation and supposed holiness. . . .

It is a glorious destiny to be a member of the human race, though it is a race dedicated to many absurdities and one which makes many mistakes: yet, with all that, God Himself gloried in becoming a member of the human race! To think that such a commonplace realization should suddenly seem like news that one holds the winning ticket in a cosmic sweepstake.[1]

In March 1958, in his seventeenth year at the Trappist monastery at Gethsemani, Kentucky, Thomas Merton was startled by a vision marking a spiritual death and resurrection. The young monk who scorned the world had died, so slowly he had barely noticed. Solitude and the monastic life drove him to renew his membership in a human race he loved. Even in this ecstatic moment he did not romanticize humanity; but the incarnation healed its sinfulness.

Merton's life had been a long separation. His parents died by the time he was sixteen; his only brother perished in World War II. Educated in English boarding schools, at Cambridge and Columbia, his unofficial "hermitage years" began in his youth. He had searched for community and solitude, a place to belong and a place to be alone. He had not known that physical isolation would bring communion.

Merton looked upon his conversion in his early twenties "as a radical liberation from the delusions and obsessions of modern man and his society." Like an adolescent running away from a deranged family, he had renounced the civilization that produced World War I and other "absurdities."[2] This became a leitmotif in his autobiographical *The Seven Storey Mountain*. His Louisville experience did not dampen his rage at the world's delusions, but his mature anger contained, and was contained within, greater pathos. His youthful indignation helped him find his identity. His fully-seasoned wrath expressed frustrated love for a self-destructive world.

Upon graduation from Columbia, Merton's search for meaning led him in three directions. He taught English literature and writing. Long fancying himself a writer, he wondered: "So many bad books get printed, why can't *my* bad books get printed?" His volunteer work at Friendship House in Harlem--a sister movement to the Catholic Worker--led Catherine de Hueck Doherty to ask him to work there full-time. Although drawn to work with the poor, he pursued the monastic life. Yet, his roads not taken left their mark. His writings on racial issues were always charged with a first-hand passion. His vocational restlessness in succeeding decades pulled him toward solitude on the one hand, and a more active ministry among the dispossessed on the other.[3]

The Franciscan Order rebuffed him, apparently because he had fathered a child while at Cambridge. After visiting the Trappist monastery in Kentucky in

1941, he entered the novitiate. At the time, he revelled equally in the joys of monasticism and in his contempt for the "world." Later, he reflected on this immature antipathy and mused that he had made himself

> a sort of stereotype of the world-denying contemplative--the man who spurned New York, spat on Chicago, and tromped on Louisville, heading for the woods with Thoreau in one pocket, John of the Cross in another, and holding the Bible open at the Apocalypse.[4]

Merton had found a place to belong and made his separate peace, entering Gethsemani at the age of twenty-six, three days after the Japanese attack on Pearl Harbor. Ordained a priest in 1949, he found a niche as novice master within the monastery and as a popular spiritual writer. His life's work seemed set. A brief but genuine romantic involvement in the 1960s caused intense vocational questioning. He incorporated his lifelong attachment to Harlem--poverty, racism, and injustice--into his life and work.

As a still conventional convert, Merton described his first experience of Gethsemani: "Presently the key turned in the door. I passed inside. The door closed quietly behind me. I was out of the world...I had entered into a solitude that was an impregnable fortress." Young man Merton thought he had left the "world" behind, but he quickly discovered its unpredictable presence within the cloister, within his own heart. The years disabused him of his naive beliefs about monasticism. He came to reject the notion of the monastery as a "spiritual dynamo." In the blush of his initial enthusiasm, he called Gethsemani the "center" of America, a binding spiritual power holding the nation together. In the 1960s, his mind's eye saw the center of America a few miles down the road at Ft. Knox. The nation had not changed; the monk had.[5]

Merton freely shared a lively sense of humor. His face balanced "mischief and wisdom." He was also sensitive to criticism, prone to pessimism, and alternately self-righteous and overly self-effacing. He confessed his pessimism, but added, "They told Jeremiah to stress the positive side of things, too." As his solitude increased, he felt compelled to communicate beyond the cloister. His voluminous letters attest to his contacts with a spectrum of correspondents (many of whom he never met) he called his "real 'community.'"[6]

There are kernels of truth in a popular two-stage outline of Merton's career. An inward-looking phase led slowly, through a deep interior life, to social concerns. Day experienced a similar pattern, although she was never satisfied separated from activism. In reality, though, when Merton embraced the world in the 1950s, he re-integrated two parts of his life torn apart by his glad discovery of the monastery. Long before he approached the Franciscans, he had been influenced by Gandhi. When fascist Italy invaded Ethiopia in 1935, Merton took part in protests. While at Columbia, he made a superficial gesture toward radicalism by joining the Communist Party. When the U.S. began its peacetime draft in 1940, the recent convert filed as one of fewer than 300 American Catholic non-combatants. Merton's later social passion was a reunion with a part of his life he had left behind.[7]

Merton's emergence as a social critic in 1961 surprised some readers, disappointed others, and embarrassed his Cistercian Order. Many resented his "new" political concerns and wanted him to return to sublime, popular, "spiritual" writings. He received angry letters and occasional threats. When--with a bemused expression--he pinned a peace button to his monk's habit, he recognized the ensemble as a statement about his vocation, connecting world peace to personal solitude much as Day had once joined Union Square with Rome.[8]

Left and right, activists and quietists, reproved Merton, but he was his own toughest critic. Out of touch with events because news of the chaotic 1960s was slow to reach his quiet hill, he resolved to write intuitively about the general social climate. In his introduction to a Vietnamese translation of *No Man Is An Island*, he wondered whether people had time to read his pious meditations with napalm showering down. Morally constrained to share more than "spiritual" thoughts, the inaccessibility of news made him feel like a blindfolded fighter with his hands tied. Accepting his limitations, he found his niche "halfway in and out of the action."[9]

Censorship quickly threatened Merton's social writings. All of his writings needed the Order's approval, and many of his superiors considered his worldly concerns an unhealthy quirk. History was on their side: it was unusual for a Trappist to publish at all. The head of the Order in France, too, was said to support enthusiastically Charles de Gaulle's militarism. At first, they toned down his polemics. Then, in April 1962, they ordered Merton to cease from publishing anything political. He submitted resentfully, citing his vow of obedience to those encouraging him to defy the ban. Yet he found ways around the gag order. Although forbidden to publish, he was free to circulate mimeographed correspondences which became known as his "Cold War Letters." He could also publish in journals with very small readerships; he began to adjust his opinion of circulation figures accordingly. Articles bearing his thought and style appeared under amusing pseudonyms: Marco J. Frisbee, Benedict Moore, and Benedict Monk.[10] While outflanking his superiors, he cautioned his friends not to print his writings on more than a limited basis. The censorship was only lifted as the Church's mood changed with Pope John XXIII's "Pacem in Terris."

Merton had not always been anxious to write about politics. In 1955, he equivocated over signing a petition against nuclear weapons, but by 1961 his signature began to adorn many statements. At first, he focused on the nuclear arms race. Then, during Vatican II, he called on his Church to validate conscientious objection and support Catholics COs. He questioned applications of the Just War theory in the nuclear era even for so-called "limited" wars. His intense interest in racial issues had never abated and showed itself in new writings on the civil rights movement. In 1964, he joined the early chorus condemning the war in Vietnam, then wrote on protests and draft card burnings.[11]

Monastic activism had its shortcomings. Merton quickly discovered that, beyond writing, all he could do was attach his name and reputation--and he doubted their worth--to peace organizations and protest statements. He became a founding sponsor of the Catholic Peace Fellowship and Pax (which later affiliated with Pax Christi). He wrote for *The Catholic Worker* and joined the largely Protestant Fellowship of Reconciliation, then an act as unusual for its ecumenicity as for its activism. Practicing from his cell what Day called the "little way" of Therese, Merton undertook small-scale works for justice, donating profits from Freedom Songs he had written to a scholarship fund for black students, selling some of his drawings to help pay for a scholarship for a black girl in Louisville.

Merton strenuously resisted suggestions from others that he return to an "active" life. An FOR staff member wrote and told him that he could contribute more to the world by leaving his cloister, that monastic life evaded responsibility. But Merton, refusing to be "appointed a scoutmaster" for activists, replied that he could best help the peace movement by seeking authentic solitude. He wrote theologian Rosemary Radford Ruether, another advocate for the active life, that while it was "damned stupid" being a monk, that was "what I have to do." He conceded that he should travel more often but, in fact, his abbot had long restricted his excursions. His decision to remain a monk was "irrevocable."[12]

Privately Merton examined other options, each one deepening his solitude, his relationship with oppressed people, or combining contemplative and active ministries. In letters to Pope John XXIII and Pope Paul VI, he asked permission to start a contemplative ministry in Latin America or a monastic apostolate as a place of retreat to encourage interfaith dialogue. In the late 1950s, he felt a "temptation" to start a monastery in Ecuador; the next year, an interest in living among Native Americans as a hermit-missionary. He was invited to join a nonviolent experiment in Brazil. In 1967, former Merton novice Ernesto Cardenal invited him to Nicaragua to be a co-founder of a lay Christian community. At the same time, he told several friends that he might start a contemplative foundation in Chile, and the American Friends Service Committee asked him to take part in a dialogue with representatives of the Vietcong.[13]

Merton also considered leaving the Cistercians for the Carthusians, an order with a more rigorous discipline of silence and greater openness to solitude. Allowed to travel in 1968, he scouted California and Alaska for a possible "hideout." Restlessness boiled within him as if he could never quite balance his dual needs for solitude and ministry. His vocational conflict never developed into "a pitched battle," yet "the entrenched, semiconscious conflict between the two needs remained, active and intense, till the end."[14]

Merton had used his research into the history of monasticism to churn up examples of the solitary life and justify his campaign to live in a hermitage; he defended solitude as a well-grounded vocation for a few with benefits for the whole monastic movement. In 1965 he was finally given permission to live apart from his community. When he entered the hermitage "full-time"--he still had brief daily interactions with his community--he believed his contacts with friends outside the monastery, and his political writings, would dwindle. Willing to sacrifice world-engagement for the sake of solitude, his official "hermitage years" were remarkably productive as he maintained a steady flow of insightful letters and commentary.[15]

Allowed to travel extensively in 1968 for the first time as a monk, Merton followed springtime visits to monastic communities in Alaska, California, and New Mexico with an autumn trip scheduled to include India, Sri Lanka, Nepal, Thailand, Indonesia, and Japan. On a journey that brought a climax to his attempts to bridge

Eastern and Western religion, he met the Dalai Lama and other Buddhist leaders. On December 10, shortly after giving a talk at a conference in Bangkok, Merton was accidentally electrocuted after a shower. On the twenty-seventh anniversary of his entry into Gethsemani, his monastic journey came to an end.

Merton has endured a fate the opposite of Muste's. In a letter to Pope John XXIII, he introduced himself as "a Cistercian monk, born in France, educated in England and in America, master of novices and author of a few paltry books."[16] But since his death Merton has been hailed as a human icon, a central figure in twentieth-century Christianity, guiding others in directions he charted. He fashioned an ecumenical Christianity in his personal faith; he began creative interfaith conversations; he charted pathways within himself and toward God; he integrated mystical and monastic traditions with social action.

Merton's form of social action was far removed from Muste's activism, Day's hands-on ministry, or King's physical risk. Yet, more often than not, Merton acknowledged his distance from events as more blessing than curse because of the perspective it offered him. It was his peculiar calling to fill a vocation in social activism by being a monk, poet, prophet, pastor, priest, and spiritual director. An artist, he painted pictures of the world in broad strokes; a poet, he evoked new ways of seeing and living in the world; a priest, he called his Church to the confessional; a pastor, he challenged activists intent on social transformation to be pure in heart.

Benedictine monk and medieval historian Jean Leclercq said, "Because he was a person of vision--not of 'visions'--. . .Merton was a prophet."[17] The roads he did not take--to Harlem, as a Franciscan or a novelist--clarified his vision and his vocation. The writer, poet, priest, and monk in him gave him a unique way of sharing that vision. He resisted the temptation to more immediate involvement in social change. To do more for the world he had to do almost nothing.

A Train to Hell

"Let me begin by describing an experience I had on a summer night in 1938. . . . .All of a sudden I saw a beautiful shining railroad train that circled around a mountain. Streams of children--and adults as well--rushed toward the train and could not be held back. I would rather not say how many adults did not join the ride. Then I heard a voice say to me: 'This train is going to hell.' Immediately it seemed as if someone took me up by the hand, and the same voice said, 'Now we will go to purgatory.' And oh! so frightful was the suffering I saw and felt, I could only have thought that I was in hell itself if the voice had not told me we were going to purgatory. Probably no more than a few seconds passed while I saw all this. Then I heard a sigh and saw a light--and all was gone."

--Franz Jägerstätter[18]

"When he opened the fourth seal, I heard the voice of the fourth living creature call out, 'Come!' I looked and there was a pale green horse! Its rider's name was Death."

--Revelation 6:7

In November 1964, when Merton hosted A. J. Muste, John Howard Yoder, James Forest, Daniel and Philip Berrigan, and others at an FOR retreat, a recurring topic was the life and witness of Franz Jägerstätter. Merton thought Jägerstätter, an Austrian peasant and a Roman Catholic who refused even non-combatant service in Hitler's army, a significant modern Christian witness. The peasant's neighbors believed his actions eccentric, unfortunate, or plain stupid. His priest and bishop urged him, as part of his Christian duty, to submit to the authority of the State. His wife asked him to compromise and save his life for the sake of their children. Five years after his dream, he was beheaded.

The train in Jägerstätter's dream symbolized the National Socialist Folk Community. Almost everyone but the peasant leapt on board. His nightmare, reminiscent of biblical apocalyptic's pattern of vision and voice, experience and explanation, and its polarities of good and evil, symbolized Merton's vision of the world a generation later.

Merton saw the world of the 1950s and 1960s "speeding downhill without brakes." Like Jägerstätter's train, decorated in affluence, glistening with the wizardry of technology, it headed toward hell. Even heads of state could not halt the blind forces propelling their societies. The greatest tragedy was not the malice of those sworn to evil but the futility of those committed to good. Eastern and Western blocs suffered from a common, demonic "political vertigo"; they were out of balance, out of control.[19]

When Muste and Merton came together in 1964, two men met who had long feared that the world reeled on the brink of doom. The powers-that-be asserted that they were reasonable, orderly, cultured, sane. Merton revealed each pose as a deception: Order masked violence; sanity disguised amorality; a culture claiming to feed really poisoned; a thin veneer of reason covered an abyss of chaos.

Someone compiling a book entitled *Success* wrote and asked the famous recluse to contribute a statement on how he had become successful. Merton "replied indignantly" that he did not consider himself a success; he had steadfastly tried to avoid it. He had once, accidentally, written a best-seller; he would be careful not to let it happen again. His message was simple: "Be anything you like, be madmen, drunks, and bastards of every shape and form, but at all costs avoid one thing: success." He did not believe his reply was published.[20]

Merton agreed with William Faulkner that people were caught in a "frantic steeplechase toward nothing" in which they lived simulated lives in an unconscious mass conspiracy. The pursuit of success was a "complete and systematic sham," a "pursuit of shadows." American society marketed all things necessary to happiness--God, peace, and salvation. It equipped each person with a "cave"--of entertainment, of anesthesia, of business, of forgetfulness. In society, people could avoid the one thing necessary in life--contact with their own selves. People had become so averse to solitude that they desperately created what Pascal called *divertissement*, systematic distractions "so mercifully provided by society, which enable a man to avoid his own company for twenty-four hours a day." The culture dealt in drugs: "People are fed on myths, they are stuffed up to the eyes with illusions. They CAN'T think straight."[21]

The "free world" was really a place where business could exploit without inhibition; democracy a fad of the transitory prosperity of the 1920s when it seemed that anyone could own an expensive car. The collective fantasies of materialistic culture masked implosive hopelessness.[22]

Each person became distorted. Each postulant, Merton thought, arrived at Gethsemani "systematically deprived of a serious identity." American culture fed its people spiritual poisons. The average worker spent a day with a machine, an evening with a TV in a "radical deprivation" of humanity. Society's "approved way" was a mirage. Delusions of success and endless diversions made it impossible to think about whether or not to board the train to hell. Well before becoming controversial, Merton believed American culture was "rotting from within" and antithetical to Christ. He altered his attitude to the people in Louisville's shopping district, not to commercial America.[23]

The U.S. misapprehended the meaning of law. It equated "order" with the-way-things-are. As King discovered, most Americans thought challenges to the status quo created unnecessary turmoil; they implicitly assumed a kind of political natural law. God had ordained things to be as they are, or to change at a comfortable pace.

In this belief, the U.S. was not alone. In 1931, Gandhi was a living, breathing contradiction for England when he arrived in London for a conference only months after being in prison: "What was the meaning of the fact that one could be holy, and fast, and pray, and be in jail, and be opposed to England all at the same time?" Could holiness oppose the Empire? Could civil rights righteousness stand against the U.S.?[24]

Roman Catholics seemed especially susceptible to a political natural law, and Merton used Catholic statements on justice to reason with them. Using John XXIII's "Pacem in Terris" as an outline, he noted that Thomas Aquinas, considered the perfecter of Christian Natural Law theory, wrote that a law falling short of "right reason" became "a kind of violence." Augustine, often branded an apologist for empires, asked: "What are kingdoms without justice but large bands of robbers?"[25]

A system commits violence when it forces people to live in "conditions of abjection, helplessness, wretchedness" and "keeps them on the level of beasts." Merton characterized the mid-twentieth century as a "storm," a "tornado," in which the world suffered from "vertigo." The superpowers were the housekeepers of chaos.[26]

Order disguised violence. A few economic gestures in a rich nation could starve thousands in a poor nation. America's pre-eminent position made it obsessed with small-scale corruption: "It is a very strange thing to accuse starving workmen of petty thievery when the economic exploitation of the resources of their land by foreigners is one of the things that keeps them starving."[27] As Aquinas and Augustine had observed: law masked robbery.

In his *Asian Journal*, Merton conjured up an image of American violence based on the four-armed Hindu god Shiva: John Wayne with eight arms. In its investigation of urban violence in the mid-1960s, the Kerner Commission saw civil rights and campus-centered peace movements as greenhouses of turbulence. Merton suggested another source:

> The real focus of American violence is not in esoteric groups but in the very culture itself, its mass media, its extreme individualism and competitiveness, its inflated myths of virility and toughness, and its overwhelming preoccupation with the power of nuclear, chemical, bacteriological and psychological overkill. If we live in what is essentially a culture of overkill, how can we be surprised at finding violence in it?[28]

Violence did not explode from time to time; it was woven into the fabric of American identity. The Commission wanted to interpret violence as a series of random incidents caused by amendable flaws, but Merton saw it as the essence of society.

The U.S. was addicted to arrogance and sadism. Merton did not understand America's surprise over John F. Kennedy's assassination, for the "murder grew out of the [Southern] soil of hatred and violence." Kennedy's "death was something that had been meditated, imagined, desired, and 'needed' in a profound and savage way that made it in some sense inevitable." Americans were "nourished on a steady diet of brutal mythology and hallucinations." Street crimes were the fruit of a violent spirit in an unjust society. When the U.S. guided Japan in its post-World War II constitution to renounce rearmament and war, it never imagined that these ideals might apply at home. The American public considered nonviolence a communist deception. Early press reports on assassin Lee Harvey Oswald hinted that he had been inclined to nonviolence! Black militant H. Rap Brown said, "Violence is as American as cherry pie," and King called the U.S. the world's "greatest purveyor of violence." The public thought nonviolence suspect and bizarre; violence patriotic and normal.[29]

Merton marveled at the twisted ingenuity of weapons-makers who experimented to build nuclear bombs without fallout and bombs that would kill but leave buildings unharmed (an idea perfected in the neutron bomb, the quintessential capitalist weapon--eliminates people, preserves property). Bomb shelters also attempted to disinfect violence. In 1961, when Merton engaged in a discussion on bomb shelters--a fad that followed the demise of the civil defense drill--he said that a family defending its shelter with a machine gun after a nuclear attack was "the final exaltation of our culture: individualism, comfort, security, and to hell with everybody else." Merton scoffed at Catholics defending the shelter ethic: "The case could be made for St. Peter to kill St. Paul if there was only enough food for one of them to survive the winter in a mountain cave."[30] The bomb shelter was emblematic of America's illicit affair with violence, a conclusion Day and Muste reached in their protest the previous decade against New York's civil defense drills.

Modesty, Merton believed, partially hid violence to arouse greater prurient anticipation. As a society organized around greed and oppression, the U.S. was always dressed for violence. Street crimes were mere diversions--in Pascal's sense--to absolve society's real criminals. Street crimes stole the nation's attention away from corporate, white-collar, bureaucratized violence. King's "nice, gentle" white people started the 1960s' urban riots; the real war crimes, Merton noted, were committed in offices far from the fighting where the only blood spilled came from an occasional nosebleed.[31]

Merton deduced from constant talk of peace that the nation's leaders believed one more war could deliver lasting peace, a notion Muste had discerned decades before. Merton remembered this strategy from the Crusades, which he considered the first war to end all wars. In the midst of the deceit, the U.S. stood under God's judgment, and there found hope. God offered the truth in merciful silence to people hidden in caves, and they were free to accept redemption.[32]

A fine coating of reason concealed a hive of lies, so Merton pitted revelation against the "reason" that justified the arms race, dictated escalation in Vietnam, and required that blacks decelerate demands for an equitable society. Muste tried to fight reason with reason. Merton saw alleged reason as a deception, and dug beneath it to reveal that its presuppositions contradicted true enlightenment.

Merton was surprised to find it necessary to defend the works of William Faulkner. Although Faulkner had won the Nobel Prize for Literature, many still wrote him off as a Southern, regional writer of little general interest, and as a pessimist (like Merton--and Jeremiah). The real accusation against Faulkner, Merton said, was that "he was out of touch with the times. He did not come up with the acceptable slogans." In writing of the South, Faulkner used a scandal of particularity to unveil a more general truth: "Faulkner saw that the reason, justice, and humanity of the Enlightenment and the lunacy, injustice, and inhumanity of the South were in reality two aspects of the same thing."[33]

Some critics did not like Faulkner's placement of stories in the fictitious Southern county of Yoknapatawpha. One critic said, "As far as Yoknapatawpha is concerned, the Enlightenment might just as well have never been." Merton called this "one of the most comical remarks in all Faulkner criticism," for this was precisely Faulkner's point.

> It is precisely in the midst of the "enlightened" middle class world that we have not only Yoknapatawpha but Auschwitz, Hiroshima, the Vietnam war, Watts, South Africa, and a whole litany of some of the choicest atrocities in human history...Far from getting on as if the Enlightenment had never been, Yoknapatawpha was made necessary by the Enlightenment--and was necessary to it.[34]

The mid-twentieth century had little to do with logic; it was an age of technology without room for wisdom or truth. Merton saw passengers on a train to hell uninterested in their culture's true destination. The thin shell of reason was easily shattered.

Merton questioned the whole concept of "sanity": "In an age where there is much talk about 'being yourself,' I reserve to myself the right to forget about being

myself, since in any case there is very little chance of my being anybody else."
Most modern psychology did not face up to human evil nor account for society's
insanity. By helping people adjust to society's norms, psychology became an
accomplice in the general madness. Merton shared Muste's suspicion of
conformity, King's preference for maladjustment.[35]

Adolf Eichmann was Merton's ultimate symbol of sanity. According to his
psychological tests, the obedient bureaucrat of the Holocaust was "sane." In both
poetry and prose, Merton described the bureaucrat's sanity. Eichmann's "relations
with father mother brother/Sister most normal/Most desirable." He slept well, had
a healthy appetite, showed no signs of psychosomatic disorder. He did not dislike
Jews. He had an administrative job; field: Mass murder. The Holocaust was a
"prize-winning transaction." Repent? "Repentance," Eichmann said, "is for
children."[36]

If this was sanity, Merton urged madness. Given this recent psycho-
history, he guessed that a general planning a nuclear war could, with equal grace,
estimate the millions of victims and pass the Rorschach ink blots. The sanity of
Eichmann, politicians, and society had no connection with morality, no relation
with conscience, no notion of sin or repentance. One could be both sane and a
sociopath. As long as megamurders were politically expedient, "sanity" had lost
touch with reality. Muste had called the situation "madness."[37]

The mundane perpetrators of the Holocaust were products of an advanced
civilization and raised in "Christian" or middle-class homes (the West often
confused the two). Merton compared Nazi Germany to the American South, "No
need for monsters: ordinary policemen and good citizens will take care of
everything." The lives of Holocaust employees made him realize that "ordinary
people stimulated by an extraordinary regime" could perform "demonic" acts.[38]

All of this made Merton maintain a distance from psychology. He confirmed Erich Fromm's intuition that successful adjustment to insane social norms was not mental health. When billboards declared that people lived in bliss, what would "adjustment" mean? Without intentional self-monitoring, psychotherapy would become another of society's tools to quiet human conscience.[39]

Merton hoped that an accurate discernment of the source of alienation might lead to psychological and spiritual health. The person whose "mask" made him sweat, whose role made her itch, the ones who abhorred their divided selves, were beginning to taste freedom. Others merely yearned to exchange one mask for another or to pay psychiatrists to scratch their itch without touching their disorder. African-Americans lost freedom when all they wanted were white American masks; white-collar workers when they wanted to become hippies. Merton advised: Do not desire another mask; stop adjusting yours for comfort's sake; strip off every delusion of psychological health; get off the train.[40]

No pawn of progressivism, Merton, like Maurin, considered the modern age a great historical crisis in which evil flowed and disaster hovered low. His early book of poems, *Figures for an Apocalypse*, signalled his view that his was an age in which ordinary decisions had "terrible consequences," in which people lived "on the doorsill of the Apocalypse." In the mid-twentieth century "the tiny ripples on the reasonable surface of history are perhaps indications of sea monsters below": chaos beneath order; Yoknapatawpha within the Enlightenment; Leviathan below calm water. The vocation of the man with vision was to spot the hungry sea monsters before they consumed all.[41]

In the fourth century, the Desert Fathers fled society's horror in order to turn and see it more clearly. What good, ordinary, city people saw as normal,

Merton--in the "desert"--saw as destructive. Society rendered ordinary people senseless, unable to perceive their predicament.

Merton's essay "Day of a Stranger" begins and ends with an awareness of the possibility of mass destruction. In the morning,

> I have seen the SAC plane, with the bomb in it, fly low over me and
> I have looked up out of the woods directly at the closed bay of the
> metal bird with a scientific egg in its breast! A womb easily and
> mechanically opened! I do not consider this technological mother to
> be the friend of anything I believe in. However, like everyone else,
> I live in the shadow of the apocalyptic cherub. . . .

In the evening he looks at the "bed in which I will presently sleep alone under the ikon of the Nativity. Meanwhile the metal cherub of the apocalypse passes over me in the clouds, treasuring its egg and its message." The day of the contemplative, dotted by prayer, reading, writing, work, and silence, had its first and last punctuation marks stamped by the "apocalyptic cherub."[42]

Common decisions had uncommon consequences. Who is right is no longer important, Merton wrote Day, merely who is not criminal, for everyone living under the metal cherub's shadow sensed a world on the verge of a holocaust, a crime second only to the crucifixion.[43] Merton's was not a clinical voice. He used extreme words like "criminal," "Nazi," and "apostate" to describe world and Church. As a poet, he exaggerated to catch and transform people's imaginations.

The term "criminal" violated conventional American morality, but no word so quickly conjured up a conglomerate of despicable images as "Nazi." When Day called the Church a "harlot," she had forgivable infidelity in mind. When Merton used the term "apostate," he described the Church going beyond infidelity; it had not only turned away from Christ, it had turned against him. In apocalyptic times, exaggerated rhetoric becomes more astute than emotionally-distanced analysis: ordinary actions become criminal, national morality Nazi amorality, infidelity apostasy.

To Merton, the U.S., the West, and the world seemed bent on suicide. He wrote off-handedly about a nation whose economy thrived on the arms industry, "a fat society glutted with the profits begotten by its own death wish." In an era of suicide, what could be more natural than people worshipping war as a god? People believed in war's omnipotence, its ability to transform evil into good. War had become "the great force, the evil mystery, the demonic mover of our century, with his globe of sun-fire, and his pillar of cloud."[44]

Writing to the Mayor of Hiroshima in 1962, Merton used a Mustean metaphor: "We are all walking backward toward a precipice. We know the precipice is there, but we assert that we are all going forward." In his poem, "The Tower of Babel," the Chorus cries:

> Hide us from the fall, hide us from the fall!
> Hide us in the catacomb, hide us in the well!
> Hide us in the ground, hide us from the sky!
> Hide us from the Tower's fall![45]

The hiding places are below ground like the catacombs in Rome, as though the survivors might be true believers like the Christians who survived the fall of the Roman Empire. Or they are hiding in a well (a place from a children's story where a child's deception masks as faith). Or they merely hide in the bomb shelters Merton loathed. They hide from the sky, the bomb, the egg dropping from the SAC plane's womb. The fearful scramble for salvation from the apparatus of annihilation.

In this atmosphere, Merton found guidance for the Church and for each Christian in what the Church did *not* do for Franz Jägerstätter. Religious leaders took calculated, enlightened action. They respected order; they assumed the value of sanity; they admired the beautiful train. As with Muste, Merton's political climate required either all-out war or the abolition of war--a triumphant god or a smashed idol. Using one of Muste's favorite images, Merton remembered the

Early Church opposing the idolatries of Empire and war when it refused to burn incense to Caesar. It was again time to oppose idolatry. In spite of the odds, the Church and the Christian, community and individual, had to shape one another's conscience, stand against the train, protest and prophesy.[46]

When, in November 1965, Merton received the tragic news of Roger LaPorte's protest-suicide, he fell victim to his particular place in social activism. He reacted like a lover or parent separated by a long distance from the beloved who hears bad news and assumes the worst. Immediately he sent a telegram to New York asking that he no longer be associated with the Catholic Peace Fellowship to which LaPorte--a former Trappist, former seminarian, and member of the Catholic Worker community--belonged. Merton refused to equate LaPorte's sacrifice with the self-immolations of Vietnamese Buddhist monks, nor did he consider the young Catholic a martyr. Day considered the suicide a tragedy. Muste credited LaPorte for his sensitivity to evil. Merton saw in the event, the third protest-suicide in rapid succession, a hint of a "pathological" tendency taking over the peace movement. Merton turned his distrust on his own motivations for being in the anti-war movement.[47]

Shaken, the New York Catholic Worker community tried to explain the inexplicable. One Worker described the protest-suicide as LaPorte's way of crying out, "'murder,' 'murder.'"[48] LaPorte had taken on a role not unlike the protesting monk's. Each had become like Kurtz in Joseph Conrad's *The Heart of Darkness*. Each viewed the war and said, "The horror! The horror!" In Conrad's novella, Kurtz converts to the horror. It seemed to have overwhelmed LaPorte. Merton must have wondered if he would be overcome, if the peace movement had already been infected with society's "sanity." He honored the message, not the act which confirmed his certainty that he lived in apocalyptic times. While most of society remained insensible, he saw "horror" where others saw only what was good and decent. LaPorte had been overly sensitive. Merton hoped that some could stand against the nightmare without being dragged down in an overpowering riptide.

After a week-long flurry of angry letters, Merton apologized for being inconsiderate of those closer to the tragedy and more entitled to grief and consolation. He recanted his resignation from the CPF but made clear through a public statement that his sponsorship in no way implied his support of each member's every act for peace.[49]

Merton's pessimism made him fear that everyone would board the "train to hell," but he did not predict the future. With Muste and King, he saw a choice between barbarism or true civilization, chaos or true peace, the Antichrist or the Millennium. In placing confidence in people's freedom to choose, he hoped that the nation might choose not to dream its nightmare any longer. Even America's dominant, warlike "illusion of innocence and universal messianism" might evaporate. He spoke of a moment of "kairos" in which the power of redemption could open a way toward God's reign of peace. At these times, he resonated with Muste's optimism as he awaited the new pentecost, with King's confidence as he hoped to hasten the arrival of the beloved community. Even as peoples and nations made the wrong choices, Merton prayed: "Grant us to see your face in the lightning of this cosmic storm, O God of holiness, merciful to men."[50]

Merton's heightened sensitivity to evil distinguishes him from Muste. The contemplative found something beneath apparently disconnected events far more terrible than the eloquent King could elucidate. The spiritual root of Merton's pessimism was this ability to sense the demonic significance in events. If he was sometimes overwhelmed by evil, it was because evil now and then blocked his hopeful imagination. If King described the Promised Land to urge his people toward it, Merton tried to convince anyone who would listen that they were all in bondage in Egypt so that they would leave it.

Merton was a monk, and from its conception in the Desert the monastic tradition has had an apocalyptic consciousness. Such times make for radical choices--fidelity or apostasy, kairos or hell. Writing during the urban riots-- sacraments of a deteriorating racial crisis--Merton asserted that when others trust in nothing but their weapons, God might give the faithful "an opening toward peace and love even when the sulphur and brimstone are at their worst."[51]

In this environment of death wish and intent to commit megamurder, Merton offered a way to create order within oneself, a way to live in apocalyptic times, a way off the train, perhaps even a way to halt it. He proposed the traditional mystical path of purgation, illumination, and union. Perhaps an almost violent purge could jar the world's delusions, and its nightmare of antagonism could end--just as Merton's dream of separateness had died in Louisville.

A "Guilty Bystander"

"On the day when crime dons the apparel of innocence...it is innocence that is called upon to justify itself."

        --Albert Camus[52]

On the monk's forty-sixth birthday, "they put an ape in space" that was undisturbed by "metaphysical problems" or guilt. As a present to himself, Merton unleashed his chafing wit.

> Why should an ape in space feel guilt? Space is where there is no more weight and no more guilt. And an ape does not feel guilt even on earth, for that matter.

> Would that we on earth did not feel guilt! Perhaps if we can all get into space we will not feel any more guilt. We will pull

levers, press buttons, and eat banana-flavored pills. No, pardon me. We are not quite apes yet.

We will not feel guilt in space. We will not feel guilt on the moon. Maybe we will feel just a *little* guilt on the moon, but when we get to Mars we will feel no guilt at all.

From Mars or the moon we will blow up the world, perhaps. If we blow up the world from the moon we may feel a little guilt. If we blow it up from Mars we will feel no guilt at all. No guilt at all. We will blow up the world with no guilt at all. Tra la.[53]

The world tried to escape the pangs of guilt at breakneck speed. As a priest, Merton recommended the confessional over the space race. To be free of guilt was to be less, not more, than human. The human race had not yet been so dehumanized.

From Gethsemani Merton realized with Vietnam veterans that society's ethics had become largely "a matter of distance and technology." It was wrong to shoot a Vietnamese civilian who was walking or standing but all right to shoot one who was running. It was immoral to destroy a village with hand-thrown grenades but moral to demolish it with napalm bombs. American soldiers in Vietnam "were simultaneously witnessing, perpetrating, and being victimized by evil." People fantasized that they could escape guilt by flights into space, religion, prayer, or monastery, but from guilt there was no exit.[54]

Merton entitled his book of reflections from 1956-65 *Conjectures of a Guilty Bystander*, recognizing his participation in the world's storms--its moonshots and wars. American soldiers in Vietnam were unexceptional in their experience of evil, except for its intensity. Everyone witnesses and inflicts evil. Evil victimizes everyone. To ignore any part of this relationship misleads one into a deadly sense of innocence.

Merton's Church offered two false solutions to guilt: compartmentalization and "otherworldliness." By concentrating on individualistic salvation, it encouraged people to believe that faith was a "happiness pill," Christ's peace a "spiritual tranquilizer." Merton fought against an unchristian rugged individualism that allowed people to segregate faith from love and spirituality from life: "There is no spiritual life, only God and His word and my total response." In the Prologue to *The Silent Life*, he paraphrased Paul: We should live no longer for ourselves alone, but for Him who died for us and rose again (2 Cor 5:15), for "when a man attempts to live by and for himself alone, he becomes a little 'island' of hate, greed, suspicion, fear, desire." In that kind of religion, "God" becomes "a mere figment of the imagination. Such religion is insincere. It is merely a front for greed, injustice, sensuality, selfishness, violence."[55]

As King decried narrowly heaven-directed preachers, Merton denounced a petty piety which selfishly abandoned the world to unscrupulous power mongers. This short-sightedness contorted Christian faith and reduced charity (*caritas*) to being "nice." It could have reminded Merton of his English boarding school chaplain who rendered "charity" (in Paul's famous hymn in praise of love) as "gentlemanliness."[56]

Merton found in American Catholic prayers for a Soviet conversion a secret yearning for the USSR to adopt all of Western Catholicism's prejudices, customs, and cliches. He preferred a more traditional petition: "Thy Kingdom come," but the Church built a kingdom its own way, in its own image.[57]

While Merton agreed with Gandhi that one could not separate religion and politics, American Catholicism proclaimed a fictitious dualism. Secular political assumptions entered the Church through social osmosis while the Church kept the Gospel on a firm leash. The Church accepted capitalism's axioms about communism, and blessed idolatrous anti-communism and violence. It equated hope in God with confidence in the economy, God's promises to Abraham with American abundance. Attempts to be "modern" tempted the Church to equate Los Angeles with the New Jerusalem. Catholic opponents of this brand of piety faced being led--spiritually--to the stake. Merton suggested an emendation to the Lord's Prayer to express the spirit of the Church: Delete "Thy Kingdom come," and add "Give us time!" The Church did not leaven society as much as society leavened-- and lessened--the Church.[58]

Internally, the Church needed to become a collegial community instead of a monolith trickling down truth from on high. To Cardinal Spellman's avid support for the war in Vietnam, Merton commented that Church leaders had been blinded for so long by their own power that they had lost all moral sense. A Church bound to, and by, hierarchical power had lost touch with mercy. A Church more concerned with the right "verbal formulas" than the commandment to love had become an "illusory Christianity."[59] A voice from the Kentucky wilderness joined Muste, Day, and King in calling the Church back to a holy life based on love, to a spiritual life of undivided personal and social concerns, to a community life focused on following Christ.

Merton was also aware of temptation's many victories in his own monastery. He entered Gethsemani not knowing that materialism preceded him: the Order made money by making cheese. In a moment of whimsy, he wrote "CHEE$E" by "Joyce Killer-Diller."

> I think that we should never freeze
> Such lively assets as our cheese:
> The sucker's hungry mouth is pressed
> Against the cheese's caraway breast.
> A cheese, whose scent like sweet perfume
> Pervades the house through every room.
> A cheese that may at Christmas wear
> A suit of cellophane underwear,

> Upon whose bosom is a label,
>
> Whose habitat:--The Tower of Babel.

In a moment of frustration at being silenced on the arms race, he wrote,

> It is all right for the monk to break his ass putting out packages of
> cheese and making a pile of money for the old monastery, but as to
> doing anything that is *really* fruitful for the Church, that is another
> matter altogether.[60]

Selfish individualism and spiritual evasion were alive and well in the monastery. The monk's vow of poverty did not preclude wealth for the Order, nor encourage a poverty of spirit. Having left the deceits of the world, Merton found himself in a "sham desert," the worst of both worlds.[61]

The early 1960s' argument about bomb shelters piqued Merton even before he heard that patriotic monks in upstate New York had constructed a shelter. It was a "grim joke": individualism, evasion, and violence all rolled into one. Monastic renewal, liturgical change, ecumenism, and revived biblical scholarship would not mean much if Christians relied on the H-Bomb to deliver peace. Upon receiving the Pax Medal from the Catholic Peace Fellowship in 1963, he offered pointed words: "A monastery is not a snail's shell nor is religious faith a kind of spiritual fallout shelter into which one can plunge to escape the criminal realities of an apocalyptic age."[62]

Prayer and voluntary poverty had to be doorways into, not out of, the human race. A monastery that confirmed preconceived, bourgeois notions promoted moral corruption: "To have a vow of poverty seems to me illusory if I do not in some way identify myself with the cause of people who are denied their rights and forced, for the most part, to live in abject misery."[63]

Instead of the Church sanctifying the world, the world's illusions corrupted Church and monastery. The Church was unwilling or unable to address the arms race, the Vietnam War, race relations, consumerism, commercialism, materialism.

In his early writings, Merton's answer to the human predicament was to call for separation from the "world." Instead of being an ape in space he had become a monk in Kentucky. With time, he learned that such answers were inadequate. His questions became more probing, but his mission remained the same--to "unmask the illusions" of the world.64

In an apocalyptic age, sitting at home, meditating on the divine presence, and praying for peace were not a sufficient way of prayer or witness. If people prayed for genuine peace, God would grant it. But when people prayed for the injustice they thought was peace, God granted that instead.65

Centuries earlier, Meister Eckhart had written that "world-flight" did not assist the development of a deep spiritual life. Now Merton asserted that his hermitage would not distance him from the world. He shared the goal of the Desert Fathers--"deliberate solitude" helped one to love God and neighbor: "If you go into the desert merely to get away from people you dislike, you will find neither peace nor solitude; you will only isolate yourself with a tribe of devils." True prayer met God in the world's "awful paradoxes" and interceded for the twentieth century:

> A nun who has meditated on the Passion of Christ but has not
> meditated on the extermination camps of Dachau and Auschwitz has
> not yet fully entered into the experiences of Christianity in our time.
> For Dachau and Auschwitz are two terrible, indeed apocalyptic,
> presentations of the *reality* of the Passion renewed in our time.

The otherworldly pious deceived themselves by regarding such events as distractions, but "the contemplative above all should ruminate on these terrible realities which are so symptomatic, so important, so prophetic."66 Merton had always had an eye for crosses. His 1946 collection of poetry included "Aubade--Harlem," a poem filled with images of crucifixion reflecting the Passion in his own city. Prayerful contemplation did not dilute pain nor deliver respectability; it awakened unanswerable questions and anguish. It opened new wounds.67

False innocence may have been the cruelest illusion to cripple the Church, its monasteries, and its prayers. Like the pacifist Muste, Merton accepted his personal responsibility for World War II. All were "implicated" in the crimes of the age. A "witness" to a crime who pretends to be an "innocent" bystander becomes an accomplice. A healthy monastic community recognizes its involvement in destructive social structures, and prays accordingly. Those who let the world blow up while pursuing a private spirituality are in "secret complicity" with the overt destruction. They could deny their involvement in "crime," but they could not shake an unconscious awareness of guilt. Justice-seekers ought to be conscious of their guilt "above all."[68]

> In compressed prose, he described to Day society's anti-values:
> We despise everything that Christ loves, everything marked with His compassion. We love fatness health bursting smiles the radiance of satisfied bodies all properly fed and rested and sated and washed and perfumed and sexually relieved. Anything else is a horror and a scandal to us. How sad. It makes me more and more sad and ashamed, for I am part of the society which has these values and I can't help sharing its guilt, its illusions. Whether I like it or not I help perpetuate the illusion in one way or other. . . .

The "illusion of spirituality" just made people "more smug on the rebound."[69] In Merton's "Chant to be used in Processions around a site with Furnaces," the commandant of Auschwitz speaks out:

> So I was hanged in a commanding position with a full
> view of the site plant and grounds
> You smile at my career but you would do as I did if you
> knew yourself and dared. . . .
> Do not think yourself better because you burn up friends
> and enemies with long-range missiles without ever seeing
> what you have done. . . .[70]

Merton could not deny his guilt:

That I should have been born in 1915, that I should be the contemporary of Auschwitz, Hiroshima, Viet Nam and the Watts riots, are things about which I was not first consulted. Yet they are also events in which, whether I like it or not, I am deeply and personally involved.

Anyone who pretended to ignore the Holocaust or Vietnam was "bluffing." Public statements opposing the war and racism did not keep him from bearing part of the blame. In 1967 he turned down a chance to leave the U.S. so that he could "stay where the guilt is." Every American traveller was an "ambassador of affluence and napalm." When in Calcutta in 1968, a woman begged him for money. He lost the "contest," giving her a rupee; for she was poor and he--with his vow of poverty-- was a "Rich Daddy" from the West.[71]

The concept of the "guilty bystander" had spiritual and social significance. A political "spiral of violence" begins with oppression which foments rebellion which then causes repression. Merton saw a spiritual spiral of violence beginning in the human heart and escalating to nuclear war. It began with guilt and, as people experience a self-hatred too powerful to face, they project it onto others, exaggerating the difference between--for instance--American good and Soviet evil. Projecting evil onto a person, place, or nation conveniently destroys the scapegoat and the evil in one blow. Denied guilt leads to nuclear war. To remedy guilt and end war, one must despise "the criminal, bloodthirsty arrogance of his own nation or class, as much as that of the enemy," one's own "self-seeking aggressivity as much as that of the politicians who hypocritically pretend they are fighting for peace."[72]

Merton turned on their heads the cliches about loving oneself in order to love one's enemies. In order to break the spiral of violence and love one's enemies, one must first despise those things about oneself and one's nation that cause scapegoating. Merton applied the wisdom of the Desert Fathers to modern politics: view others with charity, yourself ruthlessly. With Muste, he called nation and Church from self-righteousness to humility. Purgation begins at home.

The modern Desert Father renounced all disguises of guilt. Even though some blacks saw him as a sympathetic white person, Merton felt shame because whites had for so long made blacks ashamed of themselves. The pain of being a non-participant during the racial crisis made him question whether his vocation justified his inaction.[73]

Merton recognized sin and evil in others because he saw it so clearly in himself. The solitary life led him into solidarity with the human condition in all of its ugliness. As a Christian, priest, and monk, he had to renounce the blessings provided by a world whose illusions would grant him premature absolution. To be saved, he had to be at one with a world almost beyond salvation.[74]

His sensitivity to sin and evil led, ironically, to hope. Day spoke of penance, Muste a politics of repentance, King a prodigal civilization, and Merton of stripped away illusions of innocence. When America's guilt exploded into race hatred, class conflict, and war, one could stand aside from the conflagration, yet non-participation was not enough. Merton quoted St. John Chrysostom: "It is vain for you to fast and sleep on the ground, to eat ashes and to weep without ceasing. If you are no use to anybody else, you are doing nothing of any importance."[75] Chrysostom's words could easily haunt a monk so distant from activism. His vocation might be a way of becoming a kind of ape in space, of seeking an illusory remoteness from insanity profiting no one. One had to act on behalf of others. The Christian mystical tradition had for centuries advocated the way of detachment and re-attachment in love.

Merton offered no program to alleviate guilt. He could only "recognize myself as part of a society both sentenced and redeemed: a society which, if it can accept sentence and redemption, will live." Muste said: Turn and live. King's prodigal nation could come to itself. Merton called for confession--accepting responsibility for sins--and absolution.[76]

"The Pursuit of Marginality"

"A monk is one who is separated from all and united to all."

> --Evagrius Ponticus

"It is obvious, then, that the useless has its use."

> --Chuang Tzu[77]

"God did not send the Son into the world to condemn the world, but in order that the world might be saved through him."

> --John 3:17

At the beginning of *The Seven Storey Mountain*, young man Merton described his spiritual predicament:

> Free by nature, in the image of God, I was nevertheless the prisoner of my own violence and my own selfishness, in the image of the world into which I was born. That world was the picture of Hell, full of men like myself, loving God and yet hating Him; born to love Him, living instead in fear and hopeless self-contradictory hungers.[78]

The image of God battled the world and Hell. He had to renounce the world, turn away, and flee from it.

His turning back to the world, signified in his illumination and feelings of union in Louisville, had been prepared for by years of prayer and purgation. The event sacramentalized the new direction in his life and fulfilled solitude's promise. The words he uses to describe the experience are like the language of the Old

Testament covenants in which God takes Israel as "my people" and becomes "your God." From God's mouth and Merton's, these words sound like marriage vows.

> In *The Seven Storey Mountain*, young Merton wrote,
> if Adam had never fallen, the whole human race would have been a series of magnificently different and splendid images of God, each one of the millions of men showing forth His glories and perfections in an astonishing new way, and each one shining with his own particular sanctity. . . .[79]

The possibility of transfigured humanity was forever extinguished by the Fall.

By the time of his Louisville experience, the balance between Transfiguration and Fall had shifted. Though addicted to absurdities, people walk around "shining like the sun." In spite of sin, with the incarnation the human race has been transfigured to glisten with the glory of God. It was as though the Orthodox emphasis on incarnation and transfiguration had imploded into the crowd in front of Merton, as though Muste's Quaker vision of light had filled human faces. Merton's only lament was that others seemed blind. If only they could see what he had seen, there would be no more hatred, greed, cruelty, or war. The only problem would be that "we would fall down and worship each other." The incarnation re-defined humanity, filling flesh with hope and glory. Seeing the human race for the first time as it really was, Merton had fallen in love.[80]

As Day rebuffed the Church before entering it, Merton rejected the world before loving it. Day's illumination of human solidarity came as she was going to work with striking seamen. She interpreted her experience in light of the Mystical Body of Christ, the unity of the human family, the incarnation. Both Day and Merton had essentially the same experience, but her commitment was reinforced, his renewed.

Merton understood the threefold mystical path of purgation, illumination, and union in relationship to God, but in his early, romantic monasticism--as sentimental as Maurin's view of Irish monks, as Muste and King's idealization of the pre-Constantinian Church--purgation meant renouncing the world. His acidic scorn for non-monastic living cloaked in religious garb his desire to demean others.

In solitude he unearthed a second mystical path in relation to humanity. How could it not be so if Christ was fully human as well as fully divine? On this second path, his Louisville vision purged his illusion of separation, illumined his neighbors, and united them together, compressing three stages into one. Day felt united with humanity long before her baptism. Merton walked first with God before seeing God shine in human flesh. The people of Louisville had been strangers when Merton entered the monastery. Now they were his and he theirs.

When Francis of Assisi knelt before the crucifix in the deserted church at San Damiano, he met Christ in a place the medieval mind considered uniquely godforsaken. Churches and monasteries were oases of God's presence in an alien and hostile world; an abandoned church represented a place from which God had withdrawn, a place God had forgotten. The corner of Fourth and Walnut sat in Louisville's commercial district, a symbol to Merton of alienation and materialism. Standing at that corner, he discovered "the horror" cohabiting with the incarnation. God was in godforsaken places, inhabiting the uninhabitable.

The ending of Merton's "dream" parallels the transformation stories of Paul and Peter at the heart of the Book of Acts. Paul's persecution of Jesus had cut him off from God. After his vision on the road to Damascus, scales fall from his eyes. By an amazing grace, once blind, now he sees. Merton had treated people as if Christ had not become human for their sake. Now, like Paul, his persecuting days were over. The ritual piety of Jewish law made Peter exclude himself from table fellowship, communion, with Gentiles. Only after God reveals to him in a dream that nothing is unclean does Peter renounce his legalism and begin a new relationship with Gentiles. Merton's monastic formalism had relegated the outside world to a lesser fate; now he realized that he needed to be at one with those he had shunned, the non-monastics and pagans of the world. God was in the midst of godforsaken people. Muste called the Church the "great" Fellowship of Reconciliation; now Merton had discovered the greatest fellowship of reconciliation.

As recorded in *Conjectures of a Guilty Bystander*, Merton felt love, then articulated the experience in traditional language. As he noted elsewhere, both Buddhism and Christianity made use of "ordinary everyday human existence as material for a radical transformation of consciousness." Christian dogma developed a vocabulary about those experiences. Merton naturally ascribed the communion he felt to an understanding of the incarnation.[81]

Two events in Merton's life bracket his vision in Louisville. Standing at mass in 1940 in Cuba, as the children in the congregation joined in the Creed, "something went off inside me like a thunderclap" and "I knew with the most absolute and unquestionable certainty" and "delight" that there before unseeing eyes God was radiantly present. "And so the unshakable certainty, the clear and immediate knowledge that heaven was right in front of me...lifted me clean up off the earth." The experience was not extraordinary, he explained, simply more vivid than at other times. He had found "heaven," God's presence, in church.[82]

Just a few days before his death, standing before the huge sculptures of Buddha at Polonnaruwa in Sri Lanka, Merton had another powerful experience.

> Looking at these figures I was suddenly, almost forcibly, jerked clean out of the habitual, half-tied vision of things, and an inner clearness, clarity, as if exploding from the rocks themselves, became evident and obvious. . . .The thing about all this is that there is no puzzle, no problem, and really no "mystery." All problems are resolved and everything is clear, simply because what matters is clear. The rock, all matter, all life, is charged with dharmakaya [the

essence of all beings]. . .everything is emptiness and everything is compassion.

Although experimenting with a Buddhist vocabulary, Merton put his experience into familiar words. His Asian pilgrimage had "come clear and purified itself."[83]

The children's voices bound Merton to Christ's divinity, to God in heaven. The Louisville vision bound him to Christ's humanity, to all people on earth. The rocks in Sri Lanka bound him to Christ through whom all things were made and who holds all matter together. Merton had once written an essay, "Everything That Is Is Holy." Now he knew--as Day knew when she worked with wool--the sacramental quality of matter. All matter was divinized, charged with God's being.

The words with which he described the experience in Sri Lanka applied as well in Louisville. There, too, he had been "jerked clean out of the habitual, half-tied vision of things" and had received an "inner clearness." There, his monastic pilgrimage had "come clear and purified itself." He had entered the monastery to repudiate the world, but discovered that true renunciation had to be born of love. As he became more precise in what he disowned, his focused anger became like a sharpened scalpel.

Merton revealed a selective renunciation when he imagined a weapon that might evolve from the neutron bomb.

It should destroy books, works of art, musical instruments, toys, tools, and gardens, but not destroy flags, weapons, gallows, electric chairs, gas chambers, instruments of torture or plenty of strait jackets in case someone should accidentally survive.[84]

It would destroy the good and the beautiful and preserve the destructive. So now Merton tried to shake a spiritually sleeping giant from its spurious dreams as though, by the power of his words, he could wrest it free from its illusions.

In his talk on the day he died, Merton spoke of the monk's dialectic of world refusal and world acceptance. He had previously likened the modern monk to the Desert Fathers who rejected a "decadent imperial society in which the Church has become acclimated" to idolatry. With his own withdrawal, the monk refused "self-hypnosis" and removed himself from a cloud of dust so that he could see and breath clean air. He did not reject the human race; he repudiated its perverted standards that spoiled creation. He did not renounce the world; he rejected the things that maimed its people. He did not denounce the world; he decried sin, evil, untruth. His withdrawal was a special form of love; his vocation a way to find his right place in the world. He now distinguished between "renunciation" and "denunciation." Denunciation denigrated. Renunciation preceded annunciation as purgation preceded illumination and union. Monastic renunciation was a sweeping liberation from society's status quo. Any social movement breaking from established social patterns was, in this respect, "monastic."[85]

Young Merton's attempt to leave the world had been illusory. The world's mirages were more subtle than he had imagined. The Desert Fathers discovered the "world" with them in the desert, and fought it with their acts of charity. The more mature Merton recognized his own flight from the "world" as an escape into private fantasy--he had left nothing behind. The monk interested only in his own profit, peace, or perfection had taken the world into the cloister. In reality, to leave the "world" is to live for others. The monastery and the hermitage helped Merton face his narrow rigidity and grow in true charity.[86]

Less alienated from himself, Merton felt himself in "gentle sympathy" even with those unaware of their sinfulness, the world's plight, or their "blind desperate hope of happiness." Because God had given him "the grace to taste a little of what all men really seek," he had an obligation to pray and to love.[87] Because he loved the human race, he refused to share its delusions. Because he had renounced the world's strivings, he could present an alternative. His announcement was ontological; God intended the solitary Christian to be a living sign of humanity's true capacity for freedom and peace.

> It is my intention to make my entire life a rejection of, a protest against the crimes and injustices of war and political tyranny which threaten to destroy the whole race of man and the world with him. By my monastic life and vows I am saying NO to all the concentration camps, the aerial bombardments, the staged political trials, the judicial murders, the racial injustices, the economic tyrannies and the whole socio-economic apparatus which seems geared for nothing but global destruction.[88]

The monastic life did not reject the books, the toys, the art, the gardens, the things uplifting humanity; it renounced the power of Death, the wars and oppression, the subtle alienation at the corner of Fourth and Walnut. Merton admitted ambiguities. From its historical inception, monastic renunciation was "a denial of a world that has not been penetrated with the light of the Resurrection, in order to see the world that *has* been transfigured and illuminated."[89]

In his Bangkok talk, Merton spoke of true monasticism's power to save. Perhaps the monks--the detached community--more than the SCLC, FOR, or Catholic Worker would be the leaven of redemption and hope. He described the vocation of monasticism: if someone is drowning, you do not jump in to drown together; you stand on a rock and pull that person out. Twentieth century monks were to stand on the rock and pull others out of their deadly delusions, not into the monastery. "In order to liberate" the world, monks had to be liberated from it.[90]

In a decade of political opportunity, Merton was harried with questions about the significance of monasticism. Like the Desert Fathers, who entered the desert to find others in God, he found in solitude a way to be more deeply involved with humanity, a way to live for, care for, and serve others. He experienced in the contemplative's anguish for the world a source of human unity.

Merton found his neighbor through his immersion into God, his search within himself, and his sympathetic entry into foreign cultures. In loving God he recognized and loved strangers as neighbors. When Rosemary Ruether urged him to leave Gethsemani, he reminded her that he was not avoiding evil by looking deeply into himself: "I assure you that whatever else it is it is not complacency, because there is ample material for not being complacent." King described a civil war in each person; Merton felt wars raging in his own heart. His solitude had been "modified by contact with other solitudes," "a solitude that is really shared by everyone." "There is One Solitude in which all persons are at once together and alone."[91]

The Benedictine Rule taught the monk to accept Christ's command to see Himself in every pilgrim and enemy, every prisoner and sinner. Like Day, Merton knew that faith was not a tool to discern whether a person resembled Christ. Faith helped Christians to love others just as they loved Christ.[92]

In his milieu of social polarity, his age of conscious and unconscious feelings of racial, national, and ideological superiority, Merton believed that he had not really found Christ in himself until he had found Christ in a part of humanity remote from his own: "Our task now is to learn that if we can voyage to the ends of the earth and there find *ourselves* in the aborigine who most differs from ourselves, we will have made a fruitful pilgrimage." When you meet foreigners and aliens, and find yourself in them, the stranger is revealed as Christ.[93]

While his society persisted in its pursuit of nothingness, Merton began a "pursuit of marginality." To leave Gethsemani for an active ministry would have betrayed monasticism's "marginal role" in the Kingdom. Monks viewed themselves as people "marginal" to, freed from, "implicitly critical" of, yet open to society. In 1968, the Year of Relevance, he told a gathering in Calcutta that monks were "deliberately irrelevant," almost a state of value-suicide. The poet posed and answered his own question about relevance:

Who would dare to go nameless in so secure a universe?
Yet, to tell the truth, only the nameless are at home in it.

There was usefulness in being useless, a name in being nameless.[94]

In becoming marginal, nameless, useless, and irrelevant, Merton maintained a certain consistency. His mother's death, long separations from his father, and his father's death left him an adolescent orphan perpetually out of place. In his pre-conversion "hermit" life, he wandered in and out of uncloistered communities. His religious tradition proclaimed that good news came first to the marginal, to shepherds, desert-dwellers, and nomads, to the contemplatives who were their spiritual descendants.[95] He contrasted the efficiency of American power with the inefficiency of the monastery; one produced Vietnam, the other "only some milk, some cheese, some bread, some music, a few paintings, and an occasional book." God bless the nonviolence of inefficiency! Merton did not rave about the production of Trappist cheese, but it beat the destruction of war.[96]

Uselessness typified the contemplative life. Social critics judged Mt. Athos, a center of monasticism for a millennium, much as literary critics had condemned Faulkner--for being out of touch with the times. Merton countered that it was precisely because it was out of touch that Mt. Athos could transcend the times. It could help redeem the world because it was not drowning with the times. In his Asian talks, Merton underlined the way the monk's marginality deliberately questioned society's claims. Irrelevant marginality gave Mt. Athos redemptive credibility.[97]

Merton found a fundamental paradox in usefulness. Society demanded that each person perform, and find an identity in, a function. Each person was a worker, a general, a priest, "a prisoner of necessity." Each had a use. In "Rain and the Rhinoceros," the hermit reveled in the useless noise of quails and in his own useless pleasure in hearing them. One could not understand art without comprehending "the usefulness of the useless and the uselessness of the useful." The story of Martha and Mary showed that sitting inactively but attentively at Jesus' feet was preferable to getting things done. Thus Merton found much of Zen and Chuang Tzu congenial. The lot of the hermit, even more so than the monk, is to lose significance to become significant.[98]

Merton believed his lack of utility to be in direct proportion to his capacity for compassion. A friend confirmed that Merton "had the deepest sense of empathy with the oppressed and the bullied that I had ever encountered." If there was a point to pointlessness, it was in the monk's freedom to enter into the heart and pain of the alienated.[99]

The contemplative's monotonous life emulated that of "poor, uninteresting, forgotten people." Like the poor, the monk sits and waits and has nothing to say about the things that happen to him. In his hermitage, Merton shared electric power lines with poor farmers. He identified with the obliterated: "The victims of Hiroshima and Nagasaki are before me and beside me every day when I say Mass. I pray for them and I feel they intercede for me before God." He credited whatever empathy he felt for African-Americans to his experiences as an orphan and a Trappist, from being passed around as a "thing" from family to family, from living without civil rights in the monastery. To identify with those the world deemed nothing, he had to become--like Christ--"no-thing."[100]

Merton saw himself as a "pilgrim" and an "exile." Even as a monk, he had a function, an identity. Only when he returned to his hermitage in the woods was he "nobody." Wanting to be more than a friend to the world he became a stranger. In entitling an essay "Day of a Stranger," he kept in mind his intended Spanish audience. The Spanish for "stranger" is "extraño," which connotes alienation, not belonging, being extraneous.[101]

Merton became more specific about his renunciations as he realized the goal of marginality--to become a friend and brother to exiles and victims. In "Taking Sides on Vietnam," he did not ally himself with any ideology or nation. In sentiments reminiscent of Day's thoughts on the Korean War, he said,

> I am on the side of the people who are being burned, cut to pieces, tortured, held as hostages, gassed, ruined, destroyed. They are the victims of both sides. . . .The side I take is then the side of the people who are sick of war.[102]

He was theirs and they his.

In becoming nobody, he identified with those the world disenfranchised, then discounted, and finally exterminated. Into the monastery and into the hermitage, he moved away from the perpetrators of violence to solidarity with the irrelevant, the ignored, the dehumanized, those who did not count.[103]

Divestment

> "Let the same mind be in you that was in Christ Jesus, who, though he was in the form of God, did not regard equality with God as something to be exploited, but emptied himself, taking the form of a slave, being born in human likeness. And being found in human form, he humbled himself and became obedient to the point of death--even death on a cross."
>
> --Philippians 2:5-8

> "For you know the generous act of our Lord Jesus Christ, that though he was rich, yet for your sakes he became poor, so that by his poverty you might become rich."
>
> --2 Corinthians 8:9

"In order to arrive at having pleasure in everything
    Desire to have pleasure in nothing.
In order to arrive at possessing everything
    Desire to possess nothing.
In order to arrive at being everything
    Desire to be nothing."

    --John of the Cross[104]

"Go, sell what you own, and give the money to the poor, and you will have treasure in heaven; then come, follow me."

    --Mark 10:21

Thirty days before entering the monastery, Merton wrote, "whenever I read about the young rich man in the Gospels. . .I feel terrible. . .I can't read that and sit still. It makes me very unquiet." Echoing both the world-weariness of Ecclesiastes and the detachment of John of the Cross, he recalled his pre-conversion days: "In filling myself, I had emptied myself. In grasping things, I had lost everything. In devouring pleasures and joys, I had found distress and anguish and fear." Twenty years later, Merton appreciated the sixth-century Syrian Philoxenos, who noted that wealth, for Christians, is not to own many possessions but to be without needs.[105]

Voluntary poverty was more than a private matter. With Maurin and Day, Merton discerned its profound social ramifications: only widespread voluntary poverty could end destitution and undo the intimate connection between property and war. He quoted Maximus the Confessor:

We are held by the love of material things and the attraction of pleasure, and since we prefer these things to the commandment of the Lord, we become incapable of loving those who hate us. Rather we find that because of these very things we are often in conflict with those who love us.[106]

Day referred to the Epistle of James (4:1) to make the same point.

In the spring of 1940, Merton considered America's political options: "If we go into the war, it will be first of all to defend our investments, our business, our money." What he knew of the U.S., he knew of himself.

> The knowledge of what is going on only makes it seem desperately important to be voluntarily poor, to get rid of all possessions this instant. I am scared, sometimes, to own anything, even a name, let alone coin, or shares in the oil, the munitions, the airplane factories. I am scared to take a proprietary interest in anything, for fear that my love of what I own may be killing somebody somewhere.[107]

His pre-monastic intuitions later found fruition. In one of his poems, Merton imagined meeting Von Clausewitz, the theorist of modern war, at the Stock Exchange. Upon leaving, he noted that if he ever returned, Von Clausewitz would be waiting. Society's material desires were inextricably tied to violence. People preferred lucrative war to unprofitable peace. People could not love enemies, or even friends; they loved their possessions more passionately. Any threat to anyone's material interests at any time evoked hatred. Yet Merton had to do more than rid himself of all possessions:

> instead of hating the people you think are warmakers, hate the appetites and the disorder in your own soul, which are the causes of war. If you love peace, then hate injustice, hate tyranny, hate greed --but hate these things *in yourself*, not in another.[108]

Self-stripping purgation demanded a permanent inner iconoclasm.

Philoxenos, Merton said, "had fun in the sixth century, without benefit of appliances, still less of nuclear deterrents." A story of the Desert Fathers illustrated the connection between detachment and nonviolence: Two elders shared the same cell without even a single quarrel. They agreed to have an argument so that they could be like others, but they did not know how to begin. Then one said, "I'll place this brick between us and say it's mine. Then you say, 'No, it's not. It's mine.' And then we'll fight." So the first monk put the brick between them and said, "It's mine." The second, "No. I think it's mine." The first, "I believe it's mine." And the second, "Well, if it's yours, take it."[109]

There were also non-material divestments to be made. When European Christianity, as proud of its culture as of its Savior, traveled abroad in the nineteenth and twentieth centuries, it proclaimed salvation through westernization as much as through Christ. For this reason, Merton found solace in the work of the sixteenth-century Jesuit missionary to China, Matthew Ricci. Ricci entered fully into China's Confucian culture: "Like a true missionary, he divested himself of all that belonged to his own country and his own race and adopted all the good customs and attitudes of the land to which he had been sent." In doing so, he imitated Christ who "emptied Himself, taking the form of a servant" (Phil 2:6). Ricci became a model for Merton who sought common ground with Latin American cultures, with Zen and Buddhism.[110]

Violence resulted from clinging to possessions and appetites, to "our culture," "our side." Merton observed early in World War II that the Allies were disappointed that God did not act like a Nazi to wipe out Germany. He noticed that in the story of the Temptation Jesus turns away from food, money, honors, security, and power--anything that could replace love. Faced with reforms, monks grasped desperately at "the evanescent aspects of life" instead of their vocation's essentials. No one was immune from the need to divest.[111]

The Order's rule forced Merton to begin divestment, yet he knew he ought to rid himself of other continuing needs. The circuitous route through which daily news reached him was both a curse and a blessing. He likened his distance from news to living without cigarettes. In not needing to hear it immediately, he could respond to it differently, and discern events from "pseudo-events."[112] Like Muste's nonconformity, divestment was more than self-defense; it created an environment of freedom.

Periodically, Merton thought of giving up his writing. Trappists did not write, so he assumed upon entering Gethsemani that his writing days were over. Only the wisdom of his abbot amended this tradition. When he entered the hermitage in 1965, he foresaw a deceleration in his writing. In the 1950s, he thought of stopping because he feared that writing might obscure or corrupt his thoughts; the writer "tends to become rich in his own eyes," and he wanted "to enter more deeply" into spiritual poverty.[113]

Writing tempted Merton with honors and reputation, to see himself as "rich." He tried to give up part of his nature, part of his vocation, to center his life on God. He did not want this source of identity, this "name," to be an obstacle. To have a "proprietary interest in anything," even so strong an interest in oneself, even in his most direct ministry to others, was a temptation to violence. King hesitantly gave up his popularity; Merton pondered giving up writing. To use his gifts rightly, he had to assess their dangers and pray that, though tainted with sin, God would use them.

As Day's "precarity" included and exceeded voluntary poverty, Merton's divestment was a way of life both spiritual and material. Merton poked fun at popular writers who wrote "as if union with God were something put up for sale in monasteries like ham or cheese, a kind of secret bargain offered to men on the contemplative black market."[114] If you think of contemplation in terms of attaining or possessing, he said, you are on the wrong track. The regular failure to attain mystical experiences could lead to a feeling that one has paid good money to see a bad movie. Echoing John of the Cross, Merton counseled: Do not yearn for blessings or warmth or comfort or insight; seek God; "desire to be without desire."[115]

Clinging to interior possessions, to one's own purity or righteousness, was a spiritual danger. Even a passionate belief in the truth might provoke a violent defense: "If we really sought truth we would begin slowly and laboriously to divest ourselves one by one of all our coverings of fiction and delusion."116 Perhaps he remembered his early religious writings clothing his adolescent anger in a monk's habit. Only later did he replace his condescension with a sense of tragic absurdity.

Merton had wrongly believed that when he entered the "impregnable fortress of solitude" at Gethsemani, he had left the world. This "fortress" soon turned into open roads leading in many directions at once. It did not make one safe from temptations: "The solitary should not seek to replace his lost possessions by merely numerical accumulation of prayers and good works over which he can gloat like a happy miser at the end of each day."117 When one can no longer collect material possessions, one hoards things spiritual.

Meeting God in "darkness," Merton had his thoughts, motives, and purest desires stripped away.

> God, my God, God Whom I meet in darkness, with You it is always the same thing! Always the same question that nobody knows how to answer!

> I have prayed to You in the daytime with thoughts and reasons, and in the nighttime You have confronted me, scattering thought and reason. I have come to You in the morning with light and with desire, and You have descended upon me, with great gentleness, with most forbearing silence, in this inexplicable night, dispersing light, defeating all desire. I have explained to You a hundred times my motives for entering the monastery and You have listened and said nothing, and I have turned away and wept with shame.

> Is it true that all my motives have meant nothing? Is it true that all my desires were an illusion?

> While I am asking questions which You do not answer, You ask me a question which is so simple that I cannot answer. I do not even understand the question.118

God always steals the initiative. God speaks; the monk listens. God strips; the Christian stands naked. Life is generated by God's unfathomable question.

As a young monk, Merton sought personal purity. Later, he understood that one must destroy self-righteous attitudes, self-serving images. Too strong an attachment to nonviolence might make one ego-threatened, strident, violent. Thus, Muste insisted on the pacifist's humility. One had to detach from spiritual possessions. Self-emptying brought freedom.

Some perceived a trace of masochism in Merton's spiritual ablutions, a "contempt for his own identity group." But Merton's lack of gentlemanliness toward his nation, race, and class owed more to hating their appetites than themselves. He applied the self-criticism of the Desert Fathers--"that man hates evil who hates his own sins, and looks upon every brother as a saint, and loves him as a saint"--to groups.[119]

> Merton ended *The Silent Life* with a statement on divestment:
> For he who has left all things possesses all things, he who has left all men dwells in them all by the charity of Christ, and he who has left even himself for the love of God is capable of working for the salvation of his fellow-man with the irresistible power of God.[120]

Divestment replaces a cold clutching to property and its propensity to violence with a passionate embrace of all that God loves. The goals of the divested life are God, solidarity, and love--the only riches that matter.

Acts of divestment are the first steps of purgation. They strip away all one can grasp. Merton sought to purge himself of money, self-righteousness, even a "name." He became intensely iconoclastic. If he had to hate his appetites, nation, class, or Church, he was simply hating the "family" he might prefer to Jesus (Lk 14:26). Like Day, he assaulted himself with a loving ruthlessness so he could love God and neighbor more freely.

Merton wanted Christ to cleanse him so that he could offer true worship. Entering the monastery merely cleared his mind and spirit for the real work ahead. The continuing work of purgation made possible illumination and union. All three were part of the pilgrim's way.

Silence and Speech

"I will now allure her, and bring her into the wilderness, and speak tenderly to her."

--Hosea 2:14

"For everything there is a season, and a time for every matter under heaven:. . .a time to keep silence, and a time to speak."

--Ecclesiastes 3:1, 7b

Merton fought two simultaneous and apparently contradictory battles with his Order and his abbot. In one, he sought greater silence; in the other, he wanted to travel, teach, and learn, to write about civil rights, the arms race, the war in Vietnam. More than desires for free silence and free speech, these were yearnings to bring the contemplative and the prophetic together by stretching his vocation to its extremes of silent solitude and social action. He fought these personally bitter battles over the nature of monasticism and of his calling.

Merton's desire for solitude began early in his monastic career. In the 1950s, he tried to enter an Order that would allow him more silence.[121] By the early 1960s, his quest for solitude coincided with his determination to speak out on the arms race. This two-way pull went back to his pre-Trappist thoughts of working in Harlem, living with and writing for the poor, accepting a vocation like Day's. Although drawn there, Merton chose a different set of mundane horrors and joys. His inquiry into the Franciscans may have anticipated his need for travel and active ministry. The Trappist in him stood side-by-side with the Franciscan and the lay worker in Harlem.

To Merton, silence was a way to pull back from the world's distracting verbosity. In his poem "The Tower of Babel," when one angel asks another if they should learn that city's language, the other answers: "No, we must stand apart./If we learn their language/We will no longer understand/What is being said," for words "have almost made an end of reality." Merton's first full-time year in the hermitage put him "in direct confrontation with and obedience to God's word." God's Word emerged from silence, for God's speech was "no-speech."[122]

When permission finally came, Merton entered the hermitage joyfully. In 1965, he wrote that the solitary life led him further away from indifference. Silence was a protest against politics and propaganda, against a functionalist, task- and consumer-oriented society. "Illusions finally dissolve" in solitude.[123]

Four years earlier Merton had begun to write prolifically on nuclear war. It must have seemed ironic to his superiors that when they wanted him to speak, he wanted silence; when they wanted him mute, he spoke. He knew his political writings exasperated many in the Church, but a "moral obligation"--a term he used frequently--drove him to explain his outcry. The Church's silence on the arms race compelled him to speak. Its silence was unhealthy, a "grave scandal," a form of "complicity." And his superiors demanded his "silent complicity."[124]

Merton did not seek this conflict with any eagerness. Although willful, he felt cowed by the complexity of issues and his distance from information. When censored in 1962, he decided--almost relieved--to obey, yet the episode disturbed him. The Church had evaded responsibility, defaulted on its faith, instructed its clergy to follow the marching orders of "the Pentagon and *Time* magazine," advised its laity to fight. Like Muste, Merton felt that, in leaving moral decisions to the

State, the Church had surrendered Christian conscience "to nefarious and anonymous secular power."[125]

> Censorship evoked sarcasm:
> My peace writings have reached an abrupt halt. Told not to do any
> more on that subject. Dangerous, subversive, perilous, offensive to
> pious ears, and confusing to good Catholics who are all at peace in
> the nice idea that we ought to wipe Russia off the face of the earth.
> Why get people all stirred up?[126]

When accused of writing for a communist-controlled paper--*The Catholic Worker*-- he remarked sardonically that his "card" (a membership card in the Communist Party) must have fallen out during confession. After the publication of "Pacem in Terris," he said, "I wrote to the Abbot General and said it is a good thing Pope John didn't have to get his encyclical through [Cistercian] censors: and could I now start up again?"[127]

Merton was particularly incensed that the Church tried to keep its monks in a "permanent moral coma" so that they would support the pronouncements of the ecclesiastical bureaucracy and pray that God would grant their wishes. His superiors thought that his political writings might bring "disrepute" to monasticism; Merton asserted that they might salvage its dying reputation. When the Order refused publication of a book he had edited on peace, he addressed the monk's image:

> Too controversial, doesn't give nice image of monk. Monk
> concerned with peace. Bad image. Monks in NY State have fallout
> shelter. . .: good image for monk, fine, go ahead. . . .Have been
> going back to Origen and Tertullian, where I belong. What do I
> find? Preaching non-violence. Christians never kill with the sword,
> these characters say. They haven't heard that this is a bad image.
> Fathers of the Church, bad father image.

He felt obligated to write on these issues as a Christian, a priest, and "a monk above all."[128]

The world's noise made silence necessary; the Church's complicity made speech imperative. Its acquiescence had become another numbing noise covering up a conspiracy to commit mass murder. Merton offered his silence as a protest; his speech to clarify reality.

Speech without silence was babble; contemplation without prophecy was an evasion. The hierarchy wanted Merton to quietly ignore the world; activist friends called him to be a prophet at the barricades. He could not fulfill either half of his vocation without the other. A sympathetic writer condescended that Merton understood the world well "for a monk."[129] He would have answered: It was *because* he was a monk that he understood the world at all.

A monk could not forget the struggles of others while he attended mass, recited the daily offices, and strove for interior perfection. The monk "owes" the world a critical vision: "The monk is called 'out of the world' in the sense that he is called to be free of its fictions, its myths, its rationalizations, its routine demands, its deceptive promises, its organized tyrannies." In every age and culture, the monk was to question life when it submitted to "a mirage" of arbitrary assumptions, social conventions, and the pursuit of temporal satisfactions. The contemplative life made it possible to see past media superficiality and remember Gandhi's injunction to see the significance of events--and God acting in history--through meditation. Meditation did not deliver privileged information; it provided perspective. The meaning of events remained as much a mystery to the contemplative, yet the contemplative might see the world as Merton, from his hermitage at midnight, saw the whole valley below "drenched in silence and dark clarity."[130]

Many people questioned Merton about the validity of monasticism; many accused him of trying to escape conflict, but the hermit's life was neither a joke nor a picnic. It was unpleasant to face his need for self-annihilation, disconcerting when God turned away from his highest thoughts, his purest motives, his deepest desires. The contemplative led a life of infinite risk as prone to anguish as certitude. Many implied that "the hermit life might be self-centered." Some asked: "Sure! Why shouldn't the hermit be happy? He lives in his own little world! He is content because he is the sole possessor of a universe of which he is himself the center." Merton answered: If it's so easy, "try it!"[131]

Merton urged monks to take more seriously the prophetic character of their lives. The monk's detachment from materialism and freedom from fictions were prophetic signs against the dehumanization of daily life. Liberated from the world's fabrications, the contemplative could see, praise, and love.[132] To those trying to lure him from his desert, Merton asserted that the contemplative's vision--made clear by emptiness, nakedness, and uselessness--was more dangerous to the status quo than undirected activism. The monk's greatest gift to the world was his marginality.

At the 1964 FOR retreat at Gethsemani on the "Spiritual Roots of Protest," Merton's presentation, "The Monastic Protest: The Voice of the Desert," provided a "monastic-desert" angle on protest, connecting contemporary social issues with the Desert Fathers.[133] The fourth-century Christians who left society for the desert believed that their society had been shipwrecked. They could, Merton believed, flee or die. They did not retreat into a self-satisfied, ecstatic interior life, nor escape to a privatized salvation, for once they gained a firm foothold they had the obligation to save the people they had left behind. Like all Christian mystics, they "sought and found not only the unification of their own being, not only union with God, but union with one another in the Spirit of God."[134] Merton's desert perspective penetrated his Bangkok address on monasticism: only by gaining a foothold away from shipwrecked society could the monk save people from drowning.

Like those Christians who exiled themselves from their too-comfortable society and State-bound Church, the monk removed himself from the flotsam of the "great fabric of illusions." Because the monk was "out" enough, his compassion could help the world. The "proximate end of all this striving was a 'purity of heart'--a clear unobstructed vision of the true state of affairs, an intuitive grasp of one's own inner reality as anchored, or rather lost, in God through Christ." Because of their positions vis-à-vis society, Merton felt greater kinship with Albert Camus than with Billy Graham.[135]

Merton's prototypical monk resembles Day as a fool for Christ on the edge of society, King's maladjusted individual, and Muste's nonconformist who resists the mores of the city-which-is and strikes out for the city-to-be. From different corners of the Christian tradition, they arrived at the same destination. For pioneers of faith, hope lies outside the city-which-is/Ur/Babel/capitalistic society.

In the 1950s, perplexed as to how to register a desert protest, Merton envisioned the monk's role as yeast to dough. The recluse did not have to speak. His battlefields were prayer and self-sacrifice. Prohibiting himself from descending into the world's battles, from yielding to the temptation to take sides, the monk could sympathize with a movement, but had to remain aloof of factions. He had not yet mastered Day's ability to take and transcend sides.[136]

The monastic witness--the contemplative life--was a protest. The contemplative lived as God intended life to be. The desert was the restoration of Paradise, the eschaton incarnate, the Garden-to-be. The Desert Fathers were signs of a life lived in right relationship with creation, a new creation, "hence, Desert Father stories about tame lions and all that jazz." Going into the desert was a political, prophetic, and eschatological act. The world perceived the solitary as a "traitor" because the monk stood against all that society held dear. Merton's personal witness announced an alternative world when he said of his fellow desert dwellers: We're here![137]

By the time of the FOR retreat, Merton's path had followed St. Antony's lead. Each entered obscurity before others came to seek their wisdom. By 1964, Merton had re-thought his form of protest and modified his insistence on standing back from factions. The incarnation--that scandal of particularity--demanded that he take sides. Yet he never abandoned the singular importance of his ontological protest, of being--like the Desert Fathers--a foretaste of harmony after an extended dissonance, a sign of the Second Advent, the coming of the new creation.

By writing about his withdrawal, Merton clarified for himself and for others the differences--and distance--between world and desert, but written communication was secondary to his witness. As he wrote Day, he could do more for the peace movement by being a monk than he could through the weight of all of his collected writings.[138]

Unmasking Illusions

"Blessed are you who are poor, for yours is the kingdom of God. . . .But woe to you who are rich, for you have received your consolation."

--Luke 6:20, 24

Perhaps no word appears so often in Merton's writings as "illusion" and his synonyms for it--delusion, fiction, myth, obsession, mirage, falsehood. Illusions threatened the world, the Church, the monastery, the spirit. True religion--prayer, silence, solitude, reading the Bible, meeting God in darkness--unmasked illusions.[139] Nurtured in silence, Merton sought to eliminate his own illusions and, with speech emanating from silence, the world's.

The contemplative prophet was like Ezekiel who saw in Israel's history more than a disconnected series of events. Its history was a story of a promiscuously unfaithful wife who turned away from her loving husband. This was no mere metaphor, no "code language for political events." This was reality. Biblical scholarship says that God did not permit Ezekiel to warn, advise or assure. He gave perspective, caught the imagination, and created awareness: "Poets have no advice to give people. They want people to see differently, to re-vision life. They are not coercive. They only try to stimulate, surprise, hint, and give nuance, not more."[140] Merton's "Message to Poets" had the same insight:

> Let us be proud of the words that are given to us for nothing, not to
> teach anyone, not to confute anyone, not to prove anyone absurd,
> but to point beyond all objects into the silence where nothing can be
> said. We are not persuaders.

The contemplative was nothing more or less than a poet.[141]

The contemplative was also an iconoclast, contemplation "a terrible breaking and burning of idols, a purification of the sanctuary, so that no graven thing may occupy the place that God has commanded to be left empty." Contemplation obliterates obsessions, slashes fictions, smashes idols, burns cliches. It does not arrive at the root of an issue by analysis but through a terrifying simplicity.[142]

In his "Letter to an Innocent Bystander," Merton re-told the story of the emperor's new clothes. Deceived by his tailors and upheld in the charade by his courtiers and the public, the emperor paraded in the street until a child pointed out the naked truth. This is the vocation of the bystander. The child's innocence saved the people from becoming "criminal." Like that child, the guilty bystander unmasks the emperor's illusion.[143]

Prophet, poet, and child merge in the Desert, a place of true innocence. Paradise allows the child to see and speak the already unveiled truth. The child-poet speaks with an "ingrained innocence"; he offers no program; he makes a clumsy surgeon. The child uncovers the truth and lets the adults gasp and plan a course of action. The view from Paradise is both pre- and post-rational. It does not deny a place for reason, but reason alone dictates apparently harmless, habitual complicity. There can be no rational debate when all are deceived by a pseudo-sanity. Non-rational assumptions must first be revealed--the emperor is naked. Then, reason can help. Many of Merton's writings have this quality about them: This is what I see; civilization is naked; now that you know, do something about it.[144]

Merton's political writings operated like King's marches, Day's protests, Muste's arguments. Muste debunked the false presuppositions that justified violence; Day's protests rebuked and enlightened; King's demonstrations revealed hidden evils; Merton's spiritual writings had political ramifications, for all political problems were--at their root--spiritual problems.

Merton exposed the delusions of commercialism, consumerism, and materialism, the fiction of psychological adjustment to an insane society. He unveiled violence beneath a false social order. He unmasked fear and hatred behind the American Church's wholehearted blessing of nuclear build-ups. He revealed the spiritual truths beneath surface events in the Vietnam War and American race relations. He tried to crack America's self-righteous messianism from his hermit's hill, just a short distance from the heart of the nation buried at Ft. Knox.

The Church and the Arms Race

"And just as the law in civilized countries assumes that the voice of conscience tells everybody 'Thou shalt not kill,' even though man's natural desires and inclinations may at times be murderous, so the law of Hitler's land demanded that the voice of conscience tell everybody, 'Thou shalt kill,' although the organizers of the massacres knew full well that murder is against the normal desires and inclinations of most people. Evil in the Third Reich had lost the quality by which most people recognize it--the quality of temptation. Many Germans and many Nazis, probably an overwhelming majority of them, must have been tempted *not* to murder, *not* to rob, *not* to let their neighbors go off to their doom...and not to become accomplices in all these crimes by benefiting from them. But, God knows, they had learned how to resist temptation."

--Hannah Arendt.[145]

In 1962, the Vatican's Apostolic Delegate to the U.S. justified the arms race as equivalent to the self-sacrificial way of the Cross: "We must be willing to suffer, even to fight, to attain the peace of Christ. Not even the ominous shadow of the atomic cloud can bring about surrender to evil." The Church had submitted to the commandment of the West:

The first and great commandment is that America shall not and must not be beaten in the cold war, and the second is like unto this that if a hot war is necessary to prevent defeat in the cold war, then a hot war must be fought even if civilization is to be destroyed.[146]

The West resisted any temptation to turn away from this "law." An "atmosphere of crusade" pervaded the popular Catholic press which fed its readers hatred in the name of religion. Catholics had prepared for a "canonization of nuclear stockpiles as a Christian duty." The Church had abused its tradition, surrendered to a pagan war ethic, committed "total interior apostasy." It was blind to its betrayal of love, its "crimes against God."[147]

Merton's poetry discovered Von Clausewitz at the Stock Exchange. Now it was as though he saw the Stock Exchange next to the Pentagon and Von Clausewitz in the Church. Americans loved nuclear weapons; their economy depended on the arms race: "The H-bomb 'gives more destructive power for the dollar,'" a perverse and irresistible bargain. While the nation spent billions of dollars on weapons that would either devastate the world or rust in obsolescence, two-thirds of the world lacked bread; but there was no economic advantage in feeding the hungry.[148]

Merton challenged the prevailing world-view that convinced nation and Church of the need for the arms race. He attacked the popular illusion that Americans were innocent and Soviets "devils incarnate." The U.S. merely projected its evil to justify its own pre-existing hatred. In truth, the two systems were "pathological varieties of the same moral sickness" which, if given the chance, would "happily merge in an abyss of total secularism." While Americans demonized communism, its real enemy was war. In a nuclear conflagration, war was the only possible winner; truth, justice, and liberty the losers.[149]

Only an adolescent immaturity could imagine "winning" a nuclear war. Merton, like Muste, characterized the Cold War as a game of "chicken," a shoot-out between good guys and bad guys, a game of cowboys and Indians. With a "scoresheet of megacorpses," policy-makers asserted that the U.S. could survive a war even if fifty million people were killed. In such an atmosphere, could anyone discuss logic, morality, or truth? In Merton's mind, the bombing of cities like Dresden near the end of World War II was "pure terrorism," but arms race architects incorporated terrorism into their strategic game, confidently defending the balance of terror as the deliverer of a new world order.[150]

SAC planes flew over Merton's hermitage at 3:30am with enough "medicine" to stretch the "hours of fun into eternities." His "Prayer for Peace"-- read in the House of Representatives in April 1962--said that, in defending its freedom, the U.S. had enslaved itself to a new master. Saying that communism had stolen human rights, the U.S. stood poised to take human lives. Hitler's followers had been deluded; those who imagined that nuclear weapons could prepare the way for a better world order were even more so; Christians who would use such weapons to defend their religion were the most deluded of all.[151]

Basing its policies on limited genocide, the U.S. deceived itself yet again into thinking that the missiles would not be used. Napoleon had said you cannot sit on bayonets, and Merton believed that the U.S. would not be able to sit on its nuclear arsenal when it promised a quick fix for the nation's illusory problems. The existence of nuclear weapons made peace impossible.[152]

Merton shared the world's relief when the Cuban missile crisis passed without cataclysm. He knew though that, with Castro's recent ascent to power, the U.S.--whose view of Latin America was already twisted--became "addicted" to viewing Cuba as a hostile adversary. He feared that the missile crisis confirmed policy-makers' use of threats to settle disputes, and set a precedent requiring America's enemies to back down in every future confrontation.[153]

Merton compared the arms race to Nazi Germany's "final solution," balance-of-terror advocates with Adolf Eichmann. Horrified that a psychological report verified that Eichmann, the dutiful bureaucrat, was sane, Merton projected possible ramifications for his own generation.

> The sanity of Eichmann is disturbing. We equate sanity with a sense of justice, with humaneness, with prudence, with the capacity to love and understand other people. We rely on the sane people of the world to preserve it from barbarism, madness, destruction. And now it begins to dawn on us that it is precisely the *sane* ones who are the most dangerous.
>
> It is the sane ones, the well-adapted ones, who can without qualms and without nausea aim the missiles and press the buttons that will initiate the great festival of destruction that they, *the sane ones*, have prepared. What makes us so sure, after all, that the danger comes from a psychotic getting into a position to fire the first shot in a nuclear war? Psychotics will be suspect. The sane ones will keep them far from the button. No one suspects the sane, and the sane ones will have *perfectly good reasons*, logical, well-adjusted reasons, for firing the shot. They will be obeying sane orders that have come sanely down the chain of command. And

because of their sanity they will have no qualms at all. When the missiles take off, *it will be no mistake.* [154]

Merton disarmed the myths that made the arms race seem sensible. Instead of engaging in a futile attempt at rational debate, he shook the unconscious foundations of the arms race's logic to reveal its insane assumptions.

The Church's endorsement of nuclear weaponry disturbed the priest as much as the arms race itself. He described the Church's complicity as pagan, a mockery, an apostasy, a scandal, a blasphemy. Merton found the crusade mentality of American Catholicism a tragic contrast to peaceful papal encyclicals. He accused theological advocates of deterrence of suspending their collective conscience through a kind of spiritual lobotomy. Ethicists who blessed the arms race made it easier for others to march to the beat of Hitler's Germany. Preaching a false patriotism, both German and American hierarchies prepared the laity for mass murder. [155]

Roman Catholic theologians uncritically accepted American axioms about the world. In their polluted world-view, they adopted "Red or Dead" as the only two possible options in a zero-sum game of "chicken." Obsessed with the pagan fury of the Cold War, they could not take peace seriously. Merton objected, "To 'kill a Commie for Christ' is to admit that one has lost all sense of the meaning of the Gospel of Christ." Church leaders based their views on the lowest level of natural law, which allowed for self-defense, and ignored the Gospel, which demanded self-sacrifice for the sake of enemies. Like Day, King, and Muste, Merton pitted Christ against the Church. Centuries of identification with civil life had done more to secularize the Church than it had to sanctify civil society. The Church was "tied up with what is dirty and demonic," "full of sham and lies." Fidelity to God demanded that Christians say "No to the lie that is in the Church.

Not canonize its sinfulness." But theologians did not want to rock ecclesiastical or ideological boats.[156]

American Catholic theologians defended their position's consistency with the Just War tradition, which Merton called "a boat that has slipped its moorings and is now floating off in midocean a thousand miles" from reality. Moralists did not lay down rules for warfare; war dictated rules for moralists who tied their thinking to "criminal" assumptions.[157]

In the early 1960s, a time as immune to disarmament as World War II was to pacifism, Merton objected when the U.S. Postal Service postmarked mail with the words, "Pray for peace."

> What is the use of postmarking our mail with exhortations to "pray for peace" and then spending billions of dollars on atomic submarines, thermonuclear weapons, and ballistic missiles? This, I would think, would certainly be what the New Testament calls "mocking God"--and mocking Him far more effectively than the atheists do...It may make sense for a sick man to pray for health and then take medicine, but I fail to see any sense at all in his praying for health and then drinking poison.[158]

This pseudo-piety revealed the arms race's senseless blasphemy.

The monastic protester deemed it a "scandal" that nations made God war's first draftee. Policy-makers "occasionally make perfunctory gestures of respect in the direction of the Deity," but they knew nothing of the Christian God. America's god blessed bombs. The whole posture of the American Church was based on an outlandish belief in a Christian West.[159]

The Church jettisoned as impossible the command to love one's enemies, and embraced nuclear war as the lesser of two evils. American Catholicism had taken leave of its gospel sense and accepted the Red-or-Dead "psychology of evasion." Merton countered that the Lord, the disciples, the martyrs and saints had managed to love their enemies. Loving one's enemies was not a "pious luxury" but the "essence" of authentic Christian discipleship. Many Church leaders discounted Pope John XXIII's gospel of peace, and Merton mused that the only way Pope John got away with pacifism was because theologians wrote him off as "old and probably soft in the head."[160] Merton, like Day and their Protestant counterparts, used Christian teaching as their moral starting point. The war theologians began with a worldview defined by American policies and then applied Christian traditions to that pre-existing view. Merton and his theological opponents played on their Catholic instruments a variation on the Muste and Niebuhr duet.

Church leaders held that the Cold War defended the "faith"; Merton that it defended the Church's privilege and affluence, an act of "spiritual apostasy."[161] He asked: Who trusts a religion that sells out its own beliefs? If concerned with preservation, the Church had taken a wrong turn.

The Church advocated "terrorism" as the lesser of two evils. Merton remembered the 1944 special issue of *Fellowship* on the obliteration bombings of German cities and that Americans favored the policy fifty to one. He also recalled that Franco's forces first used terror bombing as a policy during the Spanish Civil War, but because Franco allegedly defended the Church, Catholics, except for *The Catholic Worker*, colluded with the slaughter: "The place? Guernica, a Christian city, in the Christian province of the Basques, in Christian Spain. Date: 1937. Also please remember Nanking, China. Same year. Not so many Christians. We protested."[162] When massive destruction defended the Church, it was sanctioned. When violence was used by non-Catholics, the Church rediscovered its moral voice.

As Christians prepared for nuclear war, Merton envisioned them arming themselves with hammer and nails to crucify Christ. The Church had resurrected the noble purpose of Caiaphas who had Jesus crucified to save his religion. Nuclear war was a moral evil second only to the crucifixion. As at Golgotha, the faithful would perform the execution, Christ would die among scapegoats, and God would apparently forsake the world.163

Merton repeatedly utilized the word "scandal" to describe the Church's passivity on the arms race, its belligerence toward America's enemies, and its refusal to take seriously the Sermon on the Mount. He may have used the word in the sense of the Greek word *skandalon*, a "stumbling block," one of the most serious accusations Jesus levels against a disciple (Mt 16:23). In employing this term, Merton declared arms race supporters obstacles to conscience, to the mission of the Church, to the world's repentance. Instead of being the way, the Church was the obstacle. It had become an anti-Church.

The Church had victimized itself with "centuries of triumphalist self-deception." The Just War tradition had misappropriated the benefit of the doubt and given it to the government and the military. A Catholic could argue to dismiss the Sermon on the Mount, defend a bomb shelter after a nuclear attack, and other Catholics would rush in to agree! The Church had blessed overkill and increased a society's perception of the "death of God."164

Tucked in among Merton's rash of denunciations lay occasional annunciations of redemption. There was an alternative to the Church's "demonic" moral passivity and its responsibility for "global suicide": It could hear and follow Jesus. Christians could keep their baptismal promise to combat evil and work toward the coming of God's Kingdom. They could imitate Jesus' refusal to defend himself with a legion of angels. They could obey God, not the State or the State-directed Church. They could not incinerate a city and call it an act of love, or claim "this hurts me more than it does you." They could not salve their consciences with occasional acts of charity while prospering through uninterrupted injustice. Merton cited Day: For the sake of peace, she protested against civil defense drills, endured

physical hardships, and went to jail. This was the Christian alternative in the
nuclear era, to protest against State and Church without counting the cost.[165]

The War in Vietnam

"The logic of 'Red or dead' has long since urged us to identify
destruction with rescue--to be 'dead' is to be saved from being
'Red'...And we decide, in their place, that it is better for them to be
dead--killed by us--than Red, living under our enemies...Think
what might happen if [they] fell under Communist rule *and liked it*!"

"Vietnam is the psychoanalysis of the U.S."[166]

After his death in Bangkok, Merton's body was flown home in a plane
carrying the corpses of American servicemen killed in Vietnam. As public and
religious support kept pace with the war's escalation in the early 1960s, Merton
saw the war as a sacrifice of American and Vietnamese lives for a powerful few,
and a symptom of a psychological and spiritual crisis.[167]

America's war in Vietnam signified "national madness," "psychopathic
delusions," and an "obsession of the American mind with the myth of know-how,
and with the capacity to be omnipotent." America paid for its psychological
security in a strange currency, the "burned flesh of women and children who have
no guilt and no escape from the fury of our weapons." The U.S. called it a
defensive war, but all it defended was a bizarre national self-image.[168]

Illusions of innocence drove the U.S. to personify evil in the enemy, and
then try to destroy evil by killing the enemy. Americans had re-invented the
Western frontier so that the "inferior races" which "infested" the jungles of
Southeast Asia could again be rounded up. The frontier mentality absolved policy-
makers: they could admit without contrition or rational contradiction that they used

torture for the sake of humanity. American strategists emulated Hitler who wept over the ruins of Warsaw because those "wicked" people made him bomb them.169

"It became necessary to destroy the town in order to save it," a famous statement by an American major, encapsulated policy in Vietnam. The sentence was no aberration, as the U.S. played "Red or Dead" in someone else's backyard with other people's lives. The war brought America's obsessive fantasies--which King might have called a deadly cancer--to the surface. Merton occasionally hoped that the U.S. might learn about itself and outgrow its adolescent fantasies, but the games of war proved more fun.170

In 1965, Merton pondered President Johnson's speech that implied divine guidance for making war. What kind of "prayer" guided Johnson to commit genocide? In what kind of Church could "a Catholic Bishop praise [the war] as a 'work of love'?" Had this become "an age of ethical moronism?" The war was the product of messianic hubris, but if the U.S. would allow it, Vietnam could provide astute spiritual direction--and some content for the Church's next confession.171

Contradictions took shelter in a babel of words. What did it mean to destroy a village to save it? How did a nation escalate the war "to *limit* the violence?" How could the U.S. government tell protesters to respect the law when the U.S. violated international law in Vietnam? How could it insist that the enemy understood nothing but violence when American actions spoke of nothing else? How could the U.S. accuse the enemy of dehumanizing life when it kept its own "remote box score" of casualties? Vietnam warned of a worldwide sickness. Merton summed up the depravity, politicizing the language of John Donne: "The war in Vietnam is a bell tolling for the whole world."172

America's distorted world-perspective produced the war.
The whole picture is one of an enormously equipped and self-complacent white civilization in combat with a huge, sprawling colored and mestizo world (a majority) armed with anything they

can lay their hands on. And the implicit assumption behind it all...is that "we" are the injured ones, we are trying to keep peace and order, and "they" (abetted by communist demons) are simply causing confusion and chaos, with no reasonable motives whatever. ...In a word, the psychology of the Alabama policeman becomes in fact the psychology of America as a world policeman.[173]

King would have appreciated the observation.

The U.S. was the bastard child of white imperialists and, like its forebearers, it had become a "one-eyed giant" with a technically skilled, "quantitative" eye that lacked depth perception. The war in Vietnam and the arms race were two symptoms of the one eye.[174]

This eye was incapable of introspection. When, to the dismay of the Soviet government, Boris Pasternak received the Nobel Prize for *Dr. Zhivago*, the American public delightedly took up Pasternak's cause. In their blindness, they did not notice, as Merton did, that Pasternak threatened the West as much as the East, for the Russian author did not invest any salvific powers in political, economic, or social structures. Subconsciously, the U.S. was trying to use its public admiration of Pasternak's integrity as a cosmetic justification of its own "spiritual prostitution." The war in Vietnam was but one more episode in the life of Church and nation as prostitutes.[175]

America's Race Crisis

"Northern liberals might admire black dignity at a distance, but they still did not want all that nobility right next door: it might affect property values. Nobility is one thing and property values quite another."

"In one of the big riots of 1964, the one in Harlem in mid-July, when the streets were filled with people in confusion, running from the police, when bricks and bottles were pelting down from the rooftops and the police were firing into the air (not without killing one man and wounding many others); the police captain tried to disperse the rioters by shouting through a megaphone; 'Go home! Go home!'

A voice from the crowd answered: 'We *are* home, baby!'"[176]

When, in *Seeds of Destruction*, Merton accused white liberals of spiritual prostitution, Martin Marty--a reviewer and popular historian--took strong exception: What right did a monk have to impugn the sincerity of well-intentioned liberals? Who was he to say that when the chips were down liberals would don neo-Nazi uniforms and put blacks in concentration camps? The poet's diagnosis upset Marty's measured optimism.[177]

Merton thought white liberals totally ignorant of their own motives, the feelings of African-Americans, and the meaning of the civil rights movement. At some point, materialism would conflict with idealism: "When the game gets rough you will be quick to see your own interests menaced by [the black's] demands. And you will sell him down the river for the five hundredth time in order to protect yourself." When it came time to maintain their economic advantage, white liberals would willingly use force. Whites held powerful positions in the civil rights movement so that, if necessary, they could hit the brakes. Black Power advocates wisely ousted white liberals from the movement.[178]

As King tried to tell white America, the racial turmoil had existed all along; it had only now surfaced. Northern liberals were only too happy to cooperate with the civil rights movement's assaults on Southern segregation, but legislative changes did not heal economic woes. Nonviolence gave way to strident rhetoric and riots. Black militant Eldridge Cleaver, in *Soul on Ice*, embraced Merton's sensitivity to African-Americans,[179] but Merton found few white allies. To

Merton, racism was "a universal symptom of homicidal paranoia." After the murders of three civil rights workers in Mississippi, he compared the world-views of the Ku Klux Klan and Southern police officers to that of the caretakers of Auschwitz: in each instance, one group concluded that another group was subhuman and had no right to exist.[180]

As a former Harlem volunteer worker, Merton saw that Northern whites had missed the point of the civil rights movement. They thought they were in a position to decide whether or not to grant certain rights to African-Americans; in reality, blacks offered them redemption. But "the white man is so blinded by his self-sufficiency and self-conceit that he does not recognize the peril in which he puts himself by ignoring the offer." To Merton, whites marched to the rhythm of King's 1963 speech at the Lincoln Memorial as a sign of repentance, for white affluence was rooted in violence, injustice, and sin.[181]

In his poem "And the Children of Birmingham," Merton likened the children's march for desegregation to Little Red Riding Hood walking through the forest to see Grandma. Then they discovered Grandma's teeth: The law was a Wolf! Their heroism--their glory--was that they sought to redeem the Wolf.[182]

As rage in the black community hardened like a spasmodic muscle, Merton shared uncomfortable words with whites. Black disrespect for law and order had been learned from white citizens and their government. Whites impeded court rulings; local governments defied federal laws; the federal government moved with great deliberation but little speed. Whites interpreted nonviolence as acquiescence to injustice, yet they asked blacks to seek change nonviolently. If whites believed in nonviolence, Merton said, they should use it themselves.[183]

Merton accepted many of the discernments of the Black Power movement. Militant H. Rap Brown equated the morality of marines torching a Vietnamese village with rioters burning an American city. Merton averred that the latter was more justifiable. White racists did not care whether blacks maintained Christian dignity or cringed powerlessly while they were beaten, just as long as they took the beating. In 1963, Merton agreed with Black Muslims that it was more honorable to be shot like an animal than to be treated like an "incurable infant." African-Americans had little to lose with violence which, at least, expressed their emotions.[184]

Although never condoning the violence, Merton tried to explain it to a self-righteous and paranoid white community. He mourned the shooting of white firemen during a riot, but understood the symbolic significance of a white institution dousing fires to preserve property while allowing poverty to consume the same block (a domestic version of the neutron bomb's values--property over people). He sensed with blacks that "whitey" was not far from becoming a Nazi, and he warned African-Americans that talk of Black Power and self-defense gave whites an excuse to call out the National Guard.[185]

Looters stole televisions, furniture, clothes, liquor, and weapons. The riots had become a perverse religious war fought over the objects of consumerism. The civil rights movement had set out to redeem white America, but black America had been converted to materialism and violence. Merton had hoped that the black bourgeoisie would not seek a white middle-class "mask" just because, beneath their masks, whites did not seem to be "sweating" or "itching." He feared that blacks had joined the pursuit-of-nothing.[186]

Merton believed that King and the nonviolent movement represented the greatest example of enacted Christian faith in American history. For a few years, he pinned his hope in race relations on the civil rights' coalition. Then, like many others, he wondered if the crisis had passed nonviolence by.[187]

In *Conjectures of a Guilty Bystander*, Merton pointed to two white Christian responses to Southern integration. The glossolalia sweeping through

Southern Protestant churches at the height of the civil rights struggle conveniently avoided the "humiliating business of hearing and obeying the Word of God."[188] If one could not censor the Bible, one could at least edit ecstatic utterances. Merely suspicious of the glossolalia, he was outraged by an incident in a church in New Orleans. A young priest had applied the Gospel lesson for that Sunday--the double commandment to love God and neighbor--to integration, and said that whites and blacks ought to love one another. Halfway through the sermon, fifty people stormed out angrily: "I didn't come here to listen to this kind of junk, I came to hear Mass"; "If I miss Mass today *it's your fault.*" Merton lamented: the "fact is that one can think himself a 'good Catholic' and be thought one by his neighbors, and be, in effect, an apostate from the Christian faith." When the Summary of the Law applied to real life was "junk," and when a "good Catholic" could be an apostate, the Church had little to offer the world.[189]

Merton had sensed a moment of "kairos," an opportunity for redemption, a time when the Kingdom could break in with extraordinary power if people received God's Word in good faith. The black children of Birmingham who faced the fury of white police and the teeth of police dogs offered such a moment to the nation. But these moments pass. Middle-class blacks despaired and tried to buy white masks; militants accepted the white-American myth of cleansing violence; rage possessed rock-throwing rioters; and liberal Christians engaged in sophisticated but empty social analysis. Any real hope for change had to come from black America. Merton's intuition met King's. Arrogance kept power from trickling down; oppression kept redemption from moving up.[190]

Martin Marty considered Merton's commentary a self-indulgent outburst devoid of disciplined social analysis. He was right. Merton had been in the Desert too long to address society's problems with society's tools. He was a child among adults, a poet in a technical world, trying to purge racial illusions with illuminations. A few years after his verbal blast at Merton, Marty apologized. The Desert had something to say after all.[191]

King identified a time in the life of every civilization when it would be "too late" to turn back. By the mid-1960s, Merton inferred that the time had already come. He had shifted the tone of his prophetic speech. He had been saying: If you do not repent, then you will be judged. He even tried Isaiah's "Come now, let us reason together" with other Christians. Then came the shift. The indictment was made: Because you have not repented, judgment is at hand.

Many illusions misled white America. Most whites had lackadaisically accepted the racist status quo for hundreds of years until protests disturbed their peace. Given a chance to repent, whites did not recognize that blacks offered them redemption. They exaggerated their commitment to reform and misunderstood the tenacity of racism in their own hearts. They misinterpreted the causes of inner city violence. Violence trickled down from the White House--through American cities all the way to Vietnamese villages and back. Violence was the leaven of obstructed laws. It raged in the quiet pews of white churches indifferent to the command to love. Christians wanted only to receive; they did not want to give. They wanted to gain life, not lose it.

And the moment of kairos passed.

The Activist's Shepherd

"Peace I leave with you; my peace I give to you. I do not give to you as the world gives."

--John 14:27

In November 1968, Merton learned of three kinds of *bodhicitta* (enlightened one). The "kingly" one sought spiritual power to save himself and then others.

The "boatman" ferried himself to salvation with others. The "shepherd," the most perfect, ushered the others ahead and entered salvation last.[192] The contemplative's role, from St. Antony through the medieval anchorites to modern monasticism, has been to live and pray at the fringes of society, and to comprehend society from the edge. Solitaries have always had a specialized ministry--the shepherd's ministry of ushering the active ahead towards salvation.

Merton gave perspective to activists, guided those with troubled consciences, comforted those spun around by tumultuous events. He hosted retreatants and gave advice to individual conscientious objectors, but fulfilled much of his pastoral role, like Paul, through letters. King's plans to go to Merton's Gethsemani were upset; in 1964, he received the Nobel Prize instead; in 1968, he was murdered. Writing to Coretta Scott King the day after the assassination, Merton wondered if her husband would have used the retreat to prepare for death.[193]

Merton was realistic about what happened to people caught up in a cause. He reminded activists to consistently renew their original commitments, and warned of the dangers of action without reflection: "An activity that is based on the frenzies and impulsions of human ambition is a delusion and an obstacle to grace." A movement's momentum could sweep a participant into a riptide of activism and a loss of personal identity.[194]

Action soured without religious faith. Merton held up Gandhi as a model; *ahimsa*--the rejection of violence of spirit--as a way of life. He shared Muste's belief that tactical, secular nonviolence became just another form of coercion: "Activity is [the activists'] substitute for faith. Instead of believing in themselves, they seek to convince themselves, by their activity, that they exist"; I-do-therefore-I-am. He agreed with Day that real prayer nurtured an equal awareness of personal helplessness and God's power. One had to discern pseudo-spiritual activism from

Christian action based on the power of the Spirit. Because it took fundamental truths seriously, Danish nonviolent resistance under the Nazi occupation successfully obstructed the deportation of Jews. Political principles touched by the Gospel liberated human behavior from "the old dark gods" and transformed political action into Christian witness.[195]

Perhaps because they resembled complacent monks, Merton shared Muste's distaste for pacifists who withdrew into a witness of personal purity. The peace movement was alternately tempted to disengaged, symbolic moralism or ruthless, power politics. Roger LaPorte's self-immolation made it seem violently "pathological." The peace movement superficially preached flower-power, then "burn baby burn"; cloying sweetness one day, hell-fire the next. To Merton, some protesters appeared to act out an infantile fantasy that unconsciously invited the authoritarian security of a police state. In contrast, Gandhian nonviolence exceeded the establishment in its respect for civilization. A peace movement lumbering into violence moved toward self-contradiction.[196]

Merton urged self-criticism to combat self-righteousness: "We must be wary of ourselves." The leaven of malice easily infected causes too convinced of their own truth. In a society exalting murder, we have to "fear the void of our own heart... For are we not all tainted with the same poison?" When we "love our own ideology and our own opinion instead of loving our brother," we become pharisees. With King and Muste, Merton warned that misplaced zeal misled activists to try to defeat their opponents instead of seeking reconciliation. When the movement worked for *its* truth instead of *the* truth, it embraced "moral aggression." When an abstract "holy zeal" for humanity disguised lovelessness, the activist began to hate people who opposed an abstract, esoteric justice.[197]

> We must be on our guard against a kind of blind and immature zeal--
> the zeal of the enthusiast or of the zealot--which represents precisely
> a frantic compensation for the deeply personal qualities which are

lacking to us. The zealot is a man who "loses himself" in his cause in such a way that he can no longer "find himself" at all. Yet paradoxically this "loss" of himself is not the salutary self-forgetfulness commanded by Christ. It is rather an immersion in his own wilfulness conceived as the will of an abstract, non-personal force: the force of a project or a program. He is, in other words, alienated by the violence of his own enthusiasm.[198]

Activists had to distrust their "own hidden drive to self-assertion." With Muste, Merton prescribed humility about one's motives, one's cause, one's truth, oneself.[199]

Activists could feign nonviolent reconciliation while seeking to humiliate their opponents. They should not expect mass conversions, but willingly listen to and learn from their adversaries, challenge the national mind-set, and sow the seeds of metanoia. They needed to value truth over power, prophecy over pragmatism.[200]

Merton cautioned activists against making a fetish of results. A Christian should seek to please God and benefit others. In a theme and variation through several letters, he invited an activist to see himself as a defective instrument of God, and to resist temptations to impatience and projection.

One has to learn to see the significance of one's apparent uselessness and not be driven to frustration by it. The uselessness, the inactivity, the frustration are deliberately assumed as an important part of non-violent resistance. . . .

As you get used to this idea you start more and more to concentrate not on the results but on the value, the rightness, the truth of the work itself. And there too a great deal has to be gone through, as gradually you struggle less and less for an idea and more and more for specific people.

The "big results" were not "in your hands or mine, but they can suddenly happen, and we can share in them."[201] Still, it was pointless to build hopes on unpredictable and inessential satisfaction. Day stressed sowing over reaping; Muste valued experiments over success; and King served God with and without consolations. Good things came, not from proving oneself, but from giving oneself to God's love.

Activists had to deepen their capacity to love, let the Holy Spirit work through them to help others, or be left with nothing to give "but the contagion of [their] own obsessions." There was nothing uniquely Protestant about admonitions to imitate Christ, heed Jesus' teachings, and center one's life on the Sermon on the Mount.[202] Purify your hearts--Merton said--and leave the effects of your actions to God.

Given his propensity toward pessimism and his sensitivity to evil, Merton could be surprisingly encouraging. Asked to write a set of Freedom Songs in 1964 (later heard by Day at a memorial service for King), Merton composed eight poems which vary in tone from his other writings. While two end with questions, the others are almost unswervingly heartening. Drawing extensively from the exilic prophets and biblical themes central to the African-American religious tradition, the songs promised that freedom-seekers could trust God, their Defender and Redeemer, to be with them, and to help them overcome fear. The songs proclaimed a new, united, harmonious society, promises made to keep people from being deterred on the "way" to glory.[203]

The themes of the Freedom Songs penetrated Merton's other writings. He discerned hope hiding in frustration. In 1962, he wrote Day that the puny, fragmented peace movement reminded them to rest their hopes on God alone. The Bible led one to expect the movement to be small; God tended to work through frail instruments. The next year he advised Daniel Berrigan not to be discouraged--God gave peace of soul to the world's peacemakers. At the FOR retreat in 1964, Merton said that God willed a reign of peace. Aware of his own cynicism, he feared that feelings of powerlessness might embitter the peace movement. He did not want others to fall victim to a "negative, self-pitying 'humility,'" nor "cling desperately to dark and apocalyptic expectations." There were no beatitudes about feeling sorry for oneself.[204]

Without an ounce of faith in "progress," Merton placed hope at the spiritual center of the peace issue, urging activists to be full of a pure, childlike trust. Earthly actions created one set of expectations; God's actions another. Real hope did not emanate from human potential, but from God invisibly bringing good out of human effort. Strength came from meditating on the Lord and gazing at the Cross. Counteracting the temptation to despair, three days before King's assassination, Merton predicted a "resurrection" for the world's oppressed while acknowledging, with King's "How Long?" speech, a time of suffering. Apropos to that week, he had written: nonviolence "does not say, 'We shall overcome' so much as 'This is the day of the Lord, and whatever may happen to us, *He* shall overcome.'"[205]

Without denying doubt or loss, Merton tried to divert activists away from a one-dimensional focus on tangible results to God's past promises about the future. He offered an apocalyptic hope based solely on God's promises, God's fidelity, God's activity. In his solitude, he discerned something that might have profited King: "I have learned that one cannot truly know hope unless he has found out how like despair hope is." Hope and despair, born of the same circumstances and feelings, were almost inseparable.[206]

In this atmosphere of frustrated powerlessness, Merton spoke of courage. In his written acceptance of the 1963 Pax Medal, he claimed no great insight, no special moral qualities, no unusual intelligence. Receiving such a medal, he said, was like getting an award for going to work or paying one's bills. Yet he attributed "heroism" to those who worked for peace, for peacemaking required greater valor than war. It took courage to resolve the conflict of loyalties between heaven and earth. In apocalyptic times, ordinary bravery could have extraordinary consequences.[207]

Courage intertwined with obedience. Merton called the Sermon on the Mount a fulfillment of human nature as assumed by Christ at the incarnation and, with Protestant pacifists, a supernatural fulfillment of natural law. Christian nonviolence required "obedience to [Christ's] demand to love." The age-old dilemma of how to serve and whom to obey--most subtle in the "Christian" West, most dramatic in apocalyptic times--rested on every Christian's shoulders. Courageous, Christian obedience was invariably fraught with the threat of persecution.[208]

In Merton's mind, the peace movement both protected and restored creation. A Kingdom-spirituality, popular with Protestants, assumed that creation needed restoring. The spirit of the Desert melded creation and Kingdom, Paradise and eschaton, and emphasized the original, inherent goodness of creation that needed protection. In the Desert one experienced the eschaton "here and now" in a sacramental foretaste of what the world--encompassed by God's mercy--would become.[209]

Merton rooted Christian nonviolence in the basic affirmation that Christ has established and reigns over the Kingdom of God, and that the Kingdom is realized in relation to the way Christians presently live the life of the Kingdom. He did not share the Social Gospel's expectation that the Kingdom would come in its totality on earth, yet the Christian was to build the Kingdom in the world, though it be but a foreshadowing of what was to come. Like Day, Merton leaned toward an already/not-for-quite-awhile Kingdom. Yet the Christian had to engage the Body of Christ in the world's redemption and "cooperate" with God in shaping history. Like Maurin, Merton believed the Church ought to nurture conditions that made it possible for people to recover their humanity.[210]

While advocating nonviolent tactics that did not stiffen opponents in self-righteousness, Merton recognized that activism might not bring quick or easy reconciliation. Like Jeremiah, activists were to "break down" as often as "build" (1:10). Christian nonviolence had to be iconoclastic, destroying the "idols of power," and calling nations to repentance. At times activists, like the Hebrew prophets, might accomplish little more than a "clear separation of antagonists."[211]

Merton admonished his friends to avoid destructiveness which merely satiated their own capricious desires for power. Christians offered a unique witness to their secular allies by being examples of wisdom, independence, and integrity, qualities easily lost in crusades. The Kingdom of God was the inverse of a mass movement which took the shape of a pyramid--those at the bottom supported the leaders. In the Kingdom, the leaders died for the sake of all.[212] The Kingdom not only modeled an alternative to injustice, it revealed a different way to seek social change.

Merton applied to activism the monastic tradition's dialectic of incarnation and eschatology. The incarnation required a holy impatience with every form of degradation and a commitment to heal human misery; the eschaton made hope possible. Merton cultivated this lively dialectic: The First Advent without the Second made people weary and overwhelmed; the Second without the First made people quiescent toward suffering. Forgetting either Advent distorted one's world-involvement and disrupted the cross-fertilization of ministry and hope.[213]

Each role Merton played for activists moved them forward. As a monk, he renounced all things dehumanizing; as a priest, he invited them to confession; as a pastor, he offered hope; as a spiritual director, he unclothed their illusions; as a novice master, he taught them the basic necessities of their vocation; as a poet, he gave perspective for their struggle. One activist wrote:

> Our temptation was to ask Merton to become less than he was by concentrating him in our area of activism, by converting him from a

person of universal viewpoint to one of particular viewpoint. He
saw the patterns from a greater perspective and therefore with
greater wisdom...His fidelity to his contemplative vocation was
therefore critically important help to those of us in the active life to
remain faithful in our vocations.214

By staying in the Desert, Merton helped those in the City play their part in
redeeming the Empire.

Merton wanted to "help in some feeble way to guide and educate" and
awaken the sleeping consciences of Church and nation. Most directly, he touched
the hearts and minds of those already seeking social change. Like Muste within the
FOR, Day in the Catholic Worker, and King in the civil rights movement, Merton
encouraged his flock to retreat, pray, and meditate. He shared the hopeful side of
his imagination primarily with his already-converted friends. And, while using
every Christian resource, he always held up Gandhi as the model activist who
balanced the spiritual and the political, who sought world peace as the fruit of inner
peace.215

Peace Within

"Non-violence is not a garment to be put on and off at will. Its seat
is in the heart, and it must be an inseparable part of our very being."

--Mohandas Gandhi216

Merton posed a question at the FOR retreat: Was metanoia, total personal
renewal, a requirement for nonviolent action? All of his writings answer "yes."
Jesus gave his disciples a dual vocation to establish peace in their hearts and in the
world. Unless people nurtured their inner lives, the world could not find peace.
Merton diagnosed social problems in spiritual terms: When the world lacked
interior solitude, only violence held it together.217

On the eve of the American entry into World War II, Merton observed that people desired peace for the wrong reasons. They wanted it to avoid pain, to preserve their refrigerators, cars, houses, legs, and lives. The world unveiled its spiritual destitution by hating war, not out of moral compunction, but because it demanded personal risk and might be bad for business. The liberty praised in the U.S. was the freedom to exploit.[218]

The world's plague came from each person's interior sickness. Solitude enabled Merton to see "nests in our minds, where death hatches all kinds of eggs," even the eggs that might fall from the SAC planes overhead. The "storm of history has arisen out of our own hearts"; apocalypse begins at home. Merton personified Gog and Magog, the evil powers of the Book of Ezekiel, as the U.S. and the USSR, but "there is a little of Gog and Magog even in the best of us." In the Cold War, the Soviet Union was not the enemy. The enemies were fear, lust, and selfishness. The defeat of the USSR would not end evil. People had to fight the spiritual conditions that caused war--hatred, lies, and injustice. It is not so much the fear of others, he said, as the fear of "everything" that starts wars. Self-hatred too powerful to be faced spurred a spiral of escalating projection that finally launched missiles.[219]

This link made Merton admire Gandhi who, most convincingly among major twentieth-century figures, acted on his belief that nonviolence began in the heart. His followers used *satyagraha* (truth force) as a means, a technique, a tactic. For Gandhi, satyagraha preceded action; nonviolence was the "fruit of inner unity already achieved." Merton gave Gandhi's prescription to any who would heed it-- activists, his nation, the world. Like Muste, he advised: Choose Gandhi.[220]

Outer change required inner change. Day believed that a Christian society required faithful Christians; Merton that there could be no social metamorphosis without a "total interior revolution" to subordinate prudence and power to the wisdom of the Cross. Conversions were "inner revolutions" transforming the person into Christ, the world into the Kingdom of God.221

Although Merton preferred asking questions to providing answers, he offered a solution to the problem of violence. Only love and humility, properly directed, could "exorcise" the root of war: "Instead of loving what you think is peace, love other men and love God above all."222

"Life and death are at war within us."223 Merton glimpsed war in the world and the world within himself. He spent his life engaged in an inner war, a war raging within each person, a war from which the world's terrors emerge. The storms of history began in the human heart. The rational ripples on the surface of human behavior disguised monsters within.

God did not offer Merton a tranquilizer. Solitude was "a mixture of heavenliness and anguish."224 To perceive the reality of the incarnation was both to rejoice in endless celebration and to share God's agony that people treat one another as if they were worthless.

Merton lived in an apocalyptic world, an apostasizing Church, a criminal nation. Only silence enabled him to speak. Only love unmasked the illusions corrupting human life. Only confessed complicity brought redemption. Only hope stood against the apparent momentum of history. Only divestment kept one from clutching at the world and allowed one to embrace it. Only the Desert could save the drowning inhabitants of the Empire. It was the sight of God--in church, among the godforsaken, in the useless, in all matter--that made possible the peace that surpasses understanding.

> What was cruel has become merciful. What is now merciful was never cruel. I have always overshadowed Jonas with My mercy and cruelty I know not at all. Have you had sight of Me, Jonas My

Child? Mercy within mercy within mercy. I have forgiven the universe without end. . . .[225]

Only God could stop the train to hell.

NOTES

THOMAS MERTON

1. Thomas Merton, *Conjectures of a Guilty Bystander* (Garden City, NY, 1968), 156-57; see also Michael Mott, *The Seven Mountains of Thomas Merton* (Boston, 1984), 311-12.

2. Robert E. Daggy, ed., *Introductions East and West: The Foreign Prefaces of Thomas Merton* (Greensboro, NC, 1981), 44.

3. Thomas Merton, *The Secular Journal* (New York, 1959), 159, Thomas Merton, *The Seven Storey Mountain* (New York, 1948, 1970), 352, 358-59.

4. Thomas Merton, *Contemplation in a World of Action* (Garden City, NY, 1973), 59.

5. Merton, *The Seven Storey Mountain*, 320; Merton, *Contemplation in a World of Action*, 26, 39, 145; compare Merton, *The Seven Storey Mountain*, 318, 325, and Thomas Merton, *Day of a Stranger* (Salt Lake City, 1981), 45; also Thomas Merton, *A Vow of Conversation* (New York, 1988), 83, 111-12, 117, 197.

6. James Forest, "Thomas Merton's Struggle With Peacemaking," in Gerald Twomey, ed., *Thomas Merton: Prophet in the Belly of a Paradox* (New York, 1978), 24; Robert E. Daggy, ed., *The Hidden Ground of Love: The Letters of Thomas Merton* (New York, 1985), 318, 501.

7. Merton, *The Seven Storey Mountain*, 142, 312.

8. Mott, 412, 629; John Howard Griffin, "The Controversial Merton," in Twomey, ed., 80-81; Forest, in Twomey, ed., 25; Merton, *A Vow of Conversation*, 153.

9. Daggy, ed., *The Hidden Ground of Love*, 161, 163, 347, 298, 100, 640, 284, 289.

10. Forest, in Twomey, ed., 31; Daggy, ed., *The Hidden Ground of Love*, 147.

11. Daggy, ed., *The Hidden Ground of Love*, 213.

12. Daggy, ed., *The Hidden Ground of Love*, 149, 507-09; John Howard Griffin, *Follow the Ecstasy* (Fort Worth, 1983), 54; Daggy, ed., *Introductions East and West*, 43.

13. Daggy, ed., *The Hidden Ground of Love*, 482-83, 491, 17-18, 136, 273, 322, 401, 153, 234, 305, 515, 99.

14. Daggy, ed., *The Hidden Ground of Love*, 239, 244; John Eudes Bamberger, OCSO, "The Cistercian," *Continuum* 7:2 (Summer 1969): 229.

15. Thomas Merton, *The Monastic Journey* (Garden City, NY, 1977), 156-161, 179; Merton, *Contemplation in a World of Action*, 251-337.

16. Daggy, ed., *The Hidden Ground of Love*, 482.

17. Jean LeClercq, "Merton and History," in Twomey, ed., 231.

18. Gordon Zahn, *In Solitary Witness* (New York, 1964), 111-12.

19. Thomas Merton, *The Nonviolent Alternative* (New York, 1980), 15, 16, 18, 117-18; Daggy, ed., *The Hidden Ground of Love*, 161.

20. Thomas Merton, *Love and Living* (New York, 1979), 11.

21. Merton, *Contemplation in a World of Action*, 27; Merton, *Conjectures of a Guilty Bystander*, 339; Thomas P. McDonnell, ed., *A Thomas Merton Reader* (Garden City, NY, 1974), 182; Thomas Merton, *Faith and Violence* (Notre Dame, 1968), 117; Merton, *The Nonviolent Alternative*, 219; Thomas Merton, *Disputed Questions* (New York, 1960), 164; Merton, *The Seven Storey Mountain*, 133; Daggy, ed., *The Hidden Ground of Love*, 295.

22. Thomas Merton, *Seeds of Destruction* (New York, 1964), 23; Merton, *The Secular Journal*, 249; Daggy, ed., *The Hidden Ground of Love*, 14.

23. Thomas Merton, *Life and Holiness* (Garden City, NY, 1964), 25; Thomas Merton, *Contemplative Prayer* (Garden City, NY, 1968), 24; Merton, *Contemplation in a World of Action*, 89; Daggy, ed., *The Hidden Ground of Love*, 14, 18.

24. Merton, *Seeds of Destruction*, 221.

25. Merton, *Seeds of Destruction*, 168, 165.

26. Merton, *Faith and Violence*, 7-8; Thomas Merton, *The Collected Poems of Thomas Merton* (New York, 1977), 372, 316; Patrick Hart, ed., *The Literary Essays of Thomas Merton* (New York, 1981), 246.

27. Merton, *The Secular Journal*, 47-48.

28. Thomas Merton, *The Asian Journal* (New York, 1973), 25; Merton, *The Nonviolent Alternative*, 229-30.

29. Merton, *Seeds of Destruction*, 7; Merton, *Faith and Violence*, 41, 3, 10, 30-35, 121; Merton, *The Nonviolent Alternative*, 67; Daggy, ed., *The Hidden Ground of Love*, 292.

30. Merton, *Conjectures of a Guilty Bystander*, 194; Forest, in Twomey, ed., 21.

31. Thomas Merton, *Gandhi on Non-Violence* (New York, 1965), 9; Merton, *Faith and Violence*, 67.

32. Merton, *Collected Poems*, 374; Thomas Merton, *Mystics and Zen Masters* (New York, 1967), 104; Merton, *Conjectures of a Guilty Bystander*, 80-81.

33. Hart, ed., 121.

34. Hart, ed., 117, 120-21; Merton, *Faith and Violence*, 217.

35. Merton, *Day of a Stranger*, 31.

36. Merton, *Collected Poems*, 703-04; Thomas Merton, *Raids on the Unspeakable* (New York, 1966), 45-49.

37. Merton, *Raids on the Unspeakable*, 45-49.

38. Merton, *The Nonviolent Alternative*, 156-59.

39. Daggy, ed., *The Hidden Ground of Love*, 313; Merton, *Faith and Violence*, 116; Merton, *Conjectures of a Guilty Bystander*, 210.

40. Hart, ed., 381.

41. Thomas Merton, *The Silent Life* (New York, 1957), 173; Merton, *The Nonviolent Alternative*, 103, 111, 257, 127; Daggy, ed., *The Hidden Ground of Love*, 132, 146, 160, 583, 645; Hart, ed., 121; Merton, *The Seven Storey Mountain*, 85.

42. Merton, *Day of a Stranger*, 31, 63; Merton, *Raids on the Unspeakable*, 14; Merton, *A Vow of Conversation*, 23, 68, 103, 128-31, 158.

43. Daggy, ed., *The Hidden Ground of Love*, 136, 311.

44. Merton, *Faith and Violence*, 18; Merton, *The Nonviolent Alternative*, 94.

45. Daggy, ed., *The Hidden Ground of Love*, 380; Merton, *Collected Poems*, 253.

46. Daggy, ed., *The Hidden Ground of Love*, 180; Merton, *The Nonviolent Alternative*, 87; Merton, *Faith and Violence*, 71; Merton, *A Vow of Conversation*, 105.

47. Daggy, ed., *The Hidden Ground of Love*, 472, 422-24, 285-87.

48. William D. Miller, *A Harsh and Dreadful Love: Dorothy Day and the Catholic Worker* (New York, 1973), 324.

49. Daggy, ed., *The Hidden Ground of Love*, 23-24, 88, 425, 287-90.

50. Merton, *The Silent Life*, 173; Merton, *The Nonviolent Alternative*, 269, 218, 270; Daggy, ed., *The Hidden Ground of Love*, 221, 300.

51. Daggy, ed., *The Hidden Ground of Love*, 458.

52. Albert Camus, *The Rebel* (New York, 1956), 4.

53. Merton, *Conjectures of a Guilty Bystander*, 60-61.

54. Philip Caputo, *A Rumor of War* (New York, 1977), 218; William P. Mahedy, *Out of the Night: The Spiritual Journey of Vietnam Vets* (New York, 1986), 10.

55. Merton, *A Vow of Conversation*, 53; Merton, *Life and Holiness*, 19, 103; Daggy, ed., *The Hidden Ground of Love*, 357; Merton, *Seeds of Destruction*, 244; Merton, *The Nonviolent Alternative*, 112, 105, 65-66; Merton, *Faith and Violence*, 67-68; Merton, *Contemplative Prayer*, 115.

56. Mott, 50; Merton, *The Seven Storey Mountain*, 73; Merton, *Life and Holiness*, 20.

57. Merton, *Faith and Violence*, 55; Merton, *Seeds of Destruction*, 112; Merton, *Life and Holiness*, 88; Merton, *Conjectures of a Guilty Bystander*, 87.

58. Merton, *The Nonviolent Alternative*, 180; Merton, *Conjectures of a Guilty Bystander*, 123-24; Daggy, ed., *The Hidden Ground of Love*, 164, 175, 216.

59. Daggy, ed., *The Hidden Ground of Love*, 152, 114; Merton, *The Nonviolent Alternative*, 176.

60. Daggy, ed. *The Hidden Ground of Love*, 79; Merton, *Collected Poems*, 799-800.

61. Merton, *Conjectures of a Guilty Bystander*, 339.

62. Merton, *The Nonviolent Alternative*, 257; Daggy, ed., *The Hidden Ground of Love*, 145, 352.

63. Merton, *The Silent Life*, 174; Merton, *Life and Holiness*, 104; Merton, *Seeds of Destruction*, xvi.

64. A. M Allchin, "A Liberator, A Reconciler" *Continuum* 7:2 (Summer 1969): 362; Henri Nouwen, *Pray to Live* (Notre Dame, 1972), 54.

65. Thomas Merton, *New Seeds of Contemplation* (New York, 1962), 122.

66. Raymond Bernard Blakney, *Meister Eckhart: A Modern Translation* (San Francisco, 1941), 9; Merton, *New Seeds of Contemplation*, 152; Daggy, ed., *The Hidden Ground of Love*, 187; Thomas Merton, *Spiritual Direction and Meditation* (Collegeville, MN, 1960), 88-89; Merton, *A Vow of Conversation*, 42.

67. Merton, *Collected Poems*, 82-83; Merton, *New Seeds of Contemplation*, 13, 12; Merton, *Raids on the Unspeakable*, 58, 18.

68. Merton, *The Seven Storey Mountain*, 248; Merton, *Raids on the Unspeakable*, 55; Merton, *Conjectures of a Guilty Bystander*, 253, 5; Merton, *Life and Holiness*, 8; Merton, *Seeds of Destruction*, xiii; Merton, *The Nonviolent Alternative*, 79; Daggy, ed., *The Hidden Ground of Love*, 264, 351.

69. Daggy, ed., *The Hidden Ground of Love*, 138.

70. Merton, *Collected Poems*, 349.

71. Merton, *Contemplation in a World of Action*, 161, 165; Merton, *Faith and Violence*, 145; Daggy, ed., *The Hidden Ground of Love*, 231, 235; Merton, *The Asian Journal*, 27.

72. Merton, *New Seeds of Contemplation*, 112, 96, 115-16; Merton, *Conjectures of a Guilty Bystander*, 85; Merton, *Disputed Questions*, 173.

73. Merton, *Raids on the Unspeakable*, 54.

74. Merton, *Disputed Questions*, 180, 169.

75. Daggy, ed., *The Hidden Ground of Love*, 264; Merton, *Faith and Violence*, 181; Merton, *Life and Holiness*, 15.

76. Merton, *Conjectures of a Guilty Bystander*, 72.

77. I owe this phrase to Lawrence S. Cunningham, "Thomas Merton: The Pursuit of Marginality" *The Christian Century* 95 (Dec. 6, 1978): 1181-83; A. M. Allchin, *The World is a Wedding* (New York, 1978), 95; Burton Watson, trans., *Chuang Tzu: Basic Writings* (New York, 1964), 137.

78. Merton, *The Seven Storey Mountain*, 3.

79. Merton, *The Seven Storey Mountain*, 353. Merton's view of Louisville and "the world" was not static; for another indicator, see Edward Rice, *The Man in the Sycamore Tree: The Good Times and Hard Life of Thomas Merton* (Garden City, NY, 1972), 89.

80. Mott, 311-13; Merton, *Conjectures of a Guilty Bystander*, 157-58.

81. Thomas Merton, *Zen and the Birds of Appetite* (New York, 1968), 51, 58.

82. Merton, *The Secular Journal*, 76-79; Merton, *The Seven Storey Mountain*, 284-85.

83. Merton, *The Asian Journal*, 233, 235.

84. Merton, *The Collected Poems of Thomas Merton*, 391.

85. Merton, *The Asian Journal*, 329-30; Daggy, ed., *The Hidden Ground of Love*, 504; Merton, *Conjectures of a Guilty Bystander*, 47; Merton, *Life and Holiness*, 78; Merton, *Disputed Questions*, 178; Merton, *Seeds of Destruction*, xv; Merton, *Faith and Violence*, 151; Gerald Twomey, "Thomas Merton: An Appreciation," in Twomey, ed., 8; Merton, *Contemplation in a World of Action*, 36, 124.

86. Daggy, ed., *The Hidden Ground of Love*, 156; Merton, *Seeds of Destruction*, xiv; Merton, *The Silent Life*, 8; Merton, *Disputed Questions*, 177.

87. Merton, *Disputed Questions*, 175; Merton, *A Vow of Conversation*, 142.

88. Daggy, ed., *Introductions East and West*, 43, 45; John Howard Griffin, *Follow the Ecstasy*, 137.

89. Daggy, ed., *The Hidden Ground of Love*, 503, 644.

90. Merton, *The Asian Journal*, 341.

91. Merton, *Raids on the Unspeakable*, 18; Merton, *New Seeds of Contemplation*, 53, ix-x; Daggy, ed., *The Hidden Ground of Love*, 502; Merton, *Disputed Questions*, 174; Merton, *Love and Living*, 17.

92. Merton, *Conjectures of a Guilty Bystander*, 15; Merton, *Disputed Questions*, 124, 125.

93. Merton, *Collected Poems*, 382-83; Merton, *Mystics and Zen Masters*, 112.

94. Daggy, ed., *The Hidden Ground of Love*, 507; Merton, *Contemplation in a World of Action*, 232; Merton, *The Asian Journal*, 306; Merton, *Collected Poems*, 355; Thomas Merton, *The Way of Chuang Tzu* (New York, 1965), 153.

95. Merton, *Raids on the Unspeakable*, 69.

96. Merton, *Contemplation in a World of Action*, 243.

97. Merton, *Contemplative Prayer*, 114; Merton, *Disputed Questions*, 70; Merton, *The Asian Journal*, 305, 329.

98. Merton, *Raids on the Unspeakable*, 21-23; Merton, *Contemplation in a World of Action*, 374; Merton, *The Way of Chuang Tzu*, 153; Merton, *Disputed Questions*, 185.

99. Merton, *Disputed Questions*, 186; Griffin, "The Controversial Merton," in Twomey, ed., 86; Merton, *Contemplation in a World of Action*, 27.

100. Merton, New Seeds of Contemplation, 250; Daggy, ed., *The Hidden Ground of Love*, 261, 566, 381, 605; Daggy, ed., *Introductions East and West*, 45; Merton, *A Vow of Conversation*, 150.

101. Daggy, ed., *The Hidden Ground of Love*, 52; Merton, *Day of a Stranger*, 57, 12; Daggy, ed., *Introductions East and West*, 46.

102. Merton, *Faith and Violence*, 109-10.

103. Daggy, ed., *The Hidden Ground of Love*, 52.

104. Kenneth Leech, *Experiencing God: Theology as Spirituality* (San Francisco, 1985), 185-86.

105. Daggy, ed., *The Hidden Ground of Love*, 7; Merton, *The Seven Storey Mountain*, 164; Merton, *Raids on the Unspeakable*, 23.

106. Merton, *The Nonviolent Alternative*, 174.

107. Merton, *The Secular Journal*, 241, 101, 110-11.

108. Merton, *Collected Poems*, 623-24; Merton, *The Nonviolent Alternative*, 232, 174; Merton, *New Seeds of Contemplation*, 122.

109. Merton, *Raids on the Unspeakable*, 14; Thomas Merton, *The Wisdom of the Desert* (New York, 1960), 67.

110. Merton, *Mystics and Zen Masters*, 83.

111. Merton, *The Secular Journal*, 101-04; Merton, *The Nonviolent Alternative*, 175; Merton, *Raids on the Unspeakable*, 18; Daggy, ed., *The Hidden Ground of Love*, 467-68.

112. Merton, *The Nonviolent Alternative*, 151.

113. LeClercq, in Twomey, ed., 221; Griffin, *Follow the Ecstasy*, 122, 39, 48; Merton, *The Seven Storey Mountain*, 410-12.

114. Merton, *New Seeds of Contemplation*, 183-84.

115. Merton, *A Vow of Conversation*, 10, 154; Merton, *The Seven Storey Mountain*, 387; Daggy, ed., *The Hidden Ground of Love*, 22; Thomas Merton, *Thoughts in Solitude* (New York, 1958), 64, 67.

116. Merton, *Conjectures of a Guilty Bystander*, 68.

117. Merton, *The Seven Storey Mountain*, 321; Merton, *Disputed Questions*, 160.

118. Thomas Merton, *The Sign of Jonas* (Garden City, NY, 1956), 342-43.

119. James Baker, *Thomas Merton: Social Critic* (Lexington, KY, 1971), 113; Merton, *The Wisdom of the Desert*, 71.

120. Merton, *The Silent Life*, 176.

121. Mott, 230, 270-71.

122. Merton, *Collected Poems*, 248, 255; Daggy, ed., *The Hidden Ground of Love*, 222, 422; Merton, *Love and Living*, 23.

123. Daggy, ed., *The Hidden Ground of Love*, 86; Daggy, ed., *Introductions East and West*, 46; Merton, *Contemplation in a World of Action*, 374; Merton, *Love and Living*, 23.

124. Merton, *Seeds of Destruction*, xv, xii; Daggy, ed., *The Hidden Ground of Love*, 346-47, 410, 175, 52; Merton, *A Vow of Conversation*, 28

125. Daggy, ed., *The Hidden Ground of Love*, 272.

126. Daggy, ed., *The Hidden Ground of Love*, 74.

127. Daggy, ed., *The Hidden Ground of Love*, 20, 269, 274.

128. Daggy, ed., *The Hidden Ground of Love*, 212, 319, 267, 266.

129. Baker, 66.

130. Merton, *Contemplation in a World of Action*, 243, 25-26, 28; Merton, *The Way of Chuang Tzu*, 10; Merton, *Spiritual Direction and Meditation*, 89; Daggy, ed., *The Hidden Ground of Love*, 187; Merton, *Conjectures of a Guilty Bystander*, 77; Merton, *Contemplative Prayer*, 112; Merton, *A Vow of Conversation*, 88.

131. Merton, *Contemplation in a World of Action*, 262; Merton, *Contemplative Prayer*, 23; Daggy, ed., *The Hidden Ground of Love*, 152-53; Merton, *A Vow of Conversation*, 93; Merton, *Disputed Questions*, 171.

132. Merton, *Contemplation in a World of Action*, 8, 29, 242, 35; Merton, *Life and Holiness*, 15.

133. Sources disagree whether Merton entitled his presentation "The Monastic Protest: The Voice of the Desert," or "The Voice of the Wilderness." Mott, 406; Merton, *The Nonviolent Alternative*, 260 vs. Daggy, ed., *The Hidden Ground of Love*, 85-86.

134. Merton, *The Wisdom of the Desert*, 3, 23, 17.

135. Merton, *The Wisdom of the Desert*, 8; Merton, *Contemplation in a World of Action*, 29, 241; Daggy, ed., *The Hidden Ground of Love*, 466, 507.

136. Merton, *The Silent Life*, 172-76.

137. Daggy, ed., *The Hidden Ground of Love*, 503; Merton, *Raids on the Unspeakable*, 22.

138. Miller, *A Harsh and Dreadful Love*, 344.

139. Merton, *Raids on the Unspeakable*, 16; Daggy, ed., *The Hidden Ground of Love*, 223; Merton, *Gandhi on Non-Violence*, 10; Merton, *Faith and Violence*, 154; Merton, *The Nonviolent Alternative*, 269; Merton, *Contemplation in a World of Action*, 169.

140. Walter Brueggemann, *Hopeful Imagination* (Philadelphia, 1986), 96, 23, 51, 62, 63.

141. Merton, *Raids on the Unspeakable*, 160.

142. Merton, *New Seeds of Contemplation*, 13; Merton, *Faith and Violence*, 147.

143. Merton, *Raids on the Unspeakable*, 61-62.

144. Merton, *Raids on the Unspeakable*, 156.

145. Hannah Arendt, *Eichmann in Jerusalem: A Report on the Banality of Evil* (New York, 1963), 150.

146. Daggy, ed., *The Hidden Ground of Love*, 573, 209.

147. Daggy, ed., *The Hidden Ground of Love*, 575, 572, 398, 402, 140; Merton, *The Nonviolent Alternative*, 129.

148. Merton, *The Nonviolent Alternative*, 16, 77, 118; Merton, *Conjectures of a Guilty Bystander*, 218.

149. Merton, *Conjectures of a Guilty Bystander*, 250, 254; Daggy, ed., *The Hidden Ground of Love*, 444, 445, 76; Merton, *The Nonviolent Alternative*, 117, 94; Merton, *Faith and Violence*, 168.

150. Merton, *Faith and Violence*, 158; Daggy, ed., *The Hidden Ground of Love*, 446; Merton, *Seeds of Destruction*, 75; Merton, *A Vow of Conversation*, 180; Merton, *The Nonviolent Alternative*, 123, 17, 95.

151. Merton, *Raids on the Unspeakable*, 41; Merton, *Day of a Stranger*, 31; Merton, *The Nonviolent Alternative*, 268; Merton, *Seeds of Destruction*, 15; Merton, *Faith and Violence*, 51.

152. Merton, *The Nonviolent Alternative*, 220.

153. Daggy, ed., *The Hidden Ground of Love*, 202, 213; Merton, *The Nonviolent Alternative*, 91.

154. Merton, *Raids on the Unspeakable*, 46-47.

155. Merton, *Conjectures of a Guilty Bystander*, 228; Merton, *The Nonviolent Alternative*, 140.

156. Merton, *The Nonviolent Alternative*, 88, 92, 109, 131; Daggy, ed., *The Hidden Ground of Love*, 177, 330, 256, 649; Griffin, *Follow the Ecstasy*, 142.

157. Daggy, ed., *The Hidden Ground of Love*, 204; Merton, *The Nonviolent Alternative*, 95, 108.

158. Merton, *New Seeds of Contemplation*, 119-20.

159. Daggy, ed., *The Hidden Ground of Love*, 259; Merton, *The Nonviolent Alternative*, 100, 114; Merton, *Conjectures of a Guilty Bystander*, 277.

160. Merton, *The Nonviolent Alternative*, 130, 174, 176; Daggy, ed., *The Hidden Ground of Love*, 208.

161. Daggy, ed., *The Hidden Ground of Love*, 216; Merton, *Disputed Questions*, 148.

162. Merton, *The Nonviolent Alternative*, op. cit., p. 96-98.

163. Daggy, ed., *The Hidden Ground of Love*, 347, 349; Merton, *The Nonviolent Alternative*, 18.

164. Daggy, ed., *The Hidden Ground of Love*, 71, 83, 247, 272, 255, 260; Hart, ed., *The Literary Essays of Thomas Merton*, 237.

165. Merton, *The Nonviolent Alternative*, 18, 222, 226; Merton, *Life and Holiness*, 89.

166. Merton, *The Nonviolent Alternative*, 239; Daggy, ed., *The Hidden Ground of Love*, 296.

167. Daggy, ed., *The Hidden Ground of Love*, 281.

168. Daggy, ed., *The Hidden Ground of Love*, 296, 295; Merton, *Faith and Violence*, 92; Merton, *The Nonviolent Alternative*, 253, 69, 244; Merton, *A Vow of Conversation*, 112.

169. Merton, *The Nonviolent Alternative*, 253, 239; Merton, *A Vow of Conversation*, 126.

170. Merton, *The Nonviolent Alternative*, 238; Daggy, ed., *The Hidden Ground of Love*, 91.

171. Daggy, ed., *The Hidden Ground of Love*, 421, 419; Merton, *The Nonviolent Alternative*, 265; Mott, 527.

172. Merton, *The Nonviolent Alternative*, 238, 229, 243, 64; Hart, ed., *The Literary Essays of Thomas Merton*, 249-50; Daggy, ed., *The Hidden Ground of Love*, 295.

173. Mott, 414-15; Merton, *A Vow of Conversation*, 183, 187

174. Merton, *Gandhi on Non-Violence*, 1.

175. Merton, *Disputed Questions*, 67, 12.

176. Merton, *Faith and Violence*, 122, 136; Merton, *A Vow of Conversation*, 66-67.

177. Merton, *Seeds of Destruction*, 41-42; Daggy, ed., *The Hidden Ground of Love*, 455; Baker, 108-110; Mott, 526.

178. Baker, 107; Merton, *Seeds of Destruction*, 33, 37; Merton, *Faith and Violence*, 124; Daggy, ed., *The Hidden Ground of Love*, 456..

179. Eldridge Cleaver, *Soul On Ice* (New York, 1968), 32-34.

180. Merton, *Conjectures of a Guilty Bystander*, 73; Merton, *The Nonviolent Alternative*, 158-59; Merton, *Faith and Violence*, 132-33.

181. Merton, *Seeds of Destruction*, 64, 89, 43-45, 48; Daggy, ed., *The Hidden Ground of Love*, 602, 334; Griffin, *Follow the Ecstasy*, 136.

182. Merton, *Collected Poems*, 335-37.

183. Merton, *Seeds of Destruction*, 5; Daggy, ed., *The Hidden Ground of Love*, 458; Merton, *Faith and Violence*, 128-29.

184. Merton, *Faith and Violence*, 123, 121; Daggy, ed., *The Hidden Ground of Love*, 165, 215; Merton, *Conjectures of a Guilty Bystander*, 33.

185. Daggy, ed., *The Hidden Ground of Love*, 456, 233, 457.

186. Daggy, ed., *The Hidden Ground of Love*, 457; Merton, *Faith and Violence*, 172-73; Hart, ed., *The Literary Essays of Thomas Merton*, 381.

187. Merton, *Faith and Violence*, 130-31, 175.

188. Merton, *Conjectures of a Guilty Bystander*, 125.

189. Merton, *Conjectures of a Guilty Bystander*, 109-10.

190. Merton, *Seeds of Destruction*, 44, 69-70; Merton, *Faith and Violence*, 129; Daggy, ed., *The Hidden Ground of Love*, 592.

191. Daggy, ed., *The Hidden Ground of Love*, 455; Baker, 109.

192. Merton, *The Asian Journal*, 119-20.

193. Forest, in Twomey, ed., 35; Daggy, ed., *The Hidden Ground of Love*, 100, 219, 640, 451.

194. Forest, in Twomey, ed., 35; Merton, *Life and Holiness*, 8; Daggy, ed., *The Hidden Ground of Love*, 266.

195. Merton, *The Nonviolent Alternative*, 233, 167; Daggy, ed., *The Hidden Ground of Love*, 259, 145; Merton, *Collected Poems*, 251; Merton, *Life and Holiness*, 9; Merton, *Conjectures of a Guilty Bystander*, 82.

196. Merton, *The Nonviolent Alternative*, 90, 104, 212, 228, 127; Merton, *Conjectures of a Guilty Bystander*, 55; Daggy, ed., *The Hidden Ground of Love*, 332, 286, 270, 97; Merton, *Faith and Violence*, 8, 21, 12.

197. Merton, *Collected Poems*, 373; Merton, *Faith and Violence*, 14, 163; Daggy, ed., *The Hidden Ground of Love*, 91, 295; Merton, *Disputed Questions*, 115, 132; Merton, *The Nonviolent Alternative*, 208, 209, 211.

198. Thomas Merton, *Seasons of Celebration* (New York, 1965), 18.

199. Merton, *The Nonviolent Alternative*, 214.

200. Merton, *Conjectures of a Guilty Bystander*, 86; Merton, *Faith and Violence*, 15, 23; Daggy, ed., *The Hidden Ground of Love*, 296, 92; Merton, *The Nonviolent Alternative*, 214, 75.

201. Daggy, ed., *The Hidden Ground of Love*, 594, 261, 262, 264, 294, 296.

202. Merton, *Contemplation in a World of Action*, 178-79; Merton, *The Nonviolent Alternative*, 210, 105.

203. Merton, *Collected Poems*, 692, 775, 779, 701, 756, 669, 714; Daggy, ed., *The Hidden Ground of Love*, 589-607; Dorothy Day, *On Pilgrimage: The Sixties* (New York, 1972), 338.

204. Daggy, ed., *The Hidden Ground of Love*, 144, 325, 81, 335; Merton, *The Nonviolent Alternative*, 215, 216.

205. Merton, *The Nonviolent Alternative*, 215-16, 75; Daggy, ed., *The Hidden Ground of Love*, 117, 297, 591, 603; Merton, *Faith and Violence*, 117-18.

206. Daggy, ed., *The Hidden Ground of Love*, 156; Merton, *The Monastic Journey*, 221.

207. Merton, *The Nonviolent Alternative*, 257-58, 113.

208. Merton, *The Nonviolent Alternative*, 209; Daggy, ed., *The Hidden Ground of Love*, 142.

209. Merton, *A Vow of Conversation*, 32, 116.

210. Merton, *Disputed Questions*, 127; Merton, *Faith and Violence*, 64, 53; Merton, *Seeds of Destruction*, xiv; Merton, *The Nonviolent Alternative*, 88, 211, 209.

211. Daggy, ed., *The Hidden Ground of Love*, 263, 264; Merton, *Faith and Violence*, 255.

212. Daggy, ed., *The Hidden Ground of Love*, 98; Merton, *Disputed Questions*, 144.

213. Merton, *Contemplation in a World of Action*, 202, 210; Merton, *Conjectures of a Guilty Bystander*, 81; Merton, *Seeds of Destruction*, 96.

214. Griffin, in Twomey, ed., 84.

215. Merton, *The Nonviolent Alternative*, 106, 213.

216. Merton, *Gandhi on Non-Violence*, 24.

217. Merton, *The Nonviolent Alternative*, 260, 13; Merton, *Contemplation in a World of Action*, 155; Merton, *Thoughts in Solitude*, 13.

218. Merton, *The Secular Journal*, 121-22, 246-47; Merton, *New Seeds of Contemplation*, 122.

219. Daggy, ed., *The Hidden Ground of Love*, 283; Merton, *Collected Poems*, 372, 373; Merton, *The Nonviolent Alternative*, 220; Merton, *New Seeds of Contemplation*, 112.

220. Merton, *Gandhi on Non-Violence*, 6; also Merton, *The Nonviolent Alternative*, 181.

221. Merton, *Gandhi on Non-Violence*, 20; Merton, *The Nonviolent Alternative*, 112; Merton, *Life and Holiness*, 117; Daggy, ed., *The Hidden Ground of Love*, 405.

222. Merton, *New Seeds of Contemplation*, 122.

223. Thomas Merton, *The New Man* (New York, 1961), 3.

224. Merton, *A Vow of Conversation*, 43.

225. Merton, *The Sign of Jonas*, 351-52.

CONCLUSION

"Who are they that glorify God? Those who, having gone out of themselves, seek not their own in anything whatever it may be, whether great or small, who look for nothing under them nor over them nor beside them nor inside them, not clinging to possessions, honours, comfort, pleasure, advantage, nor inwardness nor holiness nor reward nor heaven, having gone out of all of this, all that is theirs: from these people God has glory, and they truly glorify God and render Him what is His due."

  --Meister Eckhart

"Do you know when people really become spiritual? It is when they become the slaves of God and are branded with His sign, which is the sign of the Cross, in token that they have given Him their freedom. Then He can sell them as slaves to the whole world, as He Himself was sold."

  --Teresa of Avila.[1]

The demons have not been cast out. Still out there, still within us, they are largely unrecognized. The inner anxiety that creates the panicked craving for individual security is the same fear that has launched every arrow from every crossbow and prepares every bomb and missile in every arms race. Fear lives within us, smothers the breath of life, and creates the political systems, the economic systems, and the weapons systems which distort lives and hasten deaths.

The world is a confusing and confounding place yet the Psalms make a simple observation: The wicked prosper. Their reputations and consciences are washed cleaner than Pilate's hands. People caught in the crossfire of violence are spat upon by self-righteous bystanders while war criminals are awarded peace prizes. The nice white people in the White House and on Wall Street never see the rotten fruit of their despoiled spirits; they never see a drop of blood of the inner city gang violence they initiate from afar. They do not recognize today's urban chaos as last generation's urban riots in another guise. They are blind to the monsters that feed all around them.

We are not in combat with mere flesh and blood, but with principalities and powers and the twisted spiritual forces of wickedness. If there was just one, clearly identifiable demon or power or enemy to overthrow, our task might be easy. But there are legions, armed and dangerous.

The Exodus was the crux of the Old Testament's salvation story, but the Exile was the long and painful labor that gave birth to questions about God and a reassessment of Israel's history and vocation. The Exile created Job and a new Israel. The formative experience and central expectation of the Old Testament is that life is not as God intends it to be; may it become so. The multitude of references to the exilic prophets in the Gospels is hardly incidental. It is as though the Evangelists perceived that the world itself is in exile, out of place, possessed. The Kingdom Jesus announced is coming to overthrow the legion that occupies the world like a Roman army quietly pressing Israel under its feet. Jesus' revolutionary proposition that God is now taking charge brings skeptics rushing in to amend or silence his claims. The world prefers darkness, but Jesus brings light, and darkness can never be the same.

The demons have not been cast out, but Jesus makes a counterclaim about the make-up of the world. God is not indifferent or transcendently absent or--like Baal during Elijah's battle with the false god's prophets--occupied in a cosmic outhouse. There are channels of grace, though they are often hidden from view. The Kingdom of God erupts in the midst of the legion whenever the blind are healed, the hungry fed, the prisoners freed, the naked clothed, the Good News preached. It enters the City and the Temple from the crosses outside of town. Salvation trickles in like cold water from the corners of society. Odd moments are ripe with redemptive possibility, certain years full of kairos. God was not deaf to slaves' cries in Egypt nor did God leave exiles in Babylon. The Spirituals affirm in asking: "Didn't my Lord deliver Daniel?"[2] God does not abandon the world to an endless exile.

A call comes from God that is heard in every commandment and demand that echoes off of church walls. The call is heard in every form of biblical literature, in the teachings of Jesus, the mystical tradition; it is felt in the sacraments. The call does not reach us in a secure or peaceful place. A cacophony of terrorized cries and seductive sighs suggests that there are ways to live good, decent lives that do not share God's anguish for those who suffer or God's ecstasy with those who have been touched by grace. There are diversionary voices saying that action by itself is enough and prayer a luxury for those unconcerned with the wretched of the earth. But social action without prayer is a delusion waiting to steer its passengers over a cliff, "spirituality" without social ministry an addiction to a slow-acting poison.

The call invites us to wear the armor of God, to gird our loins with truth, to put on the breastplate of righteousness, the sandals of the gospel of peace, the shield of faith, the helmet of salvation, and the sword of the Spirit. And, when so dressed, we are to "pray at all times in the Spirit" (Eph 6:11-18). When facing demons, it is always wise to pray. Christians so often feel like midgets in giant's armor, perhaps forgetful of David's prayer for deliverance as he stood before Goliath. The real problem is that we place our faith in our own slingshots, our own armaments, our own power.

The call to become co-liberators with the Trinity is both general and personal. Day called her readers to a life of "precarity" and voluntary poverty. Yet she advised the same readers to pursue peacemaking within their existing vocations. So we must live in a state of perpetual personal discomfort. If we are not specifically called to a dramatic change of direction, we are called--at least--to make our current circumstances more precarious. We are to pronounce Day's and Merton's NO and YES in the context of our lives.

We are called to be fools for the sake of Him who foolishly carried the Word of God as his only sword and wore a crown of thorns as the helmet of salvation. Each Christian is called to be a social anomaly, a misfit, purposefully irrelevant to the logic of "the world." Each one is called to deliberately become an outcast, to seek only the stability of precarious living, and to trust that our every hesitant step gives strength and courage to others when they discover they do not stand alone.

We need a Robin Hood Theology to give us balance as we seek to respond to this call, for the predicament of that old English folk story parallels the world's situation as perceived through scripture. In the King's absence the evil Prince has seized power and brought injustice to the land. Robin Hood and his followers do not have the numbers or weapons to defeat the oppressors, yet they do have the power to resist and to create oppression-free zones. They say NO to oppression and assert that--even in the present--things are being set right. At the same time, they are a feasting people, "making merry" in anticipation of a greater banquet, preparing for the time when the King will return to renew a reign of peace. Robin Hood Theology lives within the tension of the Social Gospel's hope to "speed the day" of the Kingdom's coming and Merton's insistence that only God shall overcome the Prince of Darkness.

Matthew's Gospel tells of Jesus giving the keys of the Kingdom to Peter and, through him, to the Church. Yet Christians seem to stand before a thousand locks holding a million keys without knowing where in the world to begin. Which keys will unlock the doors? The communal ministry of the Catholic Worker or the solitary witness of the monk or the social leaven of organizations? Or does each open a separate door? Muste advised a patient spirit of experimentation, yet how can we forestall frustration when faced with so many locks? Did King's profound pain increase his desire for rapid progress toward the "beloved community"? Can we walk with him in the darkness without knowing if dawn will ever break? Can we, like Muste, yearn intensely for the city-to-be without becoming addicted to tangible results? And when we fail, can we accept our failure as part of a great experiment?

The "dark night" comes for all who seek social change. At first, God may provide positive feelings and consolations of spirit to keep us on the path. But these disappear. During his trip to Europe, Muste was deprived of his sense of direction and purpose--at the age of fifty-one--until the still, small voice whispered within him. Day's ministry had few consolations. King endured the forcible removal of all moral certainties. And just as there are seasons of suffering when one can barely keep from being overcome, so there are also seasons of kairos, times to overcome. Through every season, Muste, Day, King, and Merton found that they could proceed because of the truth of their actions, because they sought to serve God and love their neighbor, because they wanted to diminish the world's sum total of misery and increase its sum total of love.

Delivered from projections, they acted for the sake of others, even their enemies. Saved from an anxious desire for security, they acted for the sake of the Kingdom. Relieved from the need to prove themselves, they lived for God's sake. For they knew--each in a dark night--that it is not until we live precariously that we are secure, not until we live radically that we are traditional, not until we live politically that we are spiritual.

There are many inevitable letdowns in seeking radical social transformation. For Christians, there is the permanent dissatisfaction with a Church created in Christ's image yet also fallen, a Church that fails its mission to fit its people with the full armor of God and becomes, at times, an instrument of the legion. We can expect the Church's infidelity, but we must not let it fail comfortably; it is also the reservoir of a holy imagination filled with death-resisting, life-giving metaphors, parables, and stories. The Church contains a peace plan of confession, prayer, the Word of God, and communion. Though often obscured, every strand of Christian tradition has a spirituality of liberation planted within it. A "Church" or "tradition" without a liberating element is not Christian.

The theology and ministry of the first generation of Social Gospellers--and of Day, Merton, Muste, and King--were challenged and changed by contact with human suffering.[3] Only when we see around us the crucifixions of our time do we begin to understand Jesus' death on the Cross. Only when we connect that ancient and eternal torture with contemporary suffering can our imaginations begin to comprehend the world, the legion, and evil. And, in a "sanctuary frame of mind," we can see others "shining like the sun," radiating God's splendor, giving us hope.

Without that vision of transfiguration we may not have the courage to become people of the margins. God has always used nomads and slaves, exiles and last-born as levers of grace. It is not simply that radical people goad more moderate and powerful allies toward social change. The thousand doors open only at the fringes of the Church and the world. It is only at the edges of society that one can gain the leverage to move society.

Muste did not understand Merton's witness, and perhaps we will not understand one another's work for social justice. Not all of us are called to Muste's grand experiments nor King's magnificent dreams nor Day's "little way" nor Merton's Desert, but we ought to be able to find and identify our own way of Christian ministry as it relates to theirs.

The sources of our spiritual guidance will not be the same as theirs, but Jesus will speak to us and the merciful, demanding shadow of the Cross will lie across our path. We will be challenged to detach ourselves from the things within us that make us cling to fear and death. Words will be engraved on our hearts as we make use of a tradition's treasures, the great pearl being Christ.

The sources of our spiritual sustenance will not be identical with theirs, but we must live within a nurturing community. With the help of other people of faith, we can structure for ourselves a sustaining rule of life. In sharing common visions, sensing that God is not excommunicated from the present, and facing up to despair, we can find hope. We do not have to look up to heaven nor across the sea for the Word of God, for it is found in the basic substance of Christian faith, already in our mouth and in our heart (Deut 30:11-14).

We will not discern the world precisely as they did, but we will have to face the demons at large and within ourselves, learning to swim next to Leviathan without pretense of innocence. Unable--because of love--to turn our backs on the world, we will be selective in what we renounce. We will have to discern how to live out our ambiguous relationship with a hot and cold and lukewarm Church and understand its part in the comedy of trickle-up redemption.

None of us will trace their paths step by step, but we can identify, as they did, the parables, the quotations, and metaphors that activate and guide us--our own personal canon within the Church's canon. We can become fools for Christ's sake and thus be wise; we can fight internal revolutions as we seek social transformations.

This is where we are fitted with the whole armor of God and sent out against the malevolent legion. We may not experience human unity in a Quaker meeting in upstate New York, or in the Montgomery airport, or on a Manhattan bus, or at a downtown Louisville street corner, but we must pray to live as though we have known that unity--and its source--all along.

NOTES

CONCLUSION

1. M. O'C. Walshe, trans. and ed., *Meister Eckhart: Sermons and Treatises* (Longmead, Shaftesbury, Dorset, 1987), vol. 2, p. 131; Teresa of Avila, *The Interior Castle* (Garden City, NY, 1961), 229.

2. Christa Dixon, *Negro Spirituals* (n. p., 1967), 173.

3. Mel Piehl, *Breaking Bread: The Catholic Worker and the Origin of Catholic Radicalism in America* (Philadelphia, 1982), 32; see also Paul M. Minus, *Walter Rauschenbusch: American Reformer* (New York, 1988), 60-61.

BIBLIOGRAPHY

"A. J. Muste." *Fellowship* 33:3 (March, 1967): 2.

"A. J. Muste Birthday Celebrated in January." *Fellowship* 16:1 (Jan. 1950): 20.

"A J. Muste Fasts; Addresses Crowd of 10,000 at U.N." *Fellowship* 28:22 (Nov. 15, 1962): 20.

"A. J. Muste Takes Tax Refusal Position." *Fellowship* 14:6 (June 1948): 20.

Ahlstrom, Sydney E. *A Religious History of the American People.* Garden City, NY, 1975.

Allchin, A. M. "A Liberator, A Reconciler." *Continuum* 7:2 (Summer 1969): 362-64.

----------.*The World is a Wedding.* New York, 1978.

Ansbro, John J. *Martin Luther King, Jr.: The Making of a Mind.* New York, 1982.

Arendt, Hannah. *Eichmann in Jerusalem: A Report on the Banality of Evil.* New York, 1963, 1965.

Baker, James. *Thomas Merton Social Critic.* Lexington, KY, 1971.

Baldwin, James. *The Evidence of Things Not Seen.* New York, 1985.

Baldwin, James. "The Highroad to Destiny," in C. Eric Lincoln, ed., *Martin Luther King, Jr.: A Profile*, 90-112. New York, 1984.

Bamberger, John Eudes, OCSO. "The Cistercian." *Continuum* 7:2 (Summer 1969): 229-34.

Blakney, Raymond Bernard. *Meister Eckhart: A Modern Translation.* San Francisco, 1941.

Boulding, Kenneth. *There is a Spirit: The Nayler Sonnets.* New York, 1945.

Brock, Peter. *Pacifism in the United States: From the Colonial Era to the First World War.* Princeton, 1968.

----------. *Twentieth Century Pacifism.* New York, 1970.

Brueggemann, Walter. *David's Truth.* Philadelphia, 1985.

----------. *Hope Within History.* Atlanta, 1987.

----------. *Hopeful Imagination.* Philadelphia, 1986.

"By Personal Protest." *The Catholic Worker* 23:1 (July-Aug. 1956): 2.

"C. W. Editors Arrested in Air Raid Drill." *The Catholic Worker* 23:1 (July-Aug. 1956): 1, 8.

Campbell, Debra. "The Catholic Earth Mother: Dorothy Day and Women's Power in the Church." *Crosscurrents* 34:3 (Fall 1984).

Camus, Albert. *The Rebel.* New York, 1956.

Caputo, Philip. *A Rumor of War.* New York, 1977.

Chatfield, Charles. *For Peace and Justice: Pacifism in America, 1914-1941.* Knoxville, 1971.

Cleaver, Eldridge. *Soul on Ice.* New York, 1968.

Cleghorn, Reese. "Crowned with Crises," in C. Eric Lincoln, ed., *Martin Luther King Jr.: A Profile,* 113-27. New York, 1984.

Coles, Robert. *Dorothy Day: A Radical Devotion.* Reading, MA, 1987.

Collum, Danny. "Clues to the Future." *Sojourners* 13:11 (Dec. 1984): 3.

Commins, Gary. "Woody Allen's Theological Imagination." *Theology Today* 44:2 (July 1987): 235-49.

Cone, James. *The Spirituals and the Blues: An Interpretation.* New York, 1972.

----------. "The Theology of Martin Luther King, Jr." *Union Seminary Quarterly Review* 40:4 (1986): 21-39.

Cornell, Tom and David McReynolds. (untitled). *WIN* 3:4 (Feb. 24, 1967): 8-9.

Cort, John C. "My Life at the Catholic Worker." *Commonweal* 107:12 (June 1980): 361-67.

Cuneen, Sally. "Dorothy Day: The Storyteller as Human Model." *Crosscurrents* 34:3 (Fall 1984).

Cunningham, Lawrence S. "Thomas Merton: The Pursuit of Marginality." *The Christian Century* 95:47 (Dec. 6, 1978): 1181-83.

Daggy, Robert, ed. *The Hidden Ground of Love: The Letters of Thomas Merton,* volume 1. New York, 1985.

----------. *Introductions East and West: The Foreign Prefaces of Thomas Merton.* Greensboro, NC, 1981.

Day, Dorothy. "A. J." *Commonweal* 86:1 (March 24, 1967): 14-16.

----------. *From Union Square to Rome.* New York, 1938.

----------. *Houses of Hospitality.* New York, 1939.

----------. *Loaves and Fishes.* San Francisco, 1963.

----------. "Message of Love." *The Catholic Worker* 17:6 (Dec. 1950): 1-2.

----------. *On Pilgrimage.* New York, 1948.

----------. *On Pilgrimage: The Sixties.* New York, 1972.

----------. "On Pilgrimage." *The Catholic Worker* 24:1 (July-Aug. 1957): 2-3.

----------. *The Long Loneliness.* San Francisco, 1952.

----------. *Therese.* Springfield, IL, 1960.

----------. "Where are the Poor? They are in Prisons, Too." *The Catholic Worker* 22:1 (July-Aug. 1955): 1, 8.

Dellinger, Dave. "Action at Omaha." *Liberation* 4:5 (Summer 1959): 3-4.

----------. "Introduction." *Liberation* 12:6-7 (Sept-Oct. 1967): 3-4.

Deming, Barbara. "'It's a Good Life.'" *Liberation* 12:6-7 (Sept-Oct. 1967): 60.

----------. Untitled. *WIN* 3:4 (Feb. 24, 1967): 16.

Dixon, Christa. *Negro Spirituals.* N.p., 1967.

Dostoevsky, Fyodor. *The Brothers Karamazov.* New York, 1957.

Douglass, Frederick. *Life and Times of Frederick Douglass.* New York, 1971.

Downing, Frederick. "Martin Luther King, Jr. as Public Theologian." *Theology Today* 44:1 (April 1987): 18-29.

DuBois, W.E.B. *Prayers for a Dark People.* Amherst, 1980.

----------. *The Souls of Black Folk.* New York, 1903, 1969.

Ellis, Marc. *A Year at the Catholic Worker.* New York, 1978.

----------. *Peter Maurin: Prophet in the Twentieth Century.* New York, 1981.

Ellsberg, Robert, ed. *By Little and By Little: The Selected Writings of Dorothy Day.* New York, 1983.

Fager, Charles E. *Selma, 1965: The March that Changed the South.* Boston, 1974.

Finn, James. *Protest: Pacifism and Politics.* New York, 1967.

F.O.R. Executive Committee. "The Course Before Us." *Fellowship* 8:1 (Jan. 1942): 2.

F.O.R. Spiritual Life Committee. "Thine is the Power." *Fellowship* 18:5 (May 1952): 8.

Forest, James. *Love is the Measure: A Biography of Dorothy Day.* New York, 1986.

----------. "Thomas Merton's Struggle with Peacemaking," in Gerald Twomey, ed., *Thomas Merton: Prophet in the Belly of a Paradox*, 15-54. New York, 1978.

Fox, George. *The Journal of George Fox.* London, 1975.

Freire, Paulo. *A Pedagogy of the Oppressed.* New York, 1970.

Garrow, David J. *Bearing the Cross: Martin Luther King, Jr. and the Southern Christian Leadership Conference.* New York, 1986.

----------. *The FBI and Martin Luther King, Jr.* New York, 1981.

----------. "The Intellectual Development of Martin Luther King, Jr.: Influences and Commentaries." *Union Seminary Quarterly Review* 40:4 (1986): 5-20.

"'Grand Old Man' of American Pacifism." *The Christian Century* 84:8 (Feb. 22, 1967): 230.

Griffin, John Howard. *Follow the Ecstasy.* Fort Worth, 1983.

Griffin, John Howard. "The Controversial Merton," in Gerald Twomey, ed., *Thomas Merton: Prophet in the Belly of a Paradox*, 80-91. New York, 1978.

Halberstam, David. "When 'Civil Rights' and 'Peace' Join Forces," in C. Eric Lincoln, ed., *Martin Luther King, Jr.: A Profile*, 187-211. New York 1984.

Hart, Patrick, ed. *The Literary Essays of Thomas Merton.* New York, 1981.

Hennacy, Ammon. *The Book of Ammon.* N.p., 1965.

Hentoff, Nat. "A. J. Continuing." *Liberation* 12:6-7 (Sept-Oct. 1967): 66.

----------. "A. J. Muste 1885-1967." *Saturday Review* 50 (April 8, 1967): 35.

----------. *Peace Agitator: The Story of A. J. Muste.* New York, 1963.

----------, ed. *The Essays of A. J. Muste.* New York, 1967.

Higginson, Thomas. "Negro Spirituals." *Atlantic Monthly* 19:116 (June 1867): 692.

Hughes, Langston and Arna Bontemps, eds. *The Book of Negro Folklore.* New York , 1958.

Johnson, James Weldon. *The Book of American Negro Spirituals.* New York, 1925.

Julian of Norwich. *Showings.* New York, 1978.

Kelly, Thomas. *The Eternal Promise.* Richmond, VA, 1988.

Kempton, Murray. "J. Edgar Hoover and the Industry of Fear." *Liberation* 2:2 (April 1957): 8-9.

"King Speaks for Peace." *The Christian Century* 84:17 (April 29, 1967).

King, Martin Luther, Jr. *Strength to Love.* Philadelphia, 1963.

----------. *Stride Toward Freedom: The Montgomery Story.* San Francisco, 1958.

----------. *The Measure of a Man.* Philadelphia, 1959.

----------. *The Trumpet of Conscience.* New York, 1967.

----------. *Where Do We Go From Here?* New York, 1968.

----------. *Why We Can't Wait.* New York, 1963.

LeClercq, Jean. "Merton and History," in Gerald Twomey, ed., *Thomas Merton: Prophet in the Belly of a Paradox*, 213-32. New York, 1978.

Leech, Kenneth. *Experiencing God: Theology as Spirituality.* San Francisco, 1985.

Lens, Sidney. "Humanistic Revolutionary." *Liberation* 12:6-7 (Sept-Oct. 1967): 5-8.

Letts, Laurence Alan. "Peace and The Gospel: A Comparative Study of the Theological and Ethical Foundations of A. J. Muste's Radical Pacifism and Reinhold Niebuhr's "'Christian Realism.'" Ph. D. Dissertation, Yale, 1975.

Lewis, David L. *King: A Biography.* Urbana, IL, 1970, 1978.

Lomax, Louis. "When 'Nonviolence' Meets 'Black Power,'" in C. Eric Lincoln, ed., *Martin Luther King, Jr.: A Profile*, 157-80. New York, 1984.

Lovell, John Jr. *Black Song: The Forge and the Flame*. New York, 1972.

----------. "The Social Implications of the Negro Spiritual," in Bernard Katz, ed., *The Social Implications of Early Negro Music in the United States*. New York, 1969.

MacGregor, G. H. C. *The Relevance of an Impossible Ideal*. Nyack, NY, 1941, 1960.

Mahedy, William P. *Out of the Night: The Spiritual Journey of Vietnam Vets*. New York, 1986.

Maurin, Peter. *Easy Essays*. Chicago, 1977.

Mayer, Milton. "The Christer." *Fellowship* 18:1 (Jan. 1952): 1-10.

McDonnell, Thomas P., ed. *A Thomas Merton Reader*. Garden City, NY, 1974.

McKane, William. *Prophets and Wise Men*. Naperville, IL, 1965.

Meier, August. "The Conservative Militant," in C. Eric Lincoln, ed., *Martin Luther King, Jr.: A Profile*, 144-56. New York, 1984.

Merton, Thomas. *A Vow of Conversation*. New York, 1988.

----------. *Conjectures of a Guilty Bystander*. Garden City, NY, 1968.

----------. *Contemplation in a World of Action*. Garden City, NY, 1973.

----------. *Contemplative Prayer*. Garden City, NY, 1969.

----------. *Day of a Stranger*. Salt Lake City, 1981.

----------. *Disputed Questions*. New York, 1960.

----------. *Faith and Violence*. Notre Dame, 1968.

----------. *Gandhi on Non-Violence*. New York, 1965.

----------. *Life and Holiness*. Garden City, NY, 1964.

----------. *Love and Living*. New York, 1979.

----------. *Mystics and Zen Masters*. New York, 1967.

----------. *New Seeds of Contemplation*. New York, 1962.

----------. *Raids on the Unspeakable*. New York, 1966.

----------. *Seasons of Celebration*. New York, 1965.

----------. *Seeds of Destruction*. New York, 1964.

----------. *Spiritual Direction and Meditation*. Collegeville, MN, 1960.

----------. *The Asian Journal*. New York, 1973.

----------. *The Collected Poems of Thomas Merton*. New York, 1977.

----------. *The Monastic Journey*. Garden City, NY, 1977.

----------. *The New Man*. New York, 1961.

----------. *The Nonviolent Alternative*. New York, 1980.

----------. *The Secular Journal*. New York, 1959.

----------. *The Seven Storey Mountain*. New York, 1948, 1970.

----------. *The Sign of Jonas*. Garden City, NY, 1956.

----------. *The Silent Life*. New York, 1957.

----------. *The Way of Chuang Tzu*. New York, 1965.

----------. *The Wisdom of the Desert*. New York, 1960.

----------. *Thoughts in Solitude*. New York, 1958.

----------. *Zen and the Birds of Appetite*. New York, 1968.

Miller, William D. *A Harsh and Dreadful Love: Dorothy Day and the Catholic Worker Movement*. New York, 1973.

----------. *All is Grace: The Spirituality of Dorothy Day*. Garden City, NY, 1987.

----------. *Dorothy Day: A Biography*. San Francisco, 1982.

Minus, Paul M. *Walter Rauschenbusch: American Reformer*. New York, 1988.

Mott, Michael. *The Seven Mountains of Thomas Merton*. Boston, 1984.

Moyers, Bill. "Still a Rebel." *Bill Moyer's Journal*. Educational Broadcasting Network, 1973.

Muste, A. J. "'A Just and Durable Peace.'" *Fellowship* 8:4 (April 1942): 62.

----------. "A Look Around." *Fellowship* 14:5 (May 1948): 3-5.

----------. "A Meditation on Assurance." *Fellowship* 7:4 (April 1941): 58.

----------. "A New Year--A New Era." *Fellowship* 12:1 (Jan. 1946): 3-4.

----------. "A Pacifist Program--1949." *Fellowship* 15:1 (Jan. 1949): 4-9.

----------. "A Partridge in a Pear Tree." *Sojourners* 13:11 (Dec. 1984): 22.

----------. "A Plea to Enlist." *Fellowship* 6:7 (Sept. 1940): 103-04.

----------. "A Strategy for the Peace Movement." *Liberation* 7:4 (June 1962): 6-8.

----------. "A Visit to Saigon." *Liberation* 11:3 (Summer 1966): 10.

----------. "Africa Against the Bomb (II)." *Liberation* 4:11 (Feb. 1960): 11.

----------. "Annihilation Without Representation." *Liberation* 5:12 (Feb. 1961): 11.

----------. "April 27--A Message to the Fellowship." *Fellowship* 8:5 (May 1942): 75-76.

----------. "Assembly of Unrepresented People: Three Views." *Liberation* 10:7 (Oct. 1965): 27.

----------. "Berlin--Solomon--Kafka." *Liberation* 6:7 (Sept. 1961): 3-4.

----------. "Catholic Workers Unite." *Fellowship* 3:6 (June 1937): 5.

----------. "Civil Defense Protest." *Liberation* 6:4-5 (Summer 1961): 3.

----------. "Conscience Against the Atomic Bomb." *Fellowship* 11:12 (Dec. 1945): 208-09.

----------. "Dumbarton Oaks or Chaos." *Fellowship* 11:4 (April 1945): 69-84.

----------. "Evanston--After Three Months." *Fellowship* 20:11 (Dec. 1954): 12-15.

----------. "Fellowship and Class Struggle," in Charles Chatfield, ed., *International War Resistance through World War II*, 560-79. New York, 1975.

----------. "Fellowship in Discovering Truth." *Fellowship* 10:11 (Nov. 1944): 189.

----------. "Fight the Good Fight?" *The American Scholar* 6:3 (Summer 1937): 334-44.

----------. "Follow the Golden Rule." *Liberation* 3:4 (June 1958): 6.

----------. "Footnote on Moscow." *Fellowship* 9:12 (Dec. 1943): 213.

----------. "Footnote to Cleveland." *The Christian Century* 70:49 (Dec. 9, 1953): 1420-22.

----------. *Gandhi and the H-Bomb: How Nonviolence Can Take the Place of War*. F.O.R. Pamphlet: New York, 1950, 1983.

----------. "I Believe." *Fellowship* 16:2 (Feb. 1950): 3-7.

----------. "If I Were in China." *Fellowship* 4:4 (April 1938): 7.

----------. "Illusion of Victory." *Fellowship* 8:12 (Dec. 1942): 201-02.

----------. "It Glows in His Heart." *Fellowship* 17:1 (Jan. 1951): 2-6.

----------. "Last Speech." *Liberation* 12:6-7 (Sept-Oct. 1967): 52-57.

---------- . "'Let Him Come Down': A Lenten Meditation for Pacifists." *Fellowship* 4:3 (March 1938): 3-4.

----------. "Letter to the Editor." *Fellowship* 10:8 (Aug. 1944): 147.

----------. "Love and Power in Today's Setting." *The Christian Century* 80:20 (May 15, 1963): 639-42.

----------. "Love in Action." *Fellowship* 16:6 (June 1950): 7-13.

----------. "Mobilize for Peace." *Liberation* 11:9 (Dec. 1966): 23-24.

----------. "Neo-Gandhian India." *The Christian Century* 70:32 (Aug. 12, 1953): 914-16.

----------. "Niebuhr on the Brink of War." *Liberation* 1:12 (Feb. 1957): 8-10.

----------. "Nonviolence--A World Movement." *Liberation* 6:12 (Feb. 1962): 10-16.

----------. *Nonviolence in an Aggressive World.* New York, 1940.

----------. *Not By Might; Christianity: The Way to Human Decency.* New York, 1947.

----------. "NOW is the Appointed Time." *Fellowship* 25:13 (July 1, 1959): 7-12.

----------. "Overcoming Fear." *Fellowship* 16:11 (Nov. 1950): 4-7.

----------. "Pacifism After the War." *Fellowship* 9:12 (Dec. 1943): 203-06.

----------. "Pacifism and the Problem of Power." *Fellowship* 16:1 (Jan. 1950): 9-14.

----------. "Pacifism Enters a New Phase." *Fellowship* 26:13 (July 1, 1960): 21-25, 34.

----------. "Pacifists Do Not Fight." *The Christian Century* 59:9 (March 4, 1942): 289-90.

----------. "Peace and the Power States." *Liberation* 7:8 (Oct. 1962): 17.

----------. "Peace is Indivisible." *Fellowship* 2:8 (Oct. 1936): 6.

----------. "'Peace is the Way.'" *Liberation* 10:3 (May 1965): 3-5.

----------. "Politics on the Other Side of Despair." *Liberation* 7:2 (April 1962): 8-9.

----------. "Prospect for Peace in 1953." *Fellowship* 19:1 (Jan. 1953): 6-9.

----------. "Reflections on the Problems of COs in Prison." *Fellowship* 10:1 (Jan. 1944): 10-14.

----------. "Return to Pacifism." *The Christian Century* 53:49 (Dec. 2, 1936): 1603-06.

----------. "Russia in World Affairs." *Fellowship* 10:7 (July 1944): 127.

----------. "Self Immolation." *Liberation* 10:9 (Dec. 1965): 7.

----------. "Some Fellowship Objectives." *Fellowship* 7:10 (Oct. 1941): 165-67.

----------. "Stalin Pulls the Strings." *Fellowship* 10:3 (March 1944): 35-37.

----------. "Steamer Letter." *Fellowship* 13:7 (July 1947): 109-10.

----------. "Thawing but Unsettled." *Fellowship* 15:7 (July 1949): 23.

----------. "The Billy Graham Crusade." *Liberation* 2:3. (May 1957): 6-7, 19.

----------. "The Course Before Us." *Fellowship* 8:1 (Jan. 1942): 2.

----------. "The C.P.L.A. States Its Case." *The World Tomorrow* 16 (Oct. 12, 1933): 569-70.

----------. "The Direction of Growth." *Fellowship* 10:9 (Sept. 1944): 158-59.

----------. "The Oxford Conference." *Liberation* 8:1 (March 1963): 25.

----------. "The Pacifist Way of Life." *Fellowship* 7:12 (Dec. 1941): 198-200.

----------. "The Price of Moral Authority." *Fellowship* 18:1 (Jan. 1952): 13-18.

----------. "The Reign of Terror." *Fellowship* 4:10 (Dec. 1938): 8-9.

----------. "The Religious Basis of Pacifism." *Fellowship* 5:9 (Nov. 1939): 5-6.

----------. "The Roosevelt-Hitler Exchange." *Fellowship* 5:5 (May 1939): 7.

----------. "The San Francisco Charter." *Fellowship* 11:8 (Aug. 1945): 136.

----------. "The Spirit of the Martyrs." *Fellowship* 6:8 (Oct. 1940): 121.

----------. "The Spiritual Menace of Russian Communism." *Fellowship* 10:6. (June 1944): 105.

----------. "The Task Ahead." *Fellowship* 9:7 (July 1943): 128-29.

----------. "The Trend--The Historical Imperative of Civilization," in Harrop A. Freeman, ed., *Peace is the Victory*, 35-57. New York, 1944.

----------. "The True International." *The Christian Century* 56:21 (May 24, 1939): 667-69.

----------. "The Vatican Council." *Liberation* 10:10 (Jan. 1966): 4-5.

----------. "The Way Forward." *Fellowship* 14:1 (Jan. 1948): 4-9.

----------. "The Way of the Cross." *The Christian Century* 55:50 (Dec. 14, 1938): 1541-43.

----------. "Their Church and Ours." *Fellowship* 24:21 (Nov. 1, 1958): 6-8.

----------. "They Made It to Moscow." *Liberation* 6:9 (Nov. 1961): 7-10.

----------. "This Senseless War." *Fellowship* 7:8 (Aug. 1941): 139-40.

----------. "Three Men at Crimea." *Fellowship* 11:3 (March 1945): 45.

----------. "To Teach Peace." *Fellowship* 15:7 (July 1949): 48.

----------. "Today! Speak Out! Bear Your Witness Now." *Fellowship* 5:2 (Feb. 1939): 14.

----------. "Twenty-five Years After." *Fellowship* 9:11 (Nov. 1943): 189-91.

----------. "USA--Arsenal." *Fellowship* 7:4 (April 1941): 60.

----------. "Utopianism in Christianity." *Fellowship* 16:5 (May 1950): 11-16, 32.

----------. "What is the FOR?" *Fellowship* 23:1 (Jan. 1957): 8-13.

----------. "What is Left to Do?" *Fellowship* 17:7 (July 1951): 11-16.

----------. "Where Are We Now?" *Fellowship* 22:1 (Jan. 1956): 12-20.

----------. "Where 'Crisis Realism' Fails." *Fellowship* 5:4 (April 1939): 4-5.

----------. "Work for the New Year." *Fellowship* 7:1 (Jan. 1941): 12.

----------. "World Government--Panacea or Promise?" *Fellowship* 12:10 (Nov. 1946): 178.

----------. "Ye Shall Receive Power': An Easter Meditation." *Fellowship* 10:4 (April 1944): 67.

"Muste on Trial for Tax Refusal." *Fellowship* 26:7 (April 1, 1960).

"Muste Refuses Tax Again." *Fellowship* 20:4 (April 1954): 24.

"Muste Testifies Against Rearmament." *Fellowship* 18:8 (Sept. 1952): 22.

Niebuhr, Reinhold. "Christian Revolutionary." *New York Times Book Review* 72:6 (April 16, 1967): 6.

----------. "Pacifism Against the Wall." *The American Scholar* 5:2 (Spring 1936): 133-41.

----------. *The Children of Light and the Children of Darkness.* New York, 1944.

----------. "Why I Leave the F.O.R." *The Christian Century* 51:1 (Jan. 3, 1934): 18-19.

Nouwen, Henri. *Pray to Live.* Notre Dame, 1972.

Oates, Stephen B. *Let the Trumpet Sound: The Life of Martin Luther King, Jr.* New York, 1982.

"Pacifists Choose New Leader." *The Christian Century* 57:31 (July 31, 1940): 640-41.

Peers, E. Allison. *Mother of Carmel: A Portrait of Teresa of Avila.* Wilton, CN, 1944.

Petry, Ray C. *Late Medieval Mysticism.* Philadelphia, 1957.

Piehl, Mel. *Breaking Bread: The Catholic Worker and the Origin of Catholic Radicalism in America.* Philadelphia, 1982.

Raboteau, Albert. *Slave Religion: The "Invisible Institution" in the Antebellum South.* Oxford, 1978.

Raines, Howell. *My Soul is Rested.* New York, 1977.

Rauschenbusch, Walter. *A Theology for the Social Gospel.* New York, 1917.

----------. *Christianity and the Social Crisis.* New York, 1907.

----------. *Prayers of the Social Awakening.* Boston, 1910.

Rice, Edward. *The Man in the Sycamore Tree: The Good Times and Hard Life of Thomas Merton.* Garden City, NY, 1972.

Rivage-Seul, Marguerite K. "Peace Education: Imagination and the Pedagogy of the Oppressed." *Harvard Educational Review* 57:2 (May 1987): 154-66.

Roberts, Nancy L. *Dorothy Day and the Catholic Worker.* Albany, NY, 1984.

Robinson, Jo Ann Ooiman. *Abraham Went Out: A Biography of A. J. Muste.* Philadelphia, 1981.

----------. *A. J. Muste: Pacifist and Prophet. His Relation to the Society of Friends.* Wellingford, PA, 1981.

----------. "The Pharos of the East Side, 1937-1940: Labor Temple Under the Direction of A. J. Muste." *Journal of Presbyterian History* 48:1. (Spring 1970): 18-37.

Rogers, Herbert W. "The Obedient but Angry Daughter of Holy Church." *America* 127:15. (Nov. 11, 1972): 389-90.

Roszak, Theodore. "A. J." *The Nation* 204:10 (March 6, 1967): 293-94.

Sawyer, Mary. "Legacy of a Dream," in C. Eric Lincoln, ed., *Martin Luther King, Jr.: A Profile*, 260-70. New York, 1984.

Smylie, James H. "On Jesus, Pharaohs, and the Chosen People: Martin Luther King as Biblical Interpreter and Humanist." *Interpretation* 24:1 (Jan. 1970): 74-91.

Speak Truth to Power: A Quaker Search for an Alternative to Violence. N.p., 1955.

Steere, Douglas, ed. *Quaker Spirituality*. New York, 1984.

Teresa of Avila. *The Interior Castle*. Garden City, NY, 1961.

----------. *The Life of Teresa of Jesus*. Garden City, NY, 1960.

Therese of Lisieux. *The Story of a Soul*. New York, 1957.

Thoreau, Henry David. "On Civil Disobedience," in *Modern Essays*. Boston, n.d.

Thurman, Howard. *Deep River: Reflections on the Religious Insight of Certain of the Negro Spirituals*. New York, 1955.

Time (July 10, 1939): 37.

"Tract for the Times." *Liberation* 1:1 (March 1956): 4-6.

Trocme, Andre. *The Politics of Repentance*. New York, 1955.

Twomey, Gerald. "Thomas Merton: An Appreciation," in Gerald Twomey, ed., *Thomas Merton: Prophet in the Belly of a Paradox*, 92-110. New York, 1978.

Underhill, Evelyn. *The House of the Soul* and *Concerning the Inner Life*. Minneapolis, 1947.

Vishnewski, Stanley. *Wings of the Dawn*. New York, n.d.

----------, ed. *Meditations* [of Dorothy Day]. New York, 1970.

Vivian, Tim. *Paphnutius: Histories of the Monks of Upper Egypt and the Life of Onnophrius*. Kalamazoo, MI, 1993.

Walshe, M. O'C., ed. *Meister Eckhart: Sermons and Treatises*. 3 volumes: Longmead, Shaftesbury, Dorset, 1987.

Washington, James M., ed. *A Testament of Hope: The Essential Writings of Martin Luther King, Jr.* San Francisco, 1986.

Watley, William D. *Roots of Resistance: The Nonviolent Ethic of Martin Luther King, Jr.* Valley Forge, PA, 1985.

Watson, Burton, trans. *Chuang Tzu: Basic Writings*. New York, 1964.

Weinberg, Arthur and Vila, eds. *Instead of Violence*. Boston, 1963.

Wilmore, Gayraud S. *Black Religion and Black Radicalism*. Garden City, NY, 1973.

Woodcock, George. "A Moral Man." *Commentary* 44:14 (October 1967): 104-10.

Woolman, John. *The Journal of John Woolman* and *A Plea for the Poor*. Secaucus, NJ, 1975.

Work, John W. *American Negro Songs and Spirituals*. New York, 1970.

Wright, Richard. *American Hunger*. New York, 1977.

Zahn, Gordon. *In Solitary Witness*. New York, 1964.

Zaroulis, Nancy and Gerald Sullivan. *Who Spoke Up? American Protest Against the War in Vietnam 1963-1975*. Garden City, NY, 1984.

INDEXES

SCRIPTURE INDEX

INDEX OF NAMES

Spellman, Cardinal Francis 120, 162,
    295.
Spender, Stephen 86, 221.
Stalin, Josef 29, 35, 58, 74.
Stephen, Caroline 57.

T
Teresa of Avila 103, 106-07, 122,
    125, 141-42, 151-52, 156,
    168, 172-74, 176, 365.
Tertullian 320.
Therese of Lisieux 106-07, 122, 127,
    142, 144-45, 151-53, 172,
    174, 176-77, 276.
Thompson, Francis 36, 101.
Thoreau, Henry David 34, 38, 41,
    43, 53-54, 251, 273.
Thurman, Howard 227.
Tillich, Paul 131, 201.
Tolstoy, Leo 167.
Trotsky, Leon 22-23, 102.
Truman, Harry 149.

U
Underhill, Evelyn 1.

V
Vaughn, Henry 21.
Vishnewski, Stanley 104, 121, 134.
Von Clausewitz 313, 327.

W
Walker, David 240.
Wayne, John 282.
Wesley, John 101.
Wilson, Woodrow 102.
Woolman, John 27, 41, 44, 48, 51-
    52, 57.
Wright, Richard 206.

Y
Yoder, John Howard 279.
Young, Andrew 192.

SUBJECT INDEX

A
"A Testament of Hope" 209.
A Theology for the Social Gospel
    208.

Albany 192, 205, 213, 220, 224,
    246-49, 255.
Amalgamated Textile Workers 21.
American Friends Service Committee
    56, 277.
American Workers' Party 22, 25 32.
"And the Children of Birmingham"
    338.
Anti-Conscription League 102, 117.
Arms Race 69, 73, 148, 275, 296,
    318-19, 326-30, 333, 336.
Asian Journal 282.
"Aubade--Harlem" 297.
Auschwitz 285, 297-99, 338.

B
Babel 28, 65, 80, 323.
"Balm in Gilead" 226.
Bangkok 278, 307, 322, 334.
Barmen Declaration 37.
Battle Hymn of the Republic 27.
Bethlehem Steel 164.
Big Three 75, 78.
Bill of Rights for the Disadvantaged
    197.
Birmingham 192, 197, 201, 205,
    213, 215, 221, 230, 235,
    245-48, 250, 254, 257, 260,
    340.
Black Muslims 229, 244, 339.
Black Power 193, 197, 212, 222,
    244, 337-39.
Bomb Shelters 284, 289, 296, 320,
    333.
Boston Tea Party 52.
Boston University 191.
Bowery 120, 128, 151.
Bread and Wine 114.
Bremen 140.
British Empire 44, 254, 282.
Brookwood Labor College 21, 24,
    29, 32, 109.

C
Cambridge University 272.
Campion Propaganda Committee
    124, 131, 133, 151.
Carthusians 277.
Catholic Peace Fellowship (CPF)
    276, 290-91, 296.
Catholic Union of the Unemployed
    105.
Catholic Worker (community/
    movement) 21, 23, 29-30,